Recovering Nonviolent History

Development of this book was supported by the
International Center on Nonviolent Conflict

Recovering
Nonviolent
History

Civil Resistance
in Liberation Struggles

edited by
Maciej J. Bartkowski

LYNNE
RIENNER
PUBLISHERS

BOULDER
LONDON

Published in the United States of America in 2013 by
Lynne Rienner Publishers, Inc.
1800 30th Street, Boulder, Colorado 80301
www.rienner.com

and in the United Kingdom by
Lynne Rienner Publishers, Inc.
3 Henrietta Street, Covent Garden, London WC2E 8LU

Library of Congress Cataloging-in-Publication Data
Recovering nonviolent history : civil resistance in liberation struggles /
   Maciej J. Bartkowski, editor.
     p. cm.
   Includes bibliographical references and index.
   ISBN 978-1-58826-870-9 (alk. paper) — ISBN 978-1-58826-895-2
   (pbk. : alk. paper)
    1. Nonviolence. 2. Civil disobedience. 3. Government, Resistance to.
4. National liberation movements. I. Bartkowski, Maciej J., 1976–
editor of compilation.
   HM1281.R435 2013
   303.6'1—dc23

                                       2012037146

British Cataloguing in Publication Data
A Cataloguing in Publication record for this book
is available from the British Library.

Printed and bound in the United States of America

∞   The paper used in this publication meets the requirements
   of the American National Standard for Permanence of
   Paper for Printed Library Materials Z39.48-1992.

5 4 3 2 1

To all those,
known and unknown,
who fought and fight for their freedom nonviolently

Contents

Acknowledgments

The birth of this volume has been—in its microcosmic way—
similar to the emergence and actions of the people's movements that the
book describes. It required collective efforts, collaborative spirit, flexibility
and resilience, creativity and responsiveness, patience and long-term commitment, and the organized and disciplined involvement of many people whose
work contributed to its success.

The idea for the book came to me in August 2009 soon after I joined
the International Center on Nonviolent Conflict (ICNC), a Washington-
based nonprofit private foundation that creates and disseminates knowledge
about civil resistance. In my informal conversations with the staff of ICNC
and a number of its outside academic collaborators, I quickly realized that
the histories of many nations have been infused with both mythical and factual narratives about violent resistance, while no less heroic and often more
effective means of nonviolent struggle have been ignored, forgotten, or acknowledged only in passing.

From the very beginning of this stimulating journey, which sheds light
on the practice and role of civil resistance in creating and defending nations,
ICNC's leadership, together with its founding chair, Peter Ackerman, and its
president, Jack DuVall, has been wholeheartedly supportive of the project—
both intellectually and materially. Without their support, this volume would
not have seen the light of day. Another person who has been instrumental in
the development of the book, and whose editing skills and historical insights
have been invaluable, is Howard Clark, the author of the chapter on Kosovo.
Many times over, Howard played the indispensable role of mentor and ghost
editor. Hardy Merriman, ICNC senior adviser, scrupulously and with a great
intellectual precision informed by his deep knowledge of strategic nonviolent conflict offered his own corrections and requested further clarification,

all of which enhanced the book. My special appreciation goes to Mary Elizabeth King, the author of the chapter on Palestine, for her unceasing encouragement and insights into nonviolent struggles. Furthermore, engaging discussions with Stephen Zunes, chair of the ICNC academic advisers' committee, enlightened me on many important aspects of civil resistance during independence struggles. Suravi Bhandary, former ICNC program associate, was a valuable behind-the-scenes manager of the project, as well as a diligent assistant in creating the appendix of conflict summaries presented at the end of the book.

I thank the anonymous reviewers whose recommendations and suggestions bear on the improved content of the book. Last but certainly not least, I extend my appreciation to Lynne Rienner and her staff, whose high-level professionalism, experience, and responsiveness made for a smooth transition from a rough manuscript toward the beautifully designed and well-edited book that you have now in hand.

Any mistakes and errors that you might find in the book are an unintended oversight on my part. Please send questions and comments regarding its content to recovernonviolenthistory@gmail.com.

—*Maciej Bartkowski*

1

Recovering Nonviolent History

Maciej J. Bartkowski

The violence of the few does not withstand the quest for freedom of the many.

—former German President Christian Wulff,
speaking on the anniversary of the construction
of the Berlin Wall, August 13, 2011

Most people look to historical accounts to understand how their own nations emerged and fought for their freedom. Such explanations, whether found in books or imparted through public ceremonies and national memories, often tell of violent battles and insurrections, victories and defeats in wars, and fallen heroes in armed struggles. These narratives support the common belief that violence is the indispensable weapon to win freedom from foreign subjugation, but they ignore the power and historical role that nonviolent civilian-led resistance has played in many national quests for liberation.

This book brings to light the existence and impact of nonviolent organizing and defiance where it has not commonly been noticed. It argues that a number of historical struggles for national self-determination might not necessarily, or even primarily, have been won through violence. Instead, these struggles were decisively waged through diverse methods of nonviolent resistance led by ordinary people.[1] Furthermore, during the unfolding process of civil resistance, it was often the force of population-driven, bottom-up, nonviolent mobilization that shaped nations' collective identities (i.e., nationhood) and formed nascent national institutions and authorities (i.e., statehood). These processes were critical for an independent nation-state—more so than structural changes or violent revolutions that dominate the history of revolutionary struggles and nation making.

1

Recovering Civil Resistance

This book reveals little-known, but important, histories of civil resistance in national struggles for independence and against foreign domination throughout the world in the past 200 years. Often, these histories have been misinterpreted or erased altogether from collective memory, buried beneath nationally eulogized violence, commemorative rituals of glorified death, martyred heroes, and romanticized violent insurrections. In recovering hidden stories of civil resistance that involve diverse types of direct defiance and more subtle forms of everyday, relentless endurance and refusal to submit, this book shows how the actions of ordinary people have undermined the authority and control of foreign hegemons—colonizers and occupiers—and their domestic surrogates. Despite extreme oppression, the repertoire of nonviolent action has often helped societies survive and strengthen their social and cultural fabric, build economic and political institutions, shape national identities, and pave the way to independence. The narrative of the book contains a heuristic inquiry into forgotten or ignored accounts of civil resistance, showing how knowledge about historical events and processes is generated, distorted, and even ideologized in favor of violence-driven, structure-based, or powerholder-centric interpretations.

Glorified violence in the annals of nations, the gendered nature of violence wielded by men, state independence that is seen as having been founded largely on violence (the view reinforced by a state monopoly on violence as a way to maintain that independence), and human attention and media focus (both centered on dramatic and spectacular stories of violence and heroic achievements of single individuals) all dim the light on the quiet, nonviolent resistance of millions. This type of struggle neither captures the headlines nor sinks into people's memories unless it provokes the regime's response and, more often than not, a violent one.

The outcomes of seemingly violent struggles with foreign adversaries have depended to a large degree on the use of political—nonviolent—means rather than arms. Materially and militarily powerful empires and states have been defeated by poorly armed or even completely unarmed opponents not because they met irresistibly violent force, but because the nations found another source of strength—a total mobilization of the population via political, administrative, and ideological tools. Thus, political organizing has been the key ingredient in the people's revolutions that have helped the militarily weaker successfully challenge powerful enemies. Examples include, among others, the Spanish insurrectionists against Napoleon, the Chinese revolutionaries against the Japanese Army, and the North Vietnamese against the United States and its South Vietnamese allies. In all of these supposedly violence-dominated conflicts, military tools were subordinated to a broader political struggle for the "hearts and minds" of ordinary people.[2]

By recovering the stories of nonviolent actions, this book goes against a tide of prevailing views about struggles against foreign domination that fail to recognize and take into account the role and contribution of civil resistance.

Power, Structure, and Agency

The study of civil resistance presented here represents a paradigmatic shift in the understanding of national struggles and the making of nation-states, which moves away from the traditional focus on structures, conditions, processes, military power, violence, and political elites. This investigation approaches historical knowledge in a novel fashion, recognizing that the force that shapes nations and propels their resistance lies in the organized, purposeful, and defiant actions of an unarmed population. Its nonstate alternative to understanding political power goes against the established Weberian canon of political authority that is top down, centralized, static, material, and elite or institution centric. Instead, the people power perspective emphasizes the fragility and diffused nature of political power, its outside-of-the-state origin, and the agency of ordinary people. Regimes are sustained not merely by their material power, including mechanisms of coercion, but also or primarily by the apathy or ignorance of the common people. The dormant people power becomes apparent with a sudden or gradual collective withdrawal of consent and mass disobedience. This force, according to Mohandas Gandhi (Mahatma), gains its strength from the fact that "even the most powerful cannot rule without the co-operation of the ruled."[3]

This book shows various mobilizers of the power of agency in liberation struggles. First, there are powerful resources for the emergence and conduct of resistance that lie in culture and are used by local people to resist subjugation. They borrow from existing symbols, rituals, and customs to devise ever more effective strategies and tactics against an oppressor, particularly a foreign one. Religious or cultural ceremonies become occasions to gather and organize in a space not fully controlled by a regime. While engaging in culturally infused resistance, people also create new understandings, meanings, and identities that in turn reinforce unity and resilience of a given collective, mobilize others and spread consciousness, and help nation-building processes. Second, people have the power to independently activate existing or create new nonstate or civic institutions (e.g., religious groups, labor organizations, educational institutions, and civil society associations). These structure-building processes turn out to be a potent weapon of ordinary people in waging a protracted struggle for the transformation of their society and its eventual liberation from the control of a foreign oppressor—often without directly challenging the latter or raising unnecessarily its ire until the moment of the movement's own choosing. Although the book emphasizes the role and impact of agency, it does not disregard structures as they may constitute a crucial part of nonviolent strategies. However, structures remain important insofar as the actions of agency are taken into consideration. At the same time, civil resistance, its trajectories, and even its outcomes are not circumstantial. They are driven and shaped by people's decisions and actions.

The Main Inquiries in This Book

The case studies in this volume shed light on many key questions, including: What kinds of nonviolent tactics were used in national struggles? What made some nonviolent campaigns successful despite unfavorable conditions and what made others fail or achieve only partial success? What was the impact of diverse acts of civil resistance on the further unfolding of a conflict and its eventual outcomes? How did collective nonviolent actions influence nations, their collective identities, or socioeconomic and political institutions that evolved during the national struggles? Did civil resistance have longer-term consequences on the historical development of these countries? Finally, why do the annals so often ignore the presence and role of civil resistance?

By identifying episodes, periods, and specific campaigns of nonviolent resistance that at particular points in time either constituted a dominant or a sole ingredient behind a national liberation struggle, the case studies answer these questions and so encourage new conversation about the nature, place, and role of nonviolent resistance in state and nation formation.

Civil Resistance as Nonviolent Political Contestation

This book uses the terms *civil resistance, nonviolent resistance,* and *nonviolent struggle* to refer to the same basic phenomenon defined as a form of political conflict in which ordinary people choose to stand up to oppressive structures—be it occupation, colonialism, or unjust practices of government—with the use of various tactics of nonviolent action such as strikes, boycotts, protests, and civil disobedience.[4] Such methods include not only overt confrontational actions, but also more subtle forms of cultural resistance or seemingly apolitical work of autonomous associations and parallel institution building. Whether overt or tacit, nonviolent forms of resistance are a popular expression of people's collective determination to withdraw their cooperation from the powers that be. People can refuse to follow a co-erced or internalized system of lies and deception and, thereby, intention-ally increase the cost of official control. They also can encourage divisions within an oppressor's pillars of support (e.g., in the ranks of its security forces and military) and exploit the consequences of repressive violence against unarmed resisters by turning them into a strategic advantage for a movement.

Related to its nonviolent nature comes the concept of civil resistance as a separate form of political contestation. This is because action takers wage a battle of ideas in which a movement tries to win popular legitimacy while the authorities struggle to maintain the loyalty of security forces and the neutrality or apathy of the population. The causal ideas behind civil resis-tance are thoughts and expressions of one or more concrete grievances and demands articulated in articles, pamphlets, leaflets, sermons, speeches, so-cial media, or other means of communication. The ideas and the move-ments that propagate them may galvanize mass public support, but also face brutal suppression, including physical force wielded by the army or security apparatus of the regime. In that contest, to paraphrase the writings of some authors in this volume, it remains to be seen whether a nonviolent resister such as a writer or a painter can be mightier than the tyrant under whose yoke the population lives.

Weaving Together a National Fabric

Through various creative nonviolent actions aimed at resisting foreign dom-ination, a painstaking process of autonomous state building occurs—both underground and tacit as well as overt and explicit with the skillful use of allowable and available legal and political space. A multitude of repeated acts of participatory and constructive disobedience practiced by ordinary people creates and re-creates a territory-wide architecture of cultural, social, economic, and political alternative practices and norms, often accompany-ing and supporting more direct and coercive forms of nonviolent tactics.

Next to state building, the practice of civil resistance stipulates yet an-other transformational force, namely, reimagining communities and awaken-ing them to their shared values, common history, collective understanding, and unifying vision of their cultural, linguistic, social, and political roots as well as a communal life and destiny in a defined public space. Civil resistance is thus an instrument—not necessarily visible to the foreign occupier or well under-stood by those who practice it—that helps develop people's sense of patriot-ism and their attachment to their newly invented interwoven time line of memories, relations, and events that sew the fabric of an imagined nation.

Liberation Struggles Through Civil Resistance Campaigns

This book looks at cases that can be classified as *popular liberation* or *self-rule struggles,* which include struggles for independence or self-determination and against occupation, colonial control, or foreign domination—the latter often represented by an indigenous government subservient to outside interests. These cases might otherwise share common issues (e.g., mobilizing unarmed people and challenging oppressive and violent systems) with *rights-based* or *rule-of-law struggles*—but covering these two types of struggle that also include recent anti-dictatorship upheavals in the Arab world is beyond the scope of this book.[5]

Historically, liberation or self-rule struggles in which civil resistance is a predominant method of waging resistance have been uncommon. For example, as of this writing, the most systemic and methodologically rigorous dataset on civil resistance cases that allows for scholarly validation and transferability—Nonviolent and Violent Campaigns and Outcomes (NAVCO 1.0)—identifies 106 mass-based nonviolent struggles against dictatorships, occupation, and self-determination that occurred between 1900 and 2006.[6] Of this number only twenty-one campaigns can be classified, according to the criteria of this volume, as belonging to popular liberation or self-rule struggles. This book describes in detail four of these twenty-one cases, and, in addition, includes a number of other, lesser-known, instances that date as far back as the eighteenth century, through undertaking in-depth analysis of sometimes decades-long, country-specific nonviolent resistance campaigns. What emerges is a collection of culturally, religiously, temporally, and spatially diverse cases in which the role and impact of civil resistance have historically been understudied and poorly understood.[7]

The thematic coverage of this book goes beyond single disciplinary boundaries and its research speaks to a number of scholarly streams. It examines the cases through analytical and empirical lenses of the history of revolutionary and independence struggles, nationalism studies, the sociology of social movements, comparative and contentious politics, and strategic nonviolent conflict. This book is intended for students and scholars interested in accounting in their research for the purposeful agency of ordinary people who organize social movements and the strategic dimension of the use of nonviolent action in political conflicts. In addition, this volume will be of interest to policy professionals, practitioners, activists, and nonspecialists who look for a greater historical understanding of the phenomenon of popular nonviolent uprisings in order to better comprehend the major unarmed upheavals of recent years and search for inspiration and lessons that can be derived from the nonviolent history of their own or other countries.

The Structure of This Book

Following this introductory chapter, Chapter 2 considers how mass-based nonviolent resistance can create and re-create national identities and how existing collective identities can enhance or constrain a movement's repertoire of nonviolent tactics. While focusing on the interrelationship and mutually influencing effects of nonviolent resistance and the process of national identity formation, the chapter bridges two distinct and typically segregated disciplines: those of social movements and strategic nonviolent conflict.[8] This leads to fifteen empirical cases assembled by major geographical regions: sub-Saharan Africa, North Africa and the Middle East, Asia and Oceania, Europe, and the Americas. The cases within each region are presented chronologically.

The choice of case studies emphasizes historical examples that have been relatively underresearched from the perspective of civil resistance. This is why there is no chapter on the independence struggle most commonly associated with nonviolent resistance, namely, India. That is not to say that the Indian independence movement does not warrant further study,[9] but the authors of this volume came to believe that lesser-known instances of nonviolent resistance need to be brought to light in order to inform and expand empirical and theoretical knowledge and identify areas for further inquiry. Other cases of nonviolent independence struggles not present in this book include those of the Baltic countries, whose national resistance against Soviet occupation has been described elsewhere.[10] Latin America—Cuba apart—also remains underrepresented in this book and there is an obvious need for future research to ascertain the role of nonviolent resistance against colonialism and during independence in that region. Yet another study not included in this volume but important to consider for future research—given continued violence in the region—is that of the Pashtuns who, under the leadership of Khan Abdul Ghaffar Khan, organized an unarmed militia of one hundred thousand people known as "Red Shirts" (from the color of their military-like uniform) that fought the British nonviolently throughout the 1930s in what is now the western tribal areas of Pakistan.[11]

Another important criterion used for case selection in this book was the presence in a given society of narratives that glorify military might and violent insurrection. Several chapters refer to the presence of an exaggerated narrative of violent resistance as a significant reason explaining the historical oblivion to which many stories of nonviolent resistance have been relegated. The consequences of such marginalization and amnesia surrounding nonviolent history were apparent when a respected mainstream media columnist sincerely, though naïvely, offered his recommendations about nonviolent resistance to none other than the Palestinians[12]—a population that, as Chapter 9 shows, has a rich tradition of popular nonviolent struggle and a much longer historical experience with peaceful resistance than many contemporary commentators who were mesmerized by the 2011 Arab Spring realize. Chapter 9 on Palestine and Chapter 12 on West Papua stand out as representing ongoing conflicts with largely hidden records of nonviolent resistance. West Papua warrants further comparative analysis with other struggles for independence from Indonesia, notably in East Timor and in the Aceh region.[13]

The cases in this book were also selected in an attempt to represent major geographical areas, historically different periods, diverse cultures, distinct religions, and varied systems of governance and political control ranging from the dominance of an ethnic group within a multiethnic state to countries that were subject to conquest, colonialism, occupation, partition, foreign domination, and indirect forms of foreign rule through co-opted or coerced domestic proxies.

Last, the conclusion expands on the insights derived from the empirical studies beyond the ones mentioned in this introduction, including the issue of masculinity, transnationalization, and dynamics of nonviolent resistance and forward-looking arguments about the role, impact, and development of civil resistance as a practice and a field of study. The appendix that follows the conclusion includes conflict summaries that list methods and impact of nonviolent actions discussed in the chapters.

An Overview of the Case Studies

Sub-Saharan Africa

Chapters 3, 4, and 5 on Ghana, Zambia, and Mozambique, respectively, touch briefly on a diffuse Africa-wide, anticolonial, decades-long movement known as pan-Africanism, which was instrumental in raising consciousness about imperial oppression, advocating for national liberation of colonially subjugated peoples, and creating a transnational platform of conferences where topics such as strategies and tactics to achieve independence were discussed and formulated. During the Fifth Pan-African Congress in Manchester, England, in 1945 the African participants, including Kwame Nkrumah (the leader of Ghana's independence struggle and its future president), called for mass-based, popular actions as the first and most appropriate means to fight for independence. Pan-Africanism and the solidarity and support that it engendered played an important role in popularizing nonviolent means of resistance and underscored the struggles for self-determination of the African nations.[14]

In Ghana, Zambia, and Mozambique an important element of nonviolent defiance, which often preceded more open and direct forms of nonviolent resistance, was grassroots organizing in the form of voluntary and professional self-help associations, cooperatives, and unions. Even during the national struggle in Mozambique, seemingly dominated by armed insurrection, the Mozambican Liberation Front (FRELIMO) pursued broad, mass-based strategies of organizing and building institutions that were implemented in the liberated zones. The origin of these activities can be traced to the decades of nonviolent civic mobilization, direct action, and use of parallel institutions in the form of mutual aid cooperatives that preceded armed resistance. Chapter 3 on Ghana and Chapter 4 on Zambia acknowledge the important role of their leaders and subsequent presidents, Kwame Nkrumah and Kenneth Kaunda, in ensuring nonviolent discipline and carrying out mass-based nonviolent tactics, but they emphasize even more so the collective actions led by hundreds of thousands of ordinary people that gave thrust to the work of revolutionary leaders.

North Africa and the Middle East

"Many Arabs," Ralph Crow and Philip Grant note, "think of their tradition as valuing chivalry, courage, and the open confrontation of opponents, [and therefore] they wonder how a system of resistance that rejects the use of arms can be considered part of their heritage."[15] In fact, Chapter 6 on Algeria and Chapter 7 on Egypt show the extent to which nonviolent resistance has been a recurrent feature of Arab life that is compatible with various forms of Islam and an indispensable element of the struggle against foreign invaders. Furthermore, the most recent popular revolts, now commonly referred to as the Arab Spring and the earlier Green Movement in Iran, underscore the continuing relevance of historical precedents from Egypt, Algeria, Iran, and Palestine that are reexamined in this book. Indeed, these historical examples help open up a further understanding of the regime's current politics as well as civilian organizing despite inhibiting conditions.

In Iran, a glorified narrative of political violence propagated by the Shah's regime and Islamic Republic and their censored media has reinforced a general lack of recognition in the Iranian historical and political discourse of legitimate means of struggle other than violence. Nevertheless, ordinary Iranians have frequently resorted to the use of popular nonviolent resistance. This has occurred recently (such as in the Green Movement or the 1979 Iranian revolution) as well as nearly a century earlier in the tobacco movement of 1891–1892 and the constitutional revolution of 1905–1907 to oppose foreign domination and the rulers' lack of responsiveness to people's demands. As in other struggles, many Iranians drew inspiration for their peaceful resistance from religious influences. They used nonviolent actions in a deliberate, planned form to facilitate coalition building and forge unity across sects, professions, and classes to annul tobacco concessions for foreigners and later to press for broader political and constitutional changes.

Chapter 9 on Palestine challenges conventional wisdom by showing that nonviolent resistance against occupation required not only obtaining the support of international third parties, but also inducing political and social changes in the opponent (i.e., the Israelis). As the first Palestinian intifada illustrates, an opponent's lack of constructive response can undermine advocates of nonviolent actions and strengthen the appeal of violent forms of struggle. Thus far, John F. Kennedy's famous warning that "those who make peaceful revolution impossible will make violent revolution inevitable"[16] has not been fully learned. On May 15, 2011, the Palestinian Nakba Day (day of the catastrophe) that marks the Israeli Independence Day, masses of unarmed Palestinians marched to the Israeli border from Syria, Lebanon, the West Bank, and the Gaza Strip only to face violence. Violent response can backfire against the perpetrators—as a number of examples in this volume show—but believing that nonviolent actions cannot change opponents' policies can lead to disillusionment among nonviolent activists and give more importance to advocates of armed struggle. In many nonviolent struggles, the intransigence of an opponent and the obduracy of third parties who support the opponent provide fuel for those who favor armed resistance. The issue is further complicated in situations where advocacy of nonviolent struggle might (sometimes willfully) be misinterpreted as denial of a population's right to choose its own means of struggle. Chapter 9 shows the relative effectiveness of nonviolent strategies compared with military action, particularly when framed in terms of community self-governance and basic human rights.

The narratives and images of venerated wars of independence—recounted in Chapters 5, 10, 11, 15, and 16 on Mozambique, Burma, Bangladesh, Kosovo, and the United States, respectively—have shaped thinking and writing about the Algerian self-determination struggle introduced in Chapter 6. The history of the Algerian resistance lies hidden in subtle forms of nonviolent defiance such as social boycotts, individual and collective withdrawal from the public sphere, autonomous cultural and religious activism, and more visible and direct forms of nonviolent resistance that were used by the population well before the independence war. Through the pursuit of nonviolent action and despite extremely unfavorable conditions Algerians—like Poles—managed to preserve and expand their distinctive culture and develop a sense of "Algerianness," even though—similarly to Mozambique, Kosovo, Iran, or the United States—nonviolent resistance was shunted aside by armed struggle.

When the January 25, 2011, nonviolent revolution in Egypt—using strikingly similar methods of nonviolent resistance as the forerunners in 1919–1921—brought down a dictator, the history of the Egyptian resistance against foreign domination and British colonial occupation became a more significant and symbolic legacy. Important practices of nonviolent action used by ordinary Egyptians to challenge oppression and resist colonization were apparent throughout the nineteenth century. As various forms of Christianity (e.g., in Zambia, Ghana, and West Papua) have offered either inspiration (e.g., the image of Christ who struggled nonviolently against injustice) or normative foundations (e.g., the call for equality regardless of race, color, or ethnic heritage) for nonviolent defiance, similarly Islamic teaching has played a part in shaping nonviolent resistance in countries such as Egypt, Algeria, and Iran. While describing various nonviolent tactics and their outcomes, Chapter 7 on Egypt—in the same vein as various other chapters—highlights the potential formative impact of civil resistance on Egyptian national identity and statehood.

Asia and Oceania

As described in Chapter 10, to boost its own credibility, the ruling Burmese military junta has glorified the role of the military and armed resistance in the historic anticolonial, nationalist movement against British rule. This process has been seen elsewhere, such as in the propaganda of the Algerian National Liberation Front (FLN) that invoked its victorious armed struggle to legitimize continued, undemocratic leadership. However, often overlooked is the way that Burmese nonviolent campaigns and constructive programs undermined British colonial rule from 1910 to 1940 and shaped Burmese national identity. People in Burma were inspired by and continued their activities in emulation of the Indian independence movement led by Gandhi—a fact that remains relatively unknown in Burma. Burmese, like Indians, spun and wore their own native cloth (*pinni*), a symbol of resistance against British rule. In India, Gandhi referred to homespun cloth as "the livery of freedom" because he wanted to unify all Indians in the independence struggle, including the poorest. This was also the case in the Burmese anticolonial struggle as well as in West Papua and, indeed, much earlier in civil resistance of the American colonists against the British. The Burmese national resistance in the 1920s and 1930s had also been waged with the use of a repertoire of nonviolent tactics strikingly similar to those deployed by the Burmese opposition against the military dictatorship since 1988.

The case of East Pakistan (Bangladesh) in Chapter 11 offers accounts of civil resistance movements that remain relatively unknown to non-Bengali readers. Until the nine-month-long bloody war that captured the attention of the world and led to the liberation of Bangladesh in December 1971, the struggle for the right to national self-expression and self-determination was fought through the use of civil resistance methods and strategies. Two non-violent struggles are particularly notable for their impressive mobilization and impact, namely, the Bangla language movement in the 1940s and 1950s and the March 1971 nonviolent national uprising. The language movement increased Bengalis' national awareness and fueled their continued resistance while less than a month of nationwide civil resistance in the form of civic organizing, demonstrations, strikes, and mass civil disobedience in March 1971 led to the de facto independence of East Pakistan prior to the outbreak of war—a result similar to the outcomes of the American nonviolent struggle against the British.

Chapter 12 on West Papua provides an altogether fresh venue for resistance on behalf of self-determination. Contrary to a romanticized "Avatar" vision of an indigenous population equipped with primitive weapons taking on the modern machinery of the Indonesian police and military, West Papuans developed a philosophy and practice of resisting injustice and fighting for greater autonomy and independence using nonviolent means of action. This culturally validated resistance has been fed and reinforced by the West Papuans' sense of national identity. Similar to Chapter 9 on Palestine, the West Papuan case shows that, if nonviolent resistance for independence is framed in terms of universal democratic values and human rights, it can have a stronger resonance with civil society and human rights advocates in the occupying countries as well as with the international community. This, in turn, helps the oppressed population build solidarity with other groups and empathy for its struggle.

Europe

Chapter 13 describes the Hungarian resistance against the Austrian Habsburg Empire during the 1850s and 1860s that took the form of a nonviolent, though active and coercive, national confrontation. This reality contrasts with the term *passive resistance* that had been commonly used—sometimes in a derogatory way—to describe this struggle. As in Ghana and Zambia, the case of Hungary highlights the role of a national leader—Ferenc Deák—in articulating, mobilizing, and sustaining nonviolent resistance. Even without Deák's leadership Hungarians would in all likelihood have waged a nonviolent struggle, although his guidance helped the internal integrity of the movement and ensured its robust, multiyear nonviolent discipline. The strength of the Hungarian defiance came precisely from the fact that the resistance was mass based, decentralized, and without a singular operational leader whose arrest would have jeopardized the movement's survival. Just as Ghana's nonviolent struggle enthused other African nations, the Hungarian nonviolent resistance for an equal political status in the Habsburg Empire became a transnational cause célèbre for other nationalist movements, ranging from Ireland and Finland to India.

The Polish case presented in Chapter 14 addresses a common theme of nonviolent resistance beneath valorized violence and makes explicit a truth that many chapters in this volume reveal—that formation of a nation, particularly under occupation, partition, or colonialism, is not a predetermined process. Denationalization by externally imposed partitioning—when three empires (Prussia, Austria, and Russia) divided Poland among themselves— failed because people decided to resist through sociocultural organizing and educational and commemoration campaigns, along with direct action such as petitions, civil disobedience, strikes, and demonstrations. As is apparent in examples from Africa, the United States, and Asia, civil resistance was used strategically to defend Polish society, reinforce social solidarity, and strengthen the process of national identity formation and state building.

Similar to the struggles in Mozambique and in Algeria, Kosovo's national resistance described in Chapter 15 is selectively remembered for the armed struggle led by the Kosovo Liberation Army. Yet nonviolent resistance prevented the outbreak of war at the time when it would have been most disastrous—before the other wars of Yugoslav succession and when Kosovo was internationally isolated. During their decade-long nonviolent resistance, Kosovo Albanians were able to maintain their own community in the face of Serbian repression and educate international opinion about their rights. As in Cuba, Bangladesh, and Palestine, the nonviolent resistance practiced in Kosovo laid the foundation for the emergence of civil society and a fledging democratic culture, notwithstanding the fact that these achievements were rapidly undermined by a shift from collective nonviolent action in favor of armed struggle. Though, given the Serbs' military superiority, it is doubtful that violence by the Kosovars alone could have achieved independence if not for military intervention by the North Atlantic Treaty Organization (NATO). Furthermore, the rise of independent Kosovo through violent insurgency and war brought tremendous political and socioeconomic challenges. Mozambique, Algeria, and Burma saw similar postconflict problems.

The Americas

Chapter 16 on the United States and Chapter 17 on the Cuban independence struggles address a mythologized and glorified violent version of history that suppresses narratives about the role and importance of nonviolent forms of resistance. In the case of the American Revolution, emphasis on armed struggle has largely hidden from view the reality that there was a decade-long civil resistance against British taxes and edicts that preceded the outbreak of violence. In Cuba, the exaltation of heroic guerrilla warfare led civilian reformist movements to be labeled as reactionary, lacking patriotic virtues, and undermining the cause of the armed uprising. Both chapters highlight civil and nonviolent cultural, social, economic, and political mobilization as well as the use of direct collective actions such as popular disobedience, boycotts, public processions, celebrations, demonstrations, and other acts of defiance. In the United States, these actions were effective in liberating most of the colonies from British control before the war broke out and helped to lay the basis for future political and civic institutions in the postindependence era. In the case of Cuba, such actions achieved greater constitutional rights and political autonomy, and laid important foundations for the emergence of a resilient civil society. In both examples, the successes associated with grassroots nonviolent resistance were undermined by violent revolutionary fervor that often weakened popular participation, polarized the society, and produced far more casualties and material destruction than nonviolent resistance.

The Book's Contributions

The chapters in this book make important academic and intellectual contributions in several areas:

1. *Civil resistance,* including its small acts of resistance, less visible forms of defiance through institution building, and the interplay among direct and indirect methods of nonviolent action;
2. *Liberation struggles,* including a critical analysis of violence-centric narratives of the quest for independence and consequences of romanticized violence;
3. *National identity formation and state making,* through the inclusion of a conceptual framework of civil resistance.

This book also raises a number of other, no less important, considerations and issues. Described in greater detail in the concluding chapter, these include the agency of unarmed people that overcomes adversarial conditions with nonviolent actions, the dominance of masculinist narratives that occlude the role of civil resistance and women in particular, the impact of third parties and transnational networks, the historical diffusion of knowledge about waging nonviolent conflict, the diversity of tactics and tactical innovation, the enduring impact of civil resistance, and the emergence of civil resistance as a new field of study.

Civil Resistance Study

The practice of civil resistance has opened new and more versatile opportunities for political change that regional experts and other political theorists have excluded or repeatedly failed to anticipate—as with the Arab Spring—because the possibilities of people's collective action have not been treated seriously.[17] In that sense, the fact that the phenomenon of civil resistance has been increasingly acknowledged in recent years is a triumph of reality over preconceived elite- or structure-based or violence-centric notions that usually define traditional social science disciplines.

In the period since the publication of Gene Sharp's seminal work *The Politics of Nonviolent Action* in 1973,[18] the literature on nonviolent conflict has expanded considerably. A select bibliography of English-language publications on civil resistance and related subjects is included at the end of this volume. Partly, this growth in publications is a response to events: Roberts and Garton Ash's *Civil Resistance and Power Politics* (2009)[19] contains numerous case studies of civil resistance in the 1990s and 2000s, yet since then the unarmed challenges to autocracy in North Africa and the Middle East have created a need for further inquiries into cases in the new decade.

Certain salient themes have been developed in greater depth—the study of strategy, tactics, and organizing in nonviolent resistance;[20] historical case studies and narratives of nonviolent movements;[21] the mechanisms by which repression backfires against those in power and how resisters can magnify its impact despite their opponents' attempt to attenuate it;[22] and the forms and role of transnational solidarity.[23] Additional recent research has covered the quantitative study of the relative effectiveness of nonviolent and armed campaigns;[24] the qualitative and comparative analysis of both failed and successful nonviolent movements;[25] and the disciplinary gap between social movement theory and nonviolent action analysis.[26]

The book contributes to this body of literature in a number of ways, including by emphasizing the role and impact of indirect and nonpolitical forms of civil resistance on national struggles. The lessons from the case studies reveal a complex picture of the way that people challenged oppressive foreign influence and presence. Their resistance was not always about open, direct forms of contention, but often about less glamorous, less spectacular, and sometimes indiscernible-as-resistance actions that relied on seemingly unchallenging, low-profile, everyday sociocultural activities that did, in due course, erode and shake up predatory rule, no matter how violent or thorough it was.

Indirect and direct methods of resistance. Careful analysis of the methods of nonviolent resistance found in each case study in this book uncovers rich, but subtle, methods of defiance often hidden in everyday life—a seemingly ordinary type of human action that can represent a powerful form of rejection of a dominant political reality. Many populations have resisted cultural domination and denationalization through tactics that could be described as antlike, stubborn endurance to ensure collective survival in the midst of severe oppression, within a limited public space for independent political activities. This attitude is equivalent to what the Palestinians refer to as *sumud*—steadfastness and perseverance or what is known as "existence is resistance": merely staying in place or on the land in the face of oppression becomes itself a form of defiance.[27] This subaltern type of resistance—as highlighted in a number of chapters—has often been confined to private, family, and individual spheres of life or has taken the form of less risky, lower-profile, and seemingly nonpolitical and benign actions such as celebrations of cultural figures; wearing homemade cloth; organizing street theater, public performances, artistic exhibitions; or setting up and running economic, cultural, mutual aid, sport, music, or literary clubs and circles.[28] Some observers describe this type of actions as "everyday forms of resistance" or "small acts of resistance."[29]

One version of this form of defiance is known as Svejkism—named after the actions of a fictional character of the Czech soldier Svejk enlisted in the Austro-Hungarian Army. The comedy of his botched implementation of orders, with its ambiguity between incompetence and disobedience, has given its name to the small-scale, hidden defiance of people working in political and military institutions.[30] Another version of everyday resistance is seen in colonized Egypt and Algeria where the seemingly innocent act of wearing a veil became a powerful symbol of enduring opposition against foreign authorities. In the essay "Shooting an Elephant," George Orwell—who held little faith in the power of nonviolent actions[31]—recounts, as it appears, his personal experience of living in Burma in the 1920s. As a British police officer, he was the subject of exasperating small acts of resistance that often took the form of contemptuous and mocking verbal exploits. The "natives," in the words of the essay's narrator, "baited whenever it seemed safe to do so." Orwell explains further:

> When a nimble Burman tripped me up on the football field and the referee (another Burman) looked the other way, the crowd yelled with hideous laughter. This happened more than once. In the end the sneering yellow faces of young men that met me everywhere, the insults hooted after me when I was at a safe distance, got badly on my nerves. The young Buddhist priests were the worst of all. There were several thousands of them in the town and none of them seemed to have anything to do except stand on the street corners and jeer at Europeans. [Later in the text, the narrator concludes,] and my whole life, every white man's life in the East, was one long struggle not to be laughed at.[32]

Decades later and in a different country, ingenious benevolent protests of everyday defiance are taking place on the streets of Minsk against the authoritarian regime of Belarusian president Aleksandr Lukashenko.[33] Silent and do-nothing gatherings, public clapping, phone beeping set for specific times, and stuffed rabbits and bears holding protest signs at a bus stop in the country's capital or falling down from the sky are all expressions of dissent that have provoked surreal police action (e.g., arrests of protesting teddy bears) against harmless and mundane activities, making the authorities look absurd and lose legitimacy. While striving to maintain nonviolent discipline (later overtaken by violence) and diversify their civil resistance strategies and tactics, Syrians undertook creative and lower-risk activism in the form of dyeing public fountains red to symbolize the blood of the civil protesters killed across the country since the uprising began in March 2011, releasing balloons with freedom messages, or gluing the door locks of government offices.[34] Across the world, in the more open societies of Chile and the Philippines, young people are demonstrating against their government by carrying out mass kiss-in protests, jogging around the clock, circling the presidential palace, or planking highways and state institutions.[35]

In normal times these types of action would not be considered resistance. Yet under circumstances of oppression, such obvious but nonprovocative defiance can demonstrate deep and persistent opposition and put the government in a dilemma because suppressing the actions will expose the brutality, abnormality, and autocracy of those in power. Despite their importance and force, memories of these kinds of action fade and, as Chapter 6 on Algeria emphasizes, they have left few historical records. This may be partly because these everyday forms of hidden nonviolent rebellion are often tails of the dog that did not bark and, thus, lack the overt contestation, drama, and spectacle of violent struggle.

An important element of the indirect form of resistance described in a number of chapters was the development of an autonomous society with every aspect of self-rule well before a formal independence was achieved. Often, it took the form of society's own schooling system, self-managed economic cooperatives, social services organizations, and judicial or quasi-governing institutions. The idea was not to take the fight directly—with the use of collective actions—to a more powerful and brutal adversary but rather to transform the society first and, through that transformation, liberate it from the control of the foreign occupier. This was a stealth resistance more than an open confrontation. Society was seen as a social organism that could grow, defy foreign authorities, and defend itself via its own self-organization, self-attainment, and self-improvement. Such nonviolent resistance was forceful, but gradual and protracted. It thus not only could be measured by the outcomes of undermining its adversary, but also by the process of societal work through alternative institution building that instills greater unity, solidarity, mobilization, and resilience in the society. This type of indirect resistance, through the creation and seemingly apolitical work of numerous legal, semilegal, or banned grassroots institutions in the economic, social, judicial, or educational spheres became the type of silent but salient resistance akin to Assef Bayat's notion of "quiet encroachment of the ordinary."[36] They were coercive, but nonviolent acts, in the protracted struggle of the destitute population against foreign powers, its domestic surrogates, or both.

This type of alternative institution building or associationalism has often helped to create sounder ground for waging more direct nonviolent actions against a more powerful enemy that required greater mobilization and unity. In that sense, indirect resistance through institutions of societal development and education became a tool that a well-known, nineteenth-century, Syrian-born Arab reformist, Abd al Rahman al-Kawakibi, regarded as the necessary step for setting up appropriate conditions before a fully fledged peaceful resistance takes on despotism.[37] This was also the means for civil resisters to redress a huge asymmetry of force between themselves and their adversary by rendering its military superiority useless when confronted by a withdrawn, self-organized society. Yet another feature of indirect resistance of self-organized alternative institutions was a creation of an organic link between ordinary life and work on one hand and resistance on the other. There was no life beyond resistance and no resistance beyond life. Often, a sense of people's own prospects was fused with the prospect of the movement and the struggle, creating an existential unity between the two. Finally, indirect acts of resistance in the form of self-managed institutional life that empowered people and engendered the resistance in the fabric of a nation played an important role in turning the victims of oppression into self-conscious individuals aware of their powers and the sources of their captivity. Al-Kawakibi believed that people "themselves are the cause of what has been inflicted upon them, and that they should blame neither foreigners nor fate but rather ignorance (*al-jahl*), lack of endeavor (*faqd al-humam*), and apathy (*al-taw kul*), all of which prevail over society."[38] This echoes the views of al-Kawakibi's older Polish contemporary, the philosopher Józef Szujski, who points out that the guilt of falling into the predatory hands of foreign powers lay in the oppressed society and, thus, the solution and liberation need to come from that society transformed through its work, education, and civility. Victims and the seemingly disempowered are thus their own liberators as long as they pursue self-organization, self-attainment, and development of their communities.

The chapters in this book also show an interesting dynamic between direct forms of resistance and more subtle forms of defiance, whereby everyday and barely noticed acts of civil resistance were closely intertwined with or paved the way for more direct and demonstrable forms of nonviolent actions. The latter development often exhibited a growing consolidation of national identity, a realistic assessment of costs and risks of disruptive activities, and better skills in planning and collective organizing as well as reflected the memory of lost armed insurrections, emerging new opportunities due to external geopolitical changes (i.e., regional or global wars) or development and popularization of new means of communication (at various times, print technology, the telegraph, and radio well before the communications revolution of recent years). Helped by these shifts, people have begun to devise and plan methodically and, thus, develop more direct and forceful actions in order to put overt pressure on the authorities. These more confrontational engagements often involved ever-growing participation of wider swathes of the society who directly and immediately challenged the authorities and their control over land and population. In this way, nonviolent struggle expanded beyond subtle forms of social organizing and campaigning for greater autonomy and political freedoms to encompass mass-based actions that were filled with explicit nationwide demands for self-rule and independence.

Study of Liberation Struggles

This book offers insights into the historical study of liberation and independence movements by discussing the relationship between armed and unarmed struggle during the fight for statehood.

Armed struggle and civil resistance have had different relationships in different contexts and in different phases of conflict. In some cases, both types of resistance coexisted such as in Algeria after 1952 and Mozambique after 1960. In cases of Cuba, Iran, and Egypt, civil resistance was interrupted intermittently by outbursts of violent insurrection. In Hungary, Poland, and West Papua, armed struggle was replaced by civil resistance while in the United States, Burma, Kosovo, and Algeria civil resistance preceded and was overtaken by violent rebellion. Thus, far from decontextualizing nonviolent forms of contention from violent resistance, this book offers a more nuanced and realistic perspective on nationalist movements and liberation struggles. These movements and struggles relied on an impressive repertoire of civil resistance campaigns that were sometimes interspersed temporally or spatially with violence but, in other cases, were in competition with or opposed to armed insurrection.

One groundbreaking quantitative study on the comparative efficacy of armed struggle and civil resistance evaluated the outcomes of violent and nonviolent campaigns for independence, secession, and anti-dictatorship struggles between 1900 and 2006. It found that the rate of success of civil resistance campaigns was more than two and a half times higher than the rate of its failures and more than twice as successful as their armed counterparts.[39] Those data, together with the qualitative studies included in this book, challenge a common, often exaggerated and glorified perception about the role of arms in winning a country's freedom—one borne of the influence of military historians on the nationalist imagination, the enduring legacy of Homeric literature on Western-educated political establishments, and the classism of elite refusal to acknowledge the influence of ordinary people on pivotal events in national histories.

Often, once statehood has been achieved, martyrology of violent struggle has served victorious military and political forces to amplify their own role in bringing about independence and to justify their ascent and tenure in power. However, even if martyrology has been closely linked with armed struggle, the past and present reality is more complex since the eulogization of life sacrifice may also be part of civil resistance. For example, as Chapter 11 on Bangladesh shows, the unarmed activists of the nonviolent Bangla language movement who were killed while defending their right to use Bangla became immortalized in national annals as martyrs. Nowadays, Palestinians, Egyptians, Syrians, Bahrainis, and Yemenis want to recognize their fallen nonviolent activists as martyrs. Martyrology can be seen both as a strategy to mobilize supporters and as a human, emotional response to recognize and value the courage of ordinary people who fought—whether with arms or nonviolently—against a more powerful and ruthless foe and, thereby, inspired others to rise up.

National liberation through violent contestation. Many chapters in this book suggest that national historical narratives, discourse, and commemorations fail to acknowledge the role of civil resistance in movements for self-determination. Struggles for independence against occupation or foreign control have been inextricably linked with the rise of nationalism-fueled violence, venerated military heroes, and mythologized chronicles of victimhood and glorified martyrs who fought against brutal and usually more powerful foes.[40] This, in turn, has reinforced the rarely questioned popular assumption that armed force must have been the dominant or decisive means of waging independence struggles. In addition, the tendencies to use the term *revolution* as a synonym for independence struggles and to identify revolution with violence (even some popular academic encyclopedias define "revolution" as a "fundamental and violent change"[41]) suggest a revolutionary hegemonic heritage that leads to a willful amnesia of the existence and denial of the legitimacy and viability of an alternative means of struggle other than violence. Where and when civil resistance has emerged during nationalist struggles, it often has been viewed as a somehow less manly, less consequential, and less patriotic endeavor than armed insurrection. This deprecating view of civil resistance has by no means been limited to violent revolutionaries. A prominent political theorist, Michael Walzer, for example, openly criticizes and devalues nonviolent resistance as "a disguised form of surrender" and "a minimalist way of upholding communal values after a military defeat."[42]

Therefore, it should not be surprising that mainstream media unintentionally or otherwise often propagate violence-focused interpretations of independence. For example, a columnist from a newspaper as reputable as *The Guardian* who, in defense of his argument that independence comes on the eve of important political rather than legal developments, stated that "In 1776, American independence came at the muzzle of a musket, not in the form of a lawsuit against George III."[43] Providentially, Chapter 16 on the United States addresses this common misconception by showing that, in reality, most of the American colonies gained their de facto independence before the war began through reliance on and use of nonmilitary actions of resistance. These actions were not lawsuits—the British Crown in fact considered them illegal—but neither were they shoot-outs or violent battles: they involved effective mass nonviolent noncooperation with British laws and customs and the establishment of new associations and institutions.

The conventional wisdom is that, in the struggle for statehood, there is much at stake for the local indigenous population as well as for a foreign occupier or hegemon. The former fights for its own country while the latter wants to maintain its territorial integrity and imperial dominance. An independence struggle is thus a maximalist or existential conflict for the occupied people who are fighting for their own survival against potential cultural or political, if not physical, annihilation. Conversely, a foreign power historically has invested so much of its own political capital, economic resources, and human lives in occupying or indirectly controlling a country that it perceives possible withdrawal or loss of influence over the territory as an intolerable national humiliation and a threat to global or regional hegemony that could encourage others under its colonial control to rebel. With such intense and vested interest, violence instigated and perpetrated by both sides is expected; it is common and inevitable. Because independence movements encompass such an enormous capacity for militancy, and because violence is often viewed as the strongest expression of that militancy, it is difficult for some to shift their intellectual and ontological paradigm away from violence toward the presence of nonviolent resistance and its potential historical impact.

Moreover, the cases included in this volume point to the conscious application and strategic use of nonviolent resistance, which long preceded its use by Gandhi. Many natural civil resisters before the twentieth century demonstrably understood—through their choice of nonviolent means of struggle—the futility or dire consequences of armed uprisings while also sensing the benefits of relying on nonviolent methods of struggle at a specific time of their nation's history.

Dangers of violent struggle. As a matter of fact, violent insurrections are more likely to have lethal consequences for purposeful causes than nonviolent resistance. The former has often hijacked and compromised what civil resistance had previously achieved. When military options have supplanted or supplemented nonviolent resistance, adverse consequences have included an increasingly militarized and polarized society, a destroyed socioeconomic infrastructure, weaker political institutions, and a culture of violence impregnated in politics and society during the struggle that persists even if a government transition is achieved. Armed resistance can quickly undermine nonviolent mobilization across and solidarity between various societal groups, endanger economic and social progress, and hinder or regress development of nascent autonomous democratic institutions and civil society (Cuba, Kosovo, Algeria, and Palestine). In addition to its economic toll, the human and social costs of violent struggle in many cases greatly surpass those of civil resistance (the United States). Insurgent violence also provides justification for and reduces the political legitimacy costs of repression perpetrated by a movement's adversary. Moreover, in the name of military necessity, armed struggles often abandon the very values (e.g., representing and being accountable to the nation's people) that ostensibly inspire them. This in turn engenders the type of behavior and practices conducive to the emergence of authoritarian regimes (Burma, Algeria, and Mozambique). Those who turn to violence rarely analyze dispassionately the risks and costs of their methods and fail to recognize that it is much harder to end an armed struggle than to begin one. Sometimes they mistakenly see arms as a shortcut and lack an appreciation of what has already been achieved through civil resistance: for example, the remarkable degree to which nonviolent actions have liberated societies from the control of occupiers (the United States, Bangladesh, and Burma).

Some of the case studies point to the possibility that civil resistance was also used instrumentally—at times instinctively and at other times deliberately—as a prelude (as in Poland and Kosovo) or complement (as in Mozambique and Algeria) to armed resistance. Even in such circumstances, however, the impact of civil resistance should be recognized. In some cases, civil resistance had a direct role in forcing foreign authorities to grant these countries formal independence (Ghana, Zambia, and Egypt) or equal political status within an empire (Hungary). More often, it accelerated the gradual process of liberation from foreign domination relative to the outside-imposed subjugation that the populations endured earlier (as in almost all cases included in this book). The point of these histories is not to suggest that the countries could not have gained independence without nonviolent struggle or that civil resistance alone was responsible. Rather, independence came as soon as it did—and often the societies and nascent civic and state institutions had been developed and thus were better prepared for independence—partly because of reliance on civil resistance, which had a profound effect on nation and state building. (For illustrations of the latter point, see the following subsection on national identity formation and state making; the analysis of the impact of civil resistance on collective identities in Chapter 2; and Chapters 14 and 16 on Poland and the United States, respectively, among others.)

National Identity Formation and State Making

In addition to explaining the dynamics of civil resistance in liberation struggles, this book also analyzes its impact on nation building.[44] The power of nonviolent conflict must be understood broadly since civil resistance itself is more than just a set of physical or material techniques or the instrumental use of certain tactics. The experience of waging nonviolent struggle can itself be a transformational societal force on multiple levels: economic, social, political, cultural, and psychological. Furthermore, resisters often devise nonviolent actions instinctively while relying intuitively on their knowledge, experience, and interpretation of the society that surrounds them—thereby making their resistance even more organically connected with the people who rally beside them. This noninstrumental view of civil resistance, ontologically embedded in a social environment yet autonomous and constitutive, is essential in understanding its influence on collective consciousness and national identity.

The emergence of new nation-states has been associated with either great and volatile upheavals or long-term structural changes. Accordingly, some modern nation-states were formed through violent state implosions—revolutions, foreign invasions, wars, or the decline or breakup of empires. Others were created as a result of the cumulative effects of industrialization, urbanization, the development of capitalism, mass migration, and the invention of new communication and transportation technologies. Still others came about as a result of internal domestic policies such as universal conscription, free compulsory education in a national language, the buildup of national bureaucracies, or functioning party politics.[45]

However, such nation-forming forces have often been seen as macro level, top down, elite driven, and almost deterministic. In contrast, the empirical chapters of this volume suggest that a number of subjugated nations underwent often unnoticed, but no less significant and transformative, bottom-up changes driven by continued overt or tacit civilian-based mobilization, organizing, and activism despite direct or indirect foreign domination, ethnic or cultural denationalization, and forceful integration or assimilation. Under the heavy weight of foreign domination, nation formation was far from being a forgone conclusion, as the nationalist-boosting processes such as raising a national army, building a national bureaucracy, or developing national education were often banned by foreign powers while nationalist advocates were killed, imprisoned, or exiled. Under such oppressive conditions, subjugated nations could have simply disappeared, as indeed was the fate of many first nations. Through mass-based civil resistance, ordinary people (more so than abstract or imperceptible forces) performed and created a sense of stateness. They bestowed their collective legitimacy on new forms of alternative cultural, social, economic, and political activities and organizations, thus wrenching political control out of the hands of foreign states or their local surrogates. They created greater awareness about and ownership of a common national collective with a strong belief that they could develop and prosper only in an independent state free of foreign intervention.

Thus, through the deployment of a rich repertoire of nonviolent tactics, the resisters engaged in challenging the powerholders that be. And by doing so, they solidified a sense of the national selfhood, created autonomous institutions, and established quasi-independent structures often outside the purview of foreign forces. Mass nonviolent mobilization and participation enabled societies to reject foreign dominance and indoctrination while practicing self-governance and building the nucleus of a new civil society. Through civil resistance, people became vividly conscious of their belonging, identity, language, and culture—the process that George Lakey, a leading educator in nonviolent social change, has referred to as "cultural preparation," or, translating from Paolo Freire, "conscientization" through which personal destiny becomes interwoven with that of a collective life.[46] In this sense, civil resistance, through its transformative force, functioned as an instrument of state making often long before such states were formally open for business. It laid foundations for the emergence of a nationally conscious and politicized citizenry and nationwide institutions of economic, civic, and political governance necessary for running a country after its independence, even if democratic changes in these newly independent states might have left much to be desired.

Civil resistance contributed to and shaped national identity during the spread of nationalism in the nineteenth and twentieth centuries. The nonviolent strategies used to defend society and undermine foreign oppression and control reinforced people's own affinity with their yet-to-be-independent nations, which in turn strengthened their collective resistance. Chapter 2 elaborates on this mutually recursive relationship, which has in some cases also inadvertently paved the way for a narrower, ethnically focused, and exclusive understanding of nationhood. Examples include the nation of Poles, but with restricted political rights for Ukrainians, Jews, or Belarusians; the nation of Kosovars, but without Serbs; the nation of Hungarians, but with exclusion of other ethnic minorities living in the Austro-Hungarian Empire; the nation of American colonists that had little room for Native Americans; or the nation of Bangladesh with a limited public space for Hindu or Christian minorities and the continued de facto disenfranchisement of most Biharis.[47] Nonviolent methods of resistance such as nationalist education, setting up ethnic organizations, or the surfeit of national commemorations and celebrations often promoted and exalted the culture, language, and history of the suppressed nation as well as glorified its military past. According to some chapters in this book, this inadvertent impact of civil resistance can be paradoxically blamed for suppressing stories of nonviolent resistance.

Would national identities in these nations have developed without recourse to the methods of civil resistance? Perhaps, but the process would have taken longer and its final outcome been less certain in the face of the forces of denationalization unleashed by dominant foreign powers. This book offers an important, but still a preliminary, study of the historic role of civil resistance—as a sort of mnemonic device—that helps restore full national consciousness and consolidate collective identity.

The nonviolent upheavals in North Africa and the Middle East that began in Tunisia in December 2010 make this volume even more timely and relevant because it offers readers historical lessons about the timeless use of civil resistance against brutal powers. In practice, civil resistance does not know cultural, ethnic, geographical, or temporal barriers. It has proved to be as equally effective against occupiers and colonizers as it now is against ruthless domestic authoritarian rulers and dictators. Thus, to understand the events of the Arab Spring and, generally, contemporary nonviolent resistance, readers are encouraged to venture into the often forgotten and hidden past of civil resistance.

Notes

1. The terms *nonviolent method* and *tactic* are used interchangeably and are understood as a limited plan of action developed and carried out to achieve a specific goal as part of a broader strategy of a nonviolent campaign.

2. Jonathan Schell, *The Unconquerable World: Power, Nonviolence, and the Will of the People* (New York: Henry Holt, 2003), in particular 63–99.

3. "Russia and India" in *The Collected Works of Mahatma Gandhi,* vol. 5, November 6, 1905–November 3, 1906, 8, http://www.scribd.com/doc/49842274 /Collected-Works-of-Mahatma-Gandhi-VOL005, accessed November 13, 2012.

4. In this book, the term *nonviolent* refers broadly to the absence of collective acts intended to use violence against an adversary or, more specifically, to a method of deliberately eschewing physical harm to an opponent. Two cases, Zambia and Egypt, also include property destruction, itself only one among a vast number of nonviolent actions identified in these chapters. The specific act did not aim to kill or maim anyone, but rather to cripple an adversary's material resources and, thus, raise the costs of political control over the territory by, for example, cutting down communication or transportation lines.

5. *Rights-based struggles* include democratic rights campaigns against dictatorship; movements for minority, labor, women's, and indigenous people's rights; and environmental campaigns and livelihood struggles for access to water and land or against deforestation. Examples of *rule-of-law struggles* are popular anticorruption, anti-mafia, or anti-gang violence campaigns. Despite the differences in the target of the popular resistance, anti-dictatorship campaigns have an interesting similarity with self-rule struggles. As Annyssa Bellal and I have argued elsewhere, anti-dictatorship resistance tends to define a dictator as an occupier and aggressor against whom the population needs to defend itself, thus extending the right of self-rule to people who struggle equally against foreign and domestic oppressors. See Maciej Bartkowski and Annyssa Bellal, "A Human Right to Resist," *Open Democracy,* May 3, 2011, http://www.opendemocracy.net/maciej-bartkowski-annyssa-bellal /human-right-to-resist, accessed May 15, 2011.

6. Nonviolent and Violent Campaigns and Outcomes (NAVCO 1.0) dataset, http://www.du.edu/korbel/sie/research/civilresistanceproject.html. Global Nonviolent

Action Database at Swarthmore College includes more than 600 cases of civil resistance campaigns as of the end of 2012, but only a dozen cases of nonviolent struggles against foreign domination. See http://nvdatabase.swarthmore.edu/.

7. For example, despite its comprehensive nature, NAVCO 1.0 does not include some major nonviolent campaigns from the past that are described in this book: Bangladesh between 1948 and 1952 and in 1971, Egypt 1919–1921, Burma prior to World War II, or the Iranian constitutional revolution, among others.

8. In his book *Unarmed Insurrections,* Kurt Schock integrates sociological insights from the political process theory and the dynamics of nonviolent action approach in an attempt to overcome the disciplinary divide. Clearly, much more research of a similar nature is needed to better understand points of interconnections and bridge the existing disciplinary gap between the social movement literature and civil resistance studies. See Kurt Schock, *Unarmed Insurrections: People Power Movements in Nondemocracies* (Minneapolis: University of Minnesota Press, 2005), particularly chapter 2.

9. For example, the forthcoming book by Mary King, *Conversion and the Mechanisms of Change in Nonviolent Action: The 1924–25 Vykom Satyagraha Case Against the Caste System* (Freedom Song, http://maryking.info/?page_id=168), suggests that there remain unexplored areas of research on the Indian national movement and nonviolent actions.

10. Mary King, *The New York Times on Emerging Democracies in Eastern Europe* (Washington, DC: CQ Press, 2009); Mark Beissinger, "The Intersection of Ethnic Nationalism and People Power Tactics in the Baltic States, 1987–91," in *Civil Resistance and Power Politics: The Experience of Non-Violent Action from Gandhi to the Present,* ed. Adam Roberts and Timothy Garton Ash (Oxford: Oxford University Press, 2009), 231–246; Lester R. Kurtz and Lee Smithey, "'We Have Bare Hands': Nonviolent Social Movements in the Soviet Block," in *Nonviolent Social Movements,* ed. Stephen Zunes, Lester R. Kurtz, and Sarah Beth Asher (Oxford: Blackwell, 1999), 96–124; Olgerts Eglitis, "Nonviolent Action in the Liberation of Latvia," Einstein Institute Monograph Series No. 5 (Boston: Albert Einstein Institution, 1993), http://www.aeinstein.org/organizations22f6.html, accessed February 6, 2011; Grazina Miniotaite, "Nonviolent Resistance in Lithuania: A Story of Peaceful Liberation," Einstein Institute Monograph Series No. 8 (Boston: Albert Einstein Institution, 2002), http://www.aeinstein.org/organizations9997.html, accessed February 5, 2011. See also the documentary, *The Singing Revolution,* directed by James Tusty and Maureen Castle Tusty (Sky Films, 2006), about the cultural resistance of the Estonians who opposed denationalization policies of the Soviet occupiers through collective folk singing, www.singingrevolution.com, accessed August 5, 2011.

11. For an excellent account of this subject see Mukulika Banerjee, *The Pathan Unarmed* (Oxford: Oxford University Press, 2001).

12. See Thomas Friedman, "Lessons from Tahrir Sq.," *New York Times,* May 24, 2011, and a response by Peter Hart, www.commondreams.org/view/2011/05/26-9, accessed June 5, 2011.

13. Maria Stephan, "Fighting for Statehood: The Role of Civilian-Based Resistance in the East Timorese, Palestinian, and Kosovo Albanian Self-Determination Movements," *Fletcher Forum of World Affairs* 30, no. 2 (2006): 57–79. See also Maria Stephan, "Nonviolent Insurgency: The Role of Civilian-Based Resistance in the East Timorese, Palestinian and Kosovo Albanian Self-Determination Movements" (PhD dissertation, Fletcher School of Law and Diplomacy 2005).

14. For more on pan-Africanism and nonviolent resistance, see Bill Sutherland and Matt Meyer, *Guns and Gandhi in Africa: Pan-African Insights on Nonviolence, Armed Struggle and Liberation in Africa* (Trenton, NJ: Africa World Press, 2000).

15. Ralph E. Crow and Philip Grant, "Questions and Controversies About Nonviolent Political Struggle in the Middle East" in *Civilian Jihad: Nonviolent Struggle, Democratization, and Governance in the Middle East,* ed. Maria J. Stephan Palgrave Macmillan Series on Civil Resistance (New York: Palgrave Macmillan, 2010), 32.

16. John F. Kennedy, president of the United States of America, address to Latin American diplomats during the first anniversary of the Alliance for Progress at the White House, March 13, 1962.

17. Various contributors to this field of study have used different terms to refer to the same phenomenon of mass-based, organized unarmed contestation: *nonviolent struggle* and *nonviolent action* (Gene Sharp, *The Politics of Nonviolent Action: Power and Struggle [Part One], The Methods of Nonviolent Action [Part Two], and The Dynamics of Nonviolent Action [Part Three]* [Boston: Porter Sargent, 1973]); *nonviolent conflict* (Peter Ackerman and Jack DuVall, *A Force More Powerful: A Century of Nonviolent Conflict* [New York: Macmillan, 2000]; and *civil resistance* (Roberts and Garton Ash, *Civil Resistance and Power Politics*).

In addition, the societies that practiced civil resistance often introduced their own terms to describe their collective nonviolent actions: *social self-defense* (Polish Solidarity movement), *people power* (Philippines), *popular resistance* (Palestine), *nonsubmission* (Spain), *political defiance* (Burma), and *positive action* (Ghana).

Gandhi began to use the term *civil resistance* after he realized that neither "passive resistance" used by Hungarians to describe their nonviolent struggle against Austrians (see Chapter 13) nor "civil disobedience" introduced by Henry David Thoreau in his 1849 essay of the same title properly reflected the nature of the resistance that Gandhi and many of his Indian compatriots waged against the British and earlier against the apartheid regime in South Africa. In his letter to P. Kodanda Rao, dated September 10, 1935, Gandhi wrote, "The statement that I had derived my idea of civil disobedience from the writings of Thoreau is wrong. The resistance to authority in South Africa was well advanced before I got the essay of Thoreau on civil disobedience. But the movement was then known as passive resistance. . . . When I saw the title of Thoreau's great essay, I began the use of his phrase to explain our struggle to the English readers. But I found that even civil disobedience failed to convey the full meaning of the struggle. I therefore adopted the phrase *civil resistance*" (emphasis added).

18. Gene Sharp, *The Politics of Nonviolent Action.*

19. Roberts and Garton Ash, *Civil Resistance and Power Politics.*

20. Sharp, *The Politics of Nonviolent Action;* Anders Boserup and Andrew Mack, *War Without Weapons: Non-Violence in National Defense* (Berlin: Schocken Books, 1975); Peter Ackerman and Christopher Kruegler, *Strategic Nonviolent Conflict: The Dynamics of People Power in the Twentieth Century* (Westport, CT: Praeger, 1994); Robert J. Burrowes, *The Strategy of Nonviolent Defense: A Gandhian Approach* (Albany: SUNY Press, 1996); Robert L. Helvey, *On Strategic Nonviolent Conflict: Thinking About the Fundamentals* (Boston: Albert Einstein Institution, 2004); Gene Sharp, ed., *Waging Nonviolent Struggle: 20th Century Practice and 21st Century Potential* (Boston: Porter Sargent, 2005).

21. Stephen Zunes, Lester Kurtz, and Sarah Beth Asher, eds., *Nonviolent Social Movements: A Geographical Perspective* (Oxford: Wiley-Blackwell, 1999); Ackerman and DuVall, *A Force More Powerful.*

22. Brian Martin, *Justice Ignited: The Dynamics of Backfire* (Lanham, MD: Rowman and Littlefield, 2007).

23. Yeshua Moser-Puangsuwan and Thomas Weber, eds., *Nonviolent Intervention Across Borders* (Honolulu: University of Hawaii Press, 2000); Howard Clark,

ed., *People Power: Unarmed Resistance and Global Solidarity* (London: Pluto, 2009); Véronique Dudouet and Howard Clark, *Nonviolent Civic Action in Support of Human Rights and Democracy* (Brussels: Directorate-General for External Policies, European Parliament, 2009), www.nonviolent-conflict.org/images/stories.pdfs/est 25679.pdf, accessed December 5, 2010.

24. Erica Chenoweth and Maria Stephan, *How Civil Resistance Works* (New York: Columbia University Press, 2011).

25. Sharon Erickson Nepstad, *Nonviolent Revolutions: Civil Resistance in the Late 20th Century* (Oxford: Oxford University Press, 2011).

26. Kurt Schock, *Unarmed Insurrections*; see also Chapter 2 in this volume.

27. For example, see Jillian Kestler-D'Amours, "In the Jordan Valley, Existence Is Resistance," Al Jazeera, July 29, 2011.

28. These tactics of nonviolent resistance stand in stark contrast to the words of Mao Zedong, according to whom a revolution was "not a dinner party, or writing an essay, or painting a picture, or doing embroidery; it cannot be so refined, so leisurely and gentle, so temperate, kind, courteous, restrained and magnanimous." However, the revolutionary struggles for statehood described in this volume were often carried out in the very form of actions that Mao Zedong so casually discarded: from festive parties, public but often banned ceremonies in the memories of significant historical figures and events, literary discussion circles and journalistic writings, poetry, and prose to historical and satirical paintings and drawings, street theater, artistic exhibitions, or indigenous cloth spinning and wearing traditional or national dress.

29. James C. Scott, *Weapons of the Weak: Everyday Forms of Peasant Resistance* (New Haven: Yale University Press, 1985); James C. Scott, "Everyday Forms of Resistance," in *Everyday Forms of Peasant Resistance*, ed. Forrest D. Colburn (Armonk, NY: M. E. Sharpe, 1989), 3–33; James C. Scott, *Domination and the Arts of Resistance: Hidden Transcripts* (New Haven: Yale University Press, 1992); Steve Crawshaw and John Jackson, *Small Acts of Resistance: How Courage, Tenacity, and Ingenuity Can Change the World* (New York: Union Square Press, 2010).

30. Jaroslav Hasek, *The Good Soldier Svejk: And His Fortunes in the World War* (London: Penguin Classics, 2005).

31. See Ralph Summy, "Nonviolence and the Case of the Extremely Ruthless Opponent," *Pacifica Review: Peace, Security and Global Change* 6, no. 1 (1994): 1–29. In the article Summy quotes George Orwell who expressed his doubts about the power of a nonviolent movement, particularly if this type of organizing faces a brutal opponent.

32. George Orwell, "Shooting an Elephant" (London: New Writing, 1936), http://eslreading.org/shootinganelephant.pdf, accessed March 20, 2011.

33. Ellen Barry, "Sound of Post-Soviet Protest: Claps and Beeps," *New York Times,* July 14, 2011; Ilya Mouzykantskii, "In Belarus, Just Being Can Prompt an Arrest," *New York Times,* July 30, 2011; Michael Schwirtz, "Teddy Bears Fall From Sky, and Heads Roll in Minsk," *New York Times,* August 1, 2012.

34. Basma Atassi, "A Colourful Uprising in Damascus," Al Jazeera, December 13, 2011.

35. Alexei Barrionuevo, "With Kiss-Ins and Dances, Young Chileans Push for Reform," *New York Times,* August 4, 2011; Carla Obs, "Philippine Students Are Lying Down to Stand Up for What They Believe," *France 24: International News,* http://observers.france24.com/content/20110928-filipino-students-lying-down -planking-education-budget-cuts-philippines-manila-university-congress, accessed

October 1, 2011. In reference to civil resistance "planking" can be defined as organized, often collective, actions of lying still and face down in strategically selected locations to protest or disrupt.

36. Assef Bayat, *Street Politics: Poor People's Movements in Iran* (New York: Columbia University Press, 1997).

37. Ryuichi Funatsu, "Al-Kawākibī's Thesis and Its Echoes in the Arab World Today," *Harvard Middle Eastern and Islamic Review* 7, no. 2 (2006): 30–32.

38. Ibid., 31.

39. According to the study by Erica Chenoweth and Maria Stephan, civil resistance campaigns succeeded in 53 percent and failed in more than 20 percent of their analyzed cases in comparison with 26 percent successes and more than 60 percent failures for the violent campaigns. Chenoweth and Stephan, *How Civil Resistance Works*, particularly the tables on 8–9; Maria Stephan and Erica Chenoweth, "Why Civil Resistance Works: The Strategic Logic of Nonviolent Conflict," *International Security* 33, no. 1 (2008): 7–44.

40. Jørgen Johansen, for example, noted that violent upheavals usually gain greater scholarly and media attention than nonviolent political and territorial changes. For example, hundreds of books have been published in English about the violent breakup of Yugoslavia in the 1990s while far fewer have been written about the peaceful dissolution of Czechoslovakia in 1992–1993. Jørgen Johansen, lecturer and nonviolent trainer, personal communication with the author, West Bank, October 15, 2010.

41. "Revolution," in *The Columbia Encyclopedia*, 6th ed. (New York: Columbia University Press, 2009), 4106.

42. Michael Walzer, *Just and Unjust War: A Moral Argument with Historical Illustrations* (New York: Basic Books, 1977), 332.

43. Simon Tisdall, "The End of the Battle for Kosovo," *The Guardian*, July 22, 2010, http://www.guardian.co.uk/commentisfree/2010/jul/22/serbia-battle-for-kosovo, accessed August 1, 2010.

44. Others have already pointed out that nationalism can be viewed as a form of contentious politics and, thus, its development and impact can be studied through the analytical lenses and practice of collective actions. However, in contrast to this volume, previous analysis has not focused explicitly on *nonviolent* movements and actions or their role in nation making or identity formation. See Doug McAdam, Sidney Tarrow, and Charles Tilly, *Dynamics of Contention* (New York: Cambridge University Press, 2001), 227–263.

45. Ernest Gellner, *Nations and Nationalism* (Ithaca: Cornell University Press, 1983); Eric Hobsbawm, *Nations and Nationalism Since 1780: Programme, Myth, Reality* (Cambridge: Cambridge University Press, 1992); Benedict Anderson, *Imagined Communities: Reflections on the Origin and Spread of Nationalism* (London: Verso, 1991).

46. George Lakey, *Strategy for Non-Violent Revolution* (London: Housmans Bookshop, 1969), 1; George Lakey, *A Manifesto for Nonviolent Revolution* (Philadelphia: Movement for a New Society, 1976); Paolo Freire, *Pedagogy of the Oppressed*, 30th anniversary ed. (New York: Continuum, 2000).

47. For example, through nonviolent participatory activities in newly established economic, social, and educational associations in the villages, the national awareness of Polish peasants increased but often in opposition to ethnic others (i.e., Jews that ran village taverns or Ukrainian or Belarusian peasant neighbors). See Keely Stauter-Halsted, *The Nation in the Village: The Genesis of Peasant National*

Identity in Austrian Poland 1848–1914 (Ithaca: Cornell University Press, 2001). Heeding history's lessons, in the conclusion of Chapter 12 of this volume, Jason MacLeod warns the West Papuan nonviolent movement against an exclusivist nationalist concept of a pro-independence struggle to the detriment of a more general discourse and actions focused on defending human rights.

2

Identity Formation
in Nonviolent Struggles

Lee A. Smithey

Nationalism can be a powerful force for mobilizing participation in nonviolent civil resistance; it can also be shaped and reinforced by collective nonviolent action. The cases presented in this volume raise questions of particular social scientific importance: How are national identities shaped through nonviolent actions, and are such actions shaped by activists' shared identities? I argue that the study of social movements reveals that collective identity, perceptions of the field of struggle, and how conflict is waged are mutually recursive. Tactical choices reflect collective or national identities, and collective action catalyzes the construction of collective identities as meaning is formed through interaction with opponents, allies, and bystanding publics. Certain strategies[1] and tactics[2] will seem more likely or will only be conceivable as a function of the values and identities to which a group subscribes. Conversely, collective action and conflict can introduce new forms of identification or reinforce preexisting ones. Identities can also be strategically deployed through public symbolic actions to draw attention to a cause, to frame injustice against a group, or to generate dilemmas for opponents by playing on cultural norms.

The histories of nonviolent struggle described in this book can provide new opportunities to examine relationships between collective action and collective identity and to better understand how their interaction influences the outcomes of large-scale campaigns of nonviolent resistance. Sociologists have contributed much to the study of social movements, perhaps especially with respect to culture, but often have failed to account for strategic dimensions of nonviolent action or to fully appreciate that social movements are strategically engaged in conflicts. Conversely, most of the

31

literature on strategic nonviolent action has tended to overlook the cultural dimensions of nonviolent social movements such as collective identity. The chapters that follow, however, offer an important opportunity to build bridges between these two fields and to begin to understand better how culture and identity interact with nonviolent resistance or, more precisely, how strategic nonviolent power shapes and is shaped by nationalist groups' memories, ideologies, values, and worldviews.

In this chapter, I review theoretical developments in the study of social movements, nationalism, and strategic nonviolent action that could complement one another and help us to better appreciate the importance of tactics, their innovation, and the cultural underpinnings of nonviolent power. In particular, I focus on the relationship between the construction of collective identity, such as nationalism, and the methods of collective action that nonviolent resisters develop and deploy. Each can limit or enhance the other in crucial ways that help determine the outcome of nonviolent national struggles. I refer to the contributors' works in this volume as well as other cases to demonstrate ways in which nationalist collective identity and nonviolent tactics shape one another in conflict with opponents and how they must be reconciled with one another when they do not align easily.

Collective Identity and Nationalism

In the 1980s, identity and self became topics of increasing attention among sociologists[3] and collective identity emerged as a concept to address the perennial question of why people participate and maintain their involvement in movements. This can be a particularly important concern when a movement's ultimate goal (e.g., independence or an end to occupation or foreign domination) seems distant and while autocracy and repression persist. Defining what is meant by *collective identity* has required considerable theorizing.[4] Collective identity usually refers to a shared sense of "we-ness" that "derives" or "emerges" from shared cognitions, beliefs, and emotions among a group of individuals actively pursuing social or political change.[5] A range of closely related concepts has clustered around collective identity such as solidarity, commitment, consciousness, ideology, emotion, and self. The integral relationship between the personal and the collective is fundamental, as Francesca Polletta and James M. Jasper explain: "We have defined collective identity as an individual's cognitive, moral, and emotional connection with a broader community, category, practice, or institution. It is a perception of a shared status or relation, which may be imagined rather than experienced directly, and it is distinct from personal identities, although it may form part of a personal identity."[6]

Similarly, framing theorists have emphasized what William A. Gamson has called the "mesh between individual and cultural systems"[7] and have emphasized the critical work within movements of aligning personal and collective identities such that participation in movement activities seems natural and compelling.[8]

I focus here on one particularly prominent form of mass collective identity, *nationalism,* an identification with an extensive political community, often but not always incorporating a narrative of ethnic origin or distinction such as language.[9] Nationalism is a deeply psychocultural process that meets social psychological needs for belonging and solidarity and encourages groups to pursue the establishment of a state that represents their national identity. Interestingly, the emergence of social movements and civil resistance parallels the spread of nationalism in the eighteenth and nineteenth centuries through at least some of the same historical and material developments such as the spread of print technology and national education.[10] More importantly, however, I am interested in how the kinds of methods that nationalist groups use to advance their interests help construct their sense of national identity. A general reading of nationalism studies might conclude that national affiliation is a product of self-identification with imagined communities that has been facilitated by macro-level material changes such as the rise of capitalism, the development of print technology, the wide accessibility of print languages, the rise of the revolutionary nation-state, and the spread of state-sponsored education.[11] This book contributes to the field by examining the role of nonviolent collective action in nationalist movements for independence and, thus, provides new opportunities to study ways in which nonviolent resistance and national identities influence one another.

Integrating Conflict and Tactics into the Study of Social Movements

Until recently, the sociological study of social movements has usually been conducted in isolation from the conflicts in which the movements are involved, generally focusing on issues of movement emergence, participation, and maintenance. Nevertheless, some sociologists have acknowledged the way in which identities are constructed in opposition to other parties in conflict. Bert Klandermans situates movements' activities within a dynamic and interactive field of contesting parties and asserts that collective action events are sites of meaning construction and transformation: "Episodes of collective action have an enduring impact on the participants; their collective identities are formed and transformed."[12] I argue that tactics are an integral part of these episodes of give and take among nonviolent movements, authorities, countermovements, and the public, and the interactive nature of tactics constitutes one of the primary threads by which collective identity and collective action are tied to one another in conflict situations.

Interactivity and Identity Boundaries

Tactical choices made in response to discriminatory or oppressive political conditions have important repercussions for social movements. As Verta Taylor and Nella Van Dyke claim, "protest actions are one of the means by which challenging groups develop an oppositional consciousness," a collective readiness to take action against the status quo.[13] Systematic discrimination, countermovement tactics, and state repression are all pressures that can encourage resistance and "oppositional consciousness."[14] Indeed, both tactics and identities are each, to a large extent, other centered. Each depends on or reacts to others in order to have meaning and purpose. Because of their creative tension with opponents, tactics contribute to "boundary formation," the process of group differentiation that creates and sustains collective identity, even as collective identities are malleable and can change.[15] Any tactic in a conflict situation is intended to influence an opponent through coercion, persuasion, or bargaining. And any individual or collective identity is defined to some extent in contrast with others, even when a group demands inclusion such as in campaigns for civil and cultural rights. In the latter situation, demands for inclusion can advocate a distinctive ethnic or national identity and coexistence within a multicultural state. In Chapter 11, Ishtiaq Hossain shows that in 1948 and 1952 the Bengalis were mobilized nonviolently, not to press for their independence but for the inclusion of Bangla alongside Urdu as a state language in Pakistan. The Bengali language movement could thus be said to exhibit an integrative dimension in relation to other Pakistanis.

Struggle can also be integrative by providing an opportunity to overcome ethnic, religious, or other divisions in opposition to a common opponent, at least temporarily. Language education, song, poetry, and commemoration all contributed to the development of a distinctive Bengali national identity that sustained a nonviolent struggle and led to the de facto independence of Bengalis from Pakistan in 1971. Systematic discrimination, countermovement tactics, and state repression are all pressures that encourage boundary formation or "oppositional consciousness."[16] Similarly, in Chapter 10, Yeshua Moser-Puangsuwan describes the way in which a unitary national identity superseded religious and ethnic divisions during the Burmese nonviolent resistance to British colonialism, though ethnic strife has reemerged since independence.

The integrative potential of nonviolent civil resistance is one of its most promising features, and the tendency of nonviolent struggles to foster democratic political systems through the building of civil society has been documented.[17] However, it is necessary to consider Manfred Steger's warning that, while nationalism may offer a powerful force for mobilization in nonviolent campaigns, it may by its exclusive nature encourage ethnic polarization (e.g., see Jason MacLeod's Chapter 12 on West Papua) and the adoption of violent strategies in the future.[18]

In some cases, symbolically rich nonviolent methods have been used not only for the construction of collective identity but as vehicles for identity deployment by which marginalized collective identities are openly expressed in order to encourage public debate or to make use of culturally resonant identities to enhance legitimacy.[19] In nonviolent independence struggles, statuses with prestige, such as motherhood, may be emphasized to challenge a regime's monopoly on legitimacy. As Amr Abdalla and Yasmine Arafa describe in Chapter 7 on Egypt, 300 women challenged British repression of nonviolent protesters by framing the event as attacks on "unarmed sons, children, boys and men." Similarly, Egyptian women wore veils to protest British occupation and successfully undermined the authorities' capacity to stop them. According to an officer in charge, "any force you use to women puts you in the wrong."[20] Similarly, women's veils in both Algeria and Egypt have constituted symbolic challenges to Westernization and foreign domination. In Algeria between 1871 and 1954, as Algerians under French colonial rule retreated into their families and traditional Islamic communities, the veil became a battleground over the legitimacy of local culture under a colonial regime. The veil signaled devotion to Islamic culture and, as such, constituted a rejection of the imposition of French culture.[21]

Parties in conflict can cultivate and deploy identity for strategic purposes, but the interplay of opponents engaged in conflict can also shape their interrelated identities. In the dialogical models of discourse theorists, opponents respond to one another's attempts to control the definition of the situation and public opinion through framing and drawing on discursive repertoires and rhetoric. In the back and forth of framing and counterframing, response and counterresponse, no single party maintains absolute control of the direction of the discourse. These dialogic processes are dynamic, shared, and often unpredictable.[22]

In Northern Ireland, republican prisoners in the 1970s and 1980s challenged the British government's determination to portray them as terrorists by wearing blankets instead of prison uniforms. The republican blanket protest initiated a process of escalation with prisoners expanding noncooperation and the prison authorities trying to make them pay for it, ultimately leading to the "dirty protests" (where prisoners smeared their cell walls with excrement) and the 1980 and 1981 hunger strikes in which ten prisoners died. The first prisoner to die, Bobby Sands, was even elected to the British Parliament in a protest vote.[23] British authorities and the leadership of the Irish Republican Army failed to anticipate the resonance of the hunger strikes among republicans or the advantage of the grassroots political mobilization that the strikes would trigger. Meanwhile, unionists and loyalists interpreted the hunger strikes as a revulsive ploy led by republican terrorists and Catholic clergy to sanctify murderers, which only deepened their sense of alienation from their Catholic neighbors.[24] Tactical choices constitute cascades of action and response that contribute in an interactive and interpretive fashion to the formation of collective identities. In the Northern Ireland case, hunger strikes broadened and deepened republican and unionist identities as prisoners and British authorities engaged in a heated dialogic battle that was waged largely in the symbolic realms of political, ethical, and religious discourse.

Interactivity and Tactical Choice

Introducing an interactive or conflict dimension to identity construction leads to questions about how social movements and other actors interact, including the kinds of tactics that movements employ and how those choices influence the construction of identity boundaries. The finding that social movements tend to select from stable limited sets of tactics or "repertoires of contention" has inspired the most significant coverage of tactics in the social movement literature.[25] Most social movement scholars, however, have not fully addressed the wide array of methods that have been developed by nonviolent activists or the ways in which tactics exert pressure on or induce other actors (opponents, allies, and bystanders) in fields of contention.

The tactical combination of diverse nonviolent methods (e.g., protests, sit-ins, religious services, boycotts, and commemorations) can persuade or coerce and will invite different responses from opponents and third parties. Burning one's opponent in effigy will evoke a different interpretation and response compared with a respectful funeral to commemorate victims. Each is a symbolic indictment, but they project different messages that are likely to be interpreted in different ways by opponents and bystanders. Furthermore, if collective identities are indeed constructed in relation to others, we can expect that, as tactical engagements between nonviolent movements and their targets change, their collective identities will also be subject to change. For example, selective targeting of factions within a regime is an important strategic concern for nonviolent resisters who can modulate their actions to cultivate identity or loyalty shifts among important groups such as the police and military. Unlike more coercive methods such as blockades or occupying buildings, methods of symbolic protest and persuasion that incorporate humor or highlight cultural similarities between resisters and security forces can play critical roles in challenging assumptions about regime legitimacy on which agents of the regime base their obedience. Distributing flowers and food to security forces or normalizing resistance by incorporating familiar activities into demonstrations, such as prayers, weddings, and musical performances, are time-tested ways to create social psychological dilemmas for a regime's agents and encourage them to identify with nonviolent resisters.[26]

Fortunately, I am not alone in proposing that there is considerable promise in a marriage of conflict theory, nonviolent action theory, and sociologists' work on collective identity in social movements. James M. Jasper wisely calls for a "conflict lens" through which to study social movements:

> There are regularities, a logic, to conflict that is partly independent of resources, biography, and cultural meanings. Finding the right alliances, inventing tactics that surprise one's opponents, or forcing one's foe into a publicly recognized error all have an impact, whatever one's taste in tactics. Similarly, your own tastes, beliefs, and emotions can help you or trip you up strategically. Strategic choices depend so much on the interactions between various players that we need a "conflict" lens to relate social movements to the broader strategic field. The apparatus developed to explain movement emergence—frame alignment, identity, resource mobilization, moral shocks—helps us surprisingly little in accounting for success; we must switch to a different vocabulary, of tactical innovation, vulnerabilities, blunders, credibility, and rules.[27]

Jasper also prudently warns us to strike a balance between studying social movements as military and nonviolent action strategists might do and recognizing that movements are eminently social phenomenon: "Strategic interaction is crucially important, the very stuff of protest, but if it is the only lens, then 'conflict' replaces 'social movements' as the appropriate framework. A purely strategic lens misses much of the 'why' of protest."[28] Jasper invites movement scholars to incorporate strategy and tactics more fully into their research when he classifies "artful strategies" as one of the primary dimensions of protest.[29] He notes that strategic tactical choices are conditioned by the cultural environments in which they are made, but they are also creative and often effective acts developed by those who can proficiently interpret their cultural and political scene. In short, both the conflict approach represented by the nonviolent action literature's focus on strategy and tactics and the work on culture and identity fill gaps in each other to produce a more comprehensive picture of social movements, as I explain more fully in the next section.

Collective Identity and Nonviolent Tactics

Since the late 1980s, cultural models that emphasize the role that social movements play as "staging areas" for the construction of meaning and identity have become increasingly prevalent in the study of social movements and can help us understand tactical choice in nonviolent civil resistance movements.[30] The concept of repertoires that has been used to describe tactical choices has also been adopted to describe the way in which movements' persuasive use of rhetoric or "symbolic repertoires" are constrained and enabled by the cultural environment in which they are embedded.[31] We may expect the same cultural constraints and opportunities to influence nonviolent activists' tactical choices and their ability to mobilize participants and sustain their engagement. Readers of this book will find narratives from regional, historical, religious, and philosophical traditions provide familiar and emotive languages that call citizens to sustained nonviolent action in the name of values that transcend the propaganda of colonial and autocratic regimes.

The case of nineteenth- and early-twentieth-century Poland presented by Maciej Bartkowski in Chapter 14 demonstrates how the currents of national patriotism closely associated with military struggle could also be associated with nonviolent resistance. The martyrdom and sense of sacrifice around which Poland's national identity was built became a vehicle for the development of nonviolent campaigns of resistance known as organic work that aimed both to develop national economy and, through preservation of language and culture, to "awaken patriotism." Interestingly, in this case, a sense of Polish identity was fused with a new positivistic intellectual trend that harnessed national fervor in the service of strategic nonviolent resistance.

In other cases, religious traditions have played important roles by providing new rationales for resistance, even if the primary methods of action were essentially secular such as economic strikes and boycotts. In Chapter 8, Nikki R. Keddie notes the way in which the emergence of the Babi and Baha'i sects within Iranian Shiism in the middle of the nineteenth century challenged the centuries-old quietism of Shia leaders and introduced new ideas about political involvement and, in the case of the Baha'i, the imperative of using nonviolent methods to press for major constitutional reforms. Similarly, Abdalla and Arafa report in Chapter 7 that Islamic law played a fundamental role in legitimizing Egyptian resistance in 1805 against an Ottoman governor and was used to encourage nonviolent discipline during massive demonstrations and a four-month siege of the governor's citadel. Understanding the framing resources (e.g., culture, history, tradition, and religion) available to nonviolent activists is important and, as these examples illustrate, it is also important to understand the impact that participation in nonviolent action has on communicating and internalizing meaning within movements.

The Cultural Power of Nonviolent Tactics

One might expect that strategic collective actions would figure more prominently in work on social movements. But this is an interesting oversight since the relationship between culture and action sits at the core of the sociology of culture and, as I have already noted, the construction of collective identity takes place in relation with others to whom tactics are addressed.[32]

Most research on social movement identity work has focused on text, narratives, and discourse. According to Scott A. Hunt and Robert D. Benford, "Fundamentally, collective identities are talked into existence . . . personal and collective identities shape and are shaped by collective action and the subsequent identity talk."[33] They acknowledge the capacity of participation in collective action to influence identity construction, but the visual, temporal, and spatial dimensions of collective action tactics—often underestimated or ignored altogether—also play an important role. In many cases, texts or scripts are incorporated into strategic collective action through declarations, song lyrics, speeches, visual projections, and theater, but also there often can be found a rich and meaningful choreography or dramaturgy of colors, symbols, clothing, movement, and sounds.[34]

Even noncooperation and nonviolent intervention (e.g., strikes, sit-ins, and occupations), which are designed to interrupt institutions and social systems, can be laden with symbolic meaning. In Chapter 12, MacLeod describes the role that indigenous and religious rituals have played in nonviolent resistance in West Papua, first against Dutch colonialism and then against Indonesia after 1963. Nonviolent methods such as collective tax resistance and withholding of labor were undertaken alongside collective singing, dancing, and drinking palm wine. These kinds of cultural activities (e.g., choices of dress and food) continue to serve as everyday markers of identity and resistance among committed nationalists.[35] Even as recently as July 2010, simple public demonstrations featuring traditional dress and dance evolved into a merchants' strike and the occupation of the parliament building. In such instances, symbolic protest and persuasion become almost seamless with nonviolent noncooperation (e.g., strikes) and nonviolent intervention (e.g., occupying the parliament building).

Experienced organizers make sure that the symbolism of a collective action is not lost on the media and, thus, interpreting or narrating events for the public through television and radio interviews and print outlets is important. However, in order to account more fully for the power and influence of nonviolent action, the study of the capacities of carefully choreographed and symbolically rich tactics to convey shared ideology and national patriotism should accompany the textual or narrative framing and identity work that has attracted much attention among social movement scholars.[36] In fairness, one of the reasons that the relationships between collective identity and nonviolent tactics have been understudied is because they are so difficult to disentangle. People engage in collective action out of shared emotional commitments to ideologies and identification with groups, but collective action often encourages participants to express and experiment with new identities. At the same time, tactics are inspired and constrained by the availability of resources, political opportunities, in-group conflict, group history, and opponents' tactical moves. Thus, it is often difficult to attribute causality in the relationship between tactical choices and collective identity. There is also much ground to cover in documenting the vast array of tactics that are used by social movement organizations as well as the many ways in which tactics interact with organizational dynamics and induce opponents to capitulate and third parties to collaborate, processes that feed back and shape collective identity.

Collective Identity Shapes Tactical Choices

A group's history and ideology shape the repertoire of tactics on which it might call, influenced by the opportunity structures and the kinds of institutions that the movement encounters.[37] In his work on "taste in tactics," Jasper describes the important relationship between the ways in which actors perceive themselves and the tactics they are inclined to deploy: "Tactics are rarely, if ever, neutral means about which protestors do not care. Tactics represent important routines, emotionally and morally salient in these people's lives. Just as their ideologies do, their activities express protestors' political identities and moral visions."[38]

Movement organizations are inclined to adopt tactics that express or reflect their shared identity, beliefs, and experience. Song has played an important role in several of the movements discussed in this book, circumventing prohibitions, communicating messages not understood by colonial occupiers, or reaching less literate sectors of the population as in Burma and West Papua. The Burmese independence struggle, presented by Moser-Puangsuwan in Chapter 10, also involved several of the symbolic nationalist tactics of its contemporary sister movement, the Indian independence movement. In the 1920s, the Buddhist monk U Ottama encouraged the founding of cultural associations across Burma committed to Wunthanu, meaning, "to love and cherish its own culture, country, and people." As in India, strategies of nonviolent noncooperation became linked to a "constructive program" based on practices such as the wearing of local homespun cloth (*pinni*) and the eating of Burmese foods. It is often difficult to disentangle instances in which collective identity inspires the development of tactics that seem natural within activists' frames of reference and those in which the stirring of national fervor through carefully choreographed tactics is largely pragmatic as leaders seek to tap into preexisting wells of national identification. In the empirical world, both alternatives are probably in operation at the same time.[39]

Tactics Shape Collective Identity

Tactics serve as valuable expressions of identity that re-create and sustain collective identity, but they are also influential at critical moments in which identities can be renewed or transformed.[40] Some tactics are adopted because they are particularly suited to building collective identity and studies have documented the important roles that strategic collective action methods (including marches, rallies, and parades) can serve as political activities and as vehicles for building solidarity, even if that may lead to factionalism within social movements.[41]

Tactical choices also shape collective identities by inspiring or requiring new rationales and justifications for novel or controversial actions. In the 1950s, Algerian women, who had formerly worn the veil as a form of communal cultural resistance to French colonialism, adopted Western dress and manners to evade French counterinsurgency measures and smuggle contraband for the resistance. In the process, women who had been confined to domestic spheres developed new identities independent of patriarchal Islam and became known as national heroes. The tactical imperative to abandon the veil forced both men and women to reconstruct the roles and status of women in Algerian society.[42]

Collective identities, including national identities, can be shaped in fundamental ways during nonviolent movements for self-determination. As Walter H. Conser Jr. points out in Chapter 16 about nonviolent resistance against the British, the United States has over time eulogized violence in its story of national origin, but a careful historical review shows that, during colonial resistance, national identity and nonviolent strategy were closely related to one another. Exploitative British tax policies incited widespread refusal to pay taxes and boycotts of dutied items and their merchants, heightening colonists' sense of difference from Britain, instilling confidence, and catalyzing the formation of a unique American identity that views taxes with great suspicion.

As Hossain reveals in Chapter 11 on Bangladesh, the potential for widespread public participation in nonviolent resistance can broaden and amplify the impact of collective action on national identity. People of all ages participated in the defense of the Bangla language and heightened their sense of national identity through language education, attending rallies, reciting poetry, and singing anthems to commemorate the martyrs of the language movement.

Reconciling Identity and Tactics

We have established that tactical choices reflect and shape identities, but the close dialectical relationship between collective identity and collective action also produces tension that can be constructive or disruptive. Since the collective identities to which nonviolent resisters subscribe are never monolithic and coexist with their many personal and social identities, any tactical choice is likely to offer a better fit for some social movement organizations than for others.[43] External factors, such as political opportunity and countermoves by opponents, can produce strategic imperatives that recommend some tactics over others. In such circumstances, movement leaders can be encouraged to introduce new, unfamiliar, and sometimes uncomfortable tactics. Internal debate within social movements over reconciling collective identity with innovative tactics can:

1. Limit tactical repertoires when tactics violate norms. Though the Working Committee of the Indian National Congress overruled him, Mohandas Gandhi (Mahatma) proposed in 1939 that Indians nonviolently support their colonizer, Britain, in its war effort against Germany. He felt that a principled concern for one's opponent might require suspending the use of civil disobedience, especially if it jeopardized opportunities to win over an opponent.[44]

2. Instigate shifts in the content of collective identities to incorporate new forms of collective action. In Chapter 15, Howard Clark reports that the threat of Serbian attacks in Kosovo in the early 1990s generated a compelling strategic imperative among Albanians to counter stereotypes of them as dangerous Muslim fundamentalists. Kosovo Albanian Muslims therefore began to recognize Catholic festivals and the central humanitarian organization was symbolically named after Mother Teresa of Calcutta (herself an Albanian). One group even considered a mass conversion to Catholicism! We can only imagine the debates among Albanians over the theological and ethnic ramifications of such a proposal. The strategy was never realized as it would have appeared a blatantly opportunistic ploy to cultivate potential Western allies. Even so, this openness to Catholicism required a reconceptualization of Albanian Muslim identity.[45]

3. Lead to contention within and among social movement organizations.[46] Analyzing anticolonial resistance in Mozambique in Chapter 5, Matt Meyer uncovers a contentious and hidden history of grassroots nonviolent organizing and constructive work that ultimately came to define a unique Mozambican national identity. In Mozambicans' struggles against the Portuguese, guerrilla tactics were favored over nonviolent tactics. However, Meyer reveals that "two lines of struggle" existed in the Mozambique Liberation Front (FRELIMO) under the leadership of Eduardo Mondlane and his successor Samora Machel. Repression by the Portuguese elevated armed struggle over nonviolent action but not without friction between Mondlane and Leninists in FRELIMO. Nevertheless, through a legacy of cooperative organizing from the 1940s to the 1960s and the work of organizations such as the Organization of Mozambican Women (OMM) in the 1960s and 1970s, FRELIMO's zones of occupation became areas with strong civic infrastructure and grassroots empowerment that left an indelible mark on Mozambican national identity. Today, conflict repertoires in Mozambique reflect

a "'resistance and reconciliation' consciousness" that is unique across Africa, but it emerged only out of the tension between violent and nonviolent strategies that were negotiated in the midst of conflict.

Conclusion

Collective action (such as nonviolent resistance) and collective identity (including nationalism) are closely related, especially with regard to tactical choices made in a field of contention. By examining lost histories of nonviolent nationalist and independence movements, we gain access to cases that begin to reveal the intersection of the construction of nationalist identity and strategic nonviolent campaigns for national independence and freedom from foreign occupation or colonization. In the process, we can better understand how collective identities and nonviolent collective action mutually reconstitute and shape one another.

While trying to influence opponents and bystanders, nonviolent resistance movements express and define the boundaries of their collective identities. The tactics they choose are shaped by their worldview and ideology. As contributors to this collection show, some tactics can create significant material dilemmas for opponents, but others can convey meaning through symbols and careful choreography. The latter thus play important roles in the interactive framing battles through which nonviolent resistance movements mobilize, construct collective identity, instill discipline, motivate participants, bring public pressure to bear on opponents, and shape popular political cultures.

Although previous research has indicated that movements tend to draw from familiar tactical repertoires that reflect their participants' worldviews and tastes, both external opportunities and opponents' moves can encourage the use of novel nonviolent tactics that do not align perfectly with shared identities, requiring that tactics, identities, or both be modified. A movement's power through nonviolent resistance may be enhanced or internal conflicts may ensue, either of which may impact the movement's sustainability and outcomes.

The nonviolent struggles presented in subsequent chapters offer a promising opportunity for scholars to synthesize what we know about movement cultures, strategies, and outcomes, and the interdisciplinary mix that this volume represents promises to raise new questions and directions for research. The interaction of culture and nonviolent strategy is rich and untapped. Future researchers will do well to gather more ethnographic data on the activities of nonviolent movements to better capture the intricate work of framing identities and the tactical choice of choosing methods that reflect nonviolent resisters' biographies and collective identities.

Notes

This chapter draws from and expands on a previously published article: Lee A. Smithey, "Social Movement Strategy, Tactics, and Collective Identity," *Sociology Compass* 3 (2009): 658–671. I thank Maciej Bartkowski, Gregory Maney, and Lester Kurtz for feedback on earlier drafts. All errors, however, remain mine.

1. Strategy in nonviolent conflict can be understood as a general plan of action that addresses important questions such as why, when, and how best to achieve an overall goal. Gene Sharp, *The Politics of Nonviolent Action*, part 3: *The Dynamics of Nonviolent Action* (Boston: Porter Sargent, 1973), 493.

2. In this chapter, "tactics" refers to the strategic actions that movement organizations undertake. Gene Sharp, one of the foremost scholars of the study of nonviolent resistance, has developed a now-famous list of 198 "methods" that correspond with the kinds of actions that I refer to as "tactics." Sharp defines a "tactic" as the strategic application of "methods" in a particular engagement with opponents. This distinction in terminology is not generally recognized or followed meticulously in the social movement literature, perhaps to avoid confusion when the term "methods" often refers to research methods. See Gene Sharp, ed., *Waging Nonviolent Struggle: 20th Century Practice and 21st Century Potential* (Boston: Porter Sargent, 2005), 444–459. For greater insight into different categories of "methods," see the concluding chapter and conflict summaries in this book.

3. Sheldon Stryker, Timothy J. Owens, and Robert W. White, eds., *Self, Identity, and Social Movements* (Minneapolis: University of Minnesota Press, 2000), 3–4.

4. Ibid., 5–6; Francesca Polletta and James M. Jasper, "Collective Identity and Social Movements," *Annual Review of Sociology* 27 (2001); Scott A. Hunt and Robert D. Benford, "Collective Identity, Solidarity, and Commitment," in *The Blackwell Companion to Social Movements*, ed. David A. Snow, Sarah Anne Soule, and Hanspeter Kriesi (Malden, MA: Blackwell, 2004).

5. William A. Gamson, "The Social Psychology of Collective Action," in *Frontiers in Social Movement Theory*, ed. Aldon D. Morris and Carol McClurg Mueller (New Haven: Yale University Press, 1992), 55; Alberto Melucci, "The Process of Collective Identity," in *Social Movements and Culture*, ed. Hank Johnston and Bert Klandermans (Minneapolis: University of Minnesota Press, 1995), 44–45; Viktor Gecas, "Value Identities, Self-Motives, and Social Movements," in *Self, Identity, and Social Movements*, ed. Sheldon Stryker, Timothy J. Owens, and Robert W. White (Minneapolis: University of Minnesota Press, 2000), 99–100.

6. Polletta and Jasper, "Collective Identity and Social Movements," 285.

7. Gamson, "Social Psychology of Collective Action," 55.

8. David A. Snow and Doug McAdam, "Identity Work Processes in the Context of Social Movements: Clarifying the Identity/Movement Nexus," in *Self, Identity, and Social Movements*, ed. Sheldon Stryker, Timothy J. Owens, and Robert W. White (Minneapolis: University of Minnesota Press, 2000), 46–53.

9. In Chapter 11, Ishtiaq Hossain presents the central role that the Bengali language movements of 1948 and 1952 played in laying the ethnic nationalist foundations for Bangladesh's successful independence bid in 1971.

10. Sidney G. Tarrow, *Power in Movement: Social Movements and Contentious Politics*, 2nd ed., Cambridge Studies in Comparative Politics (New York: Cambridge University Press, 1998), 43–53.

11. Ernest Gellner, *Nations and Nationalism (New Perspectives on the Past)* (Oxford: Blackwell, 1983); Benedict R. O. G. Anderson, *Imagined Communities: Reflections on the Origin and Spread of Nationalism* (New York: Verso, 1991); Anthony D.

Smith, *Nations and Nationalism in a Global Era* (Cambridge, MA: Polity Press, 1995). Interestingly, as a number of chapters in this volume show, national or patriotic education was often conducted illegally and against the wishes of the authorities.

12. Bert Klandermans, "The Social Construction of Protest and Multiorganizational Fields," in *Frontiers in Social Movement Theory,* ed. Aldon D. Morris and Carol McClurg Mueller (New Haven: Yale University Press, 1992), 93.

13. Verta Taylor and Nella Van Dyke, "'Get up, Stand up': Tactical Repertoires of Social Movements," in *The Blackwell Companion to Social Movements,* ed. David A. Snow, Sarah Anne Soule, and Hanspeter Kriesi (Malden, MA: Blackwell Publishing, 2004), 270.

14. Mansbridge and Morris, *Oppositional Consciousness.*

15. Melucci, "The Process of Collective Identity," 47–48; Hunt and Benford, "Collective Identity, Solidarity, and Commitment," 442–447.

16. Mansbridge and Morris, *Oppositional Consciousness.*

17. Adrian Karatnycky and Peter Ackerman, "How Freedom Is Won: From Civic Resistance to Durable Democracy" (New York: Freedom House, May 24, 2005), http://www.freedomhouse.org/uploads/special_report/29.pdf.

18. Manfred B. Steger, *Gandhi's Dilemma: Nonviolent Principles and Nationalist Power* (New York: St. Martin's Press, 2000), 186–191.

19. Mary Bernstein, "Celebration and Suppression: The Strategic Uses of Identity by the Lesbian and Gay Movement," *American Journal of Sociology* 103, no. 3 (1997): 531–565; "Identity Politics," *Annual Review of Sociology* 31 (2005).

20. Margot Badran, *Feminists, Islam, and Nation: Gender and the Making of Modern Egypt* (Princeton: Princeton University Press, 1995), 76.

21. Rick Fantasia and Eric L. Hirsche, "Culture in Rebellion: The Appropriation and Transformation of the Veil in the Algerian Revolution," in *Social Movements and Culture,* ed. Hank Johnston and Bert Klandermans (Minneapolis: University of Minnesota Press, 1995), 144–159.

22. Marc W. Steinberg, "Tilting the Frame: Considerations on Collective Action Framing from a Discursive Turn," *Theory and Society* 27, no. 6 (1998): 845–872; Anne Kane, "Reconstructing Culture in Historical Explanation: Narratives as Cultural Structure and Practice," *History and Theory* 39, no. 3 (2000): 311–330.

23. Two other prisoners were elected to the Dail, the Irish parliament.

24. Padraig O'Malley, *Biting at the Grave: The Irish Hunger Strikes and the Politics of Despair* (Boston: Beacon Press, 1990), 160–171.

25. Charles Tilly, "Contentious Repertoires in Great Britain, 1758–1834," in *Repertoires and Cycles of Collective Action,* ed. Mark Traugott (Durham: Duke University Press, 1995), 26.

26. John A. Gould and Edward Moe, "Searching Under the Light: A Critique of the Rational Choice Analysis of Strategic Non-Violent Anti-Regime Movements," paper presented at the annual meeting of the International Studies Association, Montreal, March 2011.

27. James M. Jasper, *The Art of Moral Protest: Culture, Biography, and Creativity in Social Movements* (Chicago: University of Chicago Press, 1997), 296.

28. Ibid., 46.

29. Ibid., 319.

30. Gary Alan Fine, "Public Narration and Group Culture: Discerning Discourse in Social Movements," in *Social Movements and Culture,* ed. Hank Johnston and Bert Klandermans (Minneapolis: University of Minnesota Press, 1995), 129–130.

31. Rhys H. Williams, "Constructing the Public Good: Social Movements and Cultural Resources," *Social Problems* 42, no. 1 (1995): 124–144; Rhys H. Williams,

"From the 'Beloved Community' to 'Family Values': Religious Language, Symbolic Repertoires, and Democratic Culture," in *Social Movements: Identity, Culture, and the State,* ed. David S. Meyer, Nancy Whittier, and Belinda Robnett (New York: Oxford University Press, 2002), 247–265; Taylor and Van Dyke, "'Get up, Stand up.'"

32. Ann Swidler, "Cultural Power and Social Movements," in *Social Movements and Culture,* ed. Hank Johnston and Bert Klandermans (Minneapolis: University of Minnesota Press, 1995), 25–40; Hunt and Benford, "Collective Identity, Solidarity, and Commitment," 437–438.

33. Hunt and Benford, "Collective Identity, Solidarity, and Commitment," 445.

34. Lee A. Smithey and Lester R. Kurtz, "Parading Persuasion: Nonviolent Collective Action as Discourse in Northern Ireland," *Research in Social Movements, Conflicts and Change* 24 (2003): 319–359.

35. In Chapter 5, Matt Meyer describes similar ethnically inspired tactics that occurred in Mozambique during the 1920s and 1930s. Singing, dancing, and carving served as forms of noncooperation and symbolic protest.

36. Robert D. Benford and David A. Snow, "Framing Processes and Social Movements: An Overview and Assessment," *Annual Review of Sociology* 26 (2000): 611–639.

37. Swidler, "Cultural Power and Social Movements"; Charles Tilly, *Regimes and Repertoires* (Chicago: University of Chicago Press, 2006). As in any nonviolent campaign, corporations, states, churches, and other institutions present different vulnerabilities, which recommend more or less persuasive symbolic methods or more coercive acts of noncooperation or intervention.

38. Jasper, *The Art of Moral Protest,* 237.

39. The documentary film, *The Singing Revolution,* offers a compelling example of the way in which a traditional activity, in this case choral singing of Estonian folk songs, came to constitute a social movement tactic as it allowed Estonians to signal national solidarity and defy Soviet hegemony. James Tusty and Maureen Castle Tusty, *The Singing Revolution* (New York: Docurama Films, 2008), http://www.singingrevolution.com/.

40. Rick Fantasia, *Cultures of Solidarity: Consciousness, Action, and Contemporary American Workers* (Berkeley: University of California Press, 1988); Klandermans, "The Social Construction"; Polletta and Jasper, "Collective Identity and Social Movements," 285; Sharon Erickson Nepstad, *Convictions of the Soul: Religion, Culture, and Agency in the Central America Solidarity Movement* (New York: Oxford University Press, 2004); Taylor and Van Dyke, "'Get up, Stand up,'" 270.

41. Mary Ryan, "The American Parade: Representations of the Nineteenth-Century Social Order," in *The New Cultural History (Studies on the History of Society and Culture),* ed. Lynn Hunt (Berkeley: University of California Press, 1989); Mary Ryan, *Civic Wars: Democracy and Public Life in the American City During the Nineteenth Century* (Berkeley: University of California Press, 1997); Verta Taylor and Nancy Whittier, "Collective Identity in Social Movement Communities: Lesbian Feminist Mobilization," in *Frontiers in Social Movement Theory,* ed. Aldon D. Morris and Carol McClurg Mueller (New Haven: Yale University Press, 1992), 120; Dominic Bryan, *Orange Parades: The Politics of Ritual, Tradition, and Control* (London: Pluto Press, 2000); Verta Taylor, Leila J. Rupp, and Joshua Gamson, "Performing Protest: Drag Shows as Tactical Repertoire of the Gay and Lesbian Movement," *Research in Social Movements, Conflict, and Change* 25 (2004): 105–137; Lee A. Smithey and Michael P. Young, "Parading Protest: Orange Parades in Northern Ireland and Temperance Parades in Antebellum America," *Social Movement Studies* 9, no. 4 (2010): 393–410.

42. Fantasia and Hirsche, "Culture in Rebellion."

43. Francesca Polletta, "Strategy and Identity in 1960s Black Protest," *Research in Social Movements, Conflict, and Change* 17 (1994): 85–114; see also Melucci, "The Process of Collective Identity," 50.

44. Mahatma Gandhi, ed. Louis Fischer, *The Essential Gandhi, an Anthology* (New York: Random House, 1962), 337–338; Mohandas K. Gandhi, ed. Krishna Kripalani, *All Men Are Brothers: Autobiographical Reflections* (New York: Continuum, 2005), 31–32.

45. Howard Clark, *Civil Resistance in Kosovo* (London: Pluto Press, 2000), 66.

46. Neil J. Smelser, *Theory of Collective Behavior* (New York: Free Press of Glencoe, 1963); Jasper, *The Art of Moral Protest,* 240–242.

Part 1

Nonviolent Resistance in Sub-Saharan Africa

3

Ghana: Nonviolent Resistance in the Independence Movement, 1890s–1950s

Gail Presbey

Ghanaians have a rich and long history of civil resistance that is rooted in both a philosophy and strategic practice of nonviolent action.[1] Relatively unknown to outsiders, this history is also little heralded within Ghana despite its importance in the independence struggle. That is partly because Ghanaians won their independence using boycotts, strikes, associations, and intelligent compromise, but they usually do not describe these as methods of nonviolent action. The term popularized by Kwame Nkrumah, leader of the independence struggle, was *positive action*. Additionally, positive action is identified with Nkrumah himself: later as president of Ghana, he actively supported armed struggle elsewhere in Africa while resorting to authoritarianism at home.[2]

In this chapter, I highlight the role of ordinary people in carrying out nonviolent resistance that paved the road to independence. I trace the roots of nonviolent actions to deeply held traditions of intra-ethnic nonviolent political behavior, as well as growing awareness about people power combined with an increasing resentment toward specific colonial policies. Ghanaians practiced and refined nonviolent tactics to pressure the British to grant independence; the strategy proved successful.

Early Democratic, Participatory, and Nonviolent Strategy in Ghanaian Political Traditions

Nonviolent resistance in Ghana can trace its roots to the political tradition of governance. In West Africa in general, there traditionally were systems

51

of checks on chiefly powers. The forms of governance of the Akan king-doms (Fante, Ashanti, and others) were broadly democratic. Public forums in small towns and villages offered everyone the opportunity to partici-pate—men and women, royal or not, youths and elders.[3] At the same time, the rulers' powers were effectively constrained by the community. At the enstooling of a new chief or king, the queen mother ceremonially advised the new chief not to be "hard of hearing" or act on his or her own initiative. Chiefs who disregarded the people faced removal—destooling. A metaphor depicting the chief's cautious use of power was an egg held in a hand.[4]

The Akan also practiced decisionmaking by consensus: if all opinions were heard and all parties agreed, then there was no disgruntled minority to become permanent outsiders liable to turn to violence.[5] The Akan use of deferential and indirect speech in courts, and their addressing the chief through the mediation of the *okyeame* (spokesperson), reflected their pref-erence for less conflictual communication and their fostering of social and political harmony.[6]

Despite such constraints, Akan government could be autocratic—the Asante in particular had a reputation for militarism. Rosy historical narra-tives remain open to debate, but nevertheless played a historic role in the evolution of the Gold Coast's collective nonviolent resistance.[7] The Akan practice of wide-ranging consultation and the development of rhetorical skills fostering intergroup peace combined with the right to destool chiefs provided their descendants with a set of attitudes and skills essential in waging nonviolent struggle.

Colonial Governance, Growing Resistance, and the Rise of Nationalist Unity

By purchase, conquest, and diplomacy, British interests expanded in the Gold Coast in the nineteenth century, establishing the Gold Coast colony in 1874 and later incorporating the Ashanti kingdom. The Asante, who con-trolled much of the territory that is now Ghana, fought against British colo-nialism, their independent kingdom itself having all the attributes of a mod-ern nation, including territory, central government, police and army, national language, and law.[8] Osei Tutu, the first Asantehene in 1701, created the Ko-toko Council (a consultative assembly) and the Golden Stool as a symbol to give a strong sense of identity.

As there was little British settlement, the British relied on the coopera-tion of traditional chiefs and kings, initially the Fante whom the British supported as a counterweight to the Asante. The bond that was agreed in 1844 between Britain and eight Fante chiefs, including King Joseph Ag-grey, offered British protection to the Fante while respecting the internal rule of chiefs and kings. Law and order was to be maintained by a combination of British officials and district chiefs, "moulding the customs of the country to the general principles of British law."[9] In 1852, in the spirit of this bond, Governor H. Worsley Hill proposed a poll tax, agreed to by the chiefs, in order to improve life on the coast, especially schooling. The tax was a fiasco, provoking armed rebellion and widespread noncompliance, and ultimately was abandoned in 1862.[10]

In the 1860s, intellectuals in the Gold Coast, such as J. Africanus Beale Horton (an army medical officer from Sierra Leone), openly discussed the need for self-government. However, when in 1865 King Aggrey challenged British usurpation of kingly powers, he was promptly exiled to Sierra Leone for "sedition."[11] In 1869, subsequent Fante chiefs formed a Fante Confederation to assert their independence, adopting a constitution, collecting their own poll tax, creating a government seal, and mustering an army. The confederation engendered a nationalist spirit but collapsed, partly due to internal rivalries inflamed by the British.[12] Eventually, the British Gold Coast colony was proclaimed in 1874 as the culmination of a process of buying out or negotiating with imperial competitors such as the Dutch, allying with predominantly coastal African peoples, and fighting wars with others, notably the Asante. The military balance of power was changed dramatically in 1874 through British use of Enfield rifles and their demonstration of the Gatling gun.[13] In 1877, the seat of government was moved from Cape Coast to Christiansborg Castle in Accra. In 1902, the annexation of the Northern Territories completed British territorial expansion.

In 1896, Britain again tried to introduce direct taxation—the house tax. Women in Accra protested nonviolently, marching to Government House and noisily refusing to disperse when Governor William Maxwell would not meet them. They next sent a petition to the colonial secretary in London.[14] While this did not change British policy (neither did the 1898 Hut Tax War in Sierra Leone), it succeeded in rallying the support of King Tackie and other Accra kings. The first explicitly political organization in the colony was the Aborigines Rights Protection Society (ARPS), founded in 1897 to campaign against a bill ceding control of "all waste and unoccupied lands" to colonial authorities. Roger S. Gocking comments that, "in a remarkable show of unity, ARPS brought together both the colony's chiefs and educated elite" as well as gained support from British commercial interests who were fearful for their investments.[15] In 1898 ARPS sent a delegation to London to meet the colonial secretary, and succeeded in having the bill withdrawn—according to Desmond George-Williams "a major victory of African nonviolent strategic action."[16]

Even before the foundation of ARPS, some of its future leading figures were a thorn in the flesh of the colonial administration, notably John Mensah Sarbey who founded the *Gold Coast People* in 1890. Its allegations that the courts were corrupt and unprofessional prompted the first restrictions on freedom of the press, the 1893 Newspaper Registration Ordinance.[17] Publications linked with the growing number of voluntary associations became a vital outlet for criticism of colonial rule. Usually they needed to be subsidized by wealthy professionals,[18] but they eventually reached beyond the educated elite through the practice of literate people retelling what they had read.[19] In 1902, Mensah Sarbah and others established the Mfantsi National Education Fund in order to set up independent primary and secondary schools where pupils would read and write in Fante and, consequently, establish a Fante literature and history.[20]

Voluntary associations with mixed European and African members had begun in Ghana as early as 1787, but ARPS's success encouraged emulation. Benevolent societies, first founded in 1902, flourished and grew after 1930. Women founded charitable associations. While some associations were responses to a specific grievance and usually founded by the urban educated elites, they quickly grew to encompass a wide range of fraternal and mutual benefit associations (some based on ethnicity), charitable organizations, professional associations, trade unions, youth groups, women's groups, farmers' groups and cooperatives, and finally political parties. In the 1920s, associations such as the Gold and Silver Smith's Association, the Colony and Ashanti Motor Union, and the Carpenters and Masons Union were in existence, but dormant. Eventually these groups combined to become a countervailing force against the colonial status quo and for nationalist mobilization. Through voluntary associations the less educated became "conscious of their strength vis-à-vis the political leaders" and aware of their ability to influence and, if necessary, to resist the government.[21]

From 1895 onward, Britain increasingly practiced "indirect rule," setting up a Native Administration in its West African colonies, a policy criticized as a maneuver setting traditional chiefs against the rising demands of the educated elite.[22] The British used various means to assert their control over chiefs and kings, refusing to recognize some, deporting and reinstating others—all the while insisting that they were not interfering with the native order. In the Gold Coast, the governorship of Gordon Guggisberg (during the economic boom of 1919–1927) brought a rapid expansion of secondary and technical education to meet the needs of a modernizing economy together with constitutional reform in 1925.[23] The Trinidadian promoter of pan-Africanism, George Padmore, remarked that the only good thing about the Gold Coast's 1925 Constitution was that it "gave recognition for the first time in the history of British tropical Africa of the elective principle, as far as officers are concerned." But it also had the impact of transforming "the status of the chiefs, from elected servants of the people into paid agents of British imperialism," thereby dividing chiefs and the ARPS.[24] For a time, the ARPS withheld cooperation from the new legislative and district councils, but ultimately the organization itself split and the most significant cooperator with the new system was none other than its vice-president, J. E. Casely Hayford, one of the prime movers of pan-Africanism in West Africa.

Casely Hayford was perpetually working for a wider alliance against colonialism. In 1920, he convened the first National Congress of British West Africa (NCBWA), which involved activists from all four British colonies and drew up a charter of eighteen demands. Ghana's foremost historian, A. Adu Boahen, wrote that Casely Hayford's "idealism, political vision and faith in the unity of African peoples . . . injected a flavour of pan-Africanism into West African politics matched only by Kwame Nkrumah's efforts 25 years later."[25] Padmore too considered Casely Hayford a "John the Baptist" to a younger generation of leaders, but regretted his failure "to realize that without the active support of the plebeian masses, especially the peasantry, who form the bulk of the population, the middle-class intellectuals, small in number and disunited among themselves, were ineffective."[26]

The NCBWA faded out after Casely Hayford's death in 1930; however, linked youth initiatives thrived. The most prominent youth organizer was the Comintern-trained Sierra Leonean, Wallace Johnson, who contributed to Padmore's *The Negro Worker,* a publication that featured articles like "A Few Hints on How to Carry Out a Strike." However, when Johnson got to Ghana in 1933 (after being deported from Nigeria for his political activities), he did not suggest striking since there were too many unemployed willing to take strikers' jobs. Instead, he helped illiterate people who sought redress against employers. Despite his rhetoric of mass action, perhaps his most enduring contribution to Ghanaian politics was the connections he forged with British anticolonialist parliamentarians whom he briefed with information for parliamentary questions to the colonial secretary, especially about issues affecting Gold Coast workers. Johnson even once posed as a miner to investigate hazardous conditions down in the mines.[27]

Johnson also cofounded the West African Youth League, cooperating with a study group of former ARPS members. In Leo Spitzer and LaRay Denzer's view, "his efforts raised political expectations throughout the general public, confirming the belief of the middle elite that they had a right to influence decisions which concerned them, teaching the working class and the farmers that they might share that right."[28]

A. Adu Boahen considered the interwar years a "transitional period" in Ghanaian politics "during which both chiefs and intelligentsia participated in agitational politics," but that unfortunately was plagued by conflict among the leaders:

> Neither the NCBWA nor the youth movement ever commanded a mass following nor did any significant linkage occur between urban and rural politics. The leaders could therefore be written off by the colonial rulers as

being unrepresentative of the people. . . . There were certainly elements of radicalism in the mid-1930s but in general these movements were moderate nationalist movements, conducting their politics within the colonial framework. Political independence was decidedly not on their programme.[29]

Two ordinances in 1934 did provoke concerted resistance. The Waterworks Bill imposed rates on previously free supplies of water and Ordinance 21 (the Sedition Amendment) further curbed press freedom. "The intelligentsia, the African legislators, and the chiefs all united in opposition against these ordinances, and the populace came to feel that these groups were keenly concerned with public opinion."[30] A Gold Coast and Ashanti delegation and an ARPS delegation went to London to petition against the Waterworks Bill. Although neither ordinance was repealed, organizing against them "clearly revealed . . . the potential political strength of the masses when they were mobilized in opposition to an action which directly and adversely affected their best interests."[31]

The first Gold Coast trade union was founded in 1939 and by 1941 the colonial government had a system of registration that steered trade unions into a British model where industrial action had to be apolitical and limited to employment issues.[32]

Boycotts, Protests, and Developments Abroad

The events highlighted below were immediate precursors of the 1950s independence movement. They offered practical experience of nonviolent actions that proved invaluable in organizing later resistance.

The 1937 Cocoa Boycott

Britain had invested in Ghanaian infrastructure by building railroads and deepening Takoradi harbor to expand cocoa exports, which had become about 60 percent of the colony's income. In the global economic depression, prices plunged to one-third of their 1927 level. Therefore, European companies formed a price-fixing cartel: the United Africa Company.[33] Farmers and traders responded by organizing a refusal to sell cocoa combined with a boycott of imported goods in 1930–1931, but this first boycott lasted only two months. It failed because it was not universally observed.[34] Yet seven years later, an alliance of brokers, market women, and chiefs organized a much more successful holdup of cocoa. This second holdup lasted seven months, from October 1937 to April 1938, and reached participation levels of around 80 percent, particularly in rural areas.[35] Farmers and chiefs visited areas where the holdup and boycott of European goods was weak. Native tribunals took account of the hardships incurred by not pressing cases against farmers for repayment of debts. Market women reinforced the boycott against foreign goods by refusing to buy them. Truck drivers refused to deliver goods and even fishermen refused to fish. Under this pressure, small importers found their stocks piling up while, back in Britain, textile workers were laid off due to reduced cloth exports.[36]

When London instructed Governor Arnold Hodson to enforce the cartel, there occurred something "almost unprecedented: he decided not to carry out the instructions."[37] Instead, he advised the British government to defuse the situation by appointing a Commission of Inquiry. This commission, reporting in 1938, condemned the European firms. Contemporary historians now acknowledge the cocoa boycott as "a major event in the political history of Ghana," posing a threat to the entire colonial system,[38] and representing "a spirited, morale-boosting and novel form of resistance against white power and private foreign interests."[39] Padmore later referred to it as a pre-Nkrumah example of nonviolent positive action.[40]

Interlude: Developments Abroad

The Fifth Pan-African Congress met in Manchester, England, in October 1945, organized by Padmore and aided by the young Nkrumah.[41] Of the ninety delegates, twenty-six were from Africa, including future leaders of independent countries. As Nkrumah explained later, the 1945 Congress agreed on a plan of action "based on the Gandhist technique of non-violent non-cooperation, in other words, the withholding of labour, civil disobedience, and economic boycott."[42] The congressional declaration, "Colonial and Coloured Unity," called on colonial workers and farmers to organize:

> Colonial workers must be in the front of the battle against Imperialism. Your weapons—the Strike and the Boycott—are invincible. We also call upon the intellectuals and professional classes of the Colonies to awaken to their responsibilities. By fighting for trade union rights, the right to form cooperatives, freedom of the press, assembly, demonstration and strike, freedom to print and read the literature which is necessary for the education of the masses, you will be using the only means by which your liberties will be won and maintained. Today there is only one road to effective action—the organisation of the masses. And in that organisation the educated Colonials must join.[43]

Impressed by the success of nonviolent resistance in India, the African movements carried a real concern that colonial reprisals against violence would take a high toll. This was also a time of optimism because the victorious World War II Allies had reaffirmed the right to self-determination. Many of these influences reached Ghana through returning ex-servicemen.

The Ex-Servicemen

Britain, as other European powers, relied heavily on colonial recruits during the two world wars—11,000 Gold Coast recruits served in the British forces in World War I and 65,000 in World War II.[44] The returning ex-servicemen, as they were known, brought home ideas and aspirations acquired through their experiences in the world outside.[45] Ex-serviceman Geoffrey Aduamah, housed at a large camp in Durban, recalls being challenged by South African Indians: "Why are you fighting for Britain? Are you yourselves free?"[46]

Ex-servicemen mimeographed their own *Kintampo Camp Weekly* in 1945–1946, reflecting their own political discussions with Indian nationalists in both India and Burma.

> The war has generated new ideas and created a new sense of values throughout the world, and West Africa too has caught the spirit of the age. Her sons have gone to other lands; they have seen; they have conquered. They have conquered not only the physical, but also those habits of thought fostered by the ancient forces of reaction. There is every indication that they would not take tamely to the old order of things.[47]

John Baku, an ex-serviceman interviewed by Adrienne Israel, remembers drinking at bars with Indian soldiers:

> They had obtained a "leave pass" and gone into Bombay in order to try and get a glimpse of [Mahatma] Gandhi. . . . People were so crowded that we couldn't find the man, so we had to climb the hill. Climb upstairs [in] a four-storey building . . . I saw him, with all his party members moving together with him, creating noise, singing. . . . He was there with all his people, an old man with glasses. . . . I found out he was a hero, a great man.[48]

Likewise, Frank W. Aidoo explained,

> We didn't see much difference in how we were being governed and how the Indians were being governed by the British. When we came back [to the Gold Coast] negotiations started for Indian independence. We who were fortunate to go to India to learn first-hand the conditions there and compare it to the conditions here, we saw no reason why India should be granted independence and not our African colonies, because we didn't see much difference between India and Ghana. . . . And that actually brought this political awakening.[49]

Such encounters stiffened Ghanaian determination to seek independence. Although ex-servicemen had economic grievances, their demand for independence had its roots in a profound, ideational change about becoming free men in an independent country.[50]

Most accounts of Ghana's independence struggle focus too narrowly on the leading role of J. B. Danquah, the founder of the United Gold Coast

Convention (UGCC) party, and especially on Nkrumah.[51] For all of Nkrumah's organizing skills and his awareness of the need to include the poorer members of society in a widespread grassroots movement, he could not have succeeded unless the Ghanaian people had the necessary will, skills, and discipline. When the Ex-Servicemen's Union called a march to Christiansborg Castle, on February 28, 1948, both Danquah and Nkrumah were addressing a political meeting outside of Accra at Saltpond. About 2,000 marchers turned up, but police would not let them proceed. In the confusion, stones were thrown and the police opened fire, killing one ex-serviceman outright and wounding others (two later died).[52]

The distraught marchers ran to another section of Accra where people had gathered to conclude a month-long boycott of foreign merchants organized by Nii Kwabena Bonne III, a prominent merchant and UGCC leader.[53] With emotions running high, the crowd turned to violence, looting and burning shops. Police opened fire. A crowd battered down the gate to Ussher Fort Prison in order to let prisoners escape. As the news spread, rioting broke out in Kumasi where it continued for two weeks. According to British figures, 29 people died and 237 were injured within a month.[54]

Nkrumah and Danquah seized the moment, issuing telegrams that argued the riots showed Britain could no longer effectively rule the country and proposed that the UGCC form an interim government to restore order.[55] Several days later, trying to calm the crowds and channel their outrage into more productive political goals, the UGCC leaders addressed a 9,000-strong rally where Nkrumah urged that "people should fight with unity, not guns for independence."[56] Partly through the guidance of Nkrumah and other leaders, and partly through deeply held values, the future people's movement for independence for the most part was able to avoid violence. However, on March 11, 1948, the governor ordered the arrest of six UGCC leaders, including Danquah, Nkrumah, and Nii Kwabena Bonne III. This quickly backfired, raising the popularity of the "Big Six" to national heights.[57]

Mass Organizing and the Positive Action Campaign

Due to their different opinions of how best to organize the movement for independence, Nkrumah broke with Danquah and the UGCC and, in July 1949, formed the Convention People's Party (CPP), sometimes called the "verandah boys" (those who had no home and slept on the verandahs of the rich). The CPP mainly consisted of elementary school leavers (that is, students who finished elementary school but did not go on to secondary school), people with just enough education to read and with English as a common language. They spread the nationalist message with slogans that had wide appeal such as "We Have the Right to Live as Men," "Seek Ye First the Political Kingdom, and All Things Will Be Added unto It," and

"Self-Government Now."[58] Bankole Timothy describes Nkrumah's approach: "The farmer, the fisherman, the petty trader and the labourer were made to feel that they were equally as important as the lawyers in contributing to the progress of the country."[59]

Nkrumah worked closely with CPP organizers such as K. A. Gbedemah and Kojo Botsio to organize the youth into political action for independence. Youth groups like the Asante Youth Organization and Accra Youth Study Group were later federated into the Committee of Youth Organizations (CYO).[60]

Market women were major supporters, supplying the CPP with funds and vehicles. Nkrumah remembered a rally where a Kumasi woman slashed her own face with a razor blade: "Then, smearing the blood over her body, she challenged the men present to do likewise in order to show that no sacrifice was too great in their united struggle for freedom and independence."[61] The CPP supported three newspapers, the *Accra Evening News,* the Cape Coast's *Daily Mail,* and Sekondi's *Morning Telegraph,* but also saw that the CPP could reach people through couching its message in religious terms or using religious symbols such as manner of dress, speech, honorifics, and ascriptive titles.[62]

The positive action campaign of 1950–1951 envisaged strikes, boycotts, and noncooperation. As Nkrumah later explained, "We had no guns, but even if we had, the circumstances were such that non-violent alternatives were open to us, and it was necessary to try them before resorting to other means."[63] Nkrumah learned about Gandhi's nonviolent methods of struggle during his studies in the West as well as through his involvement in pan-Africanism. His 1949 pamphlet, *What I Mean by Positive Action,* in which he outlined the nonviolent methods for independence struggle, was modeled closely on C. V. H. Rao's 1945 *Civil Disobedience Movements in India.*[64] Britain had to be pressured to respect Ghana's right to self-government.

Nkrumah delineated three categories of positive action: (1) legitimate constitutional political agitation; (2) newspaper and educational campaigns, including political education, agitation, platform speeches, and establishing independent schools and colleges; and (3) "as a last resort, the constitutional application of strikes, boycotts, and non-cooperation on the principle of absolute nonviolence."[65]

The colonial government greeted Nkrumah's call for positive action by fining him £400 and arresting several newspaper editors. In fact, Gocking reports that the Trades Union Congress (TUC) rather than Nkrumah himself took the lead in starting positive action "by calling for a general strike in support of the Meteorological Employees Union," thereby forcing the CPP's hands.[66] The next day Nkrumah made his declaration that positive action would begin at midnight. Everyone should stay home from work. On

January 8, at a crowded rally at Accra's West End Arena, he explained that enemies of the CPP—the imperialists' "concealed agent-provocateurs and stooges"—had spread rumors that positive action really meant "riot, looting, and disturbances, in a word violence."[67] His speech, echoing his 1949 pamphlet, said, "There are two ways to achieve Self-government: either by armed revolution and violent overthrow of the existing regime, or by constitutional and legitimate non-violent methods. In other words: Either by armed might or by moral pressure."[68] His speech continued to stress his movement's commitment to "absolute nonviolence," explaining that the education stage of the campaign had already begun through newspapers, Ghanaian schools and colleges, and traveling speakers, but that it might escalate to "Nationwide Non-Violent Sit-Down-at-Home Strikes, Boycotts, and Non-Cooperation."[69]

Nkrumah's own newspaper, the *Accra Evening News,* carried many articles warning that, if necessary, people would resort to positive action as a last recourse against British intransigence, but it less often explained what positive action was. An article signed by "Agitator" argued that "agitation is, after all, the civilized peaceful weapon of moral force. It is preferable to violence and brute physical force . . . to agitate means to inform."[70] On May Day 1949, Gandhi was held up as an inspiration to Ghana's movement for freedom and democracy.[71] Sometimes there were overtones or symbols of violence, such as a cartoon where a figure crying for help personifying "imperialism" was being crushed under the boot of the CPP.[72]

The *Gold Coast Observer* reported a public lecture by Bankole Renner, who argued that to free the country from imperialism "hatred should be in our hearts" and, while this hatred should be aimed at a system rather than individuals, when individuals identified with the system "we must hate that person too."[73] This rousing speech was followed by a less inflammatory explanation that positive action used methods of boycott and general strike. Other articles had a more pronounced insistence on nonviolence. J. Ahinful Quansah urges that "the fundamental principle of non-violence be indoctrinated into the people. Yes, non-violence, for we are a religious race!"[74] Articles also castigated British violence. "Tell Britain that we as Youths have tasted the sweetness of gun bullets and we entertain no fear. We are now on brainy warfare. We believe in the maxim of 'The pen is mightier than the sword.'"[75] The newspaper also exhorted readers to explain these political insights and program of action to those who could not read.[76]

While the CPP-supported newspapers called for positive action, the colonial government broadcast counterpropaganda on the radio, telling people to go back to work and open their shops. Most city stores closed down on January 9, 1950, but the next day enthusiasm seemed to be waning and the day after some stores reopened. When Nkrumah took a walk through

Accra on January 11, dressed in a smock typical of Ghana's Northern Territories, people began to follow him. Before long, a large crowd gathered in front of the *Accra Evening News* offices. Nkrumah addressed the crowd, asking them to fill the arena that evening. His speech in the arena, and its favorable news coverage, resuscitated the movement and the strike.[77] To no avail, the colonial government moved against the press, suspending the three CPP newspapers and accusing their editors of sedition.

On January 17, the ex-servicemen again marched to Christiansborg Castle. During violent outbreaks provoked by the police, protesters killed two police officers. The chiefs on the Legislative Council then passed a motion deploring positive action as violent and coercive and blaming "grasshopper leaders" for inciting trouble and trying to usurp chiefly authority.[78] These criticisms pleased the colonial government, but did not sway the people who were solidly behind the CPP.

Nkrumah was arrested on charges of organizing an illegal "political" strike—called not in a labor dispute, but to pressure the government—and was blamed for the deaths of the two police officers. At his trial Nkrumah, describing himself as a disciple of Gandhi, insisted that positive action was absolutely nonviolent. Sentenced to twelve months with hard labor, Nkrumah's correspondence from jail reveals his determination to consolidate his relationship with the trade union movement, which he described as "the backbone of the party."[79]

While Nkrumah and other leaders were in jail, his mass movement sprang into action. The CPP swept all seven seats in the Accra Municipal Council election in April 1950 and almost all of the seats in the Kumasi Town Council election in November. Party branches were established everywhere so that the CPP would contest all possible seats in the February 1951 Legislative Assembly election. The CPP then engaged in a voter registration drive, overcoming the reluctance of some potential voters who had not wanted to pay the voter registration fee.

The CPP's election campaign was innovative and energetic. Local campaigns included picnics, dances, skits, and tours by loudspeaker vans decorated in CPP colors. As well as conventional rallies, public ceremonies were held to award diplomas to CPP "prison graduates" (those who served time in prison for their actions of political protest). The CPP adapted well-known hymns, prayers, and biblical phrases with an anticolonial message.[80]

Nkrumah was in jail during the campaign and elections. But when the CPP won thirty-four of the thirty-eight seats[81] (with Nkrumah's gaining 22,780 of the 23,122 votes in Accra Central constituency), Governor Charles Arden-Clarke released him, recognizing that "Nkrumah and his party had the mass of the people behind them . . . [while] no other party [had] appreciable public support."[82] CPP processions through streets were "dominated by women adorned with a sea of Nkrumah cloth"; that is, cloth printed with

Nkrumah's picture.[83] Also evident at this point in history was that ethnic-based antagonism had been abandoned in the struggle for independence.

Arden-Clarke asked Nkrumah to take the position of leader of government business. Nkrumah accepted and, in 1952, the constitution was amended to rename this post prime minister. Now, argued Nkrumah, the time was ripe to switch from positive to tactical action, from noncooperation to a compromise testing the limits of reform possible within the system. Nkrumah's government built roads, bridges, harbors, railways, municipal housing, water supplies, and hospitals; extended free compulsory primary education; set up teacher training colleges; and supported secondary schools. The University of Ghana at Legon was established. Many of these initiatives were made affordable by the fact that world cocoa prices soared in the 1950s, increasing the government budget fourfold.[84]

But during the 1950s, there was some internal opposition to Nkrumah. In the Ashanti region, some opposed the fixing of cocoa prices in order to fund development projects. Various close followers left the CPP and joined the National Liberation Movement (NLM), a group active in Ashanti areas that used mass political action as well as paramilitary "action groupers." The former CPP members were able to steer the NLM away from violence.[85]

Yet in the 1956 election, the CPP won 71 of 104 seats with some 57 percent of the popular vote. Not long afterward, Britain announced that Ghana would receive its independence on March 6, 1957, and Nkrumah became Ghana's first president.[86]

Conclusion

The newly independent state of Ghana took a leading role in advocating and using civil resistance. In December 1958, independent Ghana hosted the All-African Peoples' Conference, a follow-up to the 1945 Pan-African Congress. Patrice Lumumba and Tom Mboya were there along with a large Algerian contingent. In his opening speech, Nkrumah attributed the success of the Ghanaian independence movement to nonviolent positive action.[87] Kojo Botsio, who led the CPP delegation, told countries still struggling for liberation that, "with the united will of the people behind you, the power of the imperialists can be destroyed without the use of violence."[88] Some delegations were unhappy with the emphasis on nonviolent resistance, especially the Algerians and Egyptians who "regarded the very word 'nonviolence' as an insult to brothers fighting and dying for freedom."[89] Ultimately, the congress declared its support for peaceful means in territories where democratic means were available, but also supported those in circumstances where arms were the only protection from colonial violence.[90]

In 1959, after hearing that France planned to test nuclear weapons in the Sahara Desert at Regan, Algeria, a group of eleven Ghanaians along with British and other international activists attempted to intervene nonviolently, but were ejected from French territory in Upper Volta and ended up back in Ghana. Another conference to discuss the way forward for positive action was held in Accra in April 1960, Positive Action for Peace and Security in Africa. While Nkrumah opened the conference with a speech advocating "nonviolent positive action" as the main tactic, after the criticisms of Frantz Fanon and pressure from some other African delegates, the conference's emphasis on continent-wide nonviolent positive action was muted.[91] Nevertheless, Bill Sutherland and Matt Meyer describe positive action as being "a phenomenal success for Gandhian strategy."[92] Nonviolent tactics were used as part of a self-conscious overall nonviolent strategy that led Ghana quickly to independence with minimal casualties. They included consciousness-raising among the people about their right to self-government, a determination to act in concert with each other through a variety of associations, and a willingness to accept imprisonment. Boycotts and strikes showed the people that withdrawing cooperation leaves colonial forces powerless (and that cooperation reinforces subjection). Many marginalized sectors of society were mobilized in a common cause, including the youth, market women, and elementary school graduates. Newspapers and popular songs spread the message of the movement and the leaders' emphasis on the need for nonviolent discipline resonated with people's deeply held value systems. There was the grace to accept compromise in certain situations as well as the determination to go the harder way of strikes and imprisonment when sacrifice was required. The impact of mass nonviolent civil resistance on shaping Ghanaian nationalism needs further exploration, but it is clear—if rarely acknowledged—that it facilitated this process of nation building.

Notes

I would like to gratefully acknowledge inspiration for this study from Anil Nauriya and Matt Meyer, both through their published works and personally. I thank Nancy Benignus, Lonn Monroe, Stephen Roberts, and Emmanuel Asiedu-Acquah for help in finding sources, and the University of Detroit Professor's Union for a grant supporting this research. I thank Rodopi and editors David Boersema and Katy Gray Brown for permission to draw on several paragraphs of an earlier published paper, "Strategic Nonviolence in Africa: Reasons for Its Embrace and Later Abandonment by Nkrumah, Nyerere, and Kaunda," in *Spiritual and Political Dimensions of Nonviolence and Peace,* ed. David Boersema and Katy Gray Brown (Amsterdam: Rodopi, 2006), 75–101.

1. "Ghanaian" refers to the territories that now constitute Ghana that were home to more than 100 different ethnic groups, the major ones now being the Akan (including the Asante and Fante), Ewe, Mole-Dagbane, Guan, and Ga-Adangbe. J.

B. Danquah is credited with suggesting the name "Ghana," referring back to a medieval African empire, while it was Nkrumah who argued before the Parliament in British-ruled Gold Coast (on May 18, 1956) that the country should be renamed Ghana. See Ebenezer Obiri Addo, *Kwame Nkrumah: A Case Study of Religion and Politics in Ghana* (Lanham, MD: University Press of America, 1999), 184.

2. Gail Presbey, "Strategic Nonviolence in Africa: Reasons for Its Embrace and Later Abandonment by Nkrumah, Nyerere, and Kaunda," in *Spiritual and Political Dimensions of Nonviolence and Peace,* ed. David Boersema and Katy Gray Brown (Amsterdam: Rodopi, 2006), 75–101.

3. Kofi A. Busia, "The Political Heritage of Africa in Search of Democracy," in *Readings in African Philosophy: An Akan Collection,* ed. Safro Kwame (New York: University Press of America, 1995), 207–220; Kwame Gyekye, "Traditional Political Ideals, Their Relevance to Development in Contemporary Africa," in *Person and Community: Ghanaian Philosophical Studies,* vol. 1, ed. Kwasi Wiredu and Kwame Gyekye (Washington, DC: Council for Research in Values and Philosophy, 1992), 243–256; Kwasi Wiredu, "Democracy and Consensus in African Traditional Politics: A Plea for a Non-Party Polity," in *Postcolonial African Philosophy: A Critical Reader,* ed. Emmanuel C. Eze (Oxford: Blackwell, 1997), 303–312. Kwesi Yankah's study provides Akan examples of female chiefs, queen mothers who have extensive leadership roles, and even female *akyeame* (orators). Kwesi Yankah, *Speaking for the Chief: Okyeame and the Politics of Akan Royal Oratory* (Bloomington: Indiana University Press, 1995), 68–83.

4. Gyekye, "Traditional Political Ideals," 251.

5. Wiredu, "Democracy and Consensus," 304, 310–311.

6. Yankah, *Speaking for the Chief,* 54–56.

7. See Gail Presbey, "Akan Chiefs and Queen Mothers in Contemporary Ghana: Examples of Democracy, or Accountable Authority?" *International Journal of African Studies* 3, no. 1 (2001): 63–83.

8. Basil Davidson, *The Black Man's Burden: Africa and the Curse of the Nation State* (London: James Currey, 1992), 62.

9. Roger S. Gocking, *The History of Ghana* (Westport, CT: Greenwood, 2005), 32.

10. Ibid.

11. Kwaku Nti, "Actions and Reactions: An Overview of the Ding Dong Relationship Between the Colonial Government and the People of the Cape Coast," *Nordic Journal of African Studies* 11, no. 1 (2002): 1–37, at 3–4.

12. "Protest Movements and the Fante Confederation, 1830–1874" (Accra: Ministry of Local Government and Rural Development and Maks Publications and Media Services, 2006), www.ghanadistricts.com/home/?_=49&sa=4768&ssa=709, accessed November 4, 2012.

13. The British finally defeated the Ashanti militarily in 1901 and incorporated them into the Gold Coast. See Adu Boahen, *Topics in West African History* (London: Longman, 1974); Anthony Smith, *Machine Gun: The Story of the Men and the Weapon That Changed the Face of the Earth* (New York: St. Martin's Paperbacks, 2004), 67–69.

14. Desmond George-Williams, *Bite Not One Another: Selected Accounts of Nonviolent Struggle in Africa* (Addis Ababa: University for Peace, Africa Program, 2006), 30.

15. Gocking, *History of Ghana,* 44.

16. George-Williams, *Bite Not One Another,* 32–33.

17. Fred I. A. Omu, "The Dilemma of Newspaper Freedom in Colonial Africa: The West Africa Example," *Journal of African History* 9, no. 2 (1968): 279–278.

18. S. Ekwelie, "The Press in Gold Coast Nationalism" (PhD dissertation, University of Wisconsin, 1971), 258–269.

19. Stephanie Newell, *Literary Culture in Colonial Ghana: "How to Play the Game of Life"* (Manchester: Manchester University Press, 2002).

20. Nti, "Actions and Reactions," 5.

21. Immanuel Wallerstein, *The Road to Independence* (Paris: Mouton, 1964), 67, 88–94, 112, 123.

22. The following sources describe how the British through "indirect rule" tried to bypass popular control of chiefs: Wallerstein, *The Road to Independence,* 110, 151; Roger S. Gocking, "Indirect Rule in the Gold Coast: Competition for Office and the Invention of Tradition," *Canadian Journal of African Studies* 28, no. 3 (1994): 421–446; Mahmood Mamdani, *Citizen and Subject: Contemporary Africa and the Legacy of Late Colonialism* (Princeton: Princeton University Press, 1996), 122, 125, 168; Kofi Nyidevu Awoonor, *Ghana: A Political History from Pre-European to Modern Times* (Accra: Sedco; Woeli, 1990), 127.

23. Gocking, *History of Ghana,* 59–60.

24. George Padmore, *The Gold Coast Revolution: The Struggle of an African People from Slavery to Freedom* (London: Dennis Dobson, 1953), 92.

25. A. Adu Boahen, "Politics and Nationalism in West Africa 1919–35," in *Africa Under Colonial Domination, 1880–1935,* ed. A. Adu Boahen (Berkeley: University of California Press, 1985), 633.

26. Padmore, *Gold Coast Revolution,* 52.

27. Leo Spitzer and LaRay Denzer, "I. T. A. Wallace-Johnson and the West African Youth League," *The International Journal of African Historical Studies* 6, no. 3 (1973): 413–452, 425, 429.

28. Ibid., 423–424.

29. Boahen, "Politics and Nationalism," 641–642.

30. Ray Y. Gildea Jr., *Nationalism and Indirect Rule in the Gold Coast, 1900–1950* (New York: William-Frederick Press, 1964), 12.

31. Stanley Shaloff, "The Gold Coast Water Rate Controversy 1909–1938," *Institute of African Studies: Research Review* 8, no. 3 (1972): 30. Ordinance 21 was turned against Wallace Johnson as well as Nnamdi Azikwe, who later became Nigeria's first president. The governor argued that the people "in their present stage of development should be protected from disloyal intrigue and subversive propaganda." Quoted in Stanley Shaloff, "Press Controls and Sedition Proceedings in the Gold Coast, 1933–39," *African Affairs* 71, no. 284 (1972): 241–263, at 243. Even before Ordinance 21, the governor had ordered the investigation of anyone in touch with Padmore who at this time worked with the Comintern. (Padmore later argued that the Comintern put the interests of the Soviet Union above those of colonized peoples.)

32. Wallerstein, *The Road to Independence,* 67, 88–92, 112; Ekwelie, "The Press in Gold Coast Nationalism," 258–269.

33. Gocking, *History of Ghana,* 64–68.

34. Benjamin Acquaah, *Cocoa Development in West Africa: The Early Period with Particular Reference to Ghana* (Accra: Ghana Universities Press, 1999), 50. Although the cocoa holdup cost United Africa Company (of Unilever) about £1 million in profit, the companies remained profitable. See George Padmore, "West Africans, Watch Your Land," *International African Opinion* 1, no. 3 (1938): 11; see also George Padmore, "Gold Coast Report," *International African Opinion* 1, no. 5 (1938): 6.

35. Gocking, *History of Ghana,* 67–68.

36. Acquaah, *Cocoa Development,* 52.

37. Ibid.

38. Bjorn Beckmann, *Organizing the Farmers: Cocoa and the Politics of National Development in Ghana* (Uppsala: Scandinavian Institute of African Studies, 1979), 41, 48.

39. Barbara Bush, *Imperialism, Race, and Resistance: Africa and Britain, 1919–1945* (London: Routledge, 1999), 108.

40. Padmore, *Gold Coast Revolution*, 9.

41. The first Pan-African Congress was held in Paris in 1919. Spearheaded by the African-American W. E. B. Du Bois, the pan-African movement worked for the liberation of Africa from European colonization, through strengthening global solidarity among members of the African diaspora.

42. Kwame Nkrumah, *Africa Must Unite* (London: Heinemann, 1963), 134–135; Anil Nauriya, *The African Element in Gandhi* (New Delhi: Gyan Publishing House and National Gandhi Museum, 2006), 82–83.

43. George Padmore, ed., *Colonial and Coloured Unity, A Programme of Action: A History of the Pan African Congress* (London: Hammersmith Bookshop, 1947), parts 6 and 7, www.marxists.org/archive/padmore/1947/pan-african-congress/index.htm, accessed August 27, 2010.

44. Gocking, *History of Ghana*, 75.

45. Adrienne Israel interviewed and collected writings of many ex-servicemen. Scholars such as David Killingray argue that the ex-servicemen were apolitical, that their concerns were narrowly self-interested (focused on improving benefits for veterans), and that they were basically used by those like Nkrumah and Danquah. David Killingray, "Soldiers, Ex-Servicemen, and Politics in the Gold Coast, 1939–50," *Journal of Modern African Studies* 21, no. 3 (1983): 523–524. In contrast, Israel sees the two groups (nationalists and ex-servicemen) as mutually influencing each other and other Ghanaians. Interviewees deny that they were unwittingly used by the UGCC, but decided for themselves to march in protest at the colonial government. See Adrienne M. Israel, "Ex-Servicemen at the Crossroads: Protest and Politics in Post-War Ghana," *Journal of Modern African Studies* 30, no. 2 (1992): 359–368.

46. Geoffrey Aduamah, "Freedom Now: 1947–1990," PBS People's Century Series, 2000, www.pbs.org/wgbh/peoplescentury/episodes/freedomnow/aduamah transcript.html, accessed November 4, 2012.

47. *Kintampo Camp Weekly,* March 24, 1946. Anonymous, quoted in Adrienne M. Israel, "Measuring the War Experience: Ghanaian Soldiers in World War II," *Journal of Modern African Studies* 25, no. 1 (1987): 160.

48. Israel, "Measuring the War Experience," 167.

49. Ibid.

50. Ibid., 160, 162.

51. See, for example, Basil Davidson, *Black Star: A View of the Life and Times of Kwame Nkrumah* (New York: Praeger, 1973); Bankole Timothy, *Kwame Nkrumah: His Rise to Power* (Evanston: Northwestern University Press, 1963).

52. Vincent N. Okyere, *Ghana: A Historical Survey* (Accra: Vinojab, 2000), 154; Kwame Nkrumah, *Ghana: The Autobiography of Kwame Nkrumah* (New York: International, 1971 [1957]), 76–77.

53. This "anti-inflation" boycott opposed unfair British pricing policies. Nii Kwabena Bonne III, *Autobiography of Nii Kwabena Bonne III* (London: Diplomatist, 1953), 64.

54. Colonial Office, *Report on the Commission of Enquiry into Disturbances in the Gold Coast, 1948* (London: H. M. Stationery Office, 1948), 85, cited in F. M.

Bourret, *Ghana: The Road to Independence* (Stanford, CA: Stanford University Press, 1960), 169.

55. Dennis Austin, *Politics in Ghana, 1946–1950* (London: Oxford University Press, 1964), 74–75.

56. Kwame Nkrumah, quoted in Israel, "Ex-Servicemen at the Crossroads," 364, see also 367.

57. Austin, *Politics in Ghana,* 77.

58. Ibid., 17; see also Dennis Austin, *Ghana Observed: Essays on the Politics of a West African Republic* (Manchester: Manchester University Press, 1976), 21–22.

59. Timothy, *Kwame Nkrumah,* 67.

60. Nkrumah, *Autobiography,* 97–100; Bourret, *Ghana: The Road,* 172–174.

61. Kwame Nkrumah, quoted in Addo, *Kwame Nkrumah,* 90.

62. Addo, *Kwame Nkrumah,* 183.

63. Nkrumah, *Autobiography,* 103, 111, 114; Bill Sutherland and Matt Meyer, *Guns and Gandhi in Africa: Pan-African Insights on Nonviolence, Armed Struggle and Liberation in Africa* (Trenton, NJ: Africa World Press, 2000), 30.

64. Austin, *Politics in Ghana,* 87.

65. Kwame Nkrumah, *What I Mean by Positive Action* (Accra: Ministry of Information and Broadcasting, 1963 [1949]), 2–3. Nkrumah regarded political oppression as, by its very nature, illegitimate and unconstitutional. Hence, in his view, nonviolent resistance should be considered "constitutional" and part of the democratic tradition.

66. Gocking, *History of Ghana,* 93–94.

67. Timothy, *Kwame Nkrumah,* 88.

68. Kwame Nkrumah, quoted in ibid., 89–90.

69. Timothy, *Kwame Nkrumah,* 91.

70. "Agitation," *Accra Evening News,* September 3, 1948, 1.

71. "Light Spirited Leadership," *Accra Evening News,* May 1, 1949, 1.

72. Front page cartoon, *Accra Evening News,* October 6, 1951, 1.

73. "Hatred as a Weapon," *Gold Coast Observer* 9, no. 49, April 8, 1949, 583–584.

74. J. Ahinful Quansah, "A Clarion Call for Still Greater Unity: Imperialism Is a Die-Hard Not Yet Dead," *Accra Evening News,* June 5, 1950, 2.

75. Komfo Atta, "A Very Dangerous Maxim Indeed," *Accra Evening News,* January 8, 1949, 2; Kobina Egyir, "Tell Britain: Dedicated to the Coussey Committee," *Accra Evening News,* February 25, 1949, 1.

76. Kofi Annan, "The Tenser the Struggle, the Sweeter Its Gains," *Accra Evening News,* October 29, 1949, 1.

77. Nkrumah, *Autobiography,* 117–119.

78. Timothy, *Kwame Nkrumah,* 93–94.

79. Kwame Nkrumah, *Dr. Kwame Nkrumah's Directives for Running of the Convention People's Party and the Evening News from James Fort Prison, Accra, 22 January 1950–12 February 1951.* Public Records and Archives, National Archives, Accra, Ghana. Letter dated June 17, 1950, from Kojo Botsio to Kobina Sekyi.

80. Gocking, *History of Ghana,* 96; Addo, *Kwame Nkrumah,* 101–103.

81. The Legislative Assembly of 1951 had eighty-four members, thirty-eight elected and forty-six nonelected. The CPP had the support of twenty-two nonelected members, hence, a majority of fifty-four. Only two UGCC candidates were elected and the party subsequently disbanded.

82. Charles Arden-Clarke, *African Affairs* 57, no. 226 (1958): 29–37, quoted in Bourret, *Ghana: The Road,* 175.

83. Janet Berry Hess, "Imagining Culture: Art and Nationalism in Ghana" (PhD dissertation, Harvard University, 1999), 33.

84. Gocking, *History of Ghana,* 97–101.

85. Ibid., 104, 106.

86. Ibid., 108–111.

87. Sutherland and Meyer, *Guns and Gandhi,* 35.

88. Patrick Duncan, "Nonviolence at Accra," *Africa Today* 6, no. 1 (1959): 31.

89. Ibid., 32.

90. Ibid.

91. Sutherland and Meyer, *Guns and Gandhi,* 36–41.

92. Ibid., 31.

4

Zambia:
Nonviolent Strategies Against
Colonialism, 1900s–1960s

Jotham C. Momba and Fay Gadsden

Zambia, previously known as Northern Rhodesia, is one of the five southern African countries, together with Malawi, Botswana, Lesotho, and Swaziland, that achieved independence without recourse to armed resistance. From the second decade of the 1900s, Africans living in Northern Rhodesia began to organize themselves into civic and professional associations to improve their social and economic conditions under colonial rule. These early associations provided an important foundation for more militant political activity later. The struggle against the Federation of Rhodesia and Nyasaland and for independence waged in the 1950s and early 1960s was based primarily on nonviolent strategies and tactics. In this chapter, we examine resistance to colonial authority, the struggle against federation, and the nationalist movements that led to Zambia's independence in October 1964.[1] We describe the origin, development, and nature of the resistance movements and how they contributed toward the development of a sense of national identity and a political culture that rejects murderous violence.

Historical Background

The area comprising contemporary Zambia was colonized in the late nineteenth century and first ruled for Britain by the British South Africa Company, which united its administration over the new Northern Rhodesia in 1911.[2] The Colonial Office assumed control in 1924 over a sparsely populated and impoverished territory whose borders had been decided in Europe with no consideration of its ethnic composition. Over seventy tribes, each with its own language, inhabited Northern Rhodesia. Some of these peoples had traded with each other or raided their neighbors for slaves and cattle, some had resisted European invasion, and others had allied with the European invaders as a strategy for protection against their local enemies. But it was colonial rule that united them and created the framework of a new nationhood. It provided territorial boundaries, the experience of a unified administration, a system of communication through roads and railways, a common language of administration (English), and an educational system that at its upper levels involved the mixing of peoples from all over the country. The urban centers that grew in response to the needs of administration and the wider economy brought together peoples from all over the territory.

As a British protectorate, the responsibility for governance was held by the British colonial secretary who was accountable to Parliament in London. British colonies enjoyed freedoms of speech, assembly, and the press, but these were limited by systems of permits, registration, and fees. And the colonial government could ban any organization that, in its view, threatened the peace. In the 1920s and 1930s, Northern Rhodesia's Africans could and did form associations, call meetings, publish newspapers, and form political parties from the 1940s.

Britain's declared goals in the colonies were devolution of power and, ultimately, self-government. In practice this meant establishing institutions of representative government and at times accommodating nationalist demands, but within an overall context of resisting and slowing down the process of independence. Thus, Northern Rhodesia, like other African colonies of Britain, had a Legislative Council and an Executive Council comprising some elected members (initially Europeans) alongside government officials. The political battle was ultimately over the composition of these bodies and the qualifications for the franchise, that is, who controlled them. These parameters inclined nationalist aims to be essentially constitutional and democratic.

The political situation in Northern Rhodesia was complicated by the presence of immigrant communities, traders from the Indian subcontinent, and Europeans who came as farmers and miners after the development of copper mining in the mid-1920s. Europeans received preferential treatment. The government provided them with segregated schools and hospitals, accepted employment policies that restricted senior and better paying jobs to Europeans, and condoned a color bar in shops and cafés. Most significantly, it granted them representation on, but not control of, the Legislative Council established in 1924.

While in South Africa after the Boer War and in Southern Rhodesia in 1923, the British government had devolved power to European minorities, its declared policy for Northern Rhodesia was the paramountcy of African interests, clearly stated in the Passfield Memorandum of 1930 and reaffirmed by subsequent colonial secretaries:

the interests of African natives must be paramount, and if . . . those interests and the interests of the immigrant races should conflict, the former shall prevail. . . . His Majesty's Government regard themselves as exercising a trust on behalf of the African population, and they are unable to delegate or share this trust, the objective of which may be defined as the protection and advancement of the native races.[3]

Successive Northern Rhodesian governments obscured the meaning of paramountcy by privileging European interests, but in 1961 the colonial secretary again invoked it to justify a Northern Rhodesian constitution giving Africans a majority of seats in the legislature.

During the 1930s and 1940s, Europeans in Northern Rhodesia hoped to secure their dominance through some form of union with the European-controlled southern territories. From 1949, the British government supported such a federation in order to encourage regional economic growth and provide a buffer to apartheid South Africa. Despite the concerted opposition of the African population of Northern Rhodesia and Nyasaland, the Federation was imposed in 1953. This convinced African political leaders in Northern Rhodesia that the only strategy against perpetual European dominance was to gain immediate political independence and secede from the Federation.

Early Resistance to Colonial Rule

Early forms of resistance were organized within individual tribes and did not involve cooperation between the peoples of the new territory or any concept of a new politics. In some instances, resistance was armed. This is not remembered with any pride in nationalist mythology, if it is remembered at all, in contrast to the Shona *chimurenga* in Zimbabwe.[4] This may be because Zambians take pride in their peaceful history, because their unarmed independence struggle did not require the precedent of an armed revolt, and also perhaps because only some peoples were involved and a reference to them might challenge Zambia's fragile sense of national unity.

As colonial administration was consolidated and taxes imposed, resentment of European authority smoldered all over the new territory. There were localized tax revolts among the Lunda people in 1907 and the Gwembe Valley Tonga in 1909, and Henry Meebelo documented several cases of refusal to pay tax by the Namwanga and Bisa peoples of Northern Province. They also refused to provide forced labor and even to recognize colonial authority. Meebelo quotes one colonial official on the resistance of the Namwanga people: "In several instances the Wanyamwanga in the neighborhood have refused absolutely to obey me in any way and all along I have made clear to them that if any serious case of this kind comes to my knowledge again I would punish the offending village by turning the people out and destroying it (Bell to Dewar, 31 August, 1896, NER A8/2/2)."[5]

That this resistance was backward looking to an older form of politics is illustrated by the fact that it was often led by people who were either traditional leaders or linked to the traditional establishments. Thomas Rasmussen provides two examples from the North-West and Southern Provinces: in one, a Luvale chieftainess, dethroned a decade earlier by the colonial authorities, led 250 people in an antiadministration protest against the colonial administration; in the other, in the Mazabuka District of Southern Province, a chief was dethroned for leading his people in protests for land rights.[6] Meebelo recorded similar cases in Northern Province and suggests that the traditional authorities tried to "become popular by whipping up popular grievances against the *boma* [government centers]."[7] Much of this resistance was unsuccessful: taxes were levied, land was seized, and forced labor was exacted. But in Northern Province, chiefs and headmen succeeded in persuading the administration to reverse their decisions to abolish *chitemene* (a system of shifting cultivation) and allow a compromise between settled and shifting agricultural systems. This early resistance often involved violence, by Africans in revolt and by their colonizers in asserting their authority.

Proto-Nationalist Resistance

The growth and popularity of African-led churches and the beginning of worker solidarity in the towns reflected and strengthened the development of a sense of African identity and a rejection of the European assumption of racial supremacy. There was widespread support for Christian sects, founded originally by African Americans, which argued for African control in the church, for equality of white and black, and for the eviction of all Europeans.[8] In Northern Province in 1918–1919, thousands were converted by Watchtower and accepted the teachings of racial equality, the rejection of chiefly and colonial authority, and the departure of Europeans. In the 1920s in Luapula Province, Watchtower gained support, preaching disobedience stating that, "God only is to be respected and obeyed. Nobody on earth has the right to it: anymore Europeans than the native chiefs. The Europeans have no right whatsoever in the country."[9] The colonial government arrested "seditious" preachers and banned Watchtower in 1935 on suspicion of having influenced a strike in the Copperbelt.

The Copperbelt towns became a melting pot in terms of ethnic identity. Worker protests articulated a united African position. From the late 1920s, the newly opened mines attracted workers from all over the country and further afield, notably Nyasaland and Tanganyika.[10] The colonial government saw political dangers in urbanization and was concerned that the workers should not be detribalized. Therefore, it insisted that the workers be short-term migrants who would return to their villages. They also introduced a system of tribal elders in the mines as a channel of communication with the mines' administration to strengthen tribal authority and prevent the emergence of worker organizations. These strategies were not successful. African miners resented the contempt and violence with which they were treated and the privileges of their white supervisors. Strikes erupted in 1935 against increased taxation, and again in 1940 for higher pay at a time of inflation. In 1940 the miners elected their own leaders, the Group of 17, to negotiate with the mine owners. The national character of their action was evident in the language of their demands that assumed a united African labor force and the multiethnic composition of their leadership, "which was marked by a careful tribal balance."[11] The strikes received mass support and were generally conducted with moderation. In 1935 stone throwing at Roan Antelope mine in Luanshya in the face of armed police resulted in the deaths of six and wounding of twenty-two miners, but this experience influenced the adoption of a nonviolent strategy in 1940. Signs for strike action posted in the mine compounds urged miners not to "fight or cause disturbances because if we do, they will bring many machine guns and airplanes."[12] Again, however, strikers were provoked and shot. But advocacy of nonviolent action became a recurring theme for postwar nationalist resistance: Africans should demonstrate the power of their numbers through solidarity, but not risk death at the hands of colonial forces.

From the late 1940s, the miners were unionized and other African workers, truck drivers, shop assistants, and civil servants formed themselves into unions. During the 1950s, the colonial government accepted under pressure from both mine owners and unions that many Africans would remain in the towns as permanent workers. The development of a multiethnic urban proletariat, politicized through participation in collective action, was an important factor in the growth of a sense of national identity. Although the miners' union played a role in anti-federation campaigns, it generally distanced itself from the independence struggle, instead prioritizing economic issues.[13] Nevertheless, its struggles had strong anticolonial overtones. For example in 1956, a series of mine strikes exacerbated political tensions and anti-European feelings. More importantly, miners provided a cohesive and militant support base for nationalist parties that miners joined.

Development of Civic Organizations and a Political Leadership

From the second decade of the twentieth century, Western-educated men—teachers, clerks, evangelists, and storekeepers—organized themselves in welfare associations to improve their positions within the colonial system. The longer-lasting and most active welfare associations were town based, although some rural associations were formed. These societies were multiethnic, they were organized along democratic lines (i.e., officeholders elected, public meetings held, and resolutions debated by members), and grievances were brought to the attention of government for redress.

The first welfare association—the Mwenzo Welfare Society—was formed around 1912 in Mwenzo, a Protestant missionary station in Northern Province. Forced to close by World War I fighting in the area, it was revived in 1923. Its declared objectives were mild: "The aim of the association is neither directly or indirectly to subvert the authority of the Government or any lawful establishment, or to induce the community to do so. It is rather one of helpful means of developing the country in the hands of two necessary connecting links—the government and the governed."[14] There was rapid growth of associations in the towns between 1929 and 1931. The best-known and largest associations were established in Livingstone, Broken Hill, and Ndola in 1930, each with a couple of hundred members from different professions.[15]

Although the associations that formed in towns along the railway line were more militant than Mwenzo Welfare Society, their demands were couched in similar diplomatic language. This lack of militancy in language and the careful legality of their actions were in part tactical to avoid being banned but also perhaps due to an awareness of the power of the colonial state. From 1924 to 1953, the educated minority did not wish to overthrow the colonial state, but only to influence and participate in it.

The associations articulated African grievances. They raised health issues, pointing to the high African death rate, poor and inadequate housing in towns, lack of clean water and sanitary facilities, and shortage of clinics and hospitals. They demanded more and better schools. Associations in towns asked for garden plots for food growing while rural associations asked for better agricultural advisory services. They complained about the quality of meat and fish sold to Africans by local European shop owners and asked for more township markets. They protested against government-imposed racial discrimination, being required to carry passes and not being allowed to walk on European-only pavements, and being prohibited by the railways from buying tea and food at stations. They objected to white men taking African women as concubines and to the rudeness with which they were treated by Europeans.

The welfare associations often achieved local objectives. A government newspaper for Africans in Northern Rhodesia was started. In Ndola a government school was set up, sanitary conditions were improved, a township market was opened, and land was provided for garden plots. The railway began to stop at the African location in Ndola so that Africans, who were not allowed to move in the European sector at night, would not be stranded overnight.[16] The associations were also involved in direct action to improve the economic and social situation of Africans by leading awareness-raising campaigns among the local populations to send their children to school and to practice hygiene and sanitation.

In the 1930s the welfare associations involved themselves in political issues, opposing amalgamation with the south, and in 1933 they united to form the United African Welfare Association and planned to move into the villages. However, the colonial government blocked this attempt to create a united countrywide organization.

The achievements of the welfare societies should not be measured only by how successful they were in obtaining governmental concessions. Their importance lies also in their adaptation to the new colonial realities of territorial boundaries and political power—in 1923 the Mwenzo Welfare Society wanted to call itself the Northern Rhodesian Native Association, "indicating that they had more than a local interest"[17]—and their assumption of responsibility for improving the lives of Africans territory-wide. The associations developed a culture of political awareness and engagement, democratic organization and decisionmaking, a belief in racial equality, and a sense of African unity despite tribal and territorial differences. The first territory-wide nationalist party grew out of the welfare societies.

In the rural areas of Southern Province, especially the Plateau Tonga region, former Seventh-Day Adventist pastors and teachers, who became small-scale commercial farmers, formed the local leadership in protest politics during the 1930s and 1940s. They aimed at exerting influence on local councils and chiefs and sabotaging government programs by campaigning against local participation and cooperation with government officials.[18] Their activities culminated in the formation of a political party called the Northern Rhodesia African Congress in 1937. The party never really took off since the colonial administration denied it registration. Yet it is significant because it adopted a national posture, listing among its objectives "to keep and promote the welfare and interests of Africans in Northern Rhodesia" and "to inquire and report any matter tending to injure the welfare of Africans in Northern Rhodesia."[19] Some leaders of this aborted congress came to play a prominent role in the formation of the Northern Rhodesia Federation of Welfare Societies in 1946, which in 1948 transformed itself into the Northern Rhodesia African Congress.[20] Unlike in 1937, the 1948 Northern Rhodesia African Congress was allowed by the government to register as a political party. It also had a more national composition.

Another channel for moderate, reformist political activity after 1938 was that government advisory bodies sought to involve the new African educated elite in local government. Colonial administration had previously operated through chiefs, but in 1938 Native Authority Councils were established in rural areas (and later African urban advisory councils in towns) to incorporate educated African men into the colonial administration and thus discourage independent political action. During World War II, this system ceased to be confined to local government. The advisory councils elected representatives to provincial councils, and in 1946 a territory-wide African Representative Council (ARC) was set up that sent two members to the Legislative Council. These bodies did not satisfy African aspirations, but membership did provide experience in democratic procedures and enabled the educated to contribute to their communities on such issues as education, sanitation, and township organization. They also provided a forum to articulate African opinion. The ARC opposed federation and in 1952 both the central and local councils rejected "partnership" as conceived in the proposed Federation.[21] The relationship between these governmental councils and African political parties was not always harmonious, but their membership sometimes overlapped and at times the political parties sought to influence the councils. In 1951, the ARC elected two African National Congress (ANC) members to the Legislative Council.

Tactics of Resistance Against Federation

White settler demands for self-government and the threat of federation united popular discontent and educated Africans' opposition to colonialism into a combined movement. The multiethnic composition of the welfare associations of the 1930s and 1940s helped them to form the basis of a nationwide movement with a nationalist outlook: first the Northern Rhodesia Federation of Welfare Societies, which changed its name to the Northern Rhodesia African Congress in 1948 and was renamed in 1951 the African National Congress. Most welfare associations became branches of the Congress.

From the British government's point of view, the Federation was to be a partnership between white and black. Africans in Northern Rhodesia and Nyasaland never believed this was possible, many having experienced life in white-controlled Southern Rhodesia.[22] From 1949 to 1953 Congress led an increasingly desperate campaign to prevent Northern Rhodesia's incorporation into the Federation. The decision to impose federation in the face of popular opposition precipitated the struggle for independence, hence Congress's change of name to ANC with its leader, Harry Nkumbula, stating in 1952 that African interests could be protected only by an independent African government.[23]

Before it had organized itself as a national party, Congress was faced with the threat of federation. Anti-federation activity therefore went hand in hand with the party's formation, the establishment of branches, appointment of officials, and development of policies. From 1951 the ANC had a full-time headquarters with staff, provincial officials, branches in the towns and rural areas, and national conferences. It was strong in the north, the south, and the Copperbelt. The 1952 annual conference formed a Supreme

Action Council to direct the campaign against federation and made plans for a youth wing.[24]

One strategy against federation was to appeal directly to the British government by sending delegations to pressure the colonial and British government. At the 1951 ANC annual conference, 100 chiefs in attendance agreed to raise money for a joint delegation to London in 1952. When the delegation did not succeed, Nkumbula symbolically burned the government white paper announcing federation. Protest meetings were held throughout the territory to mobilize African opinion. In April 1953 when the British government had determined to introduce federation, Congress called a national strike that Nkumbula called a day of national prayer. The response, however, was half-hearted, although it was observed in two Copperbelt towns and in Lusaka.[25] The ANC failed to involve the largest trade union (the miners), as most people were resigned to the inevitability of federation. In his study of the nationalist movement, David Mulford argues that, although there was mass support for the ANC's anti-federation stance, the party itself was poorly organized and "failed to mount a single action which involved more than a handful of officials and sympathetic supporters."[26] Mulford suggests that the ANC's anti-federation campaign articulated public opinion rather than leading it. Africans opposed federation, but they were not united behind the ANC.

Federation plans for the Kariba Dam, a hydroelectric project on the Zambezi River that would create the world's largest artificial lake and displace tens of thousands of people, featured strongly in ANC propaganda in the mid-1950s. However, banned in the Gwembe Valley, ANC workers could not exercise open leadership of the local resistance and proved powerless to halt the Federation's most prestigious project (now notorious for its neglect of the dam's social impact). Spontaneous local noncooperation—such as vanishing into the bush or simply sitting down and refusing to move when the resettlement trucks came to a village—succeeded in delaying the project until the government became forceful in September 1958. The territorial governor tried in vain to convince Chipepo men in Chisamu to accept the resettlement of women and children before the flooding. When he ordered them to board the trucks, the Chipepo men charged the police who opened fire, killing eight and wounding at least thirty-two.[27] The Chisamu confrontation ended open defiance. In her classic study on this resettlement, Elizabeth Colson comments,

> Throughout Gwembe, people faced the fact that they could be killed or seriously injured if they defied a Government that was prepared to kill them. . . . Despite all earlier talk that Europeans cared nothing for Africans and that Government had abandoned them, they had not believed their own angry accusations until Chisamu. Momentarily people lost faith in the ANC. Many were angry with its national and local agents for leading them

into danger. . . . Mpwe villages were enthusiastic partisans of ANC until Chisamu. . . . In the aftermath they turned on their local ANC agent for reporting to the district officer their refusal to move.[28]

In the early years of nationalist activity in opposition to federation, political ideas and practices, some of them contradictory, emerged and have persisted in Zambian politics. In a 1951 speech to party workers in Kitwe in the Copperbelt, Nkumbula stated, "Our national spirit, now ripe, is an upthrust from our long suffering. . . . We are a nation and like any other nation on earth we love to rule ourselves."[29] Nkumbula's argument that the nation was born from its history of suffering could be used to support a pluralist position: one belonged to the nation by virtue of birth and experience and was as much a nationalist in a trade union or a government advisory council as in the ANC. However, cooperation and toleration of other political bodies was interspersed with opposition and hostility. While the constitution of the ANC contained clauses committing the party to nonviolent actions, this strategy was open to question. The ANC annual conference of 1953 called for a policy of "non-cooperation without violence" to any policies detrimental to African interests, yet the ANC used threats and intimidation to gain acceptance of its policies (e.g., in the enforcement of boycotts) and in 1957 Nkumbula threatened to rescind the nonviolence clause.[30]

ANC support declined in the mid-1950s, following the imposition of federation. However, it pursued its policy of noncooperation in rural areas, particularly in the north, for instance, forming action groups in Chinsali in 1955. There were some strikes, but noncooperation also took other forms. People were encouraged to refuse to feed touring government officials and to ignore regulations for compulsory communal storage of kaffir corn and cassava. Boycotts of Asian- and European-owned shops that practiced segregation were a direct challenge to the Federation's partnership policy and were perceived by both the shopkeepers and the boycotters as political action. Butchers' shops were a particular target, as were beer halls run by town councils. These boycotts had an economic impact and also were a demonstration of African unity and strength. During this period, ANC leaders were arrested for various offenses such as possession of banned literature and organizing illegal meetings.

The Radicalization of the Independence Struggle

A new urgency was brought to the nationalist movement in 1957 by proposed changes in the Federation's constitution that reduced African representation in the Federal Assembly and a new constitution for Northern Rhodesia that also gave more representation to Europeans. The heightened militancy, replicated in Nyasaland by Kamuzu Banda's Malawi Congress

Party, contributed to the split in the Northern Rhodesian nationalist movement in 1958. Younger nationalists considered Nkumbula not militant enough and formed the Zambia African National Congress (ZANC) led by Kenneth Kaunda. This split also meant that, after 1958, two nationalist parties competed for support among the African populations. Party branches were established as widely as possible, newsletters published, supporters canvassed, and opponents from the rival party harassed; thus, there began a tradition of interparty violence.

The two political parties continued the kinds of protests that had been organized in the preceding years. In 1959, the ANC sent another delegation to London to protest against constitutional plans.[31] There were public burnings of the passes that Africans were required to carry. More boycotts of shops, beer halls, tearooms, and hotels were mounted. There was an intensification of campaigns of noncooperation with government policies such as storage of grain and inoculation of cattle. In 1959, the ANC threatened to refuse to pay taxes.[32] The new organization, ZANC, also engaged in more militant forms of civil disobedience and, in 1958, it organized a successful boycott of elections for the new constitution. That boycott created a political atmosphere of tension and even violence. Mobs threw stones at police and Europeans.[33] Secondary school pupils went on strike and rioted. The Commission of Inquiry into the student disturbances reported that the two nationalist movements were not directly involved in provoking the student disturbances, but "the political climate of nationalist opposition to the colonial authorities did contribute to the local students' challenge to the school authorities" and to European teachers' being seen as a "local expression of colonial rule."[34]

The reaction of the colonial government was to increase repression. Union leaders were detained after a strike in 1956. ZANC was banned and its leaders imprisoned and exiled to remote areas after its call for an election boycott. Many ZANC party officials, including its leader Kaunda, were imprisoned. The jails were overflowing in 1959. These measures were counterproductive, backfiring on the authorities and fueling African resistance. The exiled leaders worked at gaining more popular support. ZANC branches remained intact underground.[35] Similarly, the banning of ZANC's successor, the United National Independence Party (UNIP), strengthened rather than weakened the party.

UNIP began to develop as a national party and a future government with a network of branches. It developed policies on education, health, and the economy; encouraged the few well-educated Zambians who were not already in the party to join so that they could be appointed to future government positions; and recruited members from the European and Asian communities, thereby making it a national party. Its practice of appointing rather than electing officials was seen as more efficient, but certainly was less democratic.

As other British African territories were attaining independence, UNIP in 1961 rejected a proposed constitution for Northern Rhodesia that aimed to secure white minority rule and launched a cha cha cha (after the dance) campaign in its strongholds in Luapula and Northern Provinces. The plan was a campaign of property damage to make the territory ungovernable until the proposed constitution was abandoned. In the resulting "disturbances," lasting from July 15 until October 31, 146 roads were either destroyed or blocked, 64 bridges destroyed, 64 schools destroyed, 77 other public buildings destroyed, 69 motor vehicles burned or destroyed, and 20 African protesters killed by security forces. However, the official report also acknowledged that, in Luapula, "the protesters did not contemplate any premeditated attacks upon the Bomas [government centers] or mission stations. . . . The violent reactions to the security forces . . . were a result of plans to resist interference rather than deliberate acts of aggression."[36] The property destruction ended immediately when the British government indicated that they were reconsidering the constitutional proposals that aimed to secure white minority rule. The civil unrest prompted the British government, which had already accepted that Nyasaland (Malawi) was leaving the Federation, to accept that Zambia should move to majority rule and independence. After this, a peaceful transition was assured: there were too few European settlers to attempt to seize power.

The Role of Women in the Nationalist Struggle

Women participated in the nationalist movement in Zambia, but it was controlled by men. Only within the past thirty years have women developed a movement to achieve equality. Women were active in some of the early mass protests on the mines and in the villages as vocal opponents encouraging the men to behave more aggressively. Simon Zukas, a leader of the Ndola Anti-Federation Action Group, recalls one man objecting to women attending meetings because they were dangerous: women goading men had once caused a riot.[37] Some women later joined the women's organizations of mass membership parties, but they tended to be widows and wives of party members or of men who had been persuaded by the party to allow their participation. Men decided party policy while women's primary duties were to raise funds, cater for party meetings, house nationalist leaders, run funeral committees, and recruit more women. Women participated in the boycotts and marches and joined men in solidarity actions, for example, by burning their colonial marriage certificates when their husbands were burning their identity cards. Women in Luapula Province organized political meetings and helped hide political prisoners in the 1950s. Julia Mulenga, a widow known as Mama Chikonameka, organized women to march, bare breasted, against the color bar and also to confront the colonial secretary at the airport.[38] Although women played a significant role in the independence movements, and their participation involved shaping and taking part in political society, their presence did not threaten male authority or challenge the parties' hierarchical structures and bullying culture that continued into the independence period.

Nonviolent Strategies

As in South Africa, Southern Rhodesia, and Tanganyika, Northern Rhodesian nationalism was partly inspired by the Indian National Congress Party with its Gandhian philosophy of nonviolent resistance. The African National Congress of South Africa, founded in 1911, followed a nonviolent policy until the 1960 Sharpeville massacre. The African political parties formed in Northern Rhodesia included nonviolence clauses in their constitutions and frequently repeated this commitment. In 1948, a Northern Rhodesian African Congress memorandum warning of civil war urged its followers to "be cool and non violent."[39] Zukas found it hard to explain the red stripes (representing the international working class) in the badge of the Ndola Anti-Federation Action Committee: "no blood had been spilt . . . nor was there a wish to have any spilt."[40] In 1959, the *Voice of UNIP* newspaper urged its supporters to conduct their boycotts without violence and to give no excuse for "the use of armed force upon innocent victims."[41]

Some leaders had an ethical commitment to nonviolence, but for the majority the tactics of petitions, meetings, marches, boycotts, stone throwing, and destruction of infrastructure were a pragmatic response to the prevailing situation and a strategic recognition that similar tactics had worked in other former British colonies. The militant action prior to independence often spilled into violence, frequently in response to the violence of the colonial authorities. This never involved plans to kill government officials or white residents, let alone to launch an armed struggle.

Factors Influencing a Nonviolent Strategy

Leadership

Kaunda, who led the more radical nationalist organization (UNIP) and became Zambia's president, began reading the writings of Mohandas Gandhi (Mahatma) in the early 1950s. When he visited the United Kingdom in 1956, he met pacifists through the Movement for Colonial Freedom and was in contact with the weekly *Peace News*. On release from prison in

1960, he hoped majority rule could be achieved "through a non-violent struggle. I therefore ask you all to be calm, patient and non-violent."[42] At public rallies where crowds were antagonized by the police presence, he reminded them "that our policy was one of non-violence."[43] The cha cha cha damage to physical infrastructure was referred to as "positive action and did not involve plans for attacks on people."[44] Kaunda's advocacy of nonviolent actions was perhaps a way of avoiding loss of life, particularly African life, when faced with a more powerful opponent rather than taking a principled stand. He warned Britain of violence worse than that of Mau Mau if Africans lost their patience.[45] His influence, however, was undeniably a moderating factor. During the violent, sometimes lethal, conflicts between the Lumpa Church and UNIP supporters, he refused to endorse violence. According to the district commissioner of Isoka, "Kenneth Kaunda himself did everything possible to persuade the opposing sides to resolve their differences peaceably."[46]

After independence Kaunda was committed to ending white domination in southern Africa, which included such support for the liberation struggles as providing headquarters and in some cases a rear base for guerrilla activities in Southern Rhodesia. His government's position was that, "if armed struggle is the only choice left for Zimbabwe and Namibia, we shall support it. Zambia has made it clear that we do not participate in acts of killing if peace can be attained without further bloodshed."[47] However, on several occasions, Kaunda expressed his strong views against "mindless violence." Even during the liberation wars, he was willing to negotiate with white regimes—a position that at times brought him into conflict with the leaders of the liberation movements.[48]

British Colonial Policies

British government strategy sometimes contributed to reducing confrontation as constitutional conferences and Commissions of Inquiry had the effect of keeping open hope for improvement. The UNIP leadership was also aware that there were British parliamentarians, from all parties, who were supportive of African independence. In 1960, the landmark "wind of change speech" by British prime minister Harold Macmillan offered further encouragement that Zambia could follow the path of Ghana and Tanganyika.

International Support for Nonviolent Resistance

By 1960, Zambian nationalists had obtained the active support of a number of African leaders, particularly Ghana's Kwame Nkrumah, Tanganyika's Julius Nyerere, and Egypt's Gamal Abdel Nasser, offering further assurance that independence could be achieved nonviolently. These countries helped fund UNIP in the spirit of pan-Africanism.

UNIP also received support from the international peace movement. In 1961, Kaunda was offered support from a pacifist group called the World Peace Brigade, comprised of the "Gandhian Movement, segments of the peace movement particularly in Europe and USA, groups engaged in non-violent struggles for social justice, and movements for national independence and reconstruction." The group was prepared to march from Tanganyika to Lusaka in international support of UNIP's rejection of the proposed 1961 constitution and in solidarity with its demands for independence.[49] This never happened as the violence and disruption caused by the cha cha cha protesters persuaded the British government to grant independence to Northern Rhodesia. But Kaunda's awareness of this potential support must have strengthened his negotiating position with the British government.

The Role of Christianity

Christianity has been influential in both the colonial and postcolonial periods, helping to create a sense of national identity. It also has influenced the nature of political discourse. The Christian churches ran almost all of the schools in Northern Rhodesia and, even when the government opened a secondary school, it stressed the importance of Christianity. Nationalist leaders in the preindependence period, and government leaders and senior civil servants since then, were all educated together at the same few schools.[50] Because this education was both Christian and based on a British curriculum, it influenced students to have democratic ideals, which they contrasted with the reality of Northern Rhodesia. It also inclined them to have peaceful and pragmatic aims, toward social democracy rather than socialist revolution. Nationalists integrated their Christianity with their politics. The welfare societies opened their meetings with prayer. When Nkumbula called a strike against federation he called it a day of prayer.

The Christian churches have a tradition of intervention in politics in Zambia that aims to achieve peaceful and, in their eyes, just solutions. In the early colonial period, European missionaries were appointed to represent African interests on the Legislative Council and many became critics of European exploitation of Africans. Several of the churches opposed federation. In 1951, the World Council of Churches denounced federation and called for the eventual transfer of power to Africans,[51] a position later echoed by the Catholic bishops and the United Church (Copperbelt Protestants).[52]

Conclusion

After the 1920s, there were no further plans for violent resistance to colonial authority. Strikes in 1935 and 1940 degenerated into violence in the face of provocation, but they were intended as a demonstration of worker solidarity through withdrawal of labor. This period also saw the beginning of a new form of politics in the associations formed by the educated African minority. Democratically organized and multitribal, seeking to change colonial policies through lobbying and self-organized action to improve conditions, they provided a basis for the development of the postwar nationalist party. The aims of this and subsequent nationalist parties were essentially constitutional, to prevent the introduction of a white-dominated federation, and later to pressure the colonial government to introduce a constitution for majority rule.

When petitions, meetings, and symbolic protest failed to change government policy, Africans resorted to more militant and often illegal actions—boycotting shops and beer halls, refusing to obey selected regulations, and boycotting elections. Finally and successfully, a campaign of nonlethal destruction of infrastructure made two provinces ungovernable. The nationalist parties adopted nonviolence clauses in their constitutions; their leaders continuously urged followers to be calm in the face of provocation from colonial forces. And Kaunda was a leader with a real concern to arrive at solutions through nonviolent actions. However, threats and violence became common ways to persuade people to follow the party line, to buy party cards, and to support boycotts. This was later followed by interparty violence.

The fact that Zambians have lived in peace for the forty-six years of the country's existence is a constant in political rhetoric and is indeed appreciated by the people of Zambia and the international community. Two political parties competing for power before independence provided a precedent for a rather aggressive form of pluralism. Apart from a few unsuccessful coup attempts, the politically disaffected have generally turned toward political movements. This was true even of the final years of the one-party state when a popular movement convinced Kaunda to reintroduce multiparty democracy. Robin Palmer, referring to his years in Zambia in the 1970s, notes, "Zambia was a free country, a decent, tolerant place, even within a one-party system, where people didn't kill each other because of politics. It was also an island of peace and sanity."[53]

Notes

1. Northern Rhodesia (Zambia)'s eastern neighbor, Nyasaland, gained its independence in 1963 as Malawi while Southern Rhodesia became Zimbabwe in 1980.

2. Northern Rhodesia had several provinces: Northern Province (split in the 1950s into Luapula and Northern Provinces), North-Western Province, Southern Province, Barotseland, Eastern Province, Central Province, and Western Province.

3. Statement of the Conclusions of His Majesty's Government in the United Kingdom as Regards Closer Union of East Africa, Cmd. 3574. Quoted in David Mulford, *Zambia: The Politics of Independence* (Oxford: Oxford University Press,

1967); Lord Passfield, colonial secretary in the first Labour government in Britain, is better known as Sidney Webb, the Fabian socialist and cofounder of the London School of Economics.

4. *Chimurenga* refers to the Shona people's wars against white domination. The first was the 1896 rebellion and the second against the Ian Smith regime in the 1960s and 1970s. Individuals who acted as spirit mediums of some mythical revered figures—such as Nehenda, Kagubi, and Kadungure—took a leading role in the first *chimurenga*. Charwe, Hehanda's spirit medium, was executed for her role. See David Lan, *Guns and Rains: Guerrillas and Spirit Mediums in Zimbabwe* (Harare: Zimbabwe Publishing House, 1985), 6.

5. Henry S. Meebelo, *Reaction to Colonialism: A Prelude to the Politics of Independence in Northern Zambia, 1893–1939* (Manchester: Manchester University Press, 1971), 93.

6. Thomas Rasmussen, "The Popular Basis of Anti-Colonial Protest," in *Politics in Zambia,* ed. William Tordoff (Manchester: Manchester University Press, 1974), 50–51.

7. Meebelo, *Reaction to Colonialism,* 111–113.

8. Robert Rotberg, *The Rise of Nationalism in Central Africa: The Making of Malawi and Zambia* (Cambridge: Harvard University Press, 1972).

9. Mwelwa Musambachime, "The African Voice in Northern Rhodesia: The Case of Mweru-Luapula, 1890–1930," Seminar Paper No. 1 (History Department, University of Zambia, May 22, 1987), 7.

10. Patrick Ohadike, "Development of and Factors in the Employment of African Migrants in the Copper Mines of Zambia 1940–66," Zambian Papers No. 4 (Lusaka: Institute for Social Research, 1969), 7.

11. Charles Perrings, *Black Mineworkers in Central Africa: Industrial Strategies and the Evolution of an African Proletariat in the Copperbelt, 1911–41* (London: Heinemann, 1979), 220.

12. Rotberg, *Rise of Nationalism,* 171.

13. Henry S. Meebelo, *African Proletarians and Colonial Capitalism* (Lusaka: Kenneth Kaunda Foundation, 1986), 416–420.

14. *Native Affairs Report* (Lusaka: Government of Northern Rhodesia, 1929).

15. David J. Cook, "The Influence of Livingstonia Mission upon the Formation of Welfare Associations in Zambia, 1912–31," in *Themes in the Christian History of Central Africa,* ed. T. O. Ranger and John Weller (Los Angeles: University of California Press, 1974), 98–134.

16. Ibid., 119.

17. Ibid., 109.

18. Jotham C. Momba, "Peasant Differentiation and Rural Party Politics in Colonial Zambia," *Journal of Southern African Studies* 11, no. 2 (1985): 289.

19. Mac Dixon Fyle, "The Seventh Day Adventists (SDA) in the Protest Politics of the Tonga Plateau, Northern Rhodesia," *African Social Research,* no. 26 (1978): 460.

20. Rasmussen, "The Popular Basis," 52–53.

21. Mulford, *Zambia,* 27, 33.

22. Godfrey Huggins, the Southern Rhodesian who became the first prime minister of the Federation, infamously compared the partnership between white and black with that of a rider and his horse.

23. Rotberg, *Rise of Nationalism,* 243.

24. Mulford, *Zambia,* 22.

25. Rotberg, *Rise of Nationalism,* 262–263.

26. Mulford, *Zambia,* 25.

27. *Gwembe Commission Report,* 1958 (Report of the Commission Appointed to Inquire into the Circumstances Leading up to and Surrounding the Recent Deaths and Injuries Caused by the Use of Firearms in the Gwembe District and Matters Relating Thereto (Lusaka Government Printer, 1958), 11–12, cited in Elizabeth Colson, *The Social Consequences of Resettlement* (Manchester: Manchester University Press, 1971), 40.

28. Colson, *Social Consequences,* 41.

29. Mulford, *Zambia,* 20.

30. Ibid., 37, 45, 64–65.

31. Ibid., 100.

32. Ibid., 114, 116; and Momba, "Peasant Differentiation," 287.

33. Stone throwing was perceived as political protest. In the first few decades after independence, when an individual with no obvious qualifications was appointed to a political position, the popular and slightly derogatory assumption would be that he had been "a stone thrower."

34. Rasmussen, "The Popular Basis," 44.

35. Mulford, *Zambia,* 107.

36. Northern Rhodesia Government, *An Account of Disturbances in Northern Rhodesia July to October, 1961* (Lusaka: Government Printer, 1961), 77–78. UNIP claimed more than 100 were killed. UNIP, "Grim Peep in the North."

37. Simon Zukas, *Into Exile and Back* (Lusaka: Bookworld, 2002), 71.

38. Gisela Geisler, *Women and the Remaking of Politics in Southern Africa* (Uppsala: Nordiska Afrikainstitut, 2004), 42–44.

39. Rotberg, *Rise of Nationalism,* 219.

40. Zukas, *Into Exile and Back,* 65.

41. Rotberg, *Rise of Nationalism,* 305.

42. Kenneth Kaunda, *Zambia Shall Be Free* (London: Heinemann, 1962), 139.

43. Ibid., 139–140.

44. Ibid., 153.

45. Ibid., 155. The Mau Mau rebellion was a revolt of the Kikuyu group called Mau Mau in Kenya in the 1950s against British colonial rule, conducted with much brutality on both sides.

46. John Hudson, *A Time to Mourn: A Personal Account of the 1964 Lumpa Church Revolt in Zambia* (Lusaka: Bookworld, 1999), 54–55. The Lumpa were too frightened to return to their villages of origin and went into exile in the Congo.

47. Government of the Republic of Zambia, *Official Verbatim Report of the Proceedings of the National Assembly,* January 17–March 21, 1975, 2799–2800, Lusaka.

48. Jotham C. Momba, "Change and Continuity in Zambia's Southern African Policy: Kaunda to Chiluba," *Africa Insight* 31, no. 2 (2001), 20.

49. Charles Walker, "Non-violence in Eastern Africa 1962–64: The World Peace Brigade and the Zambian Independence," in *Liberation Without Violence: A Third Party Approach,* ed. A. Paul Hare and Herbert H. Blumberg (London: Rex Collings, 1977).

50. Brendan Carmody, *The Evolution of Education in Zambia* (Lusaka: Bookworld, 2004), 150–151.

51. Rotberg, *Rise of Nationalism,* 239.

52. Kaunda, *Zambia Shall Be Free,* 145.

53. Robin Palmer, *A House in Zambia: Recollections of the ANC and Oxfam at 250 Zambezi Road, Lusaka, 1967–97* (Lusaka: Bookworld, 2008), 4. He was comparing Zambia not only to the countries of the south involved in freedom wars, but also to Banda's "murderous dictatorship" in Malawi.

5

Mozambique:
Liberation Myths and Resistance
Strategies, 1920s–1970s

Matt Meyer

Few regions of the world have experienced the depth of strategic nonviolent action and tactical nonviolent innovation in practice and deliberation as has Africa. The anticolonial era, stretching across the continent from the 1950s through the 1980s, afforded liberation leaders tremendous opportunities for discussion and debate on the merits of diverse forms of nonviolent resistance as well as armed struggle. At times, these forms were viewed as dichotomized and rival opposites. However, analysis of the seemingly clear-cut example of Mozambique's successful armed struggle offers a more nuanced view.

Mozambique stands out as an example where peaceful or civil resistance was a significant factor in the freedom movement, yet the successes of its ten-year armed struggle against Portugal (1964–1974) have overshadowed the complementary use of a range of tactics used over the long haul. In this chapter, I suggest that behind the images associated with the Mozambique Liberation Front (FRELIMO)—portraits of proud mother warriors with rifles in one arm and babies in the other, with songs and poems extolling the joys to come "when bullets begin to flower"[1]—there is a less often told story of nonmilitary combat.

In FRELIMO's perspective, the fight against colonial rule was also a struggle to reverse the severe social, political, and economic underdevelopment caused by colonialism. From 1966 onward, parcels of land—from north to south—were liberated from colonial rule and zones of popular control were established. Although these liberated zones functioned under the leadership of the guerrilla-based FRELIMO, their very existence relied more on the nonmilitary strategic concept of building parallel political processes. The liberated areas became miniature "states-in-the-making,"

89

where systems of dual power rivaled the Portuguese overseers.[2] The short- and long-term nature of this revolutionary civic project was recognized at the highest levels of Mozambican resistance. Mozambique's first president, Samora Machel, underscored this in his 1975 Independence Day speech:

> The State is not an eternal and immutable structure; the state is not the bureaucratic machinery of civil servants, nor something abstract, nor a mere technical apparatus. . . . The colonial state must be replaced by a people's State . . . which wipes out exploitation and releases the creative initiative of the masses and the productive forces. In the phase of the people's democracy in which we are now engaged as a phase of the Mozambican revolutionary process, our aim is to lay the material, ideological, administrative and social foundation of our State. . . . The new battle is only beginning.[3]

Although expressed in military terms, the "battle" Machel describes is essentially one of constructing schools and health centers, building civic organizations and structures of accountability, and setting up a popular, functioning infrastructure.[4] This project, which began long before the 1975 military victory, is the focus of this investigation.

Direct Resistance in the Early Years of Colonization

From the sixteenth to the twentieth century, the European drive for conquest exacerbated conflicts between the various peoples of what became Mozambique. After centuries of Arab, Swahili, and Portuguese rule, twentieth-century anticolonial movements began to call for unity across tribal, linguistic, and local lines. They started organizing primarily in exile, protesting against Portuguese domination and for "cultural improvement" for the majority of the uneducated population. One such group, the Liga Africana, was formed in Lisbon in 1923 during (and under the auspices of) the Third Pan-African Congress hosted by W. E. B. Du Bois.

The Liga Africana and other groups formed at this time petitioned the Lisbon government for reform. They wrote manifestos, held public meetings and forums, and sent letters and delegations to the colonial and domestic officials. These groups, however, were quickly and ruthlessly repressed, then driven underground altogether with the advent of fascism and the rise to power in Portugal of Antonio Salazar at the end of the decade.[5] Salazar's authoritarian New State (*Estado Novo*) was installed in Lisbon in 1933. Proclaiming its principles as anti-liberalism, anticommunism, and an understanding of Portugal as a pluricontinental empire, it put an end to overt anticolonial initiatives and little resistance could further develop until after World War II.[6] Nevertheless, small and localized acts of what might be called subaltern resistance took place throughout Mozambique in the late 1920s and early 1930s.

Since Portuguese colonialism was carried out with as few settlers as possible, contact between the colonizers and the colonized took place on only select occasions: when land was being seized, when people were being conscripted into labor camps, and when taxes were being collected. Noncooperation therefore was expressed most explicitly in response to these activities, and took cultural and largely ethnic-specific forms such as singing, dancing, and carving. The Chope and Makonde peoples, for example, became known for their acts ridiculing and resisting Portuguese rule.[7] To caricature the colonizers, they carved light-shaded wooden figures with distorted features. Some of the sculptures suggested greedy plantation overlords holding illegal torture instruments. Community-based performances portrayed whites as foolish thugs, but through songs in languages unidentifiable by the Europeans and choreographed movements that appeared as traditional to the untrained observer.[8]

A few cross-ethnic, regional racial and religious groups also emerged during this period, carrying out political activities that, while cloaked in social terms, were implicitly hostile to European domination. For instance, mutual aid societies were formed to provide scholarships for students and apprentices. Even some newspapers and magazines developed in the major towns and cities of 1930s Mozambique, including groupings of Africans, mulattoes, Muslims, and Indians. One of the more prominent, *The African Cry* (O Brado Africano), in 1932 brazenly called for an immediate end to colonial injustices:

> Enough! We've had to put up with you, to suffer the terrible consequences of your follies, of your demands. . . . We want to be treated in the same way that you are. We do not aspire to the comforts you surround yourselves with, thanks to our strength . . . even less do we aspire to a life dominated by the idea of robbing [one's] brother.[9]

Mozambican Resistance in the 1940s–1960s

Mozambican intellectual Eduardo Mondlane, who was to become a founder and first president of FRELIMO, was the foremost chronicler of the movements of the 1940s and beyond. He contrasted the racist political conditions faced by the small minority of educated Mozambicans such as himself and the peasant farmers who made up the majority and whose struggle was mainly against the daily violence of forced labor and inhuman economic conditions. For the elite, resistance took "a purely cultural expression," for instance, in the writings and paintings of Luis Bernardo Honwana, Noemia de Sousa, and Malangatana Ngwenya.[10] Mondlane saw that much work would be required to bridge the colonized groups. The foundation in 1949 of the student group Nucleo dos Estudantes Africanos Secundarios de Mocambique (NESAM) was to play a key role in this.

Although NESAM was a small part of the population, probably comprising several hundred members at its height, it included many future leaders, including Mondlane. Its importance lay in the ability to reach people throughout the nation, across wide geographical areas, with a nationalist understanding that advocated for the majority of Mozambicans. In fact, by reaching the core of educated black youth, NESAM provided a space for dialogue and reevaluation on questions of nationalism and indigenous culture, breaking colonial attempts at splitting the African elite away from their ethnic roots. For more than a decade, it gave current and former students a context for conceptualizing a future Mozambique separate from colonial designs. NESAM also concretely demonstrated the significance of a civic networking structure.[11]

The development of NESAM coincided with growing activity among urban workers, including dock workers in the capital, Lourenco Marques (now Maputo), and farmers on nearby plantations. A series of strikes in 1947 led to a major work stoppage and uprising a year later, aborted only when Portuguese authorities deported several hundred radicals and severely punished others.[12] Labor organizing continued formally and informally and, in 1956, forty-nine strikers were killed during a dock strike in Lourenco Marques.[13] In the early 1960s, strikes spread to the ports of Beira and Nacala, now supported by the newly formed FRELIMO's clandestine structures. Focusing on cruel working conditions, it was easy to link these grievances to colonialism. However, violent repression, including arrests and deaths, commented Mondlane, "temporarily discourage[d] both the masses and the leadership from considering strike action as a possible effective political method."[14]

Rural resistance also grew after World War II. As hundreds of thousands of peasants were forced to plant and pick cotton for the Portuguese market, noncompliance with meeting quotas and other forms of sabotage were common. In 1947, in one of Mozambique's most spectacular instances of labor resistance, 7,000 women from the town of Buzi refused to plant the colonial administrator's cotton seed, effectively ceasing crop production for a short period while demanding not only increased wages but greater control over the land they worked.[15]

In Gaza Province, in both 1955 and 1958, large-scale production boycotts were organized until cotton-picking wages were increased.[16] Farmers from Cabo Delgado Province regularly crossed the border to Tanganyika where the African National Union was organizing indigenous farming cooperatives, prefiguring the *Ujamaa* concept of future Tanzanian president Julius Nyerere.[17] In part influenced and aided by this, the African Voluntary Cotton

Society of Mozambique was formed. Based in the Mueda region under the leadership of Makonde nationalist Lazaro Nkavandame, the community-based cooperative became a model of civil resistance functioning outside of colonial control. In a special agreement negotiated with the Lisbon authorities, the Cabo cooperative gained thousands of members, ultimately tripling production from its previous level under colonial control.[18] By offering a Mozambican-led agricultural initiative, they inspired local farmers and families to intensify their efforts at earning a living wage and proving their effectiveness as workers and traders. Despite harassment and occasional arrests for this indigenous form of competition, the cooperative continued for several years, negotiating exemptions from forced labor from local authorities while operating in a narrow, semilegal climate. As neighboring Tanganyika pushed for self-rule throughout the late 1950s, the Mozambican cooperative became more radical.[19]

The Mueda Massacre and Its Aftermath

The undisputed, though often unmentioned, turning point in the movement for Mozambique's independence came on June 16, 1960, when a massive and peaceful protest was planned in Mueda. The Portuguese provincial governor of Cabo Delgado was visiting Mueda, and several thousand Africans, organized by the cooperative and by nationalist activists, had turned out to hear how he would respond to their demands for greater sovereignty. After a private meeting between the governor and several civic leaders, those members of the assembled crowd who wished to address him were asked to come forward and be recognized. However, when civic leaders came forward, provincial police seized them, bound their hands, and beat and arrested them.[20] As the crowd attempted to stop the arrests, the governor ordered a company of Portuguese troops, who had been hidden, to fire on the nonviolent assembly. Less than three months after the Sharpeville massacre in South Africa, the Mueda massacre in Mozambique claimed the lives of over 500 peaceful protesters. The cooperative officially collapsed and many surviving militants and independence activists fled the country.[21]

Mondlane's account of the massacre refers to the cooperative events preceding the demonstration as "spontaneous agitation," and decries the world's lack of attention to this "culminating" activity of years of struggle.[22] FRELIMO cadre Teresinha Mblale, whose uncle was killed at Mueda, notes bitterly, "Our people were unarmed when they began to shoot." Mondlane reflected that she was "one of thousands who determined never again to be unarmed in the face of Portuguese violence." Nothing in the north of the country would ever return to normal and, throughout Mozambique, a new course of struggle was set in motion. As in South Africa, nonviolent

strategy—which arguably had a weaker theoretical basis in Mozambique—
was officially and formally deemed irrelevant. "Throughout the region,"
Mondlane wrote, the massacre had "aroused the bitterest hatred against the
Portuguese and showed once and for all that peaceful resistance was futile."[23]

As pan-African pacifist Bill Sutherland comments concerning both
Sharpeville and Mueda, "people confuse defeat with death, and assume that
nonviolence is only valid as long as nobody gets hurt or killed."[24] Both
Sharpeville and Mueda saw dramatic examples of people power, with people not fully recognizing their strength. The fact that neither movement was
prepared for such violence or the shock caused speaks more to the limitations of the moment than to an inherent weakness in unarmed strategies. Although the massacre at Mueda demonstrated the overpowering force that
violence could play in that situation, it in no way diminished the radical
sentiments spreading across the country. It was not a coincidence, but rather
a direct consequence of the massacre that leading Mozambicans now intensified their work for unity and for the formation of a national front.

Three nationalist organizations vied for leadership between 1960 and
the formation of FRELIMO in 1962, yet there was little active talk about
armed struggle and no actual military engagement took place. To be sure,
most leaders thought an organized armed uprising would be necessary, but
they also understood some of the difficulties it would entail. Furthermore,
alongside any guerrilla campaign, it would be vital to mobilize civil resistance. Mondlane, who helped forge the unity needed to create a nationwide
front, was himself a participant in the civic protests of the 1940s and 1950s.
By the end of 1960, he had become convinced that "normal political pressure and agitation" would not win freedom for his country, but he retained
an extremely developed sense this would require a multifaceted series of
actions mobilizing the population.[25]

Tactical Debates Within the Building of the United Front

A September 1962 gathering brought together representatives of the three
main nationalist groups in Dar es Salaam, Tanzania, where each had made
its headquarters. According to George Houser and Herb Shore of the American Committee on Africa (ACOA), every Mozambican assembled "had
come to know the reprisals which immediately followed small-scale resistance or peaceful protest. . . . They were ready for unity."[26] At Nyerere's
urging, and with the support of other leading pan-Africanists, FRELIMO
was formed with broad objectives. "To build real freedom," Nyerere insisted, "demands a positive understanding and positive actions, not simply
a rejection of colonialism."[27] This First Congress of FRELIMO therefore set
forth as principles and aims the need to "encourage and support the formation

and consolidation of trade unions, youth and women's organizations"; to "promote by every method the social and cultural development of the Mozambican women"; to "promote the literacy of the Mozambican people, creating schools wherever possible"; to "mobilize popular opinion"; and to "procure diplomatic, moral and material help for the cause of the Mozambican people from the African states and from all peace and freedom loving people."[28]

Years later, Mozambican prime minister Pascal Mocumbi, a physician who took part in the First Congress of FRELIMO, underscored the general sentiment there: "We said that we would fight by all means for our liberation. . . . These words were deliberate. We wanted to reach these objectives through peaceful means."[29]

Though popular histories of FRELIMO romanticize the armed struggle,[30] a careful review of FRELIMO's early development under Mondlane's and Machel's leadership shows that the armed aspect of the revolutionary campaign was not primary.[31] In contrast to the strategies advanced by Ernesto Che Guevara, Mondlane and FRELIMO rejected outright the idea that military action (whether by a small *foco* or by a large army) could serve as a means to rally and properly mobilize masses of people. Their priority was ground-up, village-level, popular base building, as implemented in the FRELIMO-controlled zones throughout the late 1960s and throughout the entire country after independence. Through the building of energetic civic organizations and embedding in the educational curriculum, this emphasis on mass, popular participation was an organizational mandate. Mondlane was particularly adept at remaining open and flexible about any methods to improve the flow of information from the people to FRELIMO militants and cadre. In fact, when Guevara traveled in Africa spreading his experiences of the Cuban successes of small, inspirational guerrilla forces, Mondlane pointedly disagreed, arguing that, in Mozambique at least, a broader, mass-based strategy was needed.[32]

Therefore, claims that FRELIMO, "in contrast to their organizational predecessors[,] . . . abandoned existing policy-commitments to nonviolence"[33] seem dubious. It would certainly be more accurate to suggest that, in keeping with the experiences of their historic forebearers who engaged in diverse acts of civil resistance, FRELIMO was consistent in focusing its work around building civic institutions and popular, nonmilitary forms of alternatives to colonialism. The building of the Organization of Mozambican Women (OMM), the Organization of Mozambican Youth (OJM), and the Workers' Union received significant human and fiscal resources. The armed struggle, though deemed important and necessary, was of secondary concern to the majority of FRELIMO's leadership.

It was more than simple rhetoric that Mondlane, in writing about the need for self-defense and military action, began by stating that FRELIMO had been "determined to do everything in our power to try to gain independence by peaceful means."[34] For most of the 1960s, FRELIMO leaders debated between "two lines of struggle."[35] One, voiced by Mondlane and Machel, wanted to go beyond mere "flag" independence to an end to all forms of colonialism and colonial thinking. The opposing line placed greater emphasis on military means, but merely wanted to force the Portuguese out (and replace them with Mozambicans who would serve as loyal presidents and businessmen). A conventional change of political power and government, without a transformation of people's consciousness or social and economic conditions, would not require the tedious (and nonviolent) work of mass organizing.[36]

In this light, the conversations between Mondlane and Sutherland bear particular significance. Sutherland had, by the early 1960s, become an active representative of the Pan-African Freedom Movement of East and Central Africa, one of the organizations that helped push for unity among the constituent groupings in early FRELIMO. Maintaining their personal commitment to nonviolence as a philosophy as well as a tactic, Mondlane and Sutherland shared a "true, personal relationship" so Sutherland's pushing for a nonviolent approach undoubtedly played some role in those formative years.[37] Sutherland advised Mondlane on the importance of discipline within the ranks of the freedom fighters, noting that the Algerian movement, despite its reputation, had at points responded to provocative violence on the part of the French by remaining nonresponsive, not violent. Mondlane confirmed this through his own Algerian contacts and reported to Sutherland that, though both the Algerian and Mozambican movements needed their armed capacity, this nonmilitary phase of the Algerian resistance was seen as a great setback for the French. "It might be beneficial," Mondlane suggested, "[having] some training of people in nonviolent techniques" and he intended to propose this to FRELIMO's executive committee.[38] Why these seminars never took place has been a source of conjecture. Did vanguardist or hard-line elements within FRELIMO's leadership block them?[39] The evidence suggests that tactical considerations were resolved through open discussion and debate without violent confrontation among the leadership.

Armed Struggle and the Building of Parallel Civic Structures

The guerrilla war, with barely 200 combatants, started in earnest in 1964. In 1969, Mondlane was killed by a parcel bomb in Tanzania. Probably the Portuguese intelligence agents responsible expected Mondlane's death to cause confusion and defeatism in FRELIMO's leadership. However, eventually

Mondlane's colleague and friend Samora Machel succeeded him. Under Machel's watch, military tactics extended greatly, developing into a full people's war with armed propaganda at the forefront.[40]

As already mentioned, however, the liberated zones held by FRELIMO in this period were formed on the basis of a tightly woven network of strong civic associations that operated as parallel structures to the repressive Portuguese colonial government. They transformed into local engines of a people's democracy after independence, but maintained significant autonomy despite ties to the official FRELIMO organizational and governmental structures. With emphasis on literacy and education, extended traditional and modern health care, affordable and safe housing, and consumer protections, Mozambican society was led in many respects by its Organization of Mozambican Women. The OMM developed out of FRELIMO, but maintained independent functioning from it. It grew to have local associates in every province, town, and village of the country, mobilizing the countryside as well as urban factories and centers. By the early 1970s, when FRELIMO fighters numbered nearly 7,000, it is likely that OMM membership figures rivaled that number.[41]

The importance of the OMM increased after Mozambique became fully independent. It provided women, who were understood to be the center of economic and social development, with vocational training; education in family planning, literacy, and political development; and a space for social and cultural conversation. By the 1980s, the group had grown into the hundreds of thousands. In the late 1990s, the estimated membership exceeded 1 million. The OMM, by this time, had separated from FRELIMO (all civic organizations were encouraged to have full autonomy as the country moved toward multiparty direct democracy).[42] The OMM today certainly ranks as one of Africa's most dynamic and successful civic organizations.

In cooperation with Mozambican youth and workers' organizations, OMM instilled a dynamic form of participatory engagement in all its work, confirming Machel's view that "when we involve everyone in solving problems, when we make everyone feel responsible for solving problems which we face, we are collectivizing our leadership, collectivizing our lives."[43] Though smaller in number than OMM, the OJM engaged young people from all walks of life in the liberation process. Political education took place in social settings: as children were recruited into sports teams, as students were assisted in their educational endeavors, and as youth prepared for work. In sharp contrast to how youth were viewed in other burgeoning nation-states, the OJM was not simply a mechanism for recruiting young people into the armed forces. For those who did join the armed struggle, schools for learning reading, writing, and basic math were set up in the bush because these skills were deemed as important as the technical soldiering skills they had to learn.[44]

FRELIMO's preference for limited armed propaganda over military confrontation is illustrated by their strategy against the Cabora Bassa hydroelectric project in Tete Province. This 1970 scheme was a direct corporate challenge to FRELIMO's base-building work in the north of the country. The dam, financed by South Africa's Anglo-American Corporation, was to supply electricity to mainly the neighboring apartheid regime. Because it was not a genuine development project initiated to benefit the people on whose land it was being built, FRELIMO called the proposal a "crime against humanity" and mounted regional and international educational campaigns against it. For their part, the Portuguese forcibly resettled many Mozambicans living in surrounding villages, then spread defoliants and landmines around the area in order to prevent FRELIMO attacks. However, FRELIMO never planned a frontal attack on the dam, although this was a region where the armed liberation forces of Mozambique were relatively strong. Instead, it planned a war of attrition, carrying out small acts of sabotage (e.g., the cutting of transmission line cables and destruction of unstaffed transmission towers) that would be a drain on the colonial powers' fiscal and physical resources.[45] "We'll eat away at the project," noted Machel, "making it more expensive and taking longer to construct."[46] By the end of the war for independence four years later, the armies of South Africa and Rhodesia had to fly equipment in under heavy guard just to attempt to maintain work on the uncompleted plant.

Independence, Civil War, and the Development of Mythologized Histories

In the decade following the 1974–1975 independence of Mozambique, despite armed attacks from neighboring South Africa and Rhodesia, FRELIMO was as likely to draw on the "weapon of culture" as it was to promote military means.[47] In the years just prior to and immediately following independence, it is also clear that peaceful means, and an unusually sophisticated understanding of how liberation can bring about emancipation for the colonizer as well as the colonized, dominated FRELIMO's relationship with the Portuguese. Portugal's colonial struggles and the war in Mozambique in particular played a significant role in mobilizing dissent within the mother country. FRELIMO consciously tried to influence the Portuguese military. Most dramatically in 1975, after the fall of the dictatorship but before independence, it sent home captured Portuguese soldiers—utilizing the "sophisticated weapon" of class consciousness over simple race-based prejudice. As their boat arrived, the former prisoners hung a huge sign over the boat side: "Let's do it like FRELIMO—People's Power."[48] By the time of the primarily nonviolent Carnation Revolution in Portugal, which brought an end to decades of fascism and a moderate socialist government to the fore, 100,000 Portuguese men had dodged or resisted conscripted military service against the rebellious colonists.[49]

Former Mozambican minister of education and first lady Graca Machel likened the end of the war for independence to a circle. "We come back to the beginning. After those pauses of having to organize armed struggle, having people killed, having infrastructures destroyed, after this we have to come back to the beginning and start with negotiations. What we could have done if [the Portuguese] had accepted it in the first place!"[50]

Tragically, the beginning of independence marked another phase of violent warfare for the people of Mozambique, as South Africa and Rhodesia quickly set up their own army to destroy the gains made by the revolutionary process and to cut Mozambican support to neighboring liberation movements.[51] Initially the war was presented as national defense against the "armed bandits" of counterrevolution, later acknowledged as the political-military force known as the Mozambican National Resistance (RENAMO). Most of the civil war was fought, unsuccessfully, through use of traditional military strategies. FRELIMO could not, in simple military terms, counter the covert attacks supplied and aided by South African and US mercenaries that were aimed at their destabilization. However, FRELIMO also tried to establish mass-based educational campaigns. When grassroots resistance to the war began in 1990, it came not from FRELIMO structures, but from an unarmed community defense movement known as the Naparama (irresistible force). Led by a self-proclaimed spiritual healer named Manuel Antonio, it successfully established several neutral zones before the civil war ended, often scaring the antigovernment forces into laying down their arms without resorting to violence themselves.[52] The peace ultimately negotiated between FRELIMO and RENAMO relied heavily on nonmilitary negotiations and conflict resolution techniques.[53]

Much postwar research on Mozambique has focused on nonviolent mediation techniques used in attempting to end the civil conflict.[54] While some observers suggest that the intensity of the conflict derived from the armed nature of the war for independence, few recognize the extent of civil resistance or the psychosocial effects of the unarmed struggle in the decades leading to independence—before and during the development of FRELIMO.[55]

Postindependence Thoughts on the Mozambican Resistance

Military accounts indicate that by 1967, just four years after the start of armed struggle, one-fifth of Mozambique's territory was under FRELIMO control.[56] Behind these military gains, however, lay the building of civil resistance. Taking issue with the accounts of Basil Davidson,[57] Joseph Hanlon,[58] and John Saul,[59] Aquino de Braganca and Jacques Depelchin stress the role of "political and ideological solidity."[60] As the war raged on, FRELIMO's military challenges to Portugal's more numerous and better-equipped military became more and more successful. Nevertheless, Machel himself indicated in the late 1970s that the nonmilitary political and socioeconomic achievements were the key; they furnished the basis for military success.[61]

Conclusion

Judge Albie Sachs—an apartheid political prisoner exiled in Mozambique where he lost his arm and the sight of one eye in an assassination attempt, and later architect of the postapartheid South Africa constitution—is in a good position to review the Mozambique independence struggle. He says,

> The military and non-military resistance used in Mozambique to win independence cannot be separated from one another. The military dimension permitted a complete rupture with colonial hegemony, a questioning of everything and the envisaging of a totally different society. The non-military dimension ensured that having physical force at one's command was never an end in itself; that the "enemy" was a system of injustice, not a race of people; that it was never enough to fight for justice but that justice had to exist inside ourselves; that captured Portuguese soldiers should be treated with compassion rather than rancor; and that the liberation war should be transformed into political dialogue to achieve independence as soon as conditions for principled agreements could be negotiated between equals.[62]

By giving credence to the many strengths derived from the civil resistance campaigns mounted for Mozambique's independence, Sachs—and the selected accounts of his Mozambican colleagues from Mondlane to Machel, Chissano, and beyond—helps dispel the myths of liberation through militarism. Certainly this most popular of armed national liberation movements made gains through military means, but it is equally clear that nonmilitary tactics and the building for a revolutionary and nonviolent civil society played a defining and definitive role in the overall freedom process. FRELIMO's early focus on a people's democracy emboldened by strong civic institutions was directly influenced by the preceding decades of grass-roots strikes, women's federations, alternative economic cooperatives, and reformist educational campaigns.

During the decades of 1940s through 1960s, the growing civic activism and direct nonviolent resistance—waged en masse by various societal groups—both influenced and consolidated collective understandings of common identity (and shared destiny as one nation) among the majority of Mozambicans. Suddenly, intellectuals, students, peasants, and laborers, both women and men, found unity and common purpose through their non-violent civic engagements and struggle. This new and intensified feature of Mozambican life and national identity gave further impetus for collective resistance during the crucial decade of the 1970s.

Taken alongside decades of struggle using mass, nonviolent resistance and a widespread understanding of the great and horrible costs of military action during the civil war, this collective consciousness can now be seen in contemporary adherence to popular democratic electoral participation, continued high levels of involvement in community-based grassroots organizations, and an openness to an internationalism that defies traditional North-South or East-West dynamics. This resistance and reconciliation consciousness is clear in the words and deeds of national leaders and local civilians alike, as modern Mozambique helps model peaceful postwar relations throughout Africa. It is noteworthy for a country so long wracked with anticolonial and civil war that, in 2009, Maputo's social center Rua D'arte energetically hosted the carnival for the World March for Peace and Nonviolence.[63]

Academics and activists alike will do well to use the example of Mozambique, so apparently simple a story of armed victory, to understand the complexities involved in truly radical transformations. Through strikes and songs, newspapers and petitions, and organizations that grew in numbers beyond the Portuguese abilities to contain them and beyond any armed structure initiated by FRELIMO, the people of Mozambique have consistently shown the power of civil society. Mozambique's story, indeed, must be rewritten to emphasize the strategic possibilities afforded by unarmed mass resistance.

Notes

1. Margaret Dickinson, ed., *When Bullets Begin to Flower* (Nairobi: East African Publishing House, 1972), 33.

2. John S. Saul, *The State and Revolution in Eastern Africa* (New York: Monthly Review Press, 1979), 11. Mozambican vice-president and militant Marxist Marcelino Dos Santos later characterized the work beyond national liberation as one of building revolutionary nationalism. From his perspective, setting up communal structures and a mass, communal consciousness would make reversal of the gains from armed struggles profoundly difficult because the masses would rise up against these types of capitalist, antidemocratic notions (21).

3. Samora Machel, "The People's Republic of Mozambique: The Struggle Continues," *Review of African Political Economy*, no. 4 (1975): 19–20.

4. See, for example, Chris Searle, *We're Building a New School: Diary of a Teacher in Mozambique* (London: Zed Press, 1981), 49.

5. William Minter, *Portuguese Africa and the West* (New York: Monthly Review Press, 1972), 55.

6. Eduardo Mondlane, *The Struggle for Mozambique* (Middlesex: Penguin Books, 1969), 107.

7. Ibid., 103–104.

8. Zachery Kingdon, *A Host of Devils: The History and Context of the Making of Makonde Spirit* (London: Routledge, 2002), 24.

9. Mondlane, *The Struggle for Mozambique,* 106.

10. Ibid., 108.

11. Ibid., 114.

12. See Mondlane, *The Struggle for Mozambique*; as well as Teresa Cruz e Silva, "Identity and Political Consciousness in Southern Mozambique, 1930–1974," *Journal of Southern African Studies* 24, no. 1 (1998): 225.

13. Beata Mtyingizana, "Mozambique, Worker Protests," in *The International Encyclopedia of Revolution and Protest,* ed. Immanuel Ness (Oxford: Blackwell, 2009), 249.

14. Mondlane, *The Struggle for Mozambique,* 116.

15. Carmeliza Rosario, Inge Tvedten, and Margarida Paulo, *"Mucupuki": Social Relations of Rural-Urban Poverty in Central Mozambique* (Bergen: CMI Reports; Chr. Michelsen Institute, 2008), 17. See also Malyn Newitt, *A History of Mozambique* (Bloomington: Indiana University Press, 1995).

16. Allan Isaacman and Barbara Isaacman, *Mozambique: From Colonialism to Revolution 1900–1982* (Boulder: Westview Press, 1983), 66.

17. Julius K. Nyerere, *Ujamaa: Essays on Socialism* (Nairobi: Oxford University Press, 1968), 10.

18. Joseph Hanlon, *Mozambique: The Revolution Under Fire* (London: Zed Books, 1984), 23–24.

19. Hans Abrahamson and Andres Nilsson, *Mozambique—The Troubled Transition: From Socialist Construction to Free-Market Capitalism* (London: Zed Books, 1995), 22.

20. Basil Davidson, "The Prospects for the Southern Half of Africa," *Le Monde Diplomatique,* no. 176, November 1968. From an interview with Alberto Joaquim Chipande recorded by Davidson at the Second Congress of FRELIMO, Niasa Province, Mozambique, July 1968.

21. David Robinson, "Socialism in Mozambique? The 'Mozambican Revolution' in Critical Perspective," *LIMINA: A Journal of Historical and Cultural Studies,* no. 9 (2003): 135–137.

22. Mondlane, *The Struggle for Mozambique,* 117.

23. Ibid., 117–118.

24. Bill Sutherland, pan-Africanist activist, interviewed by Matt Meyer, Brooklyn, New York, November 15, 1993; excerpts of which appear in Sutherland and Meyer, *Guns and Gandhi in Africa: Pan African Insights on Nonviolence, Armed Struggle and Liberation in Africa* (Trenton, NJ: Africa World Press, 2000), 150–152.

25. Mondlane, *The Struggle for Mozambique,* 121–122.

26. George Houser and Herb Shore, *Mozambique: Dream the Size of Freedom* (New York: Africa Fund, 1975), 29–30.

27. Julius K. Nyerere, *Freedom and Socialism* (Nairobi: Oxford University Press, 1969), 102.

28. Houser and Shore, *Mozambique,* 30.

29. Sutherland and Meyer, *Guns and Gandhi,* 123. This was taken from an interview with Mocumbi, Mozambican minister of foreign affairs, by the authors, Maputo, July 24, 1992.

30. See, for example, from the government press: Edicao do Departamento de Trabalho Ideologico, *Historia da FRELIMO* (Maputo: FRELIMO, 1983), 7–9.

31. Herbert Shore, "Remembering Eduardo: Reflections on the Life and Legacy of Eduardo Mondlane," *Africa Today* 39, nos. 1–2 (1992): 41.

32. Ibid.," 41–42. Shore notes that Guevara himself visited Tanzania in late 1965, debating these points with Mondlane and others. Though this has scarcely been documented, Shore cites his own (and *Africa Today* guest editor Prexy Nesbitt's) conversations about these issues with Mondlane himself.

33. Simon Baynham, *Military Power and Politics in Black Africa* (London: Routledge, 1986), 130.

34. Mondlane, *The Struggle for Mozambique,* 123.

35. Ibid., 124.

36. Shore, "Remembering Eduardo," 42–44. For an alternate view that nonetheless confirms some of the same conclusions, see Uria T. Simango, "Gloomy Situation in Mozambique," November 3, 1969, Mocambique Para Todos, www.macua.blogs.com/mocambique_para_todos, accessed March 21, 2012. For some, the Reverend Uria Timoteo Simango, a FRELIMO founder, simply represented a pacifist-leaning democratic socialist while for others he was a traitor worthy of execution. See Walter Opello, "Pluralism and Elite Conflict in an Independence Movement: FRELIMO in the 1960s," *Journal of Southern African Studies* 2, no. 1 (1975): 66–82. Shore is of the point of view that Mondlane was also a democratic socialist.

37. Sutherland and Meyer, *Guns and Gandhi,* 115–116.

38. Ibid., 116–117.

39. Bill Sutherland, pan-African activist, interviewed by Prexy Nesbitt and Mimi Edwards, Brooklyn, New York, July 19, 2003, used as an unpublished transcript background paper by William Minter, Gail Hovey, and Charles Cobb Jr., *No Easy Victories: African Liberation and American Activists Over Half a Century, 1950–2000* (Trenton: Africa World Press, 2007); and for the American Friends Service Committee video, *Bill Sutherland: Nonviolent Warrior for Peace* (Philadephia: AFSC, 2005). Also Chude Mondlane, daughter of Eduardo Mondlane, interviewed by the authors, Brooklyn, New York, December 27, 2009.

40. Houser and Shore, *Mozambique,* 39.

41. These points are poignantly and concretely illustrated in Stephanie Urdang, *And Still They Dance: Women, War, and the Struggle for Change in Mozambique* (New York: Monthly Review Press, 1989), 111–154, 244.

42. Gisela G. Geisler, *Women and the Remaking of Politics in Southern Africa: Negotiating Autonomy, Incorporation, and Representation* (Uppsala: Nordiska Afrikainstitutet, 2004), 115.

43. Samora Machel, *Establishing People's Power to Serve the Masses* (Dar es Salaam: Tanzania Publishing House, 1977), 36.

44. Searle, *We're Building a New School,* 53.

45. Houser and Shore, *Mozambique,* 40–41. By the end of the war for independence, almost 2,000 towers needed to be replaced due to these acts of sabotage and nearly 3,000 needed to be refurbished.

46. Samora Machel, president of Mozambique, interviewed by George Houser, Dar es Salaam, June 17, 1970, as reprinted in Houser and Shore, *Mozambique,* 40.

47. See, for example, Mozambique Briefing, *The Weapon of Culture* (Maputo: Information Department, Frelimo Party Central Committee, 1987), 1–3. Also produced were briefings on the problem of children of war and President Chissano's proposed policies for a lasting peace (see supra note 33).

48. Iain Christie, *Machel of Mozambique* (Harare: Zimbabwe Publishing House, 1988), 146.

49. Richard W. Leonard, "FRELIMO's Victories in Mozambique," *Issues: A Journal of Opinion, African Studies Association* 4, no. 2 (1974): 38–46.

50. Sutherland and Meyer, *Guns and Gandhi,* 120. This was taken from an interview with Graca Machel, widow of Samora Machel and former Mozambican minister of education, by the authors, Maputo, July 25, 1992.

51. William Finnegan called this dynamic the "harrowing" of Mozambique in *A Complicated War* (Berkeley: University of California Press, 1993), 139. Also discussed in Barby Ulmer and Vic Ulmer, codirectors of Our Developing World educational agency, interviewed by Matt Meyer, February 27, 2010.

52. K. B. Wilson, "Cult of Violence and Counter-Violence in Mozambique," *Journal of Southern African Studies* 18, no. 3 (1992): 527–582. See also the work and website of NGO Conciliation Resources, www.c-r.org/our-work/accord/mozambique /key-actors.php.

53. Cameron Hume, *Ending Mozambique's War: The Role of Mediation and Good Offices* (Washington, DC: United States Institute of Peace, 1984). See also the work of Conciliation Resources and Chronology of the Mozambican War, www.c-r .org/ourwork/accord/mozambique/chronology.php.

54. See, for example, Hume, *Ending Mozambique's War*.

55. Lisa Bornstein, "Planning and Peacebuilding in Post-War Mozambique: From Narratives to Practices of Development," *Journal of Peacebuilding and Development* 4, no. 1 (2008): 38–51.

56. Brendan F. Jundanian, *The Mozambique Liberation Front,* vol. 110 (Geneva: Institut universitaire de hautes etudes internationals, 1970), 76–80.

57. Basil Davidson, *The People's Cause* (London: Longman, 1981), 127–128.

58. Hanlon, *Mozambique,* 292.

59. John Saul, ed., *A Difficult Road: The Transition to Socialism in Mozambique* (New York: Monthly Review Press, 1985), 420.

60. Aquino de Braganca and Jacques Depelchin, "From the Idealization of Frelimo to the Understanding of the Recent History of Mozambique," *African Journal of Political Economy* 1 (1986): 169. De Braganca was killed later in 1986, in the plane carrying Samora Machel and thirty-two other Mozambican officials.

61. Saul, *The State and Revolution,* 45.

62. Albie Sachs, South African Constitutional Court Justice and former ANC leader based in Maputo, Mozambique, personal communication with the authors, February 24, 2010.

63. Djamila Andrade, *Mozambique: Carnival of the World March in Maputo* (Maputo: World March for Peace and Nonviolence, 2009), www.nenasili.cz/en /3254_mozambiquecarnival-of-the-world-march-in-maputo.

Part 2

Nonviolent Resistance
in North Africa and
the Middle East

6

Algeria:
Nonviolent Resistance Against
French Colonialism, 1830s–1950s

Malika Rahal

In recent years, two important books have focused on the violence of the French conquest and colonization of Algeria that began in 1830. Olivier Le Cour Grandmaison's *Coloniser, Exterminer*[1] emphasizes the role that colonies such as Algeria played in the development of military forms of violence later imported to Europe while Benjamin C. Brower[2] presents a fine description of the violent means used by the French Army to control the Algerian desert after the conquest. In doing so, both authors go beyond the well-known episodes of Algerian armed resistance—notably the armed resistance of Amir Abd-al-Qadir in the 1830s and 1840s, and the war for independence in 1954–1962—to reemphasize the duration and intensity of violence in the resistance against French colonial occupation of Algeria. However, such discourse leaves little, if any, narrative space for uncovering the existence and discussing the role of other, nonviolent, forms of struggle developed by Algerians against the French colonial occupation.

In Algeria after independence, figures such as Amir Abd-al-Qadir, Bachagha El-Moqrani (leader of the 1871 uprising), and Shaikh Bouamama (a leader of the 1881–1908 insurrection) were celebrated in *lieux de mémoire*: streets and squares were named after them and statues were erected.[3] The most ubiquitous faces of the nationalist struggle in Algeria have undoubtedly been *shuhada* (martyrs) who gave their lives in the war for independence. Their constant commemoration occupies a large portion of public space and they are regularly recalled in official speeches and ceremonies. August 20 was chosen as Martyr Day, marking the violent uprising in the Constantine region in 1955. It was one of the main roles of the former mujahidin (veterans) ministry to publish and broadcast narratives of individual combatants. Booklets, newspaper articles, and popular films glorified armed struggle and sacralized the martyrs' sacrifice. Ceramic tiles representing figures of martyrs were used to decorate the city of Algiers; Algeria is in fact known as *blad milyun shahid* (the million-martyr country).[4] In 1988, a national monument was constructed in commemoration of their sacrifice: the Maqam Shahid, visible from all sides of the bay, has three statues at its foot. Two represent a National Liberation Army (ALN) soldier bearing weapons while the other is an armed peasant—all of them symbols of a nation united in arms. Last, in their preambles, the Algerian Constitutions of 1963, 1976, and 1987 emphasized the leading role of the National Liberation Front (FLN) and the ALN in winning independence, presented violent resistance as the ultimate liberation tool, and glorified the memory of *shuhada* and the dignity of mujahidin.

When the FLN came to power after the war for independence, its reinterpretation of past events produced an official history of the liberation struggle that was univocal and linear.[5] It was a linear narrative because it claimed that nationalism had been conveyed through a single ideological thread—a political genealogy that linked FLN with the Étoile Nord-Africaine created in 1926 among the Algerian workers in Paris, the Parti du Peuple Algérien (PPA) established in 1937, and the Mouvement pour le Triomphe des Libertés Démocratiques (MTLD) set up in 1946. The FLN was an ultimate and quintessential avatar of all these political parties. Consequently, all other political organizations were considered illegitimate and their contributions to a national struggle denied. It was also a univocal narrative because it defined *Algerianness* as Arabic in language and Muslim in religion, thus symbolically—and to some extent practically—excluding other languages (French or Berber) and religions (Christian or Jewish). Furthermore, the collective subsumed the individual to fit FLN populist ideology: as there had been but "one hero, the people," individual glorification was accepted only for martyrs.[6] As a result, until recent years, personal accounts in the form of autobiographies, biographies, and memoirs were a genre absent from modern Algerian history.

The constraints set by official history not only influenced public commemorations and vernacular narratives, but also affected the writing of academic history in Algeria and in France where much of the Algerian history was being written. Benjamin Stora's 1986 biography of Messali Hadj, leader of the Mouvement National Algerian (MNA), rival organization to the FLN, was undoubtedly a subversive endeavor both in form and topic, bringing to the foreground a figure rejected from official history. It showed how, at every turn, Messali was faced with decisions concerning tactical choices that were more complex and nuanced than a simplistic divide between legal action versus armed struggle.[7] After the censorship loosened in the 1990s, a few autobiographical narratives were published.[8] These sources are fundamental for describing and accounting for certain forms of collective resistance, in particular, more informal types of defiance. For example, they reveal ties between the workings of cultural associations, trade unions, and political parties. Childhood stories emphasize the importance of the scouting movement as a means of resistance. Autobiographies uncover how people confronted colonization on a more intimate, individual, and family level rather than the more organized level of political parties.

Classically in postcolonial states, victorious armed movements created national narratives that often helped them stay in power and shape the nation. In Algeria, after 1962, official history presented revolutionary violent methods and guerrilla warfare as the only possible means by which independence could have been achieved. This narrative was institutionalized in Algerian academia during the 1970s while state monopoly over book publication, including history textbooks, left no outlet for competing narratives.

As a result, the use of nonviolent forms of resistance, such as formation and work of cultural associations or political nonviolent organizing (in particular, during the "decade of political parties" after World War II),[9] appeared as nothing more than "dilatoriness and pointless discussion" in the words of the historian and former activist Mohammed Harbi.[10] And they have been accepted as such even by those who actively participated in and led them. Such attitudes resulted in a loss of collective memory of the nonviolent forms of action while, in reality, cultural associations and unions as well as Sufi and family networks—largely tacitly and nonviolently—had resisted and later openly challenged colonization.

The French Colonial Occupation of Algeria

The French colonial project in Algeria involved a complex subjugation strategy and its severity and intensity conditioned how the indigenous people could resist it. The territorial conquest in 1830 was followed by military occupation that lasted until 1871. As a consequence of the imposition of a new colonial regime after the defeat of Abd-al-Qadir, the power of the warrior aristocratic class—the *jawad*—was gradually reduced and the tribal system that had organized society in Algeria disintegrated. Just as significant as the defeat of military insurrections of Mohamed El-Moqrani (1871–1872) and Shaikh Bouamama (1881–1908) was the deculturalization of this Bedouin society.[11] The cultural consequences were drastic. In the first twenty years of the occupation, the number of indigenous schools was cut by half.[12] In 1914, only one indigenous child in twenty had access to French education.[13] By the end of the colonial period, French universities were graduating only a few dozen students from the colonized population annually, most of whom where illiterate in Arabic. Classical Arabic language was in fact one of the first victims of colonization: under colonial rule, there was no equivalent to the universities of the Qarawiyyin in Fes (Morocco) or the Zaytuna in Tunis. The establishment of schools with Arabic as a language of instruction was subject to various types of bureaucratic hurdles and permissions that, de facto, made it impossible.

Algeria was also a settler colony to which many French and other Europeans migrated. In 1860, 200,000 Europeans lived in Algeria and owned 340,000 hectares of land (which rose to more than 1.2 million hectares by 1881).[14] Forms of dispossession ranged from direct land purchase (of dubious legality) to expropriation and land confiscation as a form of collective punishment. Uprooting large portions of the population had long-term consequences for pastoral and farming families who were driven into poverty and forced to migrate.[15] In a country where over 90 percent of the population had been rural, the disruption was considerable. This traumatic and forceful transformation branded the memory of the conquest for the decades to come.

Last, after 1848, Algeria was legally no longer a colony but an extension of the French Republic, yet a region of France where the local population was at first excluded from French citizenship and never gained full citizenship rights. Until 1945, the indigenous population elected no representatives and the *code de l'indigénat* (indigenous law) established in 1874 created a number of offenses applicable solely to Algerians, limiting their constitutional freedoms.[16]

However, even at the peak of French colonial domination, the colonized society never ceased to resist. Between the nineteenth-century episodic outbursts of armed resistance and the armed revolution that began in 1954, nonviolent forms of enduring and resisting conquest and colonization were developed. During the long era of colonization, they evolved from an organic reaction for protecting the collective fabric of Algerian indigenous society to the demand for full citizenship and sovereignty of the people.

Resistance Against Conquest of the Land and Imposition of a New Authority

Mass Emigration as a Form of Collective Resistance

One of the forms of nonviolent resistance that most troubled the French authorities in the first years of the conquest was Algerians' emigration. Early emigrations were forced by the invasion and subsequent pacification as well as by the repression that followed every uprising. However, as early as 1830, emigration also appears to have been a form of resistance to the imposition of non-Muslim authority, according to the Muslim practice of *hijra*. According to demographer Kamel Kateb,[17] Algerians left the country mainly for Morocco, Tunisia, Syria, Palestine, or Egypt and, to a lesser extent, for other Muslim countries.

The French found these waves of emigrations troublesome and eventually took measures against them. Although emigration benefited European settlers by freeing land, it also posed problems: mass exodus had a clear political meaning that embarrassed the authorities. Further costs for the French were that the departure of tribes contributed to the breakdown of public order in Algeria and the increase of banditry while the emerging French economy in Algeria was hindered by the loss of the labor force.

Generally, these migrations were visible actions pursued by large groups of families from the same city or region, convinced of the necessity to leave in reaction to the new colonial conditions. These people fled the rule of a non-Muslim government, confiscation of their lands, and later military conscription. Emigration, they hoped, would preserve their cultural and social identities endangered by the French conquest. While the early emigration waves are impossible to measure, the later ones show the breadth of the phenomenon. The last mass emigration was the departure for Syria of 508 families of the city of Tlemcen in 1910–1911 in reaction to the threat of conscription to the French Army.

The scale of the emigration movement reveals the profoundness of social disruption in and after 1830. The year "1830 was an end of the world," notes James McDougall, referring to the domestic consequences of the conquest.[18] Seeing mass emigration as defiance of the colonial power, the French authorities carried out surveys to analyze emigration fluxes and tried to block them by refusing the necessary permissions. That, however, did not stop many families from leaving the country illegally. The authorities also threatened tribes with confiscation of their lands, thus foreclosing the possibility of their return or of benefiting from what wealth they possessed.[19] The issue was also diplomatically sensitive since it created tensions with the countries of destination. In some cases, the migrant families refused registration at the French consulate and rapidly blended with the local population. In other cases, however, local authorities sought French assistance in managing the large numbers of newly arrived migrants. Furthermore, as Kamel Kateb[20] points out, this nonviolent action threatened French-imposed security in Algeria as hostile Algerian populations began concentrating on the Moroccan and Tunisian borders at a time when these countries were not yet French protectorates.

Rejection and Boycotts

In the first decades of colonization, notably under the rule of Napoleon III and with the "civilizing mission" gaining popularity among many officers

of the Bureaux arabes[21] (colonial offices responsible for collecting and analyzing information on the colonized population and for designing a policy
toward the indigenous population), the mission of "enlightening" and reedu-
cating the indigenous population became central to several projects. Daniel
Rivet describes the efforts to settle down nomadic populations, that is, to
create new villages designed by French architects on a Western model.[22] Despite equipping them with *hammams* (bath houses) and mosques, the failure
of these settlements was resounding; for example, women rejected these new
places and refused to stay in them. The authorities also faced local refusal to
adopt medical services provided by the army. While infirmaries were installed among certain tribes, it appears that the people did not subscribe to
the preventive forms of medicine that were offered, thus limiting their visits
to times of crisis and the need for curative medicine.

Western education also encountered quiet noncooperation. The rare
Franco-Arab schools created among tribes met with no success. One Arab
Bureau head explained that "the indigenous people consider that sending
their children to school is the most burdensome duty that we impose upon
them."[23] The imperial college in Algiers stagnated while two schools,
opened for indigenous women in Algiers and Bône, failed entirely for lack
of pupils. More broadly, Yvonne Turin identifies what she calls a period of
refus scolaire (boycott of French schools) by notable Algerian families,
their intended target, that lasted at least until the 1880s.[24] These families
considered it unacceptable to entrust their children's education to non-
Muslim and non-Arabic-speaking schools. In other words, the colonialists'
attempts to seize and transform the minds and bodies of the colonized population were faced with a persistent form of mute resistance that the French
found extremely difficult to overcome. For those who remained in the country, this refusal seemed to be the way to oppose, resist, and endure in the
face of foreign domination brought by military force and economic imperialism. The French painter and writer Eugène Fromentin commented, "Unable to exterminate us, they [the local population] suffer our presence; unable to flee, they avoid us. Their principle, their motto, their method is to
remain quiet, to disappear as much as possible and to be forgotten. They demand little: they demand integrity and peace in their last refuge."[25]

Withdrawal

For those who remained under colonial rule, another means of resistance
was to define and protect a private space against the disruptions and interference of the colonial system around them. Consequently, the areas of resistance became family, home, and spiritual and religious life. These intimate spheres were places of refuge and perseverance of cultural practices
and identities from before the conquest. Anthropologist Jacques Berque

considers religion to have become a "bastion of withdrawal" for the colonized population of Algeria to preserve their identity.[26] For those who refused to flee to a foreign land, it provided the means for an internal *hijra*—a personal and deeply emotional and psychological migration and withdrawal to the "inner domain"—as a form of resistance.[27]

In this process, seemingly nonpolitical and personal practices underwent transformations that politicized them. In particular, women's practices—their behavior, clothing, and role in the family—acquired a political importance as they became symbols of cultural resistance to European domination and a reflection of a growing national identity. The fathers, husbands, and brothers now viewed Algerian women as the repository of cultural identity, which needed special protection since it preserved family and societal values in the face of gradual disintegration of local culture and encroaching "Frenchification." Because European men were particularly interested in "oriental" women—notably to paint them, later to photograph them—Algerian women were ever more under the special protection of men and more confined to their homes, reinforcing tacit resistance against foreign cultural expansion but at the same time increasing the gender gap and exacerbating masculinity.[28] In the same fashion, the veil (at that time in the form of the *haïk,* a long veil covering the whole body) acquired a new importance as a means to protect women—and with them the core of collective identity—from the gaze of Europeans. The entire body became a means of resisting foreign disruption and intrusion.

Resistance by Sufi Brotherhoods

In this context, Sufi brotherhoods came to play an important role in resisting French presence in Algeria. In several cases, they led or supported armed insurrections against the French and provided refuge to leaders of armed insurrections after their defeat. However, according to Julia Clancy-Smith, there were also episodes during which colonial tension involving Sufi brotherhoods peaked without transforming into violent resistance.[29]

At the turn of the nineteenth century, the colonized population was mobilized to protect a Sufi center, the *Rahmaniyya zawiya,* at the oasis al-Hamil near Bu Sa'ada, south of Algiers, against French attempts to control it. The French had leveled various earlier Sufi centers, but this complex, built in 1863, grew to be the most popular in Algeria, boasting a prestigious school and library surrounded by farms. Led by Shaikh Sidi Muhammad of the *Rahmaniyya* Sufi order, it attracted those who wanted to benefit from his saintly *baraka* (blessing), either by following the rich curriculum provided by the school or even by choosing to be buried on the *zawiya* grounds. People thus expressed their desire to rest in a land insulated from foreign interference. French authorities distrusted this powerful influence outside their control. They also coveted the wealth of the *zawiya*: its cash and properties of land and flocks. Sidi Muhammad had avoided confronting the French directly but resisted complying with colonial rule by insisting on his religious duty to provide refuge to fellow Muslims, including defeated military rebels and other fugitives from the French. Between Sidi Muhammad and the French, there was "an unstated, yet mutually binding, pact, whose implicit terms granted political order in return for religious autonomy."[30] However, in 1897 the French saw their opportunity to take control of the *zawiya* when Sidi Muhammad died with his succession unclear.

In the conflict over succession, the French supported the claims of Sidi Muhammad's nephew against those of his daughter, Lalla Zaynab. As a woman, they argued, she would be weak, incapable of administrating the *zawiya* effectively, and become a pliable tool in the hand of the anti-French elements. Lalla Zaynab, however, for all of her apparent frailty, successfully resisted the French until her death (in 1904). First, she protected the *zawiya* against her rival by denying him access. She later demanded French protection, using the inconsistencies in the French policies and calculating that they would not dare to evict her by force, as was indeed the case. The French found her an embarrassing character to deal with: her choices of celibacy and virginity increased her spiritual influence and social power. As Clancy-Smith points out, the story reveals "the absence of colonial mechanism for containing small-scale, nonviolent rebellions, particularly led by Muslim women,"[31] and emphasizes that this was also true in Tunisia, particularly where *zawiyas* were headed by women.

Resistance Against Exclusionary State Policies

The Jeunes Algériens (Young Algerians) Movement

The shift from religious movements or opposition limited to the private sphere to a more open and public involvement in various cultural associations and political organizations coincided with the emergence of the Jeunes Algériens movement early in the twentieth century. Its leaders and members were a small elite of Francophones, with a core of perhaps 1,000 members.[32] They were a product of French schooling who demanded that the republican principles taught at school—embodied in full French citizenship rights—be applied to the colonized population of Algeria. Their claims to citizenship, however, were always met with policies that set limitations on full citizenship. One condition for acquiring full citizenship rights was unacceptable to many who otherwise would have qualified: the requirement to relinquish Muslim legal status and thus become subject to the French civil code for personal matters such as marriage or inheritance.

This condition many Algerians considered equivalent to apostasy, a further blow to what was left of their collective identity.

In their struggle for citizenship rights, the Jeunes Algériens developed new institutions and practices: setting up and printing periodicals and newspapers, opening cultural and fraternal clubs, organizing political rallies, and carrying out local electoral campaigns that mobilized the elite.[33] More broadly, associations (particularly cultural associations) became the main tool to involve the population in forming and consolidating their collective practices separate from the French. Literature, music, geography, and sports associations multiplied in the 1920s.[34] Jeunes Algériens saw such activities as being directly linked to the vision of an aware citizen who was educated and publicly involved in leading civic and political initiatives. This bourgeois vision of the citizen was heavily influenced by the French republican ideal. Jeunes Algériens newspapers published ideas for political reforms that were also promoted in manifestos, petitions, and delegations sent to France. They demanded a representative parliament, a fairer tax system, and equal and competitive access to the positions in administration. However, the French administration in Algeria and French Algerian newspapers reviled them constantly for their "anti-French attitudes."[35] Although not successful in gaining full citizenship rights, the movement's association activities laid important foundations for the emergence of other political organizations, including Fédération des élus indigènes (Federation of Elected Indigenous Representatives) that in turn helped politicize some parts of the Algerian population and acted as one of the roots of Algerian nationalism.

Islamic Reformism and the Culture of Nationalism

In the 1930s, another movement emerged that shared the concerns of Jeunes Algériens for cultural development—the ulama movement headed by Shaikh Abdelhamid Ben Badis. Within two decades, this movement became a nationwide network of schools and associations promoting a reformed version of Islam and knowledge of the Arabic language.[36] In doing so, it took from and continued the tradition of the movements born in Egypt of the Nahda (Arab renaissance) and Islah (Islamic reform). The logic was no longer that of finding shelter in collective identity, but of reinvigorating it by going back to its supposed roots. This meant a salafi form of Islam (following the model of the forefathers, Prophet Muhammad and his companions) that was cleansed of Sufi influences (notably the cult of saints in the *zawiyas*) considered to be deviations from the purportedly original Islam, and the propagation and diffusion of Arabic (which the colonial forces had fought against) through a modernized pedagogy.

Despite refusing to enter the institutionalized political scene (for instance, as a political party), the ulama motto shows clear political implications:

"Islam Is My Religion, Algeria My Fatherland, and Arabic My Language." The movement developed what James McDougall calls a culture of nationalism that relied on a historical discourse of what it meant to be Algerian.[37] In promoting nationalist thought, the ulama schools valued greatly teachings about history of the Arab conquest in North Africa. Ulama also encouraged importation from Egypt of history books promoting Arabo-Muslim history and values. This national discourse was sustained by new practices that helped a newly invented Algerianness become embodied in music, theater performances, and religious celebrations. For example, cultural circles organized dramatizations where school children played great figures of the Muslim or North African past. Ulama believed that weakened spirituality allowed for foreign domination and continued colonization. Consequently, they aimed to cleanse religious practices of those traditional aspects viewed as unorthodox or magical and, therefore, as spiritually weakening the Algerian population in its struggle against foreign domination.

Politicization of Cultural Forms of Resistance

The decade after World War II was characterized by the integration of previously highlighted nonviolent collective practices (e.g., cultural organizing, meetings, and festivities) and their further development within the frameworks of new political parties.[38]

Political opening, although still limited as Algerians had fewer rights than European colonials, allowed the colonized population to participate in the legislative elections and encouraged political forces to organize into mass parties. This resulted in the establishment in 1946 of the Union Démocratique du Manifeste Algérien (UDMA) led by Ferhat Abbas and the MTLD led by Messali Hadj. They joined the Algerian Communist Party (PCA) in representing the colonized population.

The political parties did not limit themselves to conventional work of fighting elections and sending representatives to parliament. They became promoters of a broader form of cultural resistance not limited to the personal domain as in earlier times. This cultural resistance became genuinely collective and creative under the auspices of the parties that took up the struggle for the creation of a collective self and for the formation of an Algerian people (although they had different definitions of what this people should be). Political parties thus became entrepreneurs of national culture. For instance, while the UDMA and PCA considered that the Europeans living in Algeria would naturally be part of the independent country, the PPA and MTLD considered that Algerianness meant being Arab and Muslim. Algerian theater or musical troupes found their ways into political rallies, thus popularizing nationalist discourse. Various professional groups were often invited to political meetings to perform plays while children's associations (notably scouts or students of the ulama schools) closely linked to one or the other party were asked to play sketches with an explicitly nationalist, religious, or moral message. The police clearly understood the impact that such events could have and surveyed them closely, noting names of actors, themes, and vocabulary used. A surveillance report written by the Oran police in September 1951 described one political meeting:

> A four-act play, entitled "Union" was interpreted in Arabic by the students of the Falah school. The play showed four brothers, feuding with each other, whose father, Atlas, was arrested and put in jail by an ambitious sultan. Facing this situation, the children reconcile with each other, and manage to free their father. The allusion to the present is direct: the four children are the UDMA, the MTLD, the PCA and the Ulama association: they unite to fight off imperialism.[39]

Political parties—especially the UDMA, closely linked to ulama—gradually helped set the foundations for a new nationalist history.[40] The party newspapers published articles that contributed to the writing of a nationalist history. They commemorated nationalist figures such as Amir Abd-al-Qadir or Abdelhamid Ben Badis, historic dates (the Manifesto of the Algerian People in 1943), and promoted Arab or Islamic history. Party rallies were ritually constructed around various carefully choreographed and sequenced installments, including commemorations of past events (notably the bloody repression of May 1945) and celebrations of nationalist figures. Any party rally included a short historical lecture during which speakers rejected the notion that Algeria had been a wasteland before the arrival of the French. The rallies debunked colonial scholarship (according to which, to give but one example, Berber and Arab populations differed, with the former being closer to Christianity and European culture than the latter) and glorified Arab history by proving its value in the face of colonial domination. Party-related activities also promoted national rites, customs, and symbols. Several versions of the Algerian flag were popularized and patriotic national songs taught in the ulama schools or in the scout troups were sung during rallies. The party also held conferences pertaining to topics such as morality, religion, hygiene, and disease prevention during which the line between the political and the cultural, social, and religious was ultimately blurred. All of these nonviolent collective actions were considered necessary for shaping nationally conscious citizens by improving their education and knowledge of Algerian history and culture, their mores, and their physical well-being.

Intensity of police surveillance and its repression led all parties—including those who opposed an armed insurrection—to find means of self-protection. Many former militants tell stories of having held meetings in the woods, away from the village, to avoid the police. Archives also reveal how parties employed their younger members to ensure security of a meeting by preventing possible police informers from entering: blocking the door, checking membership cards, and warning party members of police presence to allow them to disperse. In the frequent cases where the newspapers were seized by censorship, alternative means of distribution were organized. The MTLD youth organized several campaigns during which the inscription "Algérie libre" (free Algeria) was written on the walls of the cities, leaflets were handed out rapidly and discreetly, and flash rallies were organized at market squares before the police had time to intervene.

Electoral campaigns after 1948, when the French administration systematically began to rig elections on a large scale, dramatized the conflict.[41] Nationalist parties, which never gave up entirely on participating in the elections, constantly tried to develop new strategies to neutralize administrative intervention in the electoral process. In Constantine in 1951, party militants were encouraged to prevent "even at the cost of their lives, the exchange of ballot boxes"[42]—a common form of electoral fraud. Party affiliates were also trained to be more efficient in the monitoring of polling stations; their presence on election day was such a problem for the authorities that it often led to arrests or brawls with the police.[43]

The practices described above were unconventional and involved a degree of physical engagement that went beyond traditional party politics and electoral campaigning. In a colonial context where nationalist symbolism constituted a threat to the status quo and where democracy was a mere formality, the attempts to create national narratives and define the meaning of a nation, to defend and expand autonomous political space, to protect the legality of the elections, and to guard voters from police harassment became intense forms of nonviolent resistance to colonial oppression.

Algerian Trade Unionism

Both the PCA and MTLD had close ties with trade unions after World War I. Most Algerian workers were affiliated with the French Confédération générale du travail (CGT) that did not always heed the calls of its Algerian activists to discuss the national question while its leadership was reluctant to appoint Algerian nationalists to key positions. However, according to former union leader Boualem Bourouiba, unionized Algerian workers (for example, in the docks) were not all communists and many were members of other nationalist parties (the MTLD and, to a lesser extent, UDMA) after World War II.[44] Though the question of the establishment of an Algerian union was raised, it was not until 1956 when the Union général des travailleurs algériens (UGTA), linked to the FLN, was created.

Algerian unionists had an essential role in organizing solidarity with other French occupied territories. For example, in the 1950s the Algerian dock workers' unions called on workers to stop loading weapons to be shipped to French forces in Vietnam where the French were fighting a war against a movement for independence.[45] These actions were in some cases coordinated with strikes in France itself, as in March 1952 when dock workers in both Marseille and Oran refused to load weapons for Vietnam.[46]

Various examples show creativity in the use of general strikes. April 25, 1952, was declared a day of mourning in solidarity with Tunisia where thousands of independence activists had been arrested and hundreds killed in recent months by French repression. In Algeria political parties and unions organized, throughout the country, a general strike and a series of nonviolent collective actions such as boycotts and protests. The Constantine prefecture noted that in the days prior to the general strike, "emissaries went around the Arab quarters of Constantine and invited Muslim women to remain at home on Friday, in particular those who worked in European families."[47] On April 25, collective actions took place throughout the country, with workers and shopkeepers going on strike and street demonstrations occurring even in smaller localities. Traffic in the main Algerian ports was blocked.

Despite popular support for those actions, they remained relatively rare. Three explanations might be offered for this. First, Algerian trade unionism, as an effective force in the struggle against colonialism, was weakened because of the absence of a national union and the impossibility of reaching all segments of what was not yet a working class.[48] Second, as a consequence, political parties were the main organizers of nationwide actions, but competition between the three nationalist parties was intense and blocked strategic cooperation—the April 1952 strike was a short-lived exception. Third, the political parties diverged dramatically on the advisability of mass nonviolent protest, an indecision that stemmed from the traumatic experience of the May 1945 massacres. On the day celebrating the German surrender in World War II, nonviolent demonstrations in eastern Algeria turned into riots and anti-European attacks after police shot demonstrators waving an Algerian flag in Sétif.[49] In the days and weeks that followed, both the French authorities and armed European militias roamed the Constantine region perpetrating summary executions and massacres while cruisers and aircraft carriers stationed in the Bougie Bay bombed villages. Thousands were killed and most nationalist leaders were detained for several months. In the years that followed, terrifying narratives of the violence against the colonized population were circulated, including ones concerning the burning of bodies in the lime kilns of Héliopolis.[50]

The trauma of May 1945 set back collective involvement for years. Combined with the authorities' oppressive measures to impede unified action and differences among nationalists over the use of alternative forms of mobilization and engagement outside the rules set by the colonial administration, Algerians felt their choice was either to acquiesce by participating in the rigged and discriminatory electoral process or to reject this legal form of action in favor of armed struggle.[51]

Nonviolent Actions Captured by Fervor of Violent Struggle

The FLN achieved its dominant position over other Algerian political factions through the use of violence against political adversaries in what was in fact an "Algero-Algerian war"[52] and then through both forceful and voluntary cooptation of former political rivals. It organized several nonviolent actions as a tool for mobilization and preparation for war, with the aim of securing and showing a wide popular support. The first major initiative was a permanent strike by students that began in May 1956, without explicit demands but expressing support for the FLN and its goals. While appearing to be merely a boycott of French universities, the strike in fact forced the intellectual elite and prominent families to get involved. It also politicized swathes of students available for further, more extreme actions and attracted new recruits for the ALN with new combatants. The student permanent strike raised general disagreements over the role that students and intellectuals should play in the national struggle: some argued that the student boycott of their education was wrong in principle and endangered the country's future intellectual capital; the counterargument was that intellectuals should show their organic link with the population by their readiness to engage in whatever way possible or demanded by the FLN.

Similarly, the FLN used the eight-day strike in January and February 1957 to drive the population to take a public stance in support of FLN and its actions that in turn helped the organization present itself as the legitimate voice of the Algerian people. Alongside the genuine popular support for the FLN and the national cause, there was also intensive pressure on all workers to quit their jobs, close their shops, and stay home. The strike was followed in most large Algerian cities. The chosen date, January 28, coincided with the United Nations General Assembly session adopting a resolution in favor of Algerian independence.[53] The strike marked the beginning of the so-called Battle of Algiers, also known as the Great Repression of Algiers,[54] and was in fact used to support an ongoing armed struggle and transform the entire population of Algiers into combatants in the war for independence—a task that became easier as a result of the subsequent disproportionate use of force and violence by French paratroopers that backfired and fueled insurgency all over the country. By 1957, all resistance actions served the goals of advancing armed struggle. Nonviolent strategies rather than offering an alternative to violence were hijacked by the fervor of armed insurrection and subordinated to a greater imperative of waging a war.

Conclusion

French colonization in Algeria was one of the most intense colonial encounters of the nineteenth and twentieth centuries. The severity of the socioeconomic disruption caused by the colonial regime and the harsh conditions of the French colonization in Algeria (including the massacres of May 1945) limited the range of possible forms of collective activities. The fact that political parties and unions developed later in Algeria than they did in other North African countries (Tunisia or Egypt) was undoubtedly linked to the breakdown of Algerian society in the face of colonization.

When armed insurrections failed to repel military conquest and occupation, the population adopted strategies of persistent endurance and survival. Emigration and more muted forms of resistance, such as withdrawal into more intimate and private domains of family life, are difficult for historians to assess. It was only with the emergence of the Jeunes Algériens and the development of cultural associations in the 1920s that this endurance took on public dimensions that were more constructive and collective. Collective activities became a means of moving away from simple survival to more proactive initiatives of rebuilding the social fabric and reinvigorating colonized society, despite ongoing restrictive and oppressive colonial policies.

Political parties succeeded in drawing on a repertoire of nonviolent actions to mobilize in the nationalist cause, but their lack of unity and reluctance to use more forceful nonviolent methods such as general strikes made them ineffective in securing serious political concessions. This partly explains the teleological narrative of the Algerian history promoted by the FLN after independence, according to which armed struggle was the only viable tool to obtain independence. Consequently, national identity construed after the colonial war was formed on a double denial of plurality—a plurality of political ideologies and nationalist parties and their contribution to the struggle for an independent state; and a plurality in understandings of what Algerianness meant and embodied. This kind of discourse denied in its entirety the value, role, impact, and legacy of unarmed forms of collective struggle.

It was only after the 1988 demonstrations, when civic associations and political parties became legal again, that the intensity of past experiences of nonviolent organizing and actions appeared reactivated: within a few days, dozens of political parties were founded. Nonviolent practices and activist networks with philosophical, institutional, and practical roots in the preindependence period were suddenly mobilized again. Thus, the decades of nationalist mythology had failed to erase them entirely.

Notes

1. Olivier Le Cour Grandmaison, *Coloniser, Exterminer: Sur la guerre et l'État colonial* (Paris: Fayard, 2005).

2. Benjamin C. Brower, *A Desert Named Peace: The Violence of France's Empire in the Algerian Sahara, 1844–1902* (New York: Columbia University Press, 2009).

3. Pierre Nora, *Realms of Memory: Conflicts and Divisions,* vol. 1: *The Construction of the French Past* (New York: Columbia University Press, 1996).

4. Malika Rahal, *Ali Boumendjel: Une affaire française, une histoire algérienne* (Paris: Belles Lettres, 2010), 26–28.

5. Benjamin Stora, *La Gangrène et l'oubli* (Paris: La Découverte, 1998), 121–137.

6. Ibid., 161–163.

7. Benjamin Stora, *Messali Hadj: Pionnier du nationalisme algérien, 1898–1974* (Paris: L'Harmattan, 1986).

8. Notably, Mohammed Harbi, *Une Vie debout, Mémoires politiques,* book 1: *1945–1973* (Paris: La Découverte, 2001); Henri Alleg, *Mémoire algérienne: Souvenirs de luttes et d'espérances* (Paris: Stock, 2005); Benjamin Stora and Zakya Daoud, *Ferhat Abbas: Une utopie algérienne* (Paris: Denoël, 1995); Mohammed Benamar Djebbari, *Un Parcours rude mais bien rempli: mémoires d'un enseignant de la vieille génération,* vol. 3 (Algiers: Anep, 2002).

9. Malika Rahal, "La place des réformistes dans le mouvement national algérien," *Vingtième Siècle: Revue d'histoire* 3, no. 83 (2004): 161–171.

10. Mohammed Harbi, *Le F.L.N., mirage et réalité* (Paris: JApress, 1980), 6.

11. Daniel Rivet, *Le Maghreb à l'épreuve de la colonisation* (Paris: Hachette, 2009), 295.

12. Mohamed Benrabah, *Langue et pouvoir en Algérie* (Paris: Seguier, 1999), 49.

13. Gilbert Meynier, *Histoire intérieure du FLN 1954–1962* (Paris: Fayard, 2002), 37.

14. John Ruedy, *Modern Algeria: The Origins and Development of a Nation,* 2nd ed. (Bloomington: Indiana University Press, 2005), 60.

15. Benjamin Stora, *La Guerre invisible, Algérie, années 90* (Paris: Presses de Sciences Po, 2001), 36.

16. Jean-Claude Vatin, *L'Algérie politique: histoire et société* (Paris: Presses de Sciences Po, 1983), 133.

17. Kamel Kateb, *Européens, "indigènes" et juifs en Algérie (1830–1962): Représentations et réalités des populations* (Paris: Institut national des études démographiques, 2001), 153–155.

18. James McDougall, *History and the Culture of Nationalism in Algeria: Colonialism, Historical Writing and Islamic Modernism, 1899–2001* (Cambridge: Cambridge University Press, 2006), 28.

19. Kateb, *Européens, "indigènes" et juifs,* 154.

20. Ibid.

21. Osama Abi-Mershed, *Apostles of Modernity: Saint-Simonians and the Civilizing Mission in Algeria* (Stanford: Stanford University Press, 2010).

22. This sections draws from Rivet, *Le Maghreb,* 124–129.

23. Ibid., 127.

24. Yvonne Turin, *Affrontements culturels dans l'Algérie coloniale: Écoles, médecines, religion, 1830–1880* (Algiers: Entreprise nationale du livre, 1983).

25. Rivet, *Le Maghreb,* 129.

26. Cited in Gilbert Meynier, *L'Algérie révélée* (Geneva: Librairie Droz, 1981), 245.

27. Julia Clancy-Smith, *Rebel and Saint: Muslim Notables, Populist Protest, Colonial Encounters (Algeria and Tunisia, 1800–1904)* (Berkeley: University of California Press, 1997), 7.

28. Jacques Berque, *Le Maghreb entre deux guerres* (Paris: Édition du Seuil, 1962), 324–327; Rivet, *Le Maghreb,* 301.

29. The following section draws from Clancy-Smith, *Rebel and Saint,* 214–253.

30. Ibid., 229.

31. Ibid., 239.

32. Vatin, *L'Algérie politique,* 171.

33. Meynier, *Histoire intérieure,* 51.

34. Omar Carlier, *Entre Nation et Jihad: Histoire sociale des radicalismes algériens* (Paris: Presses de la Fondation nationale des sciences politiques, 1995).

35. Charles-Robert Ageron, *Histoire De l'Algérie Contemporaine, Tome 2: De L'insurrection de 1871 à la Guerre de Libération de 1954* (Paris: PUF, 1979), 238.

36. Meynier, *Histoire intérieure,* 52–54.

37. McDougall, *History and the Culture of Nationalism,* 6–12.

38. The following section draws from Malika Rahal, "La tentation démocratique en Algérie: L'Union démocratique du Manifeste algérien (1946–1956)," *Insanyat* 12, no. 42 (2008): 79–97; Malika Rahal, "Prendre parti à Constantine: l'UDMA de 1946 à 1956," *Insanyat* 11, no. 35 (2007): 63–77.

39. Centre des Archives d'Outre-Mer, Aix-en-Provence, France (hereafter CAOM), 5I 112*, surveillance report of the Oran police, September 1, 1951.

40. Rahal, "La tentation démocratique en Algérie."

41. Meynier, *Histoire intérieure,* 71.

42. CAOM, 93/4101*, surveillance report of the police des renseignements généraux in Constantine, June 14, 1951.

43. Rahal, "La tentation démocratique en Algérie."

44. Boualem Bourouiba, *Les Syndicalistes algériens: leur combat de l'éveil à la libération* (Paris: Editions L'Harmattan, 1998), 213.

45. Henri Alleg, interviewed by the author, Palaiseau, France, January 20, 2003; Bourouiba, *Les Syndicalistes algériens,* 110.

46. CAOM, 5I 120, monthly report of the police des renseignements généraux of Oran, March 1952.

47. CAOM, 5I 115*, surveillance report of the Constantine prefecture, April 21, 1952.

48. Bourouiba, *Les Syndicalistes algériens,* 125.

49. Annie Rey-Golzeiguer provides a precise account of the demonstrations, distinguishing narratives on the "European" and on the "Muslim" side. Annie Rey-Goldzeiguer, *Aux origines de la guerre d'Algérie 1940–1945: De Mers-el-Kébir aux massacres du Nord-Constantinois* (Paris: La Découverte, 2006), 271–278.

50. Although the number of victims is impossible to calculate, estimates range from 8,000 to 20,000 victims (i.e., below the 45,000 provided in the official history, which had become a mythical figure).

51. Rey-Goldzeiguer, *Aux origines,* 366.

52. Meynier, *Histoire intérieure,* 455.

53. Ibid., 326.

54. Ibid., 322–323.

7

Egypt:
Nonviolent Resistance in the
Rise of a Nation-State, 1805–1922

Amr Abdalla and Yasmine Arafa

In this chapter, we identify and examine important episodes of Egyptians' nonviolent resistance against foreign domination in the nineteenth century, including the 1805 revolution, the 1881 Orabi movement, nonviolent organizing against the British occupation after 1882, and the 1919 revolution that led to Egypt's formal independence in 1922.

Often, the focus on the role of political elites, elite-driven events, brutal internal political strife, aggressive foreign interventions, armed resistance, and violence overshadows seemingly less visible but no less important people-driven nonviolent actions. Sometimes, the stories of mass nonviolent resistance are ignored altogether, even in well-respected academic publications. For example, *The Cambridge History of Egypt* offers only a few lines on the events of 1805, overlooking entirely the civilian-led nonviolent mobilization.[1] In this chapter, we aim to create greater awareness about the history of nonviolent actions in Egypt's struggle against foreign domination and offer insights into their role and effectiveness and their contribution to strengthening a national fabric—the process that eventually led to the emergence of a truly nationwide and nonviolent movement exemplified by the 1919 revolution. We also make some references to the 2011 revolution in order to emphasize similar nonviolent patterns that seem to have been present in both the 1919 revolution and the events that led to Egyptian president Hosni Mubarak's departure under the pressure of a popular nonviolent uprising.

Egyptian value systems generally emphasize the use of nonviolent means to fight oppression and injustice.[2] With the exception of violence in honor killings and blood feuds in Upper Egypt, both traditional and religious values emphasize that, before resorting to violence, nonviolent methods should be exhausted.[3] Furthermore, in order not to appear weak while taking nonviolent action, resisters should remind their opponents that the use of force remains a possible option. Collective nonviolent struggle as a form of self-defense and sacrificing one's life for the nation, religion, or principles has been highly valued.[4] However, martyrdom does not imply engaging in armed combat; someone who dies while struggling nonviolently can also be considered a *martyr*—the term was used, for example, to describe the non-violent protesters that were killed during the 2011 revolution.

In modern times Egypt's violent struggles against foreign occupiers, such as France, Britain, and Israel, are viewed as acts of self-defense. While violence in self-defense is justified in Egypt's national narratives, this is qualified by the recognition of a certain value in nonviolent actions. On one hand, many Egyptians often praise the successful 1952 revolution against their ailing monarchical system for being bloodless. On the other hand, they appear to celebrate national struggles against oppression and injustice, whether violent or nonviolent, regardless of how successful such struggle has been.

However, the mass-based nonviolent struggles of 1919 and 2011 seem to present a nonviolent model that was not accompanied by a threat of or use of force should nonviolent actions have failed. If the resisters used physical coercion, it was proportional and in self-defense. For example, in 2011 protesters dragged down thugs from charging camels and threw the policemen out of the shielded vehicles that were used to shoot at demonstrators. The two revolutions demonstrate that nonviolent resistance as a strategic option has its place in Egyptian national struggle. Even now, in the aftermath of the 2011 revolution, Egyptians continue to insist on using only nonviolent methods to protest against occasional outbursts of religious violence, to pressure the military to stop prosecuting demonstrators, and to move ahead more vigorously with democratic changes and bringing to justice former top-level officials of the ousted regime.

The May 1805 Revolution

Egypt had been under Ottoman rule since 1517, its walis (governors) selected by the sultan and aided by the Mamluks, a military caste. In 1798, as part of the colonial rivalry between Britain and France, Napoleon invaded and occupied Egypt. After the French departed in 1801, the Ottomans, Mamluks, and British vied for power in the country. In 1804, Egypt was once again brought under the control of the Ottoman Empire, this time under a new wali, Ahmad Khurshid Pasha, who imposed heavy indemnities and taxes. Soon afterward Egypt witnessed a unique political nonviolent action, which marked an unprecedented effort on the part of business and religious elites to take charge of the country's political destiny.

Responding to the plight of the masses,[5] Cairo's religious and intellectual leaders joined forces with the "business elites" to appeal to the wali.[6] Their grievances were about taxes, the presence of Ottoman soldiers in the capital, and the famine caused by the Mamluks' blockade of the transportation of grain from Upper Egypt.[7] The wali exacerbated the situation by dismissing their pleas. The contemporary chronicler Abdel Rahman Al Gabarti recorded that ordinary people went out in the streets to protest, beat drums, and shout. Women joined in, putting mud on their hands and hair as a visual form of dismay and disapproval of the wali and his policies. Soon many others followed with the support of respected shaikhs from the religious and academic center, Al-Azhar.[8] The soldiers on the streets were visibly moved and assured the masses that they empathized with their grievances.[9] Following these spontaneous nonviolent protests, the religious and business leaders asked religious scholars to offer a religious interpretation—a common form of consultation in making major decisions at that time—of whether it was permissible under certain circumstances to oust a ruler. This resulted in the religious scholars of Al-Azhar issuing a fatwa (ruling) stating that "according to the rules of Islamic Sharia [law], people have the right to install rulers and to impeach them if they deviate from the rules of justice and take the path of injustice."[10]

Despite this loss of legitimacy, the wali refused to resign even as the opposition pushed for his impeachment and the installation of Muhammad Ali, an Albanian Ottoman commander popular among Egyptians.[11] The Albanian troops, joined by a demonstration of 40,000 Egyptians—20 percent of the population of Cairo—surrounded Khurshid's citadel and did not relent for four months.[12] During the siege, the masses followed the orders of their religious and business leaders and those of the prospective ruler Muhammad Ali. They formed vigilante groups equipped with primitive weapons and sticks to defend against any attacks by the wali's citadel soldiers and to enforce the siege until Khurshid resigned. The leaders instructed people "to be vigilant, and to protect their locations; if a solider attacks them, they should respond proportionally. Otherwise people should refrain from provoking and attacking the soldiers."[13] Occasional skirmishes, usually started by soldiers using cannons, resulted in some deaths and injuries (of both soldiers and civilians). Yet the firm intention of the siege leaders was not to use violence. They went to great lengths in using religious arguments to persuade the representatives of the wali that, according to Islamic principles, lack of public consent made it his Islamic duty to step down.[14] Eventually, with the perseverance of a largely nonviolent mass mobilization and pressure by ordinary Egyptians, the Ottoman sultan withdrew Khurshid and appointed Muhammad Ali in his place.

The 1805 people's uprising at first followed an established political practice of making a plea to the ruler. When this failed, the people and their leaders resorted to unconventional, nonviolent methods of street demonstrations and later a siege. By directing their disobedience toward a specific wali, neither expressing hostility to the Ottoman Empire nor seeking the appointment of an Egyptian, the people avoided instigating a wider conflict against a much stronger adversary. Despite the importance of religion in rallying the people and as a source of identity, neither religious nor national awareness had yet developed sufficiently for Egyptians to challenge Ottoman rule in itself. Eventually, national identity became a more potent force, ultimately surpassing the Ottoman-led pan-Islamism. Scholars interpret the 1805 revolution as marking the first intervention by the people and their representatives (in this case, the religious and business elites) in political affairs of their state and the beginning of the rise of a modern Egyptian national identity, which was reinforced in the coming decades by the introduction of universal conscription to a national army, frequent educational missions to Europe, and the establishment of a modern school system.[15]

The Orabi Revolution of 1881

Tawfik Pasha became khedive (viceroy) in 1879, when the government was heavily in debt to Britain and France. The British and French had appointed financial controllers to oversee the Egyptian budget, which resulted in high taxation, low government salaries, and severe cuts in the army (from 124,000 in 1875 to 36,000 in 1879).[16] In this deteriorating economic situation, and with foreign, non-Muslim domination over government policy, domestic discontent grew and Tawfik faced resistance from different sectors of society.[17]

Religious scholarly institutions became increasingly active and politicized, thanks to disciples of the Iranian revivalist of Islamic thought and advocate for Muslim unity Sayyed Jamal al-Din (known as Afghani, see Chapter 8 on Iran) who had lived in Egypt from 1871. Afghani was expelled in 1879, but not before he encouraged the growth of a critical press and formed several forums where he trained future Islamist and nationalist activists.

The main challenge to Tawfik and the European interference in the country's affairs came from the Egyptian Army. Colonel Ahmad Orabi, born the son of a village shaikh at a time when only 13 percent of the population lived in towns, had become a career army officer and protested against a new law preventing peasants' becoming army officers. Summoned to see the khedive and war minister Osman Rifki, Orabi and two other peasant officers were arrested, only to be rescued by comrades from their regiment who forced the dismissal of Rifki and annulment of the law. This success put Orabi in a position to raise wider demands, not just reversing the army cuts but reestablishing a stronger Chamber of Deputies and drafting a new constitution. He also did not shy away from criticizing Ottoman as well as European interference. As such, his actions "created a platform upon which a variety of forces in civil society could agree."[18] Consequently, Orabi was successful in winning the support and active involvement of broad sectors of society, including parts of political and urban establishment, local mayors, landlords, government employees, intellectuals, peasants, and the army that all were frustrated by the worsening political and economic conditions of the country and the foreign interference.[19]

Orabi developed a process of citizens' endorsement for his further actions: "Delegations from around the country approached us and handed us authorizations which empower us to work for our country's best interest, declaring their solidarity with us in all our reform efforts and their prospects."[20] He set September 9, 1881, as the date to take the people's grievances to Khedive Tawfik. Backed by a civilian-military demonstration in front of Abdin Palace, Orabi and his colleagues confronted Tawfik and the acting British consul with the people's demands to rebuild the army, dismiss the government, and form a truly national assembly. "God has created us free," Orabi declared. "He did not create us as heritage or property. . . . So in the name of God who there is no God but him we will not be slaves any more."[21]

Tawfik bowed to their demands, expanding the powers of the representative assembly and rebuilding the army.[22] While reflecting on the successful nonviolent movement and its demonstration, Orabi wrote, "Whoever has read history knows that European countries earned their freedom by violence, bloodshed and destruction, but we earned it in one hour without shedding a drop of blood, without putting fear in a heart, without transgressing on someone's right, or damaging someone's honor."[23] The 1881 revolution relied on the nonviolent coercive pressure of both the military and civilian population. Orabi gained quick success by pursuing demands that were limited and posed no direct threat to the regime or generally to the interest of foreign powers. Successfully mobilizing broad-based support across the social strata, including some political leaders, large and small landowners, and urban guilds around the country, he effectively pressured Tawfik to accept the people's demands. However, if Tawfik was prepared to accept some reduction of khedival powers, Britain and France were firmly set against democratization. In January 1882, Britain and France reaffirmed their mutual interest in preserving the "order of things" in Egypt, pledging their support for the khedive.[24] And in the summer, Britain invaded militarily. Armed resistance proved futile; Orabi surrendered and was exiled to the British colony of Ceylon (now Sri Lanka).[25] Thus began the British occupation of Egypt.

Despite the defeat, Orabi's movement set the stage for further mass-based and largely nonviolent efforts to organize, mobilize, and build alternative institutions to directly challenge British colonial occupation a couple of decades later.

From the British Occupation to 1914

The British occupation of Egypt changed the Egyptians' struggle, yet again to one against a foreign occupier. Earlier occupation by the Ottomans included a sense of Muslim fraternity and pan-Islamism that appealed to many Egyptians, despite their growing sense of national identity. This time, however, a non-Muslim country ruled Egypt clearly for its own benefit. Britain took complete control over the state treasury, supervised tightly all government ministries, and appointed British administrators.[26] British administrators arbitrarily confiscated crops from farmers and forcibly collected excessive taxes to support their occupation and war efforts. They limited individual liberties, increased press censorship, and restricted public gatherings.[27] Egyptians were often ridiculed and abused in public particularly by Australians and New Zealanders—and their properties were ransacked by British troops.

Many nationalist leaders were either imprisoned or fled the country to avoid British persecution.[28] This oppression eventually backfired and aroused a mounting resentment among Egyptians.[29] A strategy of relying on more subtle forms of nonviolent resistance was dictated by pragmatic considerations of the weaker nation controlled by a powerful occupier and the conclusions drawn from Orabi's unsuccessful armed resistance to the British invasion.[30]

The Denshawai incident of June 1906 was a flash point that provoked outrage at the occupation. Five British officers on leave shot pigeons, which angered their owners in the village and led to a fracas after which one officer died. The British made an example of the villagers by hanging four of them, imprisoning or flogging others.[31] These events stirred national feelings and, for the first time since the Orabi revolution, many Egyptians became politically active. This increasing politicization ushered in a period where pro-independence parties were formed such as the National Party and the Party of the Nation, nationalist and pro-constitution newspapers (such as *al-Liwa* and *al-Jarida*) were launched, and private schools (including evening schools) as well as consumer cooperatives and trade unions were set up.[32]

The nationalist press nurtured a sense of national identity. In 1909 the British authorities, fearing the power of the press, revived censorship laws to control not only the domestic but also the international press and even letters and telegrams to or from abroad.[33] To elude the censors, opposition newspapers found foreign owners or editors since the censorship laws did not apply to non-Egyptians or Egypt-based entities owned by them. Petitions and protests against press censorship were organized in March and April 1909, with demonstrators chanting "down with oppression, down with the publications law, down with tyranny."[34] To circumvent censorship, some publications went underground and were distributed by hand to supporters who then passed copies to others.[35]

Journalist and founder of *al-Liwa* and the National Party, Mustafa Kamil carried his campaign against the British occupation to France and to Britain itself.[36] His untimely death in 1908 led to a collective national awakening when some 250,000 people joined "Egypt's first mass funeral demonstration, as civil servants walked off their jobs and students cut their classes to march behind his bier."[37] For the first time in modern history, ordinary Egyptians could finally visualize their movement and sense their strength in the vast number of people united in grief for their dead patriot.[38]

The 1919 Revolution and Independence of 1922

During World War I, Britain declared Egypt a protectorate, imposed martial law, and then broke a promise not to involve Egypt in the war by requisitioning buildings, crops, and animals and press-ganging peasants to serve in the Labour Corps and the Camel Transport Corps. As the war came to an end, Egypt again faced an economic crisis with raging inflation and mass unemployment.[39] In view of the discontent with the British occupation and the Allied powers' affirmation of the right to self-determination, the time seemed ripe for Egypt to renegotiate its own status. Therefore, on November 13, 1918, now celebrated as Yawm al Jihad (Day of Struggle), former government minister Saad Zaghlul and two members of the Legislative Assembly approached the British commissioner to propose the end of the British protectorate and the participation of an Egyptian delegation—Al Wafd al Misri, known as the Wafd—in the planned Versailles Peace Conference. Not only did the British reject these proposals, in March 1919 Saad Zaghlul and three colleagues were deported to Malta.[40] This repression backfired on a huge scale, provoking massive protests all over the country that continued despite lethal repression.[41] The British government was forced to release Zaghlul and his colleagues, but the movement had now gathered momentum. While denouncing the British violence, the Wafd leaders firmly opposed any use of violence by Egyptians and criticized those who turned the demonstrations violent.[42]

The following examples show the determined nonviolent action of various sectors of Egyptian society in the 1919 revolution.

Gathering of Signatures

The Wafd, after proposing the delegation to Versailles, embarked on a massive signature collection campaign in support of the proposal.[43] The authorities, fearing that this agitation would further politicize people—as it did—prohibited and confiscated the petition. This ban, too, turned against the British. People became even more eager to sign up. Signing was an act that bore little risk yet generated an almost transcendent feeling of fulfillment of patriotic duty, an electrifying sense of national unity and sheer enthusiasm for taking part in a historic event: the collective decisionmaking about their country's destiny.[44] Hundreds of thousands of petitions were secretly printed in Alexandria and circulated by hand until 100,000 signatures had been collected.[45]

Public Statements

Many public statements were issued by various professional groups, especially to condemn the British use of force against unarmed citizens. On March 15, 1919, doctors at Al Kasr Al Ainy Hospital in Cairo declared that their examination of the bodies of protesters and wounds of other victims provided irrefutable evidence of British brutality.[46] On April 9, 1919, the city council of the Directorate of Giza strongly protested against violent actions perpetrated by the British forces, including burning villages, killing innocent people, raping women, shooting livestock, extorting money, and destroying property. These crimes were documented and records appended to the statement. Determined not to be silenced, the Giza council members pledged to deliver their statement to the sultan and all other official and international authorities.[47]

Student Demonstrations and Strikes

The arrest and deportation of Wafd leaders outraged the Egyptian people. The next day a strike by the school students in Giza broke out, as they declared, "We do not study law in a country that does not respect law." The students marched peacefully, calling for independence and shouting the name of Saad Zaghlul. They headed first to the College of Engineering and Agriculture in Giza and then to the College of Medicine and Commerce in Cairo where many more students joined them, all marching together to Al Sayeda Zeinab Square in the heart of Cairo. There, police blocked the roads and tried to disperse the crowds, arresting 300 protesters.[48] The day after, March 10—as every available source says[49]—*all* students in Cairo, including the university at Al-Azhar, announced their protest and went on strike, demanding the release of the Wafd leaders and condemning the British occupation. Two students were killed, many were injured, yet the demonstrations continued unabated for weeks.[50] Students' strikes and demonstrations had an important impact in overcoming British censorship as students took home their news from Cairo. This led to growing unrest in many parts of Egypt.[51]

General Edmund Allenby, sent by London to establish order, told students to return to class by May 3. When they did not obey he threatened that, unless they returned by May 7, their schools would be closed for the rest of the year. This threat turned out to be a double-edged sword. Schools were indeed closed down but, by disobeying the British military authority, students further undermined its legitimacy and put in doubt British ability to rule the country. More importantly, students used the time away from their schools to continue demonstrations and organize protests in other parts of the country.

Workers' and Peasant Strikes

Tram workers along with railway, telegraph, and postal workers went on strike in mid-March 1919, joined by taxi drivers, lawyers who boycotted state courts, and even civil servants.[52] The workers' protests and strikes had both economic and nationalist goals. They demanded higher wages and better working conditions while, at the same time, defending Egypt's right to self-rule. The railway workers brought the train system to a halt by striking and cutting railway lines and destroying the railway switches; the telegraph workers disrupted communication lines while peasants paralyzed trade in rural goods; both actions affected traffic and communication between and within cities and towns.[53] Crippling transportation and communication lines particularly damaged the British administration, which relied heavily on them. These strikes showed that the movement now involved a coalition engaging different social strata.

Formation of National Police and Nonviolent Discipline

To maintain an order and nonviolent discipline, the demonstrators formed a special marshal group called "the national police" that was identified by a red badge worn on their left arms. Some of the national police were responsible for isolating people who tried to incite violence on demonstrations while others provided demonstrators with water and first aid if needed. They were credited with organizing effective demonstrations and keeping the protests peaceful as people voluntarily obeyed them.[54] The strikes and demonstrations remained predominantly nonviolent, but when some properties on the fringe of a protest were damaged, student organizers quickly issued a statement of apology, condemning such behavior while stressing that they wished to demonstrate loyalty to their country and support for harmonious relations between Egyptians and foreigners.[55]

Public Speeches in the Refuge of a Sacred Place

Al-Azhar's religious status among Egyptians meant that it was the only place the British could not use force. This offered a sanctuary for delivering public speeches by people from all walks of life—student leaders, scholars, priests, lawyers, and even workers—both Muslim and Christian.[56] As well as boosting morale, these speeches informed the public about decisions relevant to the conduct of protests and strikes and presented action plans agreed on earlier by the leaders.[57] As a result of this transparent decision-making, people felt ownership of the ongoing struggle that in turn influenced their readiness to continue even in the face of brutality.[58]

Public Involvement by Women

Hamidah Khalil, "a woman of the people," became the first woman martyr of the 1919 resistance on March 14, 1919, in Cairo.[59] Two days later, hundreds of women wearing veils went to the streets of Cairo to demonstrate against the British occupation. This event is seen as the first collective and public entry of women into Egyptian political life.[60] Safia Zaghlul, Saad Zaghlul's wife, and Huda Sharawi, the organizer of the Egyptian Feminist Union, led the demonstration. During the ongoing protest, the British Army surrounded the nonviolent protesters and pointed their rifles at women. Women stood their ground while one of them approached a British soldier and told him in English, "We do not fear death. Shoot me and make me Miss Cavell of Egypt."[61] Ashamed, the British soldiers stepped aside to let the demonstration proceed.[62] Women's protests posed the British authorities with a dilemma that was recorded by the police commander Sir Thomas Russell in a letter to his son: "My next problem was a demonstration by the native ladies of Cairo. This rather frightened me as if it came to pass it was bound to collect a big crowd and my orders were to stop it. Stopping a procession means force and any force you use to women puts you in the wrong."[63]

The revolution saw unprecedented participation of women from all social and economic backgrounds who were involved in all aspects of the nonviolent resistance.[64] Women and high school girls organized school strikes, distributing circulars about the protests to private homes despite heavy police surveillance; in the provinces secretly handed out pamphlets with nationalist demands; provided food and assistance to those who sabotaged the railway lines and communications in Upper Egypt; coordinated demonstrations and boycotts of British goods; and wrote and distributed petitions to foreign embassies to protest British oppressive policies in Egypt.[65]

Women's participation and experience in nonviolent actions outlived the 1919 revolution and many of them continued their public involvement in various political and social affairs, building "the bridge from a gradual pragmatic feminism discreetly expressed in everyday life to a highly vocal feminism articulated in an organized movement and a vigorous process of entering and creating modern professions."[66]

Demonstrations at Public Funerals

Public funerals were held by Egyptians to pay tribute to and honor victims of the British repression. Masses of people, representing various classes, participated in funerals where coffins were wrapped with the Egyptian flags. Such displays of public mourning were occasions for large, nonviolent gatherings and silent marches where thousands of people walked in silence that was occasionally interrupted by shouts against the occupation and British atrocities.[67]

Citizen Protest and Boycott of Milner's Mission

In spring 1919, the British government sent Lord Alfred Milner to investigate establishing "self-governing institutions" subordinate to the British protectorate. This plan fell far short of independence. On his arrival in December 1919, Milner's mission was greeted with a new wave of strikes by students, workers, merchants, lawyers, and other professionals opposed to the status quo ante and the continuation of the British protectorate. Leaflets urged Egyptians to boycott the mission, refusing contact with its members or to help in its work.[68]

Mass Prayer

Milner urged the British government to invite Zaghlul to London in May 1920. Therefore, the Wafd leader called a day of prayer for attaining full independence for Egypt and commissioned Ahmed Shawky to write a prayer.[69] The day of prayer illustrates Zaghlul's strategy for unifying Egyptians at critical moments, making the whole nation feel part of the struggle. On May 24, hundreds of thousands of Christians and Muslims converged around the houses of worship for a common prayer.[70]

Displaying a Symbolic Unity Flag

Demonstrators throughout the country waved a flag with the cross and crescent on a green background—a symbol of national unity or, more precisely, of Muslim-Christian unity. Muslim and Christian leaders jointly held meetings in mosques and churches where they alternated in delivering speeches.[71] Demonstrations included not only Christians and Muslims, but Jews as well.[72]

Drama, Music, and Literature That Advocate Resistance

Writers and poets expressed their love for free Egypt and denounced the British occupation through poems, songs, and literary works. In 1918–1919, Tawfiq Al Hakim wrote *Al Daif Al Thakeel* (An Unwelcome Guest), an allegorical play about a guest invited to stay at someone's home for a day who ends up staying for months.[73] Sometimes called "the voice of the 1919 revolution," Sayed Darwish's patriotic songs about the exiled Zaghlul were so inflammatory that the British forbade the performance of any songs with Zaghlul's name. Therefore, Darwish wrote a song about *saad* (happiness) and the fruit *zaghloul* (date).[74] The theaters of Munira al-Mahdiyya, al-Kassar, and Rihani popularized Darwish's patriotic songs with their subtle references to Zaghlul and the events of the day.[75]

When Milner's proposal of self-governing institutions failed to quiet the movement, the British reverted to authoritarianism and, once more, deported Wafd leaders.[76] Again this backfired, provoking a new wave of strikes and protests. Britain finally relented and on February 28, 1922, unilaterally declared the end of the protectorate and Egypt's formal independence. This independence was incomplete as Britain insisted on retaining a military presence and further negotiations on several other issues. Nevertheless, 1922 constituted a breakthrough in the formation of a modern Egyptian nation-state.

The 1919 revolution was a genuine people's uprising, largely nonviolent, which was not tainted by religious fanaticism or class conflict, that brought together a coalition of government officials, intellectuals, merchants, peasants, students, and, most remarkably, women. An equally significant feature of the demonstrations was the involvement of both Muslims and Christians, which illustrated a strong sense of common, national identity among ordinary Egyptians despite religious differences.

Conclusion

We do not claim that violence or armed struggle played no part in Egypt's road to independence, but rather that collective nonviolent actions constituted an important repertoire of resistance whose role, effectiveness, and impact require an appropriate acknowledgment and assessment.

Nonviolent resistance might not always be a conscious choice and neither its leaders nor other participants are necessarily guided by nonviolent principles. The leaders of both the 1805 movement and the Orabi revolution of 1881–1882 organized largely through nonviolent means, with the option of using arms mainly in the background or as a response to invasion, which occurred in 1882. The period 1882–1914, in contrast, was one of growing national awareness through spreading ideas, publishing, and educational work that built internal strength. Finally, in the 1919 revolution, violence by the British was out of proportion to any committed by protesters.[77] Egyptian leaders, not only the Wafd, but the students and the full array of protest organizers, took care to avoid violence and at no time during the revolution did they look to violence as an alternative should nonviolent action fail.

Nonviolent movements provided an opportunity for ordinary Egyptians from all walks of life to join in collective actions that spanned more than their familiar communal context and increased their participation, expanding the public space that for centuries had been reserved to a narrow group of foreign military and political elites.

The Egyptians' national struggle, irrespective of its violent or nonviolent patterns, is a reflection of a complex interaction of different value systems where violent physical coercion, as in the 1919 and 2011 revolutions, was restricted to self-defense and protection.

The strategic choice of nonviolent resistance used in the 1919 revolution was replicated even more deliberately during the 2011 revolution. Both revolutions utilized similar repertoires of nonviolent methods. There was emphasis on unity of all Egyptians regardless of different faiths (e.g., the flag with a cross and crescent in the 1919 revolution and the chants "Muslims, Christians, We Are All Egyptians" and mutual protection during prayers in the 2011 revolution); inclusion of women and children; insistence on the peaceful nature of the revolutions in slogans and posters; setting up of checkpoints to ensure that no arms be smuggled to the locations of demonstrations; and use of humor, art, songs, and satire to express the demands of the revolutions or ridicule the adversary. The following depiction of the carnival mode of the 1919 revolution can easily be used to describe Tahrir Square at the beginning of 2011:

> For Egypt's urban lower classes, women, and religious minorities, the almost spontaneous development of carnivalesque, and hence non-hierarchical, political expressions provided an important avenue of dissent. Marginalized voices were loudly heard through collective and direct action in the streets . . . public squares, cafés, bars, mosques, and churches [that] became the necessary carnivalesque spaces outside the reach of the centralized authorities, where illicit counter-hegemonic opinions were debated and exchanged.[78]

There were also differences, one of them being that, unlike the 1919 revolution, the 2011 popular uprising has been leaderless but still able to maintain an impressive degree of nonviolent discipline and cohesion.

In this chapter, we showed that the repertoire of nonviolent methods can make a decisive difference at various stages in the growth of a movement and the conduct of a struggle. The history of modern Egypt should give greater cognizance to the strategic contribution of nonviolent resistance in major political and social developments, including its contribution to the formation of the Egyptian national identity. The events of 1919 and 2011 point to a new trend of increased use of strategic nonviolent actions as the collective identity becomes stronger. This is reflected in the people's desire to take charge of their own destiny as Egyptian nationals in 1919 and as Egyptian citizens in 2011. The development of nonviolent resistance as a strategic choice of fighting for people's rights that correlates with a reinforced people-centered identity deserves further research.

Notes

1. Khaled Fahmy, "The Era of Muhammad Ali Pasha, 1805–1848," in *The Cambridge History of Egypt,* vol. 2, ed. M. W. Daly (Cambridge: Cambridge University Press, 1998), 144.
2. Resorting to violence has been governed by multiple value systems—religious, traditional, modern, and legal. The religious value system often calls for peaceful means and prefers patience and forgiveness to retaliation (see, e.g., Quran 42:40–43 and 49:9–10). Traditional values also generally favor nonviolent methods. During conflicts, people might invoke a proverb such as "people came to know God by reason"—meaning that rational discussion is better than violence—or "lucky is the one who while powerful forgives." The modern value system views dialogue and nonviolent means as a sign of civility whereas violence is considered uncivilized. The legal value system (although contentious by nature) advocates a similar approach by creating a venue (the judicial system) for parties to avoid physical conflict by settling disputes in courts of law. Nevertheless, all four value systems permit the use of violence as a last resort or in self-defense. Modern art, especially songs and films, often reflects this complex interplay between violence and nonviolent means of resistance in national struggle. See Amr Abdalla, "Inter-Personal Conflict Patterns in Egypt: Themes and Solutions" (PhD dissertation, George Mason University, 2001), 101.
3. Egyptians typically make a clear distinction between the use of "legitimate force" and the perpetration of "unjust violence." The former is usually seen as justified under conditions of self-defense or after peaceful means have been exhausted. The latter usually carries a negative connotation as it might imply brute, unprovoked, or disproportionate—essentially unjust—use of violent means against an opponent. In this chapter, we use the term *violence* broadly to encompass all types of violent acts, including those referred to by Egyptians as force. However, we also highlight that in many instances nonviolent actions became a force more powerful than both unjust violence and, for that matter, legitimate force.
4. Only in the early period of the expansion of the Muslim state can one hear stories and see images of glorified martyrdom, which were not necessarily warranted by the right to self-defense but through their contribution to the early quests of the rapidly growing Muslim state. Dying for Allah is seen as the highest form of faith.

5. Mahmoud Metwali, *Omar Makram Sout Al Horeya Wa Raed Al Demokrateya Al Masreya* (Cairo: Al Hay'a Al Ama Lel Este'lamat, 2008), 58.

6. Afaf Lotfi Al-Sayyid Marsot, *Egypt in the Reign of Muhammad Ali* (Cambridge: Cambridge University Press, 1984), 61; Metwali, *Omar Makram,* 59.

7. Metwali, *Omar Makram,* 59.

8. Al-Azhar, built in 972, has been an important religious and academic center in Egypt and in the Islamic world, serving as a safe haven for opposition leaders and protesters to Ottoman rule. Ahmed Mohamed Ouf, *Al-Azhar Fe Alf Am: Ebreel 970—Ebreel 1970* (Cairo: Matba'et Al-Azhar, 1970), 19–93; Shawky Atalla Al Gamal, *Al-Azhar Wa Dawro Al Seyasy Wal Hadary Fe Africia* (Cairo: Al Hay'a Al Masreya Al Ama lel Ketab, 1988), 11–129.

9. Abdel Rahman Al Gabarti, *Tareekh Aga'eb Al Athar Fe Al Taragem Wal Akhbar Al Goz' Al Thaleth* (Cairo: Al Matba'a Al Amera Al Sharkeya, 1904), 283.

10. Mohamed Abd el Fattah Abu el Fadl, *Alsahwa Al Masrya fi Ahd Mohammad Ali* (Cairo: Supreme Council of Culture, 1998), 12; Al Gabarti, *Tareekh Aga'eb,* 330.

11. Metwali, *Omar Makram,* 60.

12. Abu el Fadl, *Alsahwa,* 11.

13. Al Gabarti, *Tareekh Aga'eb,* 332.

14. Ibid., 331.

15. Metwali, *Omar Makram,* 62.

16. Donald Malcolm Reid, "The Urabi Revolution and the British Conquest, 1879–1882," in *The Cambridge History of Egypt,* vol. 2, ed. M. W. Daly (Cambridge: Cambridge University Press, 1998), 220.

17. Hassan Hafez, *Al Thawra Al Orabeya Fel Meezan* (Cairo: Matabe'e Al Dar Al Quawmeya, 1999), 27.

18. Juan R. Cole, *Colonialism and Revolution in the Middle East: Social and Cultural Origins of Egypt's Urabi Movement* (Cairo: The American University in Cairo Press, 1999), 235.

19. Hafez, *Al Thawra,* 35–36; Ahmed Abdel Reheem Mostafa, *Al Thawra Al Orabeya* (Cairo: Dar Al Qualam, 1961), 53; Cole, *Colonialism and Revolution,* 235.

20. Abdel Rahman Al Rafei, *Al Thawra Al Orabeya Wa Al Ehtelal Al Engeleezy* (Cairo: Dar Al Ma'aref, 1983), 120.

21. Hafez, *Al Thawra,* 36–38.

22. Arthur Goldschmidt Jr., *A Brief History of Egypt* (University Park: Pennsylvania State University, 2008), 87.

23. Al Rafei, *Al Thawra,* 148.

24. Hafez, *Al Thawra,* 41.

25. Mostafa, *Al Thawra,* 120.

26. The number of British in the Egyptian government structures quickly exceeded the number of Egyptians appointed in both the government and the army. Goldschmidt, *Brief History,* 101.

27. Ramzy Mikhail, *Al Sahafa Al Masreya Wal Haraka Al Wataneya Men Al Ehtelal Ela Al Esteklal 1882–1922* (Cairo: Al Hay'a Al Masreya Al Ama Lel Ketab, 1996), 137.

28. Mikhail, *Al Sahafa*; Goldschmidt, *Brief History,* 107.

29. Goldschmidt, *Brief History,* 101.

30. Ibid., 97.

31. Ibid., 102.

32. Ibid., 103.

33. Mikhail, *Al Sahafa,* 116.

34. Ibid., 110.

35. Ibid., 128.

36. Hussein Fawzy Al Naggar, *Ahmed Lotfy El Sayyed Ostaz Al Geel* (Cairo: Al Dar Al Masreya Lel Ta'leef Wal Targama, 1965), 132.

37. Abdel Rahman Al Rafei, *Mustafa Kamil Ba' eth Al Haraka Al Wataneya* (Cairo: Dar Al Ma'aref, 1984), 276. Goldschmidt, *Brief History,* 104.

38. Abdel Rahman Al Rafei, *Mustafa Kamil,* 276.

39. Helen Chapin Metz, ed., *Egypt: A Country Study* (Washington, DC: Government Printing Office for the Library of Congress, 1990), http://countrystudies.us /egypt/, accessed November 3, 2010.

40. Ibid.

41. On July 24, 1919, the British foreign secretary reported 800 Egyptians killed and 1,500 wounded in the March–June period, forty-nine death sentences, and thousands sentenced to penal servitude or imprisonment. http://hansard.milbank systems.com/commons/1919/jul/24/egypt (from digitized editions of Commons and Lords Hansard, the official report of debates in Parliament), accessed December 21, 2010.

42. Abbas Mahmoud Al Akkad, *Saad Zaghlool Za' eem Al Thawra* (Cairo: Dar Al Helal, 1988), 239.

43. The petition read, "We, the undersigned, hereby authorize Saad Zaghlul Pasha, Ali Sharawi Pasha, Abdel Aziz Fahmi Bey, Mohamed Ali Bey, Abdel Latif Al Mekabaty Bey, Mohamed Mahmoud Pasha, and Ahmed Lotfy Al Sayed Bey, to seek through peaceful and legitimate means the full independence of Egypt." Abdel Rahman Al Rafei, *Thawrat 1919: Tareekh Masr Al Kawmy Min 1914 Ela 1921* (Cairo: Dar Al Ma'aref, 1987), 122.

44. Ramzy Mikhail, *Al Wafd Wal Wehda Al Wataneya Fe Thawret 1919* (Cairo: Dar Al Arab Al Bostany, 1994), 26; Goldschmidt, *Brief History,* 111.

45. Mikhail, *Al Wafd,* 26; Goldschmidt, *Brief History,* 122.

46. The doctors' statement read, "We are deeply repentant to see the British forces' use of guns and rifles against peaceful and unarmed demonstrators, especially after finding among the victims women and children who cannot be considered as a threat, and finding most of the injuries fatal which proves the intention of causing harm and death." Al Rafei, *Thawrat 1919,* 290.

47. Ibid., 297.

48. Mikhail, *Al Wafd,* 40.

49. Al Rafei, *Thawrat 1919,* 195; Mikhail, *Al Wafd,* 40; Metz, *Egypt.*

50. Mikhail, *Al Wafd,* 40.

51. Al Rafei, *Thawrat 1919,* 216.

52. Metz, *Egypt.*

53. Al Rafei, *Thawrat 1919,* 216.

54. Ibid., 235.

55. Ibid., 197.

56. The list of speakers was long, including Shaikh Abdou Rabbu Moftah, Shaikh Abdel Baky Serour, Priest Markus Sergious, Priest Bolus Ghebrial, Hassan Yassin, and Mohamed Shokry, the latter two leaders of the student strikes. Ibid., 228.

57. Ibid., 229.

58. Ibid., 198.

59. Margot Badran, *Feminists, Islam, and Nation: Gender and the Making of Modern Egypt* (Princeton: Princeton University Press, 1995), 75.

60. Metz, *Egypt.*

61. Edith Cavell was a British nurse executed in 1915 after helping 200 Allied soldiers escape from German-occupied Belgium.

62. Al Rafei, *Thawrat 1919,* 211.

63. Badran, *Feminists, Islam, and Nation,* 76.

64. Ziad Fahmy, "Popularizing Egyptian Nationalism: Colloquial Culture and Media Capitalism, 1870–1919" (PhD dissertation, University of Arizona, 2007), 253.

65. Metz, *Egypt*; Badran, *Feminists, Islam, and Nation,* 77. An early petition sent by women to European officials condemned the "brutal use of force, and firing bullets at unarmed sons, children, boys and men only because they protested using peaceful demonstrations against the decision to ban Egyptians from travel to present their case at the Peace Conference." Al Rafei, *Thawrat 1919,* 211. Another petition delivered by women to the US, Italian, and French foreign delegations in Cairo read, "Egyptian ladies—mothers, sisters and wives who have fallen victims to British designs—present to Your Excellencies this protest against the barbarous acts that the peaceful Egyptian nation underwent for no wrong other than demanding freedom and independence for the country based on the principles advanced by Dr. [Woodrow] Wilson to which all countries, belligerent and non-belligerent, have subscribed." Badran, *Feminists, Islam, and Nation,* 76.

66. Badran, *Feminists, Islam, and Nation,* 74.

67. Al Rafei, *Thawrat 1919,* 235.

68. Metz, *Egypt.*

69. Mikhail, *Al Wafd,* 147.

70. Ibid., 150.

71. Ibid., 135.

72. Fahmy, "Popularizing Egyptian Nationalism," 259.

73. Mohamed Mandour, *Masrah Tawfiq Al Hakim* (Cairo: Dar Nahdat Masr, 1960), 9, 10.

74. Salah Eissa, "Birth of the Patriots: How Patriotic Song Played Out from the Revolution Through the 1973 War," *Egypt Today,* July 2005, www.egypttoday.com /article.aspx?ArticleID=5315, accessed June 3, 2010.

75. Fahmy, "Popularizing Egyptian Nationalism," 292.

76. Including Saad Zaghlul, Mostafa Al Nahass, Makram Ebeid, Fathalla Barakat, Atef Barakat, and Sinout Hanna. See Hussein Fawzy Al Naggar, *Saad Zaghlul Al Za'ama Wal Za'eem* (Cairo: Maktabet Madbouly, 1986), 167.

77. British troops killed 800 Egyptians whereas 29 British soldiers were killed (fewer than the death sentences imposed by Britain) and 114 injured, plus 31 European civilians were killed and 35 injured.

78. Fahmy, "Popularizing Egyptian Nationalism," 298.

8

Iran:
Nonviolent Revolts,
1890–1906

Nikki R. Keddie

Nonviolent resistance has played an influential role in Iranian history since the late nineteenth century, in particular, by challenging unjust rulers and their subservience to foreign interests. Critically this has involved a recurring strategic alliance between sections of the clergy; the bazaar merchants; and the secular, generally modernizing and nationalist intellectual elite. Lacking real agreement on desired goals, this alliance has largely been based on the existence of common enemies—the ruling dynasty and its foreign supporters—and it has been potent in organizing around anti-imperialist themes such as concessions made to foreign business interests.

In this chapter, I focus on the period when this alliance was first forged during the Qajar dynasty (1794–1925) and, in particular, the tobacco protests of 1891–1892 and the subsequent constitutional revolution of 1905–1911. This alliance resurfaced during the Pahlavi dynasty, especially in the oil nationalization campaign of 1951–1953, in the antigovernment protests of the early 1960s, and even in the movement in 1978–1979 that overthrew the monarchy and ultimately heralded the Islamic revolution. All of these episodes involved, to a greater or lesser extent, efforts to throw off foreign control of the Iranian economy and to build an independent society and state.

The political and economic context for the protest movements of 1890–1911 was the close relationship between the ruling dynasty and foreign powers, particularly but not exclusively Russia and Great Britain. From the early nineteenth century, Russia and Britain competed with each other to control Iran. Both intervened in Iranian politics and economics, via bribes and threats, and militarily by protecting the throne. In addition, Russia,

Britain, and France received a number of economic and cultural concessions such as lucrative contracts and low tariffs on imports. The issue of
these preferential tariffs aroused sporadic protests and petitions among
Iranian *bazaaris* (a term covering merchants and craftspeople of the traditional bazaars) whose sales were adversely affected, but these protests did
not suggest the scale of the revolts in the late nineteenth century.

Iran is hardly unique in having no major thinkers who promoted a philosophy of nonviolent resistance. Iranian history includes elements that glorify violence such as the celebration of ancient Iranian kings in the epic
Shahnameh[1] and more recent nationalist admiration for various conquering
rulers. The cultures of many nomadic tribes, who comprised much of Iran's
population until the 1920s, involved using violence to protect migration
routes and sometimes to assure rule over local settled populations. Violence
toward women, slaves, and, at times, religious or cultural minorities was
widely accepted. Countervailing trends were found in Sufi orders and poetry, including the work of the poet Jalal al-Din Rumi who endorsed the
unity of humanity and discouraged enmity toward others. However, politically these trends usually advocated *quietism,* meaning accepting rulers or
local leaders, no matter how oppressive. Those who wished to avoid violence were more likely to join mystical groups that concentrated on internal
individual and group practices than they were to advocate resistance based
on ideas that might seem to contradict the Quran. However, Iranians who
did actively resist rulers or foreigners often drew on a familiar repertoire of
nonviolent means, especially claiming sanctuary, closing bazaars, and mass
demonstrations, although they did not renounce threats or use of violence.

The protest movements that I describe in this chapter did not on the
whole reject violence, but drew on Iran's history of popular action to carry
out various forms of nonviolent resistance. Furthermore, they were influenced by new religious movements that emerged in the nineteenth century
and in turn helped to shape the protest campaigns of 1890–1911.

Quietism and the Challenge to It

For centuries the leading ulama (clergy) favored political quietism toward
the dynasties that ruled Iran, notably the Safavids (1501–1722) and the
early-nineteenth-century Qajars. However, in the mid-nineteenth century
the new Babi movement became a serious threat to both royal and ulama
power. Adherents believed that Sayyed Ali Mohammad of Shiraz was the
Bab—the gateway to the Hidden Imam (who would return as the messianic
Mahdi). In 1850 his imprisonment and execution provoked Babi uprisings
that were ruthlessly suppressed. Those who followed the original teachings
of the Bab, called Azalis, remained actively hostile to the Qajars and to the

ulama. Although some ulama became Babis or sympathizers, most remained united with the Shahs against the "apostate" Babis. In the 1860s, Baha'ullah, the half-brother of the Bab's successor, declared himself the future prophet predicted by the Bab and created the Baha'i religion, followed by the great majority of Babis and new converts. Both Babis and Baha'i branches of the religion called for reform in human relations, but the Baha'is were more influenced by Western liberal ideas. Significantly for the history of nonviolent resistance, the Baha'is—even though their renunciation of violence was generally quietist, calling for acceptance of the powers that be—often advocated major constitutional and judicial reforms.

The Babis and Baha'is influenced several Iranian non-Babi reformers, who included men with ambassadorial or ministerial posts like Mirza Hosain Khan and Malkum Khan, the latter having had close contact with Babis in the Ottoman Empire. However, the Babis were officially seen as heretics since Muslims saw Muhammad as the last Prophet, and rejected later prophetic claims. This put Babis and Baha'is in a worse position in Muslim countries than Christians, Jews, and Zoroastrians who were accepted as "people of the book" whose prophets preceded Muhammad. There were several anti-Baha'i pogroms in Qajar times, often instigated by leading ulama.

Nevertheless, hundreds of thousands of Iranians dissatisfied with the authoritarian rule of the Qajars joined these religious movements, which helped open their minds to reformist and liberal ideas. As a result, both movements and Azali Babis in particular—often without revealing their religious affiliation—played a leading role in the 1906 constitutional campaign and influenced other non-Babi participants.[2]

Developments Leading to the Tobacco Protest of 1891–1892

Before the nationwide tobacco protest of 1891–1892, there were several lesser events that contributed to making Iranians believe that resistance, including nonviolent resistance, against selfish and autocratic rulers and foreign domination might be effective. There were numerous local protests, often involving women and minorities, against arbitrary acts by provincial governors or outrageous price rises. Traditional forms of nonviolent protest included taking *bast* (inviolable refuge) in shrines, mosques, and foreign legations; closing bazaars; boycotting foreign goods; and threatening, though not carrying out, violent acts. From 1830 on, groups of merchants and craftspeople in the urban bazaars petitioned the Shah or governors to reduce competition from foreign importers, which by treaty paid low tariffs and were exempt from some local taxes. These petition protests usually failed as, given its long-term treaties, there was little the government could do short of risking war.

Sometimes successful, however, were local protest demonstrations, often by women, against high prices on basic foods, including flour and bread. It was widely believed that Islam integrated justice as a basic value (or equity), implying fair treatment, including economic fairness, for all. As a result, protests were often couched in demands for justice.[3]

In the early 1870s, nonviolent opposition resulted in canceling a huge concession giving control of nearly all Iran's economy to a British subject, Baron Julius de Reuter (of news agency fame). In return for payments to the treaty's negotiators and small royalties to the state, Reuter attained the rights to build all railways and streetcars, to create a national bank, to exploit most minerals, and to build other industrial and agricultural enterprises. A reformist Iranian prime minister, Mirza Hosain Khan, promoted this concession as a shortcut to modernization, but it was opposed by the Russians excluded from the deal, by many merchants, by a faction at court led by the Shah's favorite wife, and by the small group of progressive nationalists. Their influence was strong enough to force the dismissal of the Mirza Hosain Khan and to get the Shah to delay railroad construction (a condition of the concession) so that he had an excuse to cancel the concession.

Subsequently, however, in 1888, the British government used Reuter's claim for compensation for this cancellation to force the Shah, Naser al-Din Qajar (r. 1848–1896), to reinstate parts of the agreement. Granting the British-owned Imperial Bank of Persia the exclusive rights to issue bank notes for all monetary transactions in Iran was immediately unpopular with local merchants who lost out to the British monopoly on paper money. Even more resented was the concession granting a British company a monopoly on internal and external commerce in tobacco products throughout Iran. Merchants opposed it as taking away their profits in tobacco trading; ordinary Iranians opposed giving so much control over their lives and livelihoods to foreigners; ulama disliked the increased presence of foreigners and their ways such as gender mixing, odd dress, and modern non-Islamic ideas; and many saw it as a step toward foreign control of Iran.

Several strands of opposition began to coalesce. The Shah, after dismissing Mirza Hosain Khan, gave up all attempts at reform and discouraged education and foreign travel by Iranians. The modernizing reformers—some of whom had favored Reuter's concession, which was opposed by most merchants—now realigned themselves. Some reformers remained in the government and operated behind the scenes. Others, often living abroad, published articles or treatises favoring representative government and the rule of law and denouncing foreign concessions.

Some leading ulama responded to their followers' grievances and opposed increasing control of Iranian policies by foreign "unbelievers." One of the critics of the Shah was Sayyed Jamal al-Din Asadabadi, known as Afghani but a born Iranian. In 1890, he had to take refuge in a shrine near Tehran where he continued to preach against growing foreign control and concessions, and taught followers such means as distributing pamphlets and forming secret organizations. Eventually, the Shah violated Afghani's sanctuary and marched him to exile in Ottoman Iraq in 1891. Despite his exile, Afghani remained a powerful voice for resistance to the Shah's policies.[4]

The Tobacco Movement of 1891–1892

In 1890 following Naser al-Din Shah's third trip to Europe, a concession granting all economic control over the growing, sale, and export of Iranian tobacco products was given, for a very low price, to a British subject. The concession was kept secret until, in late 1890, the Istanbul-based Persian-language newspaper *Akhtar* published a strong critique. Unlike most other concessions, this one covered a product already widely grown and used in Iran; hence, it was bound to arouse widespread opposition among merchants, shopkeepers, and landholders as well as ordinary people. Both men and women in Iran widely used tobacco in the form of water pipes and it was also an export crop. Soon the Shiite clergy, who had close familial and ideological ties to the bazaar classes, joined in an opposition that was strengthened by their outrage against the fact that a foreign Christian company now controlled Iran's tobacco trade.

Protests occurred in various cities once the tobacco company agents began to arrive and post deadlines for the sale of all tobacco to the company. The protests took mainly nonviolent forms, such as mass demonstrations that were often addressed by clerical leaders and refusal to sell tobacco. The first major protest occurred in Shiraz, where a leading cleric preached noncompliance with the order to sell tobacco to the company. In reprisal, the government expelled the movement's main religious leader, who went to Ottoman Iraq where he met with Afghani. Subsequently, Afghani wrote to the Iraq-based leading Shia cleric Hajj Mirza Hasan Shirazi, asking him to denounce the Shah and his sale of Iran to Europeans. At this time, Shirazi responded by writing privately to the Shah, repeating many of Afghani's points against the proliferation of concessions to foreigners.

Meanwhile mass demonstrations continued to take place in Iran. The Tabriz protests, where some participants threatened to kill company and royal representatives, were so threatening that the government decided to suspend the tobacco concession there. In Mashdad too, a few protesters threatened to kill company representatives. However, elsewhere in Isfahan, Tehran, and several other cities, the spreading mass protests were organized nonviolently, appealing for top ulama to stand against the concession.

The final step was a triumph of nonviolent resistance. A fatwa (decree) was issued in the name of the Iranian leader of the Shia community, Shirazi, based in Iraq, which he confirmed when his authorship was questioned. It said that all use of and commerce in tobacco, as long as the concession existed, was against the will of the Hidden Imam. The aim of the boycott was not to stop smoking as such, but to force the cancellation of the tobacco concession. This fatwa ensured the widening of civil disobedience. The boycott of tobacco began first in Isfahan by some of its leading clerics and quickly spread to major cities and towns all over Iran. In December 1891, the movement culminated in an amazingly successful national boycott on the sale and use of tobacco, observed even by the Shah's wives and non-Muslims. Those who reported this event were unanimous in saying that nobody in Iran could be seen smoking or buying or selling tobacco in this period.

Faced with the people's unity and an unprecedented level of compliance with the boycott, the government tried to end the company's internal monopoly while leaving unchanged its monopoly on tobacco exports. A mass demonstration to protest this in Tehran, in which several people were killed by government fire, was followed by even more massive nonviolent protests. This pressure forced the government to cancel the entire tobacco concession, despite its being saddled with a large debt for extortionate repayment to the tobacco company for claimed expenses.

This struggle suggested that victories against the autocratic government, even with foreign backers, might be won with little or no violence if merchants, ulama, elite and intellectual reformers, and ordinary people worked together with a single and specific goal in mind. While some violent incidents broke out, mainly in Tabriz and Mashhad, the movement remained predominantly nonviolent. The issue of ethnic groups and minorities was not important in the movement, except to the extent that non-Muslims were seen to observe the Islamically defined tobacco boycott.

One long-term impact of the tobacco movement was in originating a tactical and strategic alliance between some of the nascent group of Iranian modernizers. These included several Babis, secularists, and nationalists, with a large number of merchants threatened by Western economic domination, and a section of the ulama that disliked the growth of Western Christian and imperial control in Iran. This alliance was to reappear in the 1905–1911 revolution. The movement also pioneered tactics that were used again during the constitutional revolution: leaflets, mass demonstrations, and telegraph contact between Iranian cities and between Iran and the Shiite shrine cities in Iraq.

For a few years after the tobacco movement, the state managed to buy off some of the ulama with subsidies and by halting foreign concessions. However, the continuing underlying problems of autocracy in collusion with imperialism meant that civil resistance, now inspired by the confidence and skills gained from the successful tobacco movement, was bound to reappear in even larger form and with more radical demands in the coming years.

Background of the 1905–1911 Constitutional Revolution

Between 1892 and 1905, discontent with the government grew. After a follower of Afghani assassinated Naser al-Din in 1896, Muzaffar al-Din (r. 1896–1907) was a weak Shah who instituted few reforms. Instead, he incurred large loans from Russia, used mainly to finance his extravagant European trips, and put Iranian customs under the control of an unpopular Belgian. Secret societies that involved reformers but also appealed to religious leaders formed and worked against Iran's autocracy and in favor of reform. Japanese victories in the Russo-Japanese War and the Russian Revolution of 1905, which granted a representative parliament, gave further impetus both to revolt and to parliamentary constitutional ideas in Iran.

In addition, a number of Iranian governmental figures and intellectuals proposed major reforms in governance. Their ideas influenced Iranians and prepared them for popular civil disobedience actions and revolt against autocratic government and foreign domination. Mirza Fath Ali Akhundzadeh (1812–1878) wrote plays, essays, and treatises against Iran's misgovernment, corrupt clergy, and the mistreatment of women that became known to many literate Iranians in Iran and the Caucasus. Mirza Aqa Khan Kermani (1853–1896) contributed to *Akhtar,* which was well known among literate Iranians in Istanbul and Iran. His writings were strongly critical of Iran's socioeconomic conditions, elites, and clergy. Mirza Malkum Khan (1833–1908), who created a Freemason-style group in Tehran, published in London a Persian-language newspaper, *Qanun,* which was smuggled regularly into Iran. It advocated the rule of law and representative government and attacked Iran's rulers. Afghani (1838–1897) advocated modernizing Muslim countries to combat British imperialism. He was influential in Egypt where his charismatic personality and ideas attracted an important group of young reformers. In Paris, in 1883–1884 he coedited a pan-Islamic newspaper distributed free throughout the Muslim world, and taught oppositionists in Iran such means as organizing secret societies and oppositional leaflets, making a significant contribution to the tobacco movement. Abd al-Rahim Talebof (1834–1911) wrote books in simple language that advocated secular reforms in education, government, and law. And finally, Zain al-abedin Maragheh'i, a merchant who lived mostly outside Iran, wrote the fictional *Travelbook of Ibrahim Beig,* bitterly critical of Iranian conditions, which was widely read, including in Iranian secret societies.

Thinkers such as these were influential among literate Iranians who were dissatisfied with Iran's economic poverty and backwardness and its subservience to Russia and Britain. Furthermore, the prior and continuing influence of religious dissidents, including Azali Babis, Baha'is, and reformist clerics, added to the receptivity of many Iranians toward secular reformers.

Also influential before and during the revolution were Iranian workers who migrated, usually temporarily, to the Russian Caucasus. While abroad they came in contact with trade unions and social democrats and, hence, were introduced to secular activism for reform or revolution.

Before the constitutional revolution, several secret and open reform-oriented political and cultural societies were formed in various cities. Prominent merchants founded societies to counter increasing European control of the country. In Tehran, they included non-Muslim Zoroastrian and Armenian merchants who helped finance new schools and a public library. Also in Tehran a group of liberal intellectuals, including a few in the government, formed the Society of Learning in 1897–1898. They helped found the National Library in 1904. Tehran reformers founded several schools while elite women set up the first girls' schools.

Azali Babis were prominent in such societies, including Mirza Aqa Khan Kermani and Shaikh Ahmad Rudi in Kerman. In later decades, these included the preachers Malek al Motakallemin and Sayyed Jamal al-Din Va'ez who was a Babi-influenced freethinker based in Isfahan. These two were prominent in the Islamic Society, which asked Iranians to boycott foreign goods and buy only goods produced in Iran. They later went to Tehran and were among the most prominent preachers early in the revolution adapting Islam to democratic constitutionalism, taking part in the founding meeting of the Revolutionary Committee, writing *The True Dream* (a book excoriating current conditions and proposing an ideal future), and, finally, meeting their deaths in the 1908 coup d'etat.

In Tabriz young intellectuals, influenced by Western liberal writings and Caucasian social democratic ideas, founded a political society. They included Sayyed Hasan Taqizadeh who later rose to prominence as a social democratic leader. The modern school that they established was closed by orthodox clerics, but they went on to set up a bookstore selling modern books and, for a year, published a weekly journal whose readership extended to Tehran.

In 1902–1903 nonviolent protests began, as several secret societies became active in Tehran and elsewhere and distributed antigovernmental leaflets, called "night letters" because they were handed out during the night. A revived and powerful movement of ulama, courtiers, *bazaaris,* and secular progressives forced the dismissal in 1903 of Prime Minister Amin al-Soltan, who was blamed for the loans and concessions that were increasing Russian control over Iran.

The Shah appointed a reactionary relative, Ain al-Dauleh, as premier but protests continued against high prices, focusing on the Belgian official in charge of customs and the treasury. In May 1904, fifty-seven intellectuals linked to the National Library held a secret meeting where they established the Revolutionary Committee. Most attending agreed that the despotic government should be replaced by a more democratic one. Although the meeting was addressed by two Babi preachers and several members were Babis, they agreed not to attend any non-Islamic meetings that opponents could use as a pretext to attack them.[5]

Another secret society, the Secret Anjoman, formed in February 1905 and was supported by progressive clerics. One member invoked the model of the 1905 Russian Revolution. The Secret Anjoman's first published statement demanded a *majles* (parliament) and laws to curb the power of governmental ministers and the ulama.[6] Secret societies grew and educated their members and others by reading and disseminating critical literature, including the *Travelbook of Ibrahim Beig* and *The True Dream*. It added to the discontent that critical Persian newspapers published abroad were now more easily available in Iran than under Naser al-Din.

Some, especially in the secret societies, began to plan action to install constitutional government. The Russo-Japanese War of 1904–1905 and the Russian Revolution of 1905 strengthened revolutionary sentiment. At the same time, Iranians saw an opportunity as the Russian state, occupied with war and revolution, would be unable to intervene in a movement that aimed at lessening Russian power in Iran. Additionally, the sight of the only Asian constitutional power defeating the main European nonconstitutional power made many Iranians see constitutions as a secret of strength.

The 1905–1911 Revolution

The Iranian revolution of 1905–1911, sometimes called the constitutional revolution, took place in two major stages. In the first stage (from 1905 to 1907), the opposition, using overwhelmingly nonviolent means, succeeded in establishing a constitution and *majles*. Mozaffar al-Din Shah died in 1907, and the next Shah, Mohammad Ali (r. 1907–1909), dissolved the *majles* and reoccupied Iran by force. Mohammad Ali was deposed through violent struggle and constitutional rule was restored, but the revolution was ultimately suppressed by Russian and British military intervention in 1911.

The revolution is often dated from December 1905, when Tehran's governor *bastinadoed* (beat the feet) of merchants he said were overcharging for sugar. As happened during the tobacco movement, the violence backfired against the government. A large group of *mollas* (a general term for mostly low-ranking clergy) and *bazaaris* took *bast* (sanctuary) in

Tehran's royal mosque. When government forces violated their sanctuary and dispersed them, they went to a nearby shrine and formulated demands for the Shah. Their numbers reached over 2,000. Their key demand was for a representative *adalatkhaneh* (house of justice), a kind of higher court representing various classes whose duties, mostly judicial, were not spelled out. This demand was a compromise between the traditional clergy, not yet ready to demand a constitution, and the constitutionalists. The *bastis* refused to disperse and bazaar strikes continued for a month, backed by ongoing popular nonviolent demonstrations. Under such pressure the Shah gave in. In January 1906, he agreed to the *adalatkhaneh* and dismissed the governor of Tehran, which the protesters had also demanded.

The Shah, however, took no steps to create the *adalatkhaneh*. Instead, the government exiled nationalist leaders, including Sayyed Jamal al-Din Va'ez, to distant cities. Several oppositionists again took sanctuary in Tehran's Friday mosque. When theology students tried to free an arrested preacher, a government officer killed a young theology student.[7] Theology students then marched to commemorate this martyr and soldiers killed over 100 people. More oppositionists came to the Friday mosque and some cried "Long Live the Nation of Iran," which joined the more religious slogans. After this, the group moved en masse to take *bast* in Qom in July 1906. Revolutionaries used these mass *basts* to educate people about constitutional government and human rights.

In July, after getting permission from the British chargé d'affaires, a crowd, which by August reached 14,000 *bazaaris,* took *bast* in the British legation in Tehran. As a result, business was brought to a standstill. By now the *bast* had become a general strike, as almost a third of Tehran's commercial labor force was involved. Thousands of supportive women demonstrated outside the legation. In the evenings, the crowd heard the story of Imam Husain ibn Ali's killing at Karbala and identified with him.[8]

The mass participation of guild members, students, and radical intellectuals of the secret societies accelerated the formulation of new demands backed by ongoing political education of ordinary Iranians in public spaces through sermons, open discussions, and free exchanges of ideas about political rights and representation. Now the protesters demanded the dismissal of the prime minister and the establishment of a *majles* and discussed a constitution. The continuing massive protest, the failure of efforts to buy off its more conservative supporters, and defections within the government meant the Shah had to give in. In late July, the Shah dismissed the premier and accepted the *majles*. The two sides reached a final agreement on August 9, 1906, calling for a national consultative assembly, *majles,* to be elected right away.

Besides religious dissidents, secularists, and progressive clergy, the trade guilds were crucial to this success. The guilds organized and financed the British legation *bast* and gained the right of major guild representation in the first *majles*. As occurred in the 1979 revolution, the heterogeneous nature of the revolutionary coalition brought further internal struggles.

The democratically organized and participatory nonviolent movement with its liberal and constitutional demands had finally won for itself an institutionalized space to turn its ideas into laws and practice. The first *majles* was quickly elected by a six-class system that gave great representation to the guilds. The first election by six "estates" ironically turned out to be more democratic in outcome than the subsequent universal male suffrage elections, which in practice resulted in landlord and elite domination, via intimidation of peasants.

The *majles* opened in October 1906 and assigned a committee to write a Fundamental Law, which the Shah signed when he was mortally ill in December 1906. In 1907 his successor, Mohammad Ali Shah, signed a longer Supplementary Law. These two laws formed the Iranian Constitution until 1979. Largely modeled on the Belgian constitution, it created a constitutional monarchy in which real power was supposed to lie with the elected *majles*. Equality before the law and personal rights and freedoms were guaranteed, subject to a few limits, despite objections by some ulama that minority religions should not have equal status with Islam.

The 1906 electoral law called for the formation of anjomans (councils) to monitor *majles* elections. In several cities, these anjomans remained in session by popular demand and took on new responsibilities, chiefly directed at defending democratic control of central and local governments. A 1907 law gave anjomans taxing and spending authority that made them into governing bodies.

In addition, nonofficial councils, also called anjomans, were formed throughout Iran—a vivid reflection of the enduring civic activism awakened by the nonviolent movements in the preceding years.[9] Almost 200 anjomans were formed in Tehran and probably about 100 elsewhere. Iranians from outside Tehran living in Tehran also formed anjomans, the most important of which was the 3,000-member Tabriz anjoman of Tehran led by Taqizadeh. Most anjomans supported constitutional government and opposed Mohammad Ali Shah's attempts to limit it. Some anjomans represented trades, ethnicities including Iranian-Armenians, or religious groups such as Zoroastrians and Jews. There were a few conservative anjomans. The anjomans formed the main base of a new civil society.

A leading role in defending the revolution was played by the National Revolutionary Committee, which had ties to Caucasian social democrats and included several Azali Babis and editors of the proliferating revolutionary newspapers. Two members, the popular preachers Sayyed Jamal al-Din Va'ez and Malek al-Motakallemin, gave frequent fiery and educational speeches to enthusiastic crowds. There were several women's anjomans that worked to set up schools, hospitals, and orphanages and to further women's legal rights.

In January 1907 the new and autocratic Shah appointed as his prime minister Amin al-Soltan Atabak, who had been prime minister through the tobacco revolt and after until his 1903 ouster. This aroused conflicts in the pro-constitutional camp. He was assassinated in August 1907 by a member of a far left group, though there is also evidence that monarchists too were planning his assassination. On August 31, 1907, Britain and Russia signed an agreement settling their conflicts and dividing Iran into a northern zone, open to the Russians; a middle neutral zone; and a southeastern zone, open to the British. The agreement clearly violated Iranian sovereignty over its territory despite the British and Russian claims otherwise.

The Shah, after an unsuccessful attempt on his life, took steps that culminated in a coup d'etat. In June 1908 he demanded the arrest of several revolutionaries, the *majles* refused, and many informal civil society groups that gathered earlier in anjomans came to defend the *majles*. Taqizadeh, after heading a delegation to meet the Shah, counseled caution and convinced the anjomans to disperse. The Shah then ordered the Cossack Brigade, which formed in 1879, was led by Russian officers, and added to Russia's power in Iran, to fire on the *majles* and the adjoining mosque, a gathering place for constitutionalists. Among those killed were Azali Babi leaders, including Malek al-Mutakallemin and others. Two *mujtahid* leaders, Sayyid Abdullah Bihbahani and Mirza Sayyed Mohammad Tabataba'i, were arrested, beaten, and put under house arrest. Taqizadeh with several others took refuge in the British legation and then left temporarily for Britain.

The Shah sent tribal forces to restore autocracy throughout Iran. This led to counterviolence and guerrilla war, beginning with guerrilla insurgency in Tabriz, to restore constitutional rule. Constitutionalist forces from north and south took Tehran in July 1909. Mohammed Ali Shah sought refuge with the Russians before going into exile and his minor son was made Shah with a constitutionalist regent. A leading *mujtahid* who had backed the coup was hanged.

A second *majles* was elected, manifesting differences between the conservative moderates and the reforming nationalist Democratic Party, led by men like Taqizadeh.[10] To deal with financial bankruptcy, the *majles* invited a US financial expert, Morgan Shuster, to be treasurer-general. However, in November 1911, Russia with British support sent an ultimatum demanding Shuster's dismissal and Iran's agreement not to engage foreigners without Russian and British consent. The *majles* refused but, as Russian troops advanced, the regent and moderate cabinet (mainly composed of members of the Bakhtiari tribal confederation) dissolved the *majles*, accepted the ultimatum, and dismissed Shuster. This marked the end of the revolution, though the constitution theoretically continued, further *majleses* were elected, and some of the reforms authorizing more modern educational, judicial, and economic systems initiated later reform measures.

The revolution showed that great changes could be brought by nonviolent protests and demands. Even after the new Shah used violence, and British help to the opposition was superseded by Russo-British support for the dynasty, nonviolent protests nevertheless advanced reformist and democratic ideas. However, nonviolent action no longer sufficed to gain democratic ends in the face of armed reaction.[11]

Iranian Attitudes Toward Violence and Nonviolent Resistance in 1890–1911

The tobacco movement and the first years of the 1905–1911 revolution showed that mass nonviolent resistance could yield victories against both an autocratic regime and foreign powers. However, later Iranian writers have generally highlighted issues other than the means of struggle used during the 1890–1911 period or the relative roles of nonviolent and violent resistance. In the Pahlavi period (1925–1979), the most popular writer on the revolution was Ahmad Kasravi, a secular populist nationalist who glorified the role in the revolution of the Azeri guerrilla leaders—Sattar Khan and Baqer Khan—and accused the nonviolent social democrat, Sayyed Hasan Taqizadeh, of cowardice.

Marxist scholars and their followers emphasized the role of social democrats in the revolution, including both guerrilla acts and nonviolent ones. Armenians and Georgian natives of both Iran and of the Russian Caucasus had a major role in the revolution, again both violent and nonviolent, and some scholars have studied and emphasized these.[12] Mehdi Malekzadeh, a scholar of Babi origin, wrote a book that gives due weight to Babi revolutionaries though he does not name them as such.[13] The great British Orientalist, Edward G. Browne, published a book on the revolution in order to arouse British subjects against their own government's support for Russian policies after 1907. He also stressed the role of nonviolent protests.[14]

Some recent scholars have traced women's activities in the revolution. While some women did pretend to be men in order to join the guerrillas, nearly all women's other activities were nonviolent, from forming committees to raising money for national causes to writing newspaper articles and publishing the first women's newspaper.[15] Recently, some scholars of Baha'ism have argued that one reason the Baha'is refrained from playing a more visible role in the revolution was so as not to taint the movement in the eyes of conservative Muslims and clerics and thereby undermine its unity.[16]

In the post-1979 period, defenses of the clergy, including attributing to them all advances achieved in the 1890–1911 period, have become common and censorship of views disliked by the ruling elite is even stronger than it was in Pahlavi times.

Today, when many Iranians want to encourage the use of nonviolent tactics in movements against the clerical and military regime, some Iranians emphasize the importance of nonviolent actions in the successes achieved in the 1890–1911 movements. This view has been expressed more in speeches than in treatises. Some writers contend that both the tobacco protest and the 1905–1911 revolution were overwhelmingly nonviolent and that their achievements were gained by nonviolent means. Most scholars would consider this an exaggeration, although certainly a great deal was achieved by nonviolent means, and these past nonviolent experiences constitute an important historical force within "receding and returning waves" of protracted social and political revolutions that Iran experienced ever since.[17]

The Heritage of Resistance

The resistance movements of 1890–1911 had a strong impact on national consciousness and collective identities. During the 1905–1911 revolution participants appealed to both Iran and Islam, but the growth of Iranian nationalist ideas during the 1890–1911 period greatly increased many Iranians' national identification. Despite the Islamic ideology of the current regime during the Iran-Iraq War (1980–1988) and after, it has had to appeal largely to the Iranian identity that was first put forward in 1890–1911. The impact of civil resistance during 1890–1911 on subsequent nationalist strategies is ambiguous. Certain leaders, such as Taqizadeh, renounced popular struggle in favor of backing the rise to power of Reza Shah Pahlavi, crowned in 1925. They saw a strong, unifying military leader as necessary to counter the power of foreign countries, especially Britain. Reza Shah suppressed popular movements and nomadic tribes. When the World War II Allies forced him to abdicate in 1941, popular movements ranging from left to right reappeared and most backed Mohammad Mossadeq's movement for the nationalization of oil. This movement used some of the tactics and strategy begun in 1890–1911, such as general strikes and boycotts, and involved more Iranians. Some participants also used violent means, including assassination, but Mosaddeq's successes should be attributed to the pressure of mass tactics. However, as in 1911, the popular movement was suppressed because of foreign intervention—in this case the 1953 coup against Mosaddeq executed by the United States with British support.

Leaders who advocated violent tactics have retained an honored place in Iranian national consciousness, including Afghani, Mirza Aqa Khan Kermani,

Mirza Reza (the assassin of Naser al-Din), and others. A number of histories and historical novels perpetuated such views. Even more striking is the almost universal valorization of periods in Iran's past when kings created large empires via conquest. There are competing Islamic and Marxist discourses, but these also often glorify men who made use of violent means and supported many elements of Iranian nationalism.

Such ideas came to include Islamic conquerors, like some Safavid rulers and the eighteenth-century conqueror, Nader Shah Afshar. Antimonarchist and anti-imperialist countertheories often invoked violent revolts against foreign tyrants. The influential newspaper *Kaveh* (1916–1922) founded in Berlin by Taqizadeh and other Iranian progressives took the name of a legendary rebel from the *Shahnameh,* Kaveh the blacksmith. And Islamic thinkers often justified defensive holy wars against attackers, including the early-nineteenth-century Russians.

The heroes of such narratives were always men; women's roles tended to be validated only as martyrs and sufferers from religious oppression or as models of obedience. The latter is the image of Fatima, the wife of Imam Ali, invoked among others by the "revolutionary" Muslim, Ali Shariati. When the Islamic Republic needed women's help in the Iran-Iraq War, its leaders invoked Imam Husain's sister, Zainab, as a symbol of resistance to her Sunni captors. The growing nonviolent women's movement of the past two decades, supported by diaspora Iranians, has revived heroic stories of women's nonviolent resistance. They refer, without noting their religion, to the Babi poet and preacher Tahereh and the Baha'i writer of the constitutional period Tayireh as well as to the early-twentieth-century feminist Sediqeh Daulatabadi and the socialist secular Qajar princess Taj al-Saltaneh.

The Iranian revolution of 1978–1979 and the oppositional Green Movement of 2009–2010 revived and broadened the massive nonviolent means employed in the 1890–1911 period. In 1977 Shah Mohammad Reza, partly under US pressure, lessened restrictions on speech, and prominent intellectuals and others signed open letters and held poetry readings demanding reforms. In 1978 a series of escalating mass protests that occurred almost automatically at standard Shiite forty-day intervals weakened the government, which was further undermined by its violent repression of one demonstration and especially by a general strike that included the oil industry. Just as earlier movements made intensive use of the telegraph, so this one utilized cassette tapes of Ayatollah Khomeini, the leader of the religious opposition in exile in France. The government was overthrown with little use of violence in February 1979.

The Green Movement, in protest at the fraudulent vote count in the June 2009 presidential election, like earlier movements combined people of many different classes and viewpoints. It operated through massive protests, overwhelmingly nonviolent, in several cities. Like earlier movements it has used the latest means of communication to reach and mobilize supporters—in the 1890–1911 movements, the telegraph and mimeographed leaflets; in 1978–1979, Khomeini's cassette tapes; and currently, the Internet, including blogs, photographs and videos, text messages, and tweets. To date it has not brought important parts of the military to its side, nor does it have a unified program or clear leader, though some movements have succeeded without a single leader.

From 1890 to the present, many Iranians have seen nonviolent action as a tactical choice in certain situations rather than a philosophy. They have usually preferred nonviolent means of struggle when possible, given the population's inability to win against the armed forces in a violent struggle. With past experience of traditional nonviolent means like boycotts, sanctuary, and general strikes, and successes in forcing concessions even from powerful opponents, Iran has experienced several predominantly nonviolent protests and revolts. When government forces have resorted to violence, however, some opponents have tended to adopt violent means, in 1908–1911 on a large scale and in other movements on a smaller scale. The current Green Movement has seen more insistence on nonviolent resistance than previous movements because of its better understanding of how strategic nonviolent tactics can work for the advantage of the seemingly powerless. Hence, today's movements appear to have learned important lessons from the past resistance.

Notes

1. *Shahnameh,* or "The Book of Kings," is the Persian-language epic written by Hakim Abul Quasim Ferdowsi Tusi in the late tenth century that chronicles Persian history and often its mythical past.

2. See Abbas Amanat, *Resurrection and Renewal: The Making of the Babi Movement in Iran, 1844–1850* (Ithaca: Cornell University Press); and Juan R. I. Cole, *Modernity and the Millennium: The Genesis of the Baha'i Faith in the Middle East* (New York: Columbia University Press, 1998). On the influence of Babis in the revolution, see Abbas Amanat, "Memory and Amnesia in the Historiography of the Constitutional Revolution," in *Iran in the 20th Century: Historiography and Political Culture,* ed. Touraj Atabaki (London: I. B. Tauris, 2009). See Vanessa Martin, *The Qajar Pact: Bargaining, Protest and the State in 19th-Century Persia* (London: I. B. Tauris, 2005).

3. See Martin, *The Qajar Pact.*

4. See Nikki R. Keddie, *Religion and Rebellion in Iran: The Tobacco Protest of 1891–1892* (London: Frank Cass, 1966); Nikki R. Keddie, *An Islamic Response to Imperialism: Political and Religious Writings of Sayyid Jamal ad-Din "Al-Afghani"* (Berkeley: University of California Press, 1983); Mangol Bayat, *Mysticism and Dissent: Socioreligious Thought in Qajar Iran* (Syracuse: Syracuse University Press, 1982); A. K. S. Lambton, *Qajar Persia: Eleven Studies* (London: I. B. Tauris, 1989).

5. Three of the nine-person core of the Revolutionary Committee were Azali Babis while one member was both a Baha'i and Muslim *mujtahid* (religious leader, nowadays usually called an ayatollah).

6. The immediate background to the revolution is well covered by Janet Afary, *The Iranian Constitutional Revolution, 1906–1911: Grassroots Democracy, Social Democracy, and the Origins of Feminism* (New York: Columbia University Press, 1996).

7. Gene Sharp, *The Politics of Nonviolent Action,* part 2: *The Methods of Nonviolent Action* (Boston: Porter Sargent, 1973), 208, writes that ordinary soldiers refused to fire on student Sayyid Husayn when he rushed the door, but an officer intervened personally.

8. Husain, the second son of Ali (Muhammad's cousin and son-in-law), was killed in the Battle of Karbala in 680 CE by the caliph's army. This martyrdom became a central event for the Shia community, which commemorated it annually.

9. In a few cases like Tabriz, the same anjoman played the official and popular roles.

10. Taqizadeh had to leave Iran after he was falsely accused of involvement in the 1910 assassination of the moderate clerical leader, Behbahani.

11. On the 1905–1911 revolution, see Afary, *Iranian Constitutional Revolution*; Mangol Bayat, *Iran's First Revolution: Shi'ism and the Constitutional Revolution of 1905–1909* (New York: Oxford University Press, 1991); and Vanessa Martin, *Islam and Modernism: The Iranian Revolution of 1906* (London: I. B. Tauris, 1989).

12. See Houri Berberien, *Armenians and the Constitutional Revolution, 1905–1911: The Love for Freedom Has No Fatherland* (Boulder: Westview Press, 2001).

13. The best brief presentation of populist and nationalist writers on the revolution is Muhammad Reza Afshari, "The Historians of the Constitutional Movement and the Making of the Iranian Populist Tradition," *International Journal of Middle East Studies* 25, no. 3 (1993): 477–494. E. G. Browne, *The Persian Revolution of 1905–1909* (Cambridge: Cambridge University Press, 1910); Mansour Bonakdarian, *Britain and the Iranian Constitutional Revolution of 1906–1911: Foreign Policy, Imperialism, and Dissent* (Syracuse: Syracuse University Press, 2006).

14. Browne, *The Persian Revolution*; Bonakdarian, *Britain and the Iranian Constitutional Revolution*.

15. On women in the revolution see Afary, *Iranian Constitutional Revolution*; and Mangol Bayat-Philipp, "Women and Revolution in Iran, 1905–1911," in *Women in the Muslim World,* ed. Lois Beck and Nikki Keddie (Cambridge: Harvard University Press, 1978).

16. See Cole, *Modernity and the Millennium*; and several chapters in *The Baha'is of Iran: Socio-Historical Studies,* ed. Dominic Parviz Brookshaw and Seena B. Fazel (London: Routledge, 2008).

17. Michael Fischer, "The Rhythmic Beat of the Revolution in Iran," *Cultural Anthropology* 25, no. 3 (August 2010): 497–543; Nader Hashemi and Danny Postel, eds., *The People Reloaded: The Green Movement and the Struggle for Iran's Future* (New York: Melville House, 2010).

9

Palestine:
Nonviolent Resistance in the
Struggle for Statehood, 1920s–2012

Mary Elizabeth King

A series of external interventions in Palestine around the time of World War I created what would become an acute and pernicious conflict. After the Ottoman Empire was divided into British and French spheres of influence, General Edmund Allenby militarily entered Palestine on December 9, 1917.[1] The League of Nations granted Britain the mandate for Palestine in 1922. Yet the most defining colonial intrusion was British foreign secretary Arthur James Lord Balfour's declaration in a November 2, 1917, letter to the leader of British Jewry, the banker Lionel Walter Lord Rothschild:

> His Majesty's Government view with favour the establishment in Palestine of a national home for the Jewish people, and will use their best endeavours to facilitate the achievement of this object, it being clearly understood that nothing shall be done which may prejudice the civil and religious rights of the existing non-Jewish communities in Palestine or the rights and political status enjoyed by Jews in any other country.

The idea of a restored Israel, with exiled Israelites returning to the Promised Land, appealed not only to the British government but to much of the West, thus planting the seeds, in David Gilmour's words, for "spectacular antagonism in Palestine through ignorance and disregard for its Arab inhabitants."[2]

Palestinian Resistance in the 1920s and 1930s

Six Palestine Arab Congresses gathered between 1919 and 1923 in opposition to Lord Balfour's pledge to the Zionists.[3] In Palestine, waves of protests broke out against its ratification[4] and opposed the separation of Palestine from what was then Greater Syria, an alliance considered by militant young Palestinians the best vehicle for independence.

During most of the 1920s, the Palestinian resistance was led by Haj Amin al-Husseini, the grand mufti (Sunni Muslim leader), and others in the often feuding Arab elites. Directed toward London and its support for the Zionist movement, it used nonviolent methods of persuasion and appeal. These included the simplest forms of protest and assertion, including assemblies, deputations, demonstrations, processions, declarations, and petitions. Continuing with these methods, the Palestinians added noncooperation to their repertoire in the form of social, economic, and electoral boycotts and resignation from jobs in the British colonial administration. They sustained protests against land grants to Zionists and escalated approaches of noncooperation as shops closed across the country. *Mukhtars* (village chiefs or mayors) refused to cooperate with government commissioners. As mosques offered prayers about the danger facing Palestine, villagers were encouraged not to pay tithes to a non-Muslim government. Those who sold land to Zionists or their brokers were excommunicated (i.e., denied access to Islamic sites).

Women were often at the forefront, as Palestinian collective nonviolent action sought abrogation of the Balfour Declaration, an end to the British mandate, and national independence.[5] Women protested against the eviction of peasants from farmland purchased by Zionist colonies and agents. In the late 1920s and early 1930s, women organized a silent procession to exhibit their disapproval of the mandate's policies, submitted statements to each diplomatic consulate, and sent protest telegrams to Queen Mary.[6]

Riots broke out on May 1, 1921, in Jaffa, the main port in Palestine. Yet generally speaking from 1920 to 1924, the Palestinian Arabs continued to apply political pressure on London and to stress that no elements of Palestinian society could cooperate with Britain while British policy was based on the Balfour language. They rejected all compromise proposals coming from London. A British colonel's contemporary account notes the "wonderful self-control and exemplary behaviour of the local [Palestinian] Christians and Arabs" in response to Lord Balfour's first and only trip to Palestine, in March and April 1925, to inaugurate the Hebrew University.[7] During the one-day strike, all Arab shops closed and Jerusalem's Arab newspapers were bordered with mourning black.[8] Nevertheless, political scientist Ann Mosely Lesch contends,

> The Arabs' attempts to influence British policy through delegations, political strikes, and election boycott appeared a failure by the mid-1920s. . . . As a result, the Arab movement began to split between those who felt that the best strategy would be to grasp any available lever of power in Palestine in order to influence policy, and those who held that total opposition and anomic violence would force the British into rethinking their policy.[9]

On September 24, 1928, Yom Kippur (the Jewish Day of Atonement), Jewish worshipers put up a partition at the outer wall of the temple in Jerusalem. Across Palestine, rumors spread that the great Jewish temple might be rebuilt on the sacred site of al-Aqsa mosque,[10] setting off spiraling events known as the uprisings of 1929[11] with hundreds of Jews and Palestinians killed and wounded.[12]

Palestinian nonviolent resistance both intensified and broadened in the 1930s. General strikes increased, as did Palestinian organizational capacity with the development of a far-reaching committee structure. Political parties evolved. When this disciplined nonviolent action failed to bring change, some groups turned to rural violence. In summer 1931, a Palestinian conference in Nablus responded to British assistance for Jewish defense not solely by discussing independence or boycotting imports, but by calling for their own defense organization and purchase of weapons.[13]

The patrician families of Jerusalem did not reject violence in principle; rather, they believed that making reasoned claims offered the best hope for a fair hearing from both Britain and the Zionists. Yet as a new generation of educated Palestinian nationalists gained influence, they disparaged the tools of protest and noncooperation chosen by the Jerusalem elite. A chief source of internal dissension was "disagreement over methods." Soraya Antonius writes, "Some leaders believed only force could attain the national goals. Others believed gradualism and diplomacy would be more effective."[14] It is clear in retrospect that, if the Palestinians' pleas and protests had been heeded, the option of armed struggle would have seemed less attractive.

Concepts of national interests or nationhood were unknown to the peasantry; the name "Palestine" had only recently replaced "Southern Syria." Absorbing shocks from successive losses caused by Jewish emigrés and British bureaucrats—both seeking jurisdiction over land considered by Muslims to be second in holiness only to Mecca and Medina—Palestinian peasants looked for solutions in Islam. The pathway to redemption and restoration would, they believed, be found in jihad, protecting the faith. Dispossessed and estranged farmers drifted to Old Haifa where Shaikh Izz al-Din al-Qassam was organizing secret armed cells. Qassam's model of guerrilla warfare through secret societies was followed in the mid- to late 1930s and continues into the present as a prototype of Islamic revivalist resistance. For evicted laborers, Islam, as interpreted by Qassam, became the starting place for the coming mass opposition, much of it violent.[15]

Strikes by Palestinians were frequent and, in 1936, possibly the longest in history occurred in Palestine. The *al-thawra al-kubra* (great revolt) of the Palestinians started with a general strike called at a nationalist conference in Nablus in April 1936. This initiated the last period of coherent, well-planned, and national nonviolent civil resistance until the 1987 intifada, a half century later.[16] National committees were quickly organized to coordinate a widespread effort to bring all economic activity to a total standstill.

The newly formed Arab Higher Committee demanded a halt to Jewish immigration, restrictions on land sales to Jews, and establishment of a national government accountable to a representative council—in other words, an independent Palestinian state. Several hundred veiled women marched in Gaza on April 25, 1936. With great speed, local committees of the national body were set up, each deciding its priorities although generally echoing the Arab Higher Committee's demands. The autonomy of these local committees contributed to the strike's resilience. As authorities locked up one area leader, another emerged. By the end of June, nearly all Palestinian businesses and transportation across the country had ground to a halt.

Britain responded with collective punishments, imposing fines, conducting mass arrests, and demolishing homes. Despite the detention of 2,598 Palestinians[17] and the imprisonment of some 400 leaders of strike committees,[18] the strike persisted. Guerrilla tactics became more evident, as underground Qassamite armed bands moved into the forefront.[19] They detonated railway lines, derailed two trains, blew up a bridge, obstructed roads, and sliced telephone wires. "Despite the success of the general strike in many parts of Palestine," Zachary Lockman concludes, "the nationalist movement's inability to make it [total] undermined its effectiveness."[20] Public fatigue set in, especially among Palestinian citrus grove owners, and the stevedores and boat owners at the Jaffa port.[21] On October 10, 1936, after 174 days—nearly six months—ostensibly at the behest of Arab monarchs, the Arab Higher Committee ended the strike that had nearly paralyzed the country.

After the strike ended, calm prevailed until a few weeks before the release of the British-appointed Peel Commission's report in July 1937, when leaked excerpts disclosed Lord Peel's intention to recommend the partition of Palestine. Rebellion recommenced.[22]

Following the assassination in Nazareth on September 26 of the acting district commissioner for Galilee, Lewis Andrews,[23] and his guards, the Arab Higher Committee was declared illegal, several leaders arrested and deported (the grand mufti fled, evading arrest), and its committees banned. Armed bands sabotaged transportation and communications by destroying train tracks, and gangs with weapons seized control of towns, collected taxes, and held kangaroo courts. By April 1938, more than 1,000 bellicose acts during a six-month period had been recorded, including fifty-five political murders and thirty-two attempted assassinations, as Palestinian insurgents killed other Palestinians that they considered traitors, including intellectuals, exacerbating kinship and other conflicts.[24]

The revised British policy, combining "appeasement" (abandoning partition) with "suppression," succeeded in putting down the rebellion after more than 1,000 deaths (mainly in the closing period).[25] The British government belatedly recognized, as the Palestinian Arabs had argued since

1917, that the situation created by London was unfeasible and irredeemable.[26] The general strike had been organized and nonviolent—its boycotts and noncooperation methods were models of disciplined implementation through local coordinating committees—but its restraint ultimately collapsed. Major turns to violence had occurred with the May 1921 riots and the 1929 uprisings, but the evidence suggests that these episodes were aberrant and not premeditated or planned, at least until the anarchic violence of 1938–1939.[27] Moreover, the British administration and leaders of the global Zionist movement disregarded the Palestinians' remarkable and more prevalent displays of restrained self-discipline, thereby strengthening those elements advocating violent resistance, including the forerunners of today's violent Islamic revivalist organizations.

Mythologies of Liberating Palestine Through Armed Struggle

On May 14, 1948, the Zionists proclaimed the state of Israel. The next day, when British forces withdrew, Egypt, Lebanon, Iraq, Syria, and Jordan invaded. Their forces outnumbered the Israelis, but were ill-equipped, poorly led, and disunited. When the armistice was signed in 1949, Israel controlled not just the 55 percent allocated by the UN partition plan but 78 percent of mandatory Palestine. The 1948 war had killed 6,000 of Palestine's Jews, 1 percent, but for the Palestinian Arabs was a catastrophe. The remaining quarter of the country—what became the West Bank of the Jordan River and the Gaza Strip—came under the control of Jordan and Egypt. The Arab state envisaged in the UN plan never materialized and approximately 750,000 Palestinian refugees (half the Palestinian population in 1948) fled their homes or property and suffered other losses during the fighting. Dispossessed, lacking the ability and tools to eke out a living in their new places of exile, they dispersed to the West Bank and Gaza or to Syria, Jordan, and Lebanon.

Palestinian refugees in the teeming camps of the 1950s could see that Arab unity had not protected their rights and were receptive to arguments for armed struggle, often promoted by the better educated and with encouragement from the Syrian government.[28] Palestinian guerrilla movements began to develop. Fateh was founded in 1957 and seized the initiative.[29] The Palestine Liberation Organization (PLO), then and now a front primarily composed of refugees, grew out of an Arab League meeting in Cairo in 1964. Its charter called for preparations for armed struggle by starting military training camps. In 1968, the PLO revised this charter, declaring "armed struggle is the only way to liberate Palestine." Almost unlimited support initially existed for the *fedayeen* (guerrillas, literally "self-sacrificers") as they began to form units in the refugee camps of Jordan, Lebanon, and Syria. Subsequently, Palestinians would carry out some of the twentieth century's most notorious attacks. Indeed, most of the PLO's operations were directed against civilians.[30] Decades of nonviolent means of struggle were repudiated, without any evidence that guerrilla methods could affect the underlying issues.

In June 1967, Israel conquered East Jerusalem, the West Bank, and the Gaza Strip—the remaining quarter of the land that the United Nations had allocated Palestinians in 1947—and placed the territories of the West Bank and Gaza under military occupation. Sociologist Rosemary Sayigh comments, "Few peoples have been more systematically kept helpless in the face of attack than the Palestinians, and it is not surprising that the symbol of their resurgence after 1967 was the gun."[31]

In February 1969, Fateh took over the PLO and Yasser Arafat was elected chair. Banned by the Israelis, the PLO's main base until 1970 was in Jordan. It relocated to Beirut (until the Israeli invasion of 1982) and then to Tunis in remote North Africa, isolated from conceptual innovations and organizational changes that were developing inside the occupied territories. In addition, the Qassamite option and support for armed struggle became entrenched as a tendency in Palestinian polity.

Many Palestinians were captivated by stories of guerrilla resistance from the Algerian war for independence (Algerian guerrilla methods had been used in Fateh's mid-1960s raids[32]); the 1959 Cuban revolution, whose appeal lay in the fact that it was perceived not as a popular movement but as action triggered by twelve *commandantes* hidden in the Sierra Maestra[33]; and the French and US defeats in Indochina. Throughout the late 1960s and 1970s, works by Mao Tse-tung, Ernesto "Che" Guevara, Régis Debray, and Frantz Fanon were circulated. Palestinian philosopher Sari Nusseibeh recalled that, in the early 1980s, "Our students were in love with that business of the cleansing power of violence."[34] Nusseibeh contended, in contrast, that these armed struggles had little relevance to their situation, not least because the Palestinians had been disarmed after 1967.

Reassertion of the Validity of Nonviolent Action: The First Intifada of 1987

Inside the territories captured in 1967, Palestinians began to organize themselves. Unseen, an incipient nonviolent mass movement began to cohere, its target the ending of Israeli occupation. In 1969, the Palestinian Communist Party (PCP) broke the Israeli ban on political organizing. Numerically small, the PCP believed that long-range political goals, such as an independent state, could be achieved only through comparably long-term changes in the social structure. Over the next two decades, this decision would unleash organizing efforts by civilian groups (including many that identified with factions of the distant PLO).

In the 1970s, new political space opened with the emergence of community-based networks and civilian mobilization. In effect, creating a fledgling civil society—a sphere of public life where citizens could interact unreservedly and more or less without intrusion from the Israeli authorities—countless self-governing voluntary professional associations, student and faculty unions, women's committees, youth groups, and even a prisoners' movement evolved to fill voids created by military occupation as well as to oppose it. According to Mahdi Abd al-Hadi, head of the Palestinian Academic Society for the Study of International Affairs, an estimated 45,000 committees were in existence by 1987.[35]

By the 1980s, the exiles' guerrilla military strikes and sorties, and some clandestine operations inside the occupied territories, no longer held much allure for the residents of the Palestinian areas. This ambivalence about armed struggle was not based on moral abhorrence of violence, but arose from the reality that cross-border sorties or forays by combat squads brought Israeli reprisals and collective punishments to rain down on the residents in the territories.[36] The formation of thousands of committees and associations into grassroots networks of popular mobilization combined with other influences at work, such as the promotion of fresh ideas about how to struggle for rights, thus facilitating a reassertion of nonviolent methods.

In 1987, civil resistance reemerged, aimed at lifting the military occupation, and was called intifada. No appropriate term for "nonviolent" exists in Arabic or Hebrew. *Sumud* (steadfastness) had after 1967 been promoted inside the territories, the idea being that the perseverance required to persist with everyday life under belligerent circumstances and staying on the land is itself a form of resistance. *Sumud* offered a nonviolent option between accepting military occupation and choosing armed struggle.[37] The word *intifada* went further. Drawn from the verb *nafada,* suggesting recovering or recuperation, it also implies "shaking off," like shaking dirt from a rug. To Palestinian cultural anthropologist Ali Hussein Qleibo, intifada "connotes the removal of unnecessary elements; shaking off preexisting weaknesses."[38] The word *uprising*—the term chosen by English-speaking Palestinians—fails to convey the sense of sloughing off passivity. Intifada is one of the few Arabic words to enter the vocabulary of international politics.[39]

The first intifada of 1987 enlisted virtually all segments of the Palestinian population. It was not spontaneous as many perceived, but a mass unarmed mobilization resulting from a decades-long spread of knowledge about nonviolent strategies throughout Palestinian society. In contrast to the PLO's military doctrine and its rubric "all means of struggle," during the 1980s activist scholars were producing and translating writings that propounded political tools as more realistic than armed struggle for the disarmed Palestinians. Changes in political thought were led by some two dozen Palestinian organizer intellectuals who argued among other points that statehood could compensate for the losses of their ancestral lands and who proffered coexistence with Israel in return for citizenship in their own state.[40] Some writings advanced a penetrating recognition: Palestinian cooperation had in part allowed Israel's military occupation to persist and such obedience could be withdrawn.[41]

Among the generative forces for the 1987 intifada were a series of joint Israeli-Palestinian committees against the occupation that began working together in 1980 around East Jerusalem. These committees had by 1985 merged into the Committee Confronting the Iron Fist, which used banners, boycotts, documentation, denunciation, demonstrations, lobbying, marches, news releases, petitions, picketing, speeches, and vigils to exert pressure for lifting the occupation.[42] All posters, pickets, and news releases were written in Arabic, English, and Hebrew.

Once the intifada started, new Israeli peace groups proliferated.[43] Perhaps 40 percent of all Israeli solidarity activity with the intifada came from newly formed groups.[44] One of the properties of nonviolent action is its ability to cause divisions within the ranks of the target group.

Palestinian nonviolent action in the 1980s was more sophisticated than in the 1920s and 1930s. A new politics developed as an entire society under military occupation unified, based on changes in popular thinking about how to transform their situation, including the withdrawal of their own cooperation with the occupation. In the first month of the intifada, harmonized actions could be seen in disparate localities: civil disobedience, fasting, general and local strikes, marches, public prayers, renaming of streets and schools, resigning from jobs, ringing of church bells, and unfurling of flags. Palestinians employed more than 100 differentiated nonviolent methods from December 1987 to March 1990.

Within the first month of the intifada, Israel placed 200,000 Palestinians under curfew in the West Bank and Gaza, which rose to 1 million by December 1989. Noncooperation was able to continue despite reprisals and crackdowns thanks to hundreds of popular committees, often started and run by women, which sustained communities under curfew or on strike. With precedents from women's collective actions in 1929 and 1933, from December 1987 to March 1988 women alone held more than 100 demonstrations. Paradoxically, Israeli-imposed curfews, school closings, and closure of six universities in February 1988 helped to spread ideas about nonviolent struggle. As 14,500 students and professors were sent home to their villages and refugee camps, a baker sat with a physics professor or a student to plan distribution of bread—or to decide the next nonviolent action against the occupation.

A leadership collective remained clandestine to evade arrest. It consisted of representatives from the four main secular-nationalist factions in the occupied territories. Despite being called the Unified National Leadership Command, it did not command the population but rather coordinated actions. Local committees could make independent decisions. The Command encouraged shifting action centers from one location to another and sought to prevent fatigue by advocating varying nonviolent methods.

None of the Command's biweekly leaflets bade the destruction of Israel or death to Jews. Rather, they presented the Palestinian strategy as aiming at peace through negotiations and built on three political aims: (1) acceptance of Israel in its pre-1967 borders; (2) removal of Israeli authority from the occupied territories; and (3) establishment of a Palestinian state. The leaflets shed light on the uprising's internal strategic deliberations, including an eighteen-month-long debate on adopting "total" civil disobedience. The relationship between the Command inside the territories and the PLO in Tunis was fraught with disagreement because the PLO did not understand nonviolent strategies or civil disobedience.

Thousands of Israeli soldiers were on active duty in the territories, thus stone throwing by youths—far from being seen as evidence of the absence of weapons—aroused Israeli fears. This practice ultimately lessened the achievements of the uprising. Actual fatalities show how the thrown stones distorted Israeli perceptions. According to an Israel Defense Forces (IDF) spokesperson, in 1988–1991 Palestinians killed a total of twelve Israeli soldiers in the West Bank and Gaza while Israelis killed 706 Palestinian civilians.[45]

Groups in the Qassamite tradition, such as Hamas (the Islamic Resistance Movement), found a place within the circumference of the intifada. In September 1990, Fateh and Hamas signed a thirteen-point pact of honor. Hamas endorsed armed struggle and refusal to recognize Israel—stances contrary to the intifada's framework of nonviolent struggle and desire for negotiations with Israel. In the pact, however, Hamas softened its position to the lifting of Israel's military occupation, thereby reversing its position on partition of Palestine.

The Command survived four waves of arrests, but chagrin began to spread among Palestinians as Israeli officials eventually imprisoned or deported the specific activist intellectuals who had laid the groundwork for the uprising and steered it, and there appeared to be only bitter fruits from the exertions of nonviolent discipline. The consensus on nonviolent strategies eventually collapsed because of threefold opposition: it took years for the Israelis to recognize that the uprising had political rather than military goals; the PLO concerned itself with preventing a new leadership from arising in the territories; and international powers failed to seize the unparalleled openings for building peace presented in 1987–1990 (an exception being the 1991 Madrid peace conference).

When the Palestinians were successful and saw positive results, it coincided with the early two and a half years of the intifada, when they were at their most disciplined in applying nonviolent methods. The first intifada's achievements include the 1991 Madrid peace conference and the opening of political space for the 1993 Oslo Accords, notwithstanding the latter's subsequent invalidation by all parties to the conflict.

Palestinian resistance during the intifada, for the first time, succeeded in converting the occupation into an economic burden, as for example, documented by the independent Adva Center in Tel Aviv. Shlomo Swirski, the institute's head, advised an Israeli newspaper that although he could not speak definitively, he estimated that the occupation had cost Israel $100 billion over the preceding forty years. Israel could withstand such high costs because of external support and funding.[46]

In December 1988, Arafat formally and publicly declared Israel's right to exist and repudiated terrorism largely as a consequence of the 1987 intifada's civil resistance. Even so, it had not been until November 1988—eleven months after the initiation of the intifada—that the PLO publicly proposed the concept of a Palestinian state side by side with Israel. This compromise was a direct outcome of the changes in political thought manifested in the uprising inside the territories.

Palestinian Statehood Forged Through Armed or Nonviolent Resistance?

An author who has written widely on the theme of Palestinian armed struggle and nationhood is Yezid Sayigh, professor of Middle East studies at King's College, London. While conceding a significant symbolic role to armed struggle and acknowledging its centrality in PLO rhetoric even as late as the 1980s, he also points out that the practice has been problematic:

> If the PLO hoped to establish a democratic secular state for Arabs and Jews in Palestine, then bombings or dramatic raids (both basically indiscriminate) hardly reassured the Israelis of the PLO's intentions. Indeed, even when the PLO's political aims were more modest—such as setting up a separate Palestinian ministate (primarily) through international diplomacy—indiscriminate military action worked against Palestinian interests. It hardened Israeli resolve and alienated the very international parties whose pressure on Israel was considered crucial by the PLO. . . . The nature of Palestinian action (especially terrorism) tended to undermine, rather than reinforce, the PLO's political and moral message to Israel and the West.[47]

Furthermore, Sayigh suggests that, even in the 1970s in the occupied territories, *sumud* was a more relevant concept while, by the 1980s, "social and political organization—dubbed 'mass action'—was an important embodiment of national identity and will in these circumstances."[48]

Fateh, the largest faction in the PLO, had a symbolic importance and certain of its activists played a vital practical role in building diffuse community-based groups throughout East Jerusalem, the West Bank, and Gaza, in the prisoners' movement and among student and faculty organizations.[49] Yet Sayigh notes the PLO's "hostile disregard for strategies of nonviolent resistance." Instead, the mainstream PLO leadership took a "statist approach" that

> viewed the population as a target audience to be co-opted through the provision of services and public goods. It strove neither for social mobilization, in the sense of assisting local communities or social groups to gain collective control over resources, nor for transformation of social relations, but rather to construct an alternative framework (to Israel) for the exercise of political power.[50]

An evolution had occurred: Palestinian civilian organizations, instead of being consigned to be support for guerrillas, had come to form the bedrock for an unarmed movement.

A formative role in promoting the nonviolent strategies of this movement was played by a circle of activist intellectuals who, over a period of years and especially in the 1980s, redefined the concepts, symbols, and discourse of retributive armed struggle. For example, they substituted *independence* for *liberation*. They framed their quest in the context of international recognition of human rights, consolidated in the period after the 1975 Helsinki Accords, rather than what they regarded as the spent dogmas of armed insurrection. Even when the emerging civilian organizations were identified with factions—a feature of Palestinian life under occupation—membership was voluntary, nominal, heraldic, and associated with families. Recruits were neither conscripted nor press-ganged.

The resultant movement of movements created the capacity for the Palestinians to endure Israeli reprisals, particularly during the intifada's productive years (1987–1990), before Israel incarcerated or deported the very activist intellectuals who had helped bring about this new thinking. The nonviolent discipline broke down as the PLO took over the intifada in March 1990. Rebel armed groups reasserted themselves. Nonetheless, for nearly three years, Palestinian organizer intellectuals around East Jerusalem and Bir Zeit University in Ramallah succeeded in overcoming the nearly insuperable predicament of factional disunity while pressing for a "white revolution" of no bloodshed and coaching their compatriots to work for entitlements through nonviolent struggle.[51] This extended, multiyear process of building nonmilitary political capability can properly be regarded as foundational in constructing a Palestinian state.

The earlier monopolistic ideologies of armed struggle, rather than reconstructing societal structures and reconstituting the body politic, had left the Palestinians weakened and beholden to Arab state sponsorship. The 1987 intifada, its predecessor movements of the 1970s and 1980s, and the work by the activist intellectuals and popular committees cumulatively opened up Palestinian society and did more for coining a model of authentic democratic governance in the Arab world than any other force to date. Not only could military command structures of the guerrilla units not protect Palestinian communities from the repressive violence of military occupation, they could not generate democratic leaders. The leadership that emerged during the birth and life of the uprising was the most egalitarian and committed to democracy in the Arab world in the twentieth century. Moreover, residual knowledge of nonviolent action and the ability of citizens to withdraw their cooperation from corrupt or unjust governance are essential prerequisites for the Palestinian people in order for them to be able to restrain any rise of internal despotism in the future.

Continuation of Nonviolent Struggle into the Early Twenty-First Century

Mirroring the pattern of the 1920s and 1930s, a number of local, nonviolent Palestinian movements are at work with restraint and perseverance, pressing for protection against further losses of their land from the Israeli barrier now colloquially called "the wall." In April 2002, the Israeli government announced its plans for constructing "separation barriers," purportedly to prevent the infiltration into Israel of suicide bombers. Regarding these suicide bombings in the second, or so-called al-Aqsa, intifada that erupted in September 2000, former US colonel Robert L. Helvey contends,

> Because the Palestinian Authority failed to aggressively dissociate itself from these terrorist acts, Israeli public support for a negotiated homeland for Palestinians evaporated, and the international community began backing away from influencing restraint on Israeli settlement policies and Israel's violent occupation of the West Bank. . . . If the objective of these terrorists' attacks was to end Israeli occupation, one must question the wisdom of confronting Israel at its strongest point—military force.[52]

In contrast, a number of small, nonviolent movements are attempting to minimize the destructiveness of the wall being erected by Israel among their communities. These dramatic local mobilizations are articulate in repudiating armed struggle as the means to a limited end. Parts of the barrier consist of twenty-five-foot-high segments of concrete—more than twice the height of the Berlin Wall. The Israeli human rights monitoring organization B'Tselem adamantly maintains that the barrier's route "defies all security logic and appears politically motivated."[53] In challenging "the wall" the Palestinians garner the support of the international solidarity networks that had not been evident in the past and revive their governance of local committees—reminiscent of the Palestinian self-organization in 1936 during the first stage of the great revolt and in the 1987 intifada.

Often missed by the established news media, these nonviolent campaigns called "the intifada of the wall" are avidly covered by Israeli, Palestinian, and joint alternative media. Such local movements are adept at citizen journalism and electronic transnational activism. They consistently benefit from direct personal participation by Israeli sympathizers and allies, as well as the presence of international supporters. Rulings made by the Israeli high court in favor of these movements are often disregarded by the IDF, and the reaction of the Israeli authorities and international onlookers is negligible. The pattern persists of ignoring the Palestinians' nonviolent action while responding to violent episodes.

An exception is the attention paid by mainstream media to several international flotillas that have sought, beginning in June 2010, to bring relief supplies by sea to Gaza, home to 1.5 million Palestinians, two-thirds of them refugees. After Hamas won parliamentary elections in 2006, the United States and European Union tightened their restrictions on aid for Gaza while Israel restricted travel and commerce and constricted entry points into the Gaza Strip. In December 2008, to halt rocket fire from Gaza, Israel launched Operation Cast Lead, in which 1,400 Gazans and 13 Israelis died. Israel's continued blockage of Gaza faced increasing international criticism, which saw a European-led "Freedom Flotilla" attempt to challenge it regularly between 2010 and 2012. An Israeli military raid on a Turkish-flagged ship in June 2010 left nine foreign activists dead, and three months later a flotilla by Jews further internationalized Palestinian nonviolent struggle against Israeli's occupation. Aziz Dweik, a Hamas parliamentarian in the West Bank, noted the countervailing logic of nonviolent action as a form of power. He told the *Wall Street Journal,* "When we use violence, we help Israel win international support; the [2010] Gaza flotilla has done more for Gaza than 10,000 rockets."[54]

A former commander of the Al-Aqsa Martyrs' Brigade in Jenin, which falls within the Qassamite tradition, Zakaria al-Zubeidi, made a personal decision that nonviolent cultural resistance was preferable to armed struggle and became cofounder of an independent playhouse. Supported by private donations, the Freedom Theatre at the Jenin Refugee Camp uses the cultural tools of drama, giant puppets, and music. In September–October 2012 the theater sponsored its first Freedom Ride, in which a Freedom Bus traveled from Jenin to the south Hebron hills, traversing the entire West Bank. At each stop, trained actors from Jenin enacted extraordinary stories of everyday people coping under occupation, including home demolitions, land confiscation, army invasions, arbitrary arrests, and violence by Israeli settlers. Most of the freedom riders were international visitors, apart from actors and crew.

A Palestinian "Empty Stomach" campaign led by the Palestinian political prisoners in Israel uses hunger strikes to press Israeli officials and popularize demands. In contrast to the historical antecedents of Palestinian hunger strikes in Israeli prisons in 1970, 1976, 1980, 1984, and 1987, such fasts now draw worldwide attention in news reports, aided by Palestinian social media and greater interest in popular resistance as a result of the Arab Awakening that began in 2010. The exact impact of hunger strikes may be uncertain, although in 2012 conditions in Israeli prisons improved as a result.

With a goal of prevailing upon Israel to conform to international resolutions pertaining to the Palestinians and end the occupation, Palestinian civic organizations launched a Boycott Divestment Sanctions (BDS) campaign in 2005 noting the historic example of tertiary sanctions applied against the antiapartheid regime of South Africa. BDS has become a globally decentralized international campaign that seeks worldwide application of third-party sanctions against Israel with corporate disinvestment and boycotts.

The Palestinian Authority (PA) appears to be evolving in its stance and sometimes leans toward supporting popular civil resistance. The PA has launched some nonviolent campaigns, for example, boycotting of products from Israeli settlements. A successful bid to recognize Palestine as a nonmember observer state at the United Nations has not been solely limited to diplomatic efforts; it has involved enlisting local and international grassroots patronage.

Conclusion

The turmoil caused by the Balfour Declaration and the UN decision on partition has never subsided. Yet Zionists and others have long contradicted the plain, observable facts of the period after World War I, which show that the Palestinians were not irredeemably committed to violence. The same internal disagreements over methods among the Palestinian leadership that characterized the decade of the 1930s are relevant in the period after 1969; they were at work during the 1987 intifada and endure today.

If only posthumously it must be acknowledged that in any acute conflict, the nonviolent challengers can control only their own actions; they cannot succeed without changes taking place in the target group. The repeated failures of Britain and the Zionists to respond to the Palestinians' nonviolent sanctions of the 1920s and 1930s cannot be laid at the feet of the civil resisters. By autumn 1938, historian J. C. Hurewitz observes, "events taught the lesson that the use of violence as a political weapon produced results which otherwise appeared unobtainable."[55] It is also often the case that the nonviolent protagonists cannot productively pursue their claims for justice without successful outside, third-party assistance.

The development of a Palestinian capacity for self-governance owes less to notions of armed revolt than to the fledgling civil society built by the civilian movements of the 1980s, which laid the groundwork and infrastructure for an overwhelmingly unarmed 1987 uprising. The 1987 intifada provided the Palestinian people with experience and mass participation in a proto-democracy. It was guided by human rights discourses, self-governing community-based organizations could transmute themselves into popular committees and make survival possible despite heavy reprisals and curfews, and understanding of the power of noncooperation was widespread. Even though undermined and splintered when Arafat and the PLO returned from exile in Tunis in 1994, an emergent Palestinian civil society is a prerequisite for the evolution of coexistence and building peace in the eastern Mediterranean.

For more than two years beginning in 1987, Palestinians waged struggle against the occupation, refusing to use firearms against the Israeli soldiers and settlers in their midst, and they succeeded in applying the most cogent pressures to date to create a Palestinian state alongside Israel, with implied acceptance of the latter's permanence.

More than any other factor, Palestinian civil resistance has been decisive in creating the foundations for Palestinian democracy and statehood. Nonetheless, the historical record continues to reveal a paucity of efforts to strengthen the influence of Palestinians who advocated civil action as opposed to military strategies to preserve their way of life and establish their oft-promised state alongside the state of Israel.

As the centenary of the Balfour Declaration approaches, an opportunity presents itself for Britain to apologize formally for its actions that set in train a deadly conflict and for world powers to assure the emergence of a just and peaceful Palestinian state alongside the state of Israel.

Notes

This chapter draws on material in Mary Elizabeth King, *A Quiet Revolution: The First Palestinian Intifada and Nonviolent Resistance* (New York: Nation Books, 2007).

1. George MacMunn and Cyril Falls, *Military Operations, Egypt and Palestine: From the Outbreak of War with Germany to June 1917* (*History of the Great War*) (London: His Majesty's Stationery Office, 1928), 260–261.

2. David Gilmour, "The Unregarded Prophet: Lord Curzon and the Palestine Question," *Journal of Palestine Studies* 25, no. 3 (1996): 67.

3. Bernard Wasserstein notes them as follows: Haifa, Damascus, Haifa, Jerusalem, Nablus, and Jaffa. Bernard Wasserstein, *The British in Palestine: The Mandatory Government and the Arab-Jewish Conflict, 1917–1929* (London: Royal Historical Society, 1978), 57, 60, 94–95, 106, 120, 125. See A. W. Kayyali, *Palestine: A Modern History* (London: Third World Centre for Research and Publishing, n.d., ca. 1971), 60, 88, 99, 113, 119. The British government forbade the second congress planned for Jerusalem. Muhammad Y. Muslih, *The Origins of Palestinian Nationalism* (New York: Columbia University Press, 1988), 204–205.

4. The Allied powers ratified the declaration at San Remo on April 25, 1920.

5. Kayyali, *Palestine,* 168; Simona Sharoni, *Gender and the Israeli-Palestinian Conflict: The Politics of Women's Resistance* (Syracuse, NY: Syracuse Studies on Peace and Conflict Resolution, 1995), 59; Soraya Antonius, "Fighting on Two Fronts: Conversations with Palestinian Women," *Journal of Palestinian Studies* 8, no. 3 (1979): 26–27.

6. Matiel E. T. Mogannam, *The Arab Woman and the Palestine Problem* (London: Herbert Joseph, 1937), 69–76; Ellen Fleischman, *Jerusalem Women's Organizations During the British Mandate: 1920s–1930s,* monograph (East Jerusalem: Palestinian Academic Society for the Study of International Affairs, 1995), 26. See also Julie M. Peteet, *Gender in Crisis: Women and the Palestinian Resistance Movement* (New York: Columbia University Press, 1991), 50–51.

7. "Beyond showing their feelings by passing the day in prayer, with closed houses and places of business shrouded in black, and shunning the precincts of the new University, the Mohammedans made no hostile demonstration of any kind; and a similar attitude was taken by the Christian population." P. H. H. Massy, *Eastern Mediterranean Lands: Twenty Years of Life, Sport, and Travel* (London: George Routledge and Son, 1928), 70.

8. Philip Jones, *Britain and Palestine, 1914–1948: Archival Sources for the History of the British Mandate* (Oxford: Oxford University Press, 1979), 40; Blanche E. C. Dugdale, *Arthur James Balfour: First Earl of Balfour, K.G., O.M., F.R.S., 1906–30,* vol. 2 (London: Hutchinson, 1936), 365.

9. Ann Mosely Lesch, "The Palestine Arab Nationalist Movement Under the Mandate," in *The Politics of Palestinian Nationalism,* ed. William B. Quandt, Fuad Jabber, and Ann Mosely Lesch (Berkeley: University of California Press, 1973), 28.

10. Sami Hadawi, *Palestinian Rights and Losses in 1948: A Comprehensive Study* (London: Saqi Books, 1988), 37; Wasserstein, *British in Palestine,* 223.

11. Historian Yehoshua Porath cites the Western Wall conflict as marking the widening of the Palestine predicament from a local issue into a pan-Arab and Muslim question. Yehoshua Porath, *The Emergence of the Palestinian-Arab National Movement,* vol. 1: *1918–29* (London: Frank Cass, 1974), 258–273.

12. The British Parliamentary Commission of Inquiry on these events (the Shaw Report) judged the violence was not premeditated and raised concerns about British failure to protect Arab rights and about Jewish immigration exceeding the "absorptive capacity" of Palestine's economy. *Report of the Commission on Palestine Disturbances of August, 1929,* Parliamentary Papers, Cmd. 3530 (London: His Majesty's Stationery Office, March 1930).

13. Zvi Elpeleg, *The Grand Mufti: Haj Amin al-Husaini, Founder of the Palestinian National Movement* (London: Frank Cass, 1993), 30, 31. Kayyali, *Palestine,* 165.

14. Antonius, "Fighting on Two Fronts," 39.

15. Nels Johnson, *Islam and the Politics of Meaning in Palestinian Nationalism* (London: Kegan Paul, 1982), 56–58.

16. This is not to say there were no episodes of nonviolent struggle. Occasional national campaigns occurred, such as the Palestinian Land Day in 1976, and episodes of sustained local resistance such as the successful nonviolent defense of the village of Battir in 1948. See Jawad Botmeh, "Civil Resistance in Palestine: The Village of Battir in 1948" (master's thesis, Centre for Peace and Reconciliation Studies, Coventry University, 2006), http://www.preparingforpeace.org/pdfpapers /s2-JawadBotmeh.pdf, accessed November 4, 2012. In the 1960s, a nonviolent campaign was instituted against land confiscation for construction of Karmiel in Galilee, a city built according to an urban master plan. See Uri Davis, *Crossing the Border: An Autobiography of an Anti-Zionist Palestinian Jew* (London: Books and Books, 1995), 63–90. More research is needed on this period. See also as examples, Mazin Qumsiyeh, *Popular Resistance in Palestine: A History of Hope and Empowerment* (London: Pluto Press, 2010); and Andrew Rigby, *Palestinian Resistance and Nonviolence* (East Jerusalem: Palestinian Academic Society for the Study of International Affairs, 2010).

17. The figure of 2,598 detentions was given in Parliament, as cited by Barbara Kalkas, "The Revolt of 1936: A Chronicle of Events," in *The Transformation of Palestine: Essays on the Origin and Development of the Arab-Israeli Conflict,* ed. Ibrahim Abu-Lughod (Evanston: Northwestern University Press, 1971), 249–250.

18. Mogannam, *Arab Woman,* 305.

19. Shai Lachman, "Arab Rebellion and Terrorism in Palestine, 1929–39: The Case of Sheikh 'Izz al-Din al-Qassam and His Movement," in *Zionism and Arabism in Palestine and Israel,* ed. Elie Kedourie and Sylvia G. Haim (London: Frank Cass, 1982), 78.

20. Zachary Lockman, *Comrades and Enemies: Arabs and Jewish Workers in Palestine, 1906–1948* (Berkeley: University of California Press, 1996), 241.

21. Yehoshua Porath, *The Palestinian Arab National Movement: From Riots to Rebellion,* vol. 2: *1929–39* (London: Frank Cass, 1977), 212.

22. The Peel Commission's partition plan would have joined the Arab portion of Palestine with Trans-Jordan, putting it under the rule of King Abdullah.

23. Andrews was regarded as the ablest of the Palestine Service and he spoke Arabic and Hebrew. Christopher Sykes, *Orde Wingate* (London: Collins, 1959), 136. The Palestinian Arabs believed that he was expediting the transfer of Galilee to the Jews, as called for in the partition plan. Nevill Barbour, *Nisi Dominus: A Survey of the Palestine Controversy* (London: George G. Harrap, 1946; reprint, Beirut: Institute for Palestine Studies, 1969), 188–189. This was the first assassination of a British administrator by Palestinians. He was the most senior British official to have been slain in Palestine. Lesch, "Palestine Arab Nationalist Movement," 221.

24. Papers of Sir Charles Tegart, box 2, file 3, Centre of Middle Eastern Studies, St. Antony's College, Oxford, as cited by Martin Kolinsky, "The Collapse and Restoration of Public Security," in *Britain and the Middle East in the 1930s,* ed. Michael J. Cohen and Martin Kolinsky (New York: St. Martin's Press, 1992), 155.

25. Kolinsky reports 547 Jews and 494 Arabs were killed in three years. Kolinsky, "Collapse and Restoration," in ibid., 162. British official data suggest 5,000 may have been killed and 14,000 wounded. See Walid Khalidi, ed., *From Haven to Conquest: Readings in Zionism and the Palestine Problem Until 1948* (Beirut: Institute for Palestine Studies, 1971), appendix 4, 846–849.

26. *Palestine Royal Commission Report,* Cmd. 549 (London: His Majesty's Stationery Office, 1937), 136–140, 362.

27. Philip Mattar concludes that political violence in 1920, 1921, 1929, and 1933 did not constitute revolts, but "localized spontaneous riots." Philip Mattar, *The*

Mufti of Jerusalem: Al-Hajj Amin al-Husayni and the Palestinian National Movement (New York: Columbia University Press, 1988), 149.

28. William B. Quandt, "Political and Military Dimensions of Contemporary Palestinian Nationalism," in *The Politics of Palestinian Nationalism,* ed. William B. Quandt, Fuad Jabber, and Ann Mosely Lesch (Berkeley: University of California Press, 1973), 56.

29. Fateh is both a palindrome and acronym for Harakat al-Tahrir al-Filistiniyya or Palestinian Liberation Movement.

30. Barry Rubin, *Revolution Until Victory? The Politics and History of the PLO* (Cambridge: Harvard University Press, 1994), 24, 26.

31. Rosemary Sayigh, *Palestinians: From Peasants to Revolutionaries* (London: Zed Press, 1979), 154.

32. Walter Z. Laqueur, *The Road to War: The Origin and Aftermath of the Arab-Israeli Conflict, 1967–68* (London: Penguin Books, 1969), 58.

33. Yehoshafat Harkabi, "Fadayeen Action and Arab Strategy," Adelphi Papers No. 53 (London: International Institute for Strategic Studies, 1969 [1968]), 17.

34. Sari Nusseibeh, president of Al-Quds University and pivotal in guiding the 1987 intifada, interviewed by the author, East Jerusalem, January 28, 1996. See Sari Nusseibeh, *Once Upon a Country: A Palestinian Life,* with Anthony David (New York: Farrar, Straus and Giroux, 2007).

35. As quoted in John Kifner, "Israelis and Palestinians Change Their Tactics but Not Their Goals," *New York Times,* May 15, 1988, 1.

36. See, for example, Alain Gresh, "Palestinian Communists and the Intifadah," trans. Diane Belle James, *Middle East Report* 157 (1989): 35.

37. See Raja Shehadeh, *The Third Way: A Journal of Life in the West Bank* (London: Quartet Books, 1982).

38. Ali Hussein Qleibo, *Before the Mountains Disappear: An Ethnographic Chronicle of the Modern Palestinians* (Jericho: Kloreus Books, 1992), 69.

39. The so-called second intifada is linguistically a misnomer as Palestinians returned to violence, including suicide bombings in Israel, far from the meaning of the original nomenclature.

40. The PLO in Tunis claimed to control social and political change within the territories. Yet key thinkers around East Jerusalem were pressing for expanding political and economic freedoms while seeking to end the military occupation, along with nonviolent struggle, as the most direct means to secure basic human rights. Three seminal works written by Sari Nusseibeh, clandestinely circulated, were influential in guiding the strategies of the intifada. The "Fourteen Points by Palestinian Personalities" was the first, corroborating the new political thinking, released at a news conference on January 14, 1988. Other activist intellectuals introducing new ideas and action strategies included Radwan Abu Ayyash, Haj Abd Abu-Diab, Ziad Abu Zayyad, Mamdouh Aker, Hanan Mikhail Ashrawi, Mubarak Awad, Mahdi Abd al-Hadi, Feisel Husseini, Muhammad Jadallah, Zahira Kamal, Ghassan Khatib, Jonathan Kuttab, Raja Shehadeh, Riad al-Malki, Khalil Mahshi, Haidar Abd al-Shafi, Raja Shehadeh, and Hanna Siniora.

41. An argument was systematically advanced that Palestinian cooperation with the occupation had permitted it to prevail. This reasoning was proffered by the Palestinian Center for the Study of Nonviolence, set up in 1984 in East Jerusalem by Mubarak Awad and Jonathan Kuttab, including through the center's distribution of translations of Gene Sharp's works.

42. In 1980, Feisel Husseini set up the Arab Studies Society in East Jerusalem and sought the Israeli journalist Gideon Spiro, a former conscript and decorated paratrooper, to begin this process of joint committees. See note 46.

43. According to Naomi Chazan, eighty-six new Israeli peace groups came into being. Naomi Chazan, interviewed by the author, West Jerusalem, June 6, 1988; Naomi Chazan, one-hour interview, interviewed by the author, East Jerusalem, November 12, 1994. Chazan is a political scientist and former Israeli Knesset Deputy Speaker.

44. David Hall-Cathala, *The Peace Movement in Israel, 1967–87* (New York: St. Martin's Press, 1990), 177, 216, 217.

45. Formal communication with author from Lt.-Col. Yehuda Weinraub, IDF head of information, Tel Aviv, pursuant to telephone request of March 18, 1997, trans. Reuven Gal. Gal is an Israeli former chief psychologist of the IDF.

46. According to Gideon Spiro, in an interview ca. 2007 Shlomo Swirski was asked by the Israeli newspaper *Yedioth Ahronoth* if he could give the costs of Israel's military occupation since 1967. Swirski responded that he could not speak conclusively, but estimated the occupation's costs to Israel at $100 billion over the preceding forty years. In Spiro's view, "without the generous American foreign aid, the occupation would not be possible." Gideon Spiro, personal communication with the author, January 17, 2011. Gideon Spiro, Israeli conscript and former paratrooper, was decorated for his role in the 1956 Suez war, having emigrated from Berlin to British-controlled Palestine in 1939. He was among the Israeli troops who took military control for Israel over Arab East Jerusalem in 1967. In 1982, he became a founding member of Yesh Gvul (There Is a Limit), a movement of Israeli reserve soldiers who refused to serve in the 1982 war in Lebanon and challenged that war's legality. He was among the Israelis and Palestinians who began to work together against the occupation in the early 1980s. The author wishes to thank Spiro for his help. See Shlomo Swirski, *The Price of Occupation* (Tel Aviv: Adva Center, 2008), 119–122, http://israeli-occupation.org/docs/shlomo-swirski_the-burden-of%20occupation _200811.pdf, accessed November 4, 2012.

47. Yezid Sayigh, "Palestinian Armed Struggle: Means and Ends," *Journal of Palestine Studies* 16, no. 1 (1986): 104, 105.

48. Yezid Sayigh, "The Armed Struggle and Palestinian Nationalism," in *The PLO and Israel: From Armed Conflict to Political Solution, 1964–1994*, ed. Avraham Sela and Moshe Ma'oz (New York: St. Martin's Press, 1997), 3.

49. By 1982, Fateh was paying attention to mass mobilization, as opposed to its tight guerrilla units, but many who sought elective office as "Fateh" in unions and associations were not Fateh in a cellular sense. Sari Nusseibeh clarified, "They were generally Fateh." For example, "Perhaps three cell members in a faculty union were Fateh, out of 150 who defined themselves as Fateh." Entire student movements were loosely allied with Fateh, but had no connection with the PLO. At then Bir Zeit College, the Fateh student movement grew "primarily by itself, independently; although there were students who were operatives in Fateh, on the whole, the student movement was not." Sari Nusseibeh, president of Al-Quds University, East Jerusalem, interviewed by the author, November 5, 1994. Hillel Frisch says that "none of these [new] movements contained an overarching secretariat or central committee that was responsible for all the organs within the movements," perhaps with the exception of the communists. Hillel Frisch, "Between Diffusion and Territorial Consolidation in Rebellion: Striking at the Hard Core of the *Intifada*," *Terrorism and Political Violence* 3, no. 4 (1991): 48.

50. Yezid Sayigh, *Armed Struggle and the Search for State: The Palestinian National Movement, 1949–93* (Oxford: Oxford University Press, 1997), 612.

51. "The Palestinians knew that violence would be counterproductive. There was very real and conscious restraint—they wanted to keep it a 'white revolution' without bloodshed, . . . for example, not paying taxes, boycotting of Israeli goods,

and burning of identity cards. If there had been support from Tunis, it would have gone further and quicker." Lucy Austin Nusseibeh, former director of the Palestinian Center for the Study of Nonviolence, East Jerusalem, one-hour interview, by the author, East Jerusalem, November 5, 1994.

52. Robert L. Helvey, *On Strategic Nonviolent Conflict: Thinking About the Fundamentals* (Boston: Albert Einstein Institution, 2004), 117–118.

53. *A Wall in Jerusalem: Obstacles to Human Rights in the Holy City* (Jerusalem: B'Tselem, 2006), 13. B'Tselem (the Israeli Information Center for Human Rights in the Occupied Territories) was founded in 1989 to document human rights violations in the occupied territories and inform the Israeli public and policymakers about them.

54. Charles Levinson, "Israel's Foes Embrace New Resistance Tactics: Hamas and Hezbollah Find Inspiration in Flotilla, Support Protest Movements," *Wall Street Journal,* July 2, 2010, http://greenhouse.economics.utah.edu/pipermail/rad-green /2010-July/039536.html, accessed November 3, 2012.

55. J. C. Hurewitz, *The Struggle for Palestine* (New York: Schocken Books, 1976), 93.

Part 3

Nonviolent Resistance in
Asia and Oceania

10

Burma: Civil Resistance in the Anticolonial Struggle, 1910s–1940

Yeshua Moser-Puangsuwan

Opponents to a new constitution in Burma called for a nation-wide *hartal* (work stoppage). In Rangoon, 1,000 demonstrators marched to show their rejection of the new constitution, carrying placards bearing the slogans "Wreck the Constitution," "Publish Newspapers with Freedom," and "Speak Without Restraint." Opposition political organizations worked jointly to organize protests in eighteen other towns around the country.[1] In the presence of armed troops the demonstrators proceeded to burn copies of the constitution and a flag.

This activity was not organized in reaction against the highly unpopular 2008 military-imposed constitution. It took place instead in 1937, against a constitution imposed by Britain following the separation of British Burma from the British raj in India.[2]

Civil resistance to British colonial rule in Burma is overshadowed by the struggle waged by Mohandas Gandhi (Mahatma) and the Indian National Congress (INC). The Indian struggle remains an inspiration to those seeking political change through nonviolent means. However, an equally impressive mass movement against colonial rule in the British Indian province of Burma was independently organized by Burmese nationalists and their activities were frequently linked with, or organized jointly with, those of the INC.

Burma was colonized by Britain through a series of wars in the mid- to late 1800s and was ruled as a part of British India until 1937 when Britain appointed a separate governor of Burma who was responsible for defense, foreign affairs, and finances while supposedly taking directions on other matters from locally elected representatives. Later events, including the

183

Japanese invasion and the change of tactics by some key leaders of the anti-colonial struggle in Burma, have all but erased the civil resistance to British colonialism from the history books.

Birth of National Consciousness

The birth of nationalist sentiments in Burma was concurrent with, and influenced by, stirrings of national conscience in other parts of South Asia, Southeast Asia, and in the world at large. Early discontent and opposition to colonial authorities took place at a time when more young men (virtually no women) were returning from European educational institutions. While this experience sometimes brought them closer to colonial values, it also opened them to wider influences of the world, allowing them to identify and articulate their second-class status in their homeland. In particular, there was much migration between Burma and India; their citizens were exposed to one another as they migrated as laborers, students, or civil servants across British India.[3]

The earliest institution in Burma to raise nationalist sentiments was the Young Men's Buddhist Association (YMBA) in 1906. Formally constituted as a cultural association, a Buddhist equivalent to the Young Men's Christian Association (YMCA), the YMBA was intended to become a platform for political ideas. From 1915 onward, the YMBA in Rangoon and branches in other towns began organizing nationwide public meetings around issues of discontent. This generated popular support, for the first time, for a political platform independent of, and as a challenge to, the colonial authorities. The YMBA's early steps were modest such as forcing Buddhist holidays onto the official register of colonial holidays, obtaining exemption of Buddhist temples from colonial land tax, and lobbying for wider access to education. These issues as well as all other aspects of governance of Burma's daily life were administered by foreign colonial authorities. A seemingly insignificant issue—that British residents failed to respect the custom of removing shoes on entering temples—turned into a national campaign against wearing footwear in Buddhist shrines. This had important lessons for political organizing because it was the first experience of people uniting to express their will and feeling the power of unity.[4] After 1917, the YMBA, conscious that experiments in other parts of the subcontinent allowed colonial subjects more access to power, began to seek some level of participation for Burmese in local governmental decisionmaking.[5]

World War I and its accompanying barbarity between European states revealed to colonized people broadly that European superiority and invulnerability was a lie. At the same time, they perceived that Allied war propaganda about "the Right to Self Determination" should apply universally—

not just in Europe.[6] In one of its last activities as a political force in May 1920, the YMBA sent a delegation to London to meet with the secretary of state for India to request inclusion of Burma in the constitutional provisions being proposed for the rest of India. Their request was granted, but they returned to Burma early in 1921 only to find that it was no longer relevant: the political momentum had gone much further.

Much of this momentum was generated by the first student strike, which the YMBA was instrumental in organizing in 1920 against the Rangoon University Act. Seeing this act as further limiting educational opportunities for Burmese people, the student strikers remained outside the university but carried on their classes independently, leading to the birth of a parallel educational institution and the founding of national schools as an alternative to colonial schools. National schools aimed to instill anticolonial and pro-independence values.[7] The YMBA now gave way to an organization of national character that it helped bring about, the General Conference of Burmese Associations (GCBA; the B originally indicating "Buddhist," but changed to "Burmese" in order to be more inclusive).

Working in Parallel with the Indian Anticolonial Struggle

A key member of the GCBA was the Burmese Buddhist monk U Ottama. Educated in Calcutta, he became closely involved with the INC.[8] U Ottama returned from India to Burma during the 1920 student strike in order to impart to the students the methods being used in India by Gandhi and the INC.[9] As did Gandhi with the INC, U Ottama turned the GCBA into a mass political struggle organization, organizing not only the first public meetings in Burma expressly against colonial rule but also introducing many of the civil resistance methods pioneered by Gandhi. U Ottama carried on a personal correspondence with Gandhi throughout this time.[10] He championed the cause of making and wearing *pinni,* the native homespun cloth of central Burma, in parallel to the INC's *khadi* campaign. This *pinni* campaign was part of a constructive program to increase self-reliance and indigenous employment while simultaneously reducing dependence on, or contribution to, the colonial power.[11] Subsequently, U Ottama toured the country, frequently under GCBA auspices, encouraging the formation of Wunthanu associations in every village he visited. *Wunthanu* is a Burmese word, which is translated as "to love and cherish its own culture, country, and people." It is similar to nationalism, but not the same. Wunthanu is considered peaceful.

Wunthanu associations pledged to use only Burmese-made products and to boycott British goods.[12] This program was easily accessible and understood by the uneducated and the poor, which resulted in widespread participation in this campaign. Village merchants displayed Wunthanu signboards to show that they were promoting homemade goods. Under U Ottama, the GCBA ran a campaign parallel to the INC's against the Rowlatt Act,[13] a boycott of the visit by the Prince of Wales, and the campaign for home rule. U Ottama became the first person in Burma to be imprisoned for the crime of making a political speech, in this case for promoting the boycott of British goods and noncooperation with colonial governance, and such "sedition" meant that he spent more time in than out of jail during the 1920s.

Gandhi visited Burma on three occasions during the anticolonial movement period. On his final visit in 1929, Gandhi traveled throughout the country, making speeches at public gatherings in Mandalay, Prome, Moulmein, and several other towns. In Rangoon itself, he stood on the steps of Shwedagon Pagoda to address a large crowd of Burmese monks and ordinary people.[14] Shwedagon Pagoda had become, and would remain, a common rallying point for rebellion. Decades later, in 1988, this would be the site of the first political speech by Aung San Suu Kyi—current-day democracy advocate, daughter of Aung San—at which she acknowledged that a "second struggle for national independence" was taking place.[15] Asked which line of action Burma should take, Gandhi replied,

> The conditions in India and Burma, so far as I can see, are much the same. I have there[fore] the same remedy to recommend to both, i.e., non-violent non-co-operation. . . . You should study our movement carefully and evolve a policy of national action in accordance with your peculiar environment and social conditions. I do not want a mere mechanical imitation on your part.

He emphasized the importance of setting up a mass struggle organization along the lines of the INC. On the boycott of foreign goods, Gandhi advised them to focus solely on the boycott of foreign cloth since that was an achievable goal.[16] The INC consistently supported nationalist activity in Burma as well as the right of Burmese to separate from India if they chose to.[17]

By the 1930s, the GCBA had achieved a significant level of mass mobilization and the boycott was having a noticeable impact on the colonial economy. However, the organization began to break down due to infighting, power struggles among movement leaders, and factional disagreements on tactics and strategies. One breakaway faction would prove lethal to the growing civil resistance movement. The GCBA elected Saya San to head a special committee to study abuse by colonial authorities of villagers living in remote areas. He compiled a dossier of 170 case studies in what would today be called a human rights abuse report. His recommendation for action by the GCBA was that it should launch nonviolent direct action in support of villagers' resistance to rural tax collection and to support their right to collect forest products for home use.[18] For reasons not recorded, the GCBA decided not to pursue this campaign. Therefore, Saya San split from the GCBA and set up a primitively armed militia to accomplish the same ends. He urged villagers in remote regions to halt tax payment and promised protection through his militia. Saya San had correctly identified an issue of widespread rural oppression and general revulsion. His actions also found fertile soil in the anger of villagers from many regions of the country who joined in forming an armed rebellion. However, colonial officials predictably reacted by bringing military forces from India and, by the end of 1932, had caught and killed a large number of rebels. The suppression of the rebellion also offered the authorities the opportunity to round up other opposition organizations, such as the Wunthanu associations, and imprison their leaders, thereby effectively eliminating both the armed and the civil resistance.

Dobama Asiayone: The Thakin Movement

For the next few years, opposition to colonial rule was minimal. However, a younger set of leaders with a more aggressive civil resistance agenda was emerging. The Dobama Asiayone (Our Burma Association) was formed by young activists in the early 1930s and came to national attention through a student strike in 1936. (This was Burma's second student strike, the first—mentioned above—having been called by the YMBA in 1920.)[19]

The Dobama movement was also known as the Thakin movement (its members addressed each other as Thakin, which is Burmese for "Lord" and was the required form for addressing colonial officials). Thakin activists explained that they wanted to instill dignity in the people by taking the title for themselves and, thus, communicate that the citizens of the country should be the lords of their own destiny.[20] To further turn the tables, they encouraged the populace to stop using colonial titles in addressing administrators and refer to them instead as public servants. They used strident rhetoric and unconventional methods to attract attention and distinguish themselves from other opposition political movements of that period. An early form of propaganda was song, especially the Dobama song, which the Thakins tried to have sung at the opening of any social event, always requesting people to stand as though it were a national anthem. This turned out to be an effective means of spreading Dobama Asiayone's political ideas. While political pamphlets reached only some of the literate population, this song was passed from person to person, its stirring lyrics deploring Burma's humiliating position and urging the populace to strive for national freedom. Within a year, it was being used widely to open football games and village festivals (and, after independence, the Dobama song did become the national anthem).

The Thakins were also the first group to unreservedly commit to the goal of independence from Britain.[21] Dobama Asiayone promoted a constructive program that included encouraging spinning with a view toward replacing foreign imported textiles with homespun. It also urged all Burmese to patronize national enterprises by using homemade goods, specifically, to smoke cheroots instead of cigarettes, use indigenous umbrellas instead of imported ones, use traditional slippers instead of foreign shoes, furnish one's home with Burmese wares, and eat Burmese instead of foreign food, which followed the earlier platform of the GCBA and the INC.[22]

Until the 1936 student strike, the Thakins were a marginal political force. However, several members infiltrated the leadership of the Rangoon University Student Union (of which Aung San became president). The strike was supported and advised by Dobama members, initially in response to the expulsion from the university of two people soon to be key leaders of Dobama Asiayone: Aung San and U Nu. Swiftly, the strike adopted larger demands, including reform of the University Act and student representation on the University Council.

The strike took place just prior to exams and the strikers set up pickets at the halls. Because this was the most important time for students in the academic year, the strike had to be approached with tact and students with quick tempers were asked not to volunteer on the picket line. The vast majority of students at Rangoon University joined the strike and set up a strike committee and strikers' camp at nearby Shwedagon Pagoda. The authorities initially ignored the strike committee's demands and then threatened to fail students who did not participate in their exams. However, the strikers held firm and the authorities were forced to back down and postpone the exams. This gave time for striking students to return to their home areas and transform a strike at a single institution into a national campaign, complete with a national student strike committee. Students at high schools and even primary schools joined the strike and parents backed the students. Negotiations between the students and the authorities were successful in gaining the changes and concessions sought. This action gained the Dobama activists national recognition and chapters of the organization began to be organized in towns across the country. Dobama Asiayone particularly attracted youth due to its militancy and uncompromising language. Dobama activists, all strikers, and the people in general learned many important lessons in the student strike, including how to manage a national campaign, how agitation can be used to the advantage of the movement and when it becomes counterproductive to the movement, and the time limit beyond which public support cannot be stretched.[23]

The Dobama movement maintained close links with the INC. In late 1935, the Dobama Asiayone president and U Ottama traveled to India to meet INC leaders and give public talks until the British authorities silenced them by charging them with sedition and sending them back to Burma. Immediately the Dobama vice-president stepped into their place, departing for India where he stayed for six months touring, taking part in anticolonial activities, and informing Indian nationalists about the situation in Burma. As well as creating ties between Burmese and Indian activists in the anticolonial struggle, these visits enabled the Dobama leaders to learn about the activities of Indian political organizations and develop an understanding of their own problems according to the international situation. Dobama Asiayone also established a political party in order to make use of political space opened by an election organized by colonial authorities. They did not seriously seek to obtain office but used this political space to campaign against the constitutional changes Britain was about to impose. The Dobama party's public platform was to "wreck the Constitution," and agitate for independence.[24]

As in India itself, where there were strategic differences inside the INC leadership about whether to boycott or to take part in the elections scheduled by the new constitution for 1937, so in Burma there was cooperation between nationalist organizations but various differences among them. Some objected that the new constitution deprived Burma of the constitutional advances offered to India. Some decided to run candidates pledged to "wreck the constitution from within." The Thakins also stood for wrecking the constitution and organized a political party, but they used the electoral campaign as a recruiting platform while organizing an electoral boycott; they then depicted the new government as a "puppet administration."

The General Strike

In 1935, when Burma separated from India, it became a member of the International Labour Organization (ILO), prompting Burmah Oil to change working conditions to fulfill ILO regulations. This, however, triggered worker protests about long-standing grievances, leading to a strike in the oil fields. Thakins were again in the lead. When Burmah Oil suspended a Thakin for attending a Dobama Asiayone meeting, workers in his section halted work and demanded his reinstatement. This work stoppage soon escalated from a single section to the entire labor force and those long-standing grievances became the platform for the strike.

To bring wider attention to their demands, the oil field workers launched a cross-country march by 1,000 workers to the capital, Rangoon. Despite the authorities' attempts to suppress the march, including implementing emergency laws in all towns through which the march would pass and seizing and jailing many of the strike's leadership, the march persevered. The strikers were supported with food, shelter, and funds by the populace of towns along the march route until they reached the capital and set up a strike camp at Shwedagon Pagoda.[25]

The Thakins were also busy organizing in the agricultural sector and encouraged peasants to form parallel marches to join the oil field workers and, thus, build momentum toward a general nationwide strike. They wanted to bring down the "government" elected under the imposed constitution, which they saw as a puppet administration, and make the country ungovernable by Britain. By January 1938, over 7,000 strikers were staying in the strike camp at Shwedagon Pagoda. A strike office of Dobama Asiayone was raided by the police who arrested all the leaders and seized all the documents they could find. However, the workers were by this time organizing themselves into a "Strikers' Parliament." At the same time, the All Burma Student Union was mobilizing support. Their first demand was the lifting of the emergency regulations invoked once the strikers started marching. They defied these by organizing a march of 2,000 students through Rangoon and sent out a call to district union members to undertake similar nonviolent civil disobedience actions in their areas, openly flouting the emergency regulations. When the authorities did not respond to this provocation, the students met to discuss how they could escalate the battle of wills. Student leaders emphasized that discipline, self-restraint, unity, and mass participation were the most important weapons of civil disobedience.

The following day the students blockaded the Secretariat, the colonial administrative center for the entire country. It was an audacious action. No group in Burma had ever organized nonviolent direct action on this scale. Each gate had rows of students blocking entry and no government employee could go to work, effectively shutting down the colonial civil administration. As the police arrived and pried loose students from the gates, other students standing nearby stepped in to fill the breach and the blockade remained in place. The central gates were blocked by women students. At noon, the students felt that they had made their point and ended the blockade by marching around the Secretariat as they collected the students at each gate. However, once they had marched away and were being addressed and congratulated by their leaders, a group of white British police fell on them with batons and rode over them in a horse charge (apparently, the colonial authorities did not feel the local police would obey). One student was killed and many were injured. This led to a new national student strike that demanded the lifting of emergency rule, freeing of political prisoners, and a negotiated settlement with the oil field and peasant strikers. Some 300,000 people violated emergency laws in Rangoon by attending the funeral of the dead student.[26]

Over the next two months, the labor strike grew. However, firms then began to offer employees various concessions, thereby persuading them to return to work and effectively withdraw from the strike. Consequently, by the third month, the student and labor strikes diminished until they finally ended. Nonetheless, the attempt at a complete general strike brought about a greater appreciation in the population of its political power. Preservation of British authority had been also made difficult because all actions happened in public, with the authorities frequently responding with unnecessary violence and brutality that led to a corresponding loss of legitimacy for the colonial government. The strikes made clear that Burmese political activists were likely to become more, not less, strident in their demands for political freedom.

World War II Comes to Burma

In 1940 Aung San, then general secretary of the Dobama movement, felt that international assistance was necessary even though the main work for liberation must be done in Burma. His strategy depended on a countrywide mass resistance movement against British rule. This, he said, should grow progressively, in the form of a series of local and partial strikes of industrial and rural workers escalating to a general and rent strike, followed by mass demonstrations, people's marches, and eventually mass civil disobedience. The next step would be to combine this with an economic campaign against British imperialism including a boycott of British goods that would lead to the nonpayment of taxes. At this point, however, he envisaged that civil resistance should be augmented with guerrilla action against military and civil police outposts and lines of communication. These combined actions, he believed, would lead to a complete paralysis of the British administration at which point the movement should make the final and ultimate move to capture power.

When Britain declared war on Germany and later Japan, Burma was declared a belligerent country without consultation with its domestic legislature. The INC and Dobama Asiayone both asked if the British war aims applied to their countries—if the aim was democratic freedom, they would join in the struggle. However, Britain said no. All Burmese nationalist political parties joined in a coalition called the Freedom Bloc and, together with the INC, instituted "No War Effort" campaigns, as it was clear to them that the war was being fought between imperialist powers.[27]

Had the Japanese occupation of Burma not occurred during World War II, a case can be made that possibly—judging by its commitment of and experience in waging widespread nonviolent resistance—the anticolonial movement in Burma might have brought about decolonization through civil resistance, in tandem with the INC in India. However, that was not to be. Japan was increasing its presence and dominance in Asia. Indian nationalist S. C. Bose broke with the INC and gained Axis backing for his Indian National Army to fight the British. These and other factors had an influence on Aung San and the faction of Thakins that had started to consider how armed struggle could be waged in conjunction with civil resistance. A majority of Thakins disagreed with the inclusion of this element of armed struggle, but

Aung San and a faction of like-minded activists went in search of arms. In seeking military assistance for this agenda of liberation, Aung San and his colleagues reached out to Japan and as a result ended up becoming a part of the Japanese war machine.[28] The Japanese invasion of Burma was accompanied by a small military force created by Aung San, which was called the Burma Independence Army. The Japanese Army succeeded in militarily displacing the British; however, much to the nationalists' disappointment, Japan made Burma its own colony. In response, Aung San's Burma Independence Army, renamed the Burma National Army, launched a guerrilla war against the Japanese, ironically with the backing of the British.

Ultimately, Aung San's military forces were not needed either for the conquest of Burma by the Japanese or for its reconquest by Britain. Furthermore, the Burma National Army was not a decisive force in eventually removing the British. Aung San's actions did, however, lead to the birth of the People's Army, which has ruled Burma as a military dictatorship for almost the entire postcolonial period.[29]

Armed Violence Displaces Nonviolent Action

One of the lasting legacies of World War II to Burma was arms. Most men had arms, training, and experience in their use and felt they deserved a share of the power.[30] All political parties, including Aung San's faction of the Anti-Fascist People's Freedom League (a political party he launched after the war), had their own armed militias separate from the national army.[31] Aung San and his inaugural cabinet were massacred by a political rival prior to forming the nation's first postcolonial government. The communists withdrew into an armed struggle and took sections of the army with them into insurgency. Ethnic leadership in the national army was purged and ethnic groups launched their own insurgencies against the now Burmese state.[32] The country's postwar political leadership was riven by factionalism and infighting and was incapable of addressing much of the postwar devastation, let alone development. One of Aung San's colleagues and army commander Ne Win seized power in 1962, and the army directly ruled the country until 2011.

Violence Institutionalized and
History of Civil Resistance Marginalized

Another legacy of the national struggle was the inheritance of a multiethnic state. The territory now known as Burma or Myanmar is home to many, distinct ethnic groups, several of whom have been at war with one another over governance of the state since independence. Ethnic Burmans,[33] the largest ethnic group, control the national army. The British used troops from non-Burman ethnic minorities to suppress the nationalist movement, especially the Karen—the third most numerous ethnic group. The Karen in particular remained loyal to Britain during the invasion by Japan and fought against Aung San's army whereas the national army claims its origin in the period when armed rebellion against the Japanese commenced. Today, the Karen remain in armed opposition to central Burman authority. Previous military regimes viewed themselves as the guardians of national independence, which was perpetually threatened by foreign-backed assaults.[34] The Burman dominance was made physically manifest in the new administrative capital built in 2005 where the government works under the watchful gaze of three gigantic statutes of armed, Burman warrior kings.

History as taught in Burma today mentions the student strikes, but does not explain their context or provide any understanding of the depth and breadth of civil resistance in the anticolonial struggle. The GCBA is given a nod for encouraging nationalism, but its nonviolent struggle and links with the Gandhian movement go unacknowledged. Prewar anticolonial efforts recorded in Burma's textbooks focus on the violent rebellion launched by Saya San in 1930. Past history focuses on warrior kings of bygone eras and their dominance over many of Burma's neighbors. Education and media within the country remained under strict control and heavily censored from 1962 to 2012, during which there was little room for the emergence of alternative historical accounts.

From 1962 until 2011 there was a continuity of military rule in one form or another and independent institutions, such as the national schools developed during the anticolonial period, were dissolved and their property seized by the state. In 1962, dissolution of the university councils and imposition of curfews on students led to a protest by the Rangoon University Student Union. The ruling Revolutionary Council sent troops to Rangoon University, which resulted in the quelling of the protest and the deaths of many students. The regime also dynamited the Rangoon University Student Union building, reducing a historic site of anticolonial resistance to dust and obliterating the role that students played in civil resistance.[35]

The demolition of the student union building also symbolized a change in the path to political power. Whereas student activism had fed the growing nationalist leadership and was the birthplace of almost all major civic and political leaders, since the 1960s attendance at military colleges was the path to elite power in Burma.[36] Despite the military elite's attempts to channel and marginalize student aspirations, student activism continued and led to confrontations in each of the following decades. The year 1974 brought a series of events marked by massive strikes and protests. Deteriorating economic conditions led to strikes in several sectors, including the oil field workers who had been prominent in the 1938 general strike. The same year, the Burmese former UN Secretary-General U Thant died. The military government refused to offer a state funeral for the veteran politician who was respected for his role in the anticolonial movement, but 50,000 people attended a simple funeral after which students seized his body and placed it in a makeshift mausoleum they constructed on the site of the former Rangoon University Student Union. Despite being surrounded by an estimated 2,000 students the military again laid siege to the site, killing and imprisoning a large number of students after which they closed all universities for four months. The following year, students commemorated the first anniversary of the 1974 labor strike by occupying the buildings of Rangoon University and calling for a national student strike. This led to another university closure for six months. In 1976, students organized a march to commemorate the birth of a leader of the anticolonial movement, which swiftly turned antigovernment. Before the students could return from the march, the government closed the universities for another six months to prevent them from being occupied.

Continuing economic problems led the government to withdraw and cease to accept most small banknotes twice in two years, which wiped out many people's savings.[37] Widespread discontent fueled a national uprising against the government in 1988. The first group to call for change was again students, but they were rapidly joined by many other sectors. A general strike and mass demonstrations spread from the capital to other cities. The government retreated and made a number of cosmetic changes, including introducing new faces as leaders, in an attempt to halt the civil rebellion. After some months, the military staged an autocoup. Through a combination of massive military force and the promise of elections, this succeeded in bringing the demonstrations to a halt.

The founders of Burma's present military were themselves a product of the anticolonial civil resistance struggle and they were keenly aware of the methods, including the need to thwart popular use of them. The military consistently stressed military values and set up various mass organizations that many sectors of the society were required to join. In the early 1990s, it set up the Union Solidarity and Development Association (USDA) to which all civil servants must belong. USDA shares the goals of the military regime and its cadres are mobilized for mass demonstrations in support of the military elite's goals or slogans, in some instances, to attack protests or signs of dissent by the populace.[38] Nevertheless, despite this lack of political space, a political opposition calling for an end to authoritarian rule developed after the military suppressed mass demonstrations in 1988. The opposition pledged itself to nonviolent methods of bringing about a change in governance in its 1990 Gandhi Hall Declaration.[39] Members wear the *pinni* cloth, which was the symbol of the anticolonial struggle, and are led by the daughter of the martyred nationalist leader, Daw Aung San Suu Kyi.[40] In 2008 the military junta imposed a new constitution that would extend its rule under a parliamentary government. In 2010 it held tightly controlled elections in which the military-organized Union Solidarity Development Alliance (renamed Party) won the majority of seats. Almost a quarter of seats in parliament are retained solely for the military. Several former generals were ordered to stand down and take up suits and high positions in Burma's new "democratic" government. The military regime formally ended in February 2011.

Conclusion

The effort of the army to reengineer history and remove the memory of Burmese civil resistance has by and large been successful. Some underground history of the student movement remains, but how little is known can be gauged from the reaction of a leader of the exiled political opposition whom I interviewed: he was surprised to learn that Gandhi had ever visited Burma.[41]

The truth is that, between 1910 and 1940, the people of Burma discovered and employed a wide variety of civil resistance techniques, including the development of mass mobilization organizations, coherent campaigns, and constructive programs. In its early phases, they shared with the Indian independence movement not just a common opponent but also a similar repertoire of methods attuned to Burmese circumstances and culture. However, the character of the movements diverged, partly through different circumstances but also through the distinctive constituencies involved. Indian students did not play the dynamizing role of their Burmese counterparts, and there was no strategic group of Indian workers with the leverage of the oil field workers. The Burmese movements that developed were adept at seizing political opportunities and then maintaining the initiative by escalating tension. They also had a clear goal—independence. However, both major growth phases of the movements in the 1920s and 1930s succumbed to factional infighting and internal power struggles just as they reached their peak. They lacked the maturity to maintain unity and discipline at key moments.

Since that time, only in 1988 has civil resistance harnessed the numbers necessary to bring about a change in power. However, even then, a lack of unity in leadership and vision again prevented the movement from capitalizing on its gains. When asked what today's movements should learn from Dobama Asiayone, one of the few surviving Thakins, Chan Htun, did not hesitate and said, "Unity," adding that "political leaders should stop fighting amongst themselves."[42]

Notes

1. Khin Yi, *The Dobama Movement in Burma (1930–1938)*, Southeast Asia Program Monograph (Ithaca: Cornell University, 1988), 50–51.

2. Burma was separated from India by the Government of India Act, 1935, followed by the Government of Burma Act, 1937, imposing the new constitution. In response to Burmese demands for increased participation in domestic governance, Burma was to have its own elected government under the executive authority of a governor responsible to London, rather than the viceroy of India. See Donald M. Seekins, *Historical Dictionary of Burma (Myanmar)* (Lanham, MD: Scarecrow Press, 2006).

3. By 1930 almost half of the population of Rangoon was Indian. Indian immigration became a source of concern for the nationalists, and tension caused by the large-scale immigration allowed by colonial authorities resulted in some race riots.

4. Fred R. Von red Menhaden, *Religion and Nationalism in Southeast Asia: Burma, Indonesia, the Philippines* (Madison: University of Wisconsin Press, 1963), 167.

5. John F. Cody, *A History of Modern Burma*, 5th ed. (Ithaca: Cornell University Press, 1978), 189–203.

6. Birendra Prasad, *Indian Nationalism and Asia (1900–1947)* (Delhi: B. R. Publishing, 1979), 69.

7. Aung San Suu Kyi, *Aung San of Burma: A Biographical Portrait by His Daughter* (Edinburgh: Escadrille, 1984), 3, 5.

8. Rajshekhar, *Myanmar's Nationalist Movement (1906–1948) and India* (New Delhi: South Asian, 2006), 43.

9. Michael E. Mendelson, *Sangha and State in Burma: A Study of Monastic Sectarianism and Leadership* (Ithaca: Cornell University Press, 1975), 203.

10. *The Collected Works of Mahatma Gandhi (CWMG)*, vols. 39 and 41, CD-ROM (Ministry of Information and Broadcasting, Government of India, New Delhi, 1999).

11. Five decades later, the wearing of *pinni* remains a symbol of resistance (now against a military regime) and is the de facto uniform for members of Aung San Suu Kyi's National League for Democracy party.

12. Rajshekhar, *Myanmar's Nationalist Movement*, 43.

13. Also known as the Anarchical and Revolutionary Crimes Act, it was called the Black Act by the INC. The act allowed for arrest and detention on suspicion of subversive activities, indeterminate detention, and trial of political offenders without jury. The INC responded to the imposition of the act by a nationwide hartal on April 6, 1916.

14. *The Collected Works of Mahatma Gandhi (CWMG)*, vol. 45, CD-ROM (Ministry of Information and Broadcasting, Government of India, New Delhi, 1999).

15. Aung San Suu Kyi, "Speech to a Mass Rally at the Shwedagon Pagoda," August 26, 1988, http://burmalibrary.org/docs3/Shwedagon-ocr.htm, accessed July 30, 2010.

16. *CWMG*, vol. 45: February 4–May 11, 1929.

17. Prasad, *Indian Nationalism*, 134–135.

18. Maung Maung, *From Sangha to Laity: Nationalist Movements of Burma, 1920–40* (New Delhi: Manohar, 1980), 83.

19. Ibid., 130–137.

20. Khin Yi, *The Dobama Movement*, 3. Also Maung Maung, *From Sangha to Laity*, 119.

21. Most political opposition groups were involved in debate about whether Burma should remain united with India under British rule; have home rule, separate from India; or have dominion status under Britain, like Canada. The Thakins dismissed these parties as debating whether it was better to live under the left or right heel of the British boot.

22. Dobama Asiayone youth wing, Third Manifesto, 1933, reprinted in Khin Yi, *The Dobama Movement*, 17.

23. Maung Maung, *From Sangha to Laity*, 135.

24. Khin Yi, *The Dobama Movement*, 38.

25. Maung Maung, *From Sangha to Laity*, 171–173.

26. Ibid., 162–168.

27. Aung San, "The Resistance Movement: Address Delivered at the Meeting of the East and West Association, Rangoon, 29 August 1945." Reprinted in Joseph Silverstein, *The Political Legacy of Aung San* (Ithaca: Department of Asian Studies, Cornell University, 1972), 42.

28. Aung San and his faction first approached the communists and the nationalists in China for support in armed struggle against the British—both groups turned them down and counseled them to stay with the British. US arms to fight Japan were being transported with British assistance through Burma to both Chinese communists and nationalists, and the Chinese feared that an insurgency in Burma would threaten this arms supply.

29. General Aung San was assassinated shortly before independence. He is remembered as the father of the nation and founder of the army. However, contemporary eulogies say little about his history as a student activist or as a delegate from Burma to the INC, or his leadership of a major civil resistance movement using nonviolent methods.

30. As the British were displaced by the Japanese, many of the former ethnic soldiers in the colonial army stayed behind, with their weapons, to form militias. The Japanese also formed and armed militias to fight the British as they reinvaded the country. Aung San's Burma Independence Army, which grew more rapidly than its chain of command, accepted arms from both at different times, with some units undertaking massacres for ethnic or other reasons. See Donald M. Seekins, *The Disorder in Order: The Army-State in Burma Since 1962* (Bangkok: White Lotus, 2002).

31. Aung San quit the army but organized his own militia, which would be more reliable. In 1949, two years after Aung San's death, this militia joined with the communists in an attempt to overthrow the elected government of U Nu. Seekins, *Disorder in Order*, 26.

32. Robert H. Taylor, *The State in Burma* (London: Hurst, 1987), 236.

33. *Burman* denotes a member of the majority ethnic group. *Burmese* refers to anyone residing in Burma.

34. *Myanmar: The Military Regime's View of the World*, Asia Report No. 28 (International Crisis Group, London, December 7, 2001), esp. chap. 3, "The Military's Outlook," 4–8.

35. Michael W. Charney, *A History of Modern Burma* (Cambridge: Cambridge University Press, 2009), 116–117.

36. David I. Steinberg, *Burma's Road Toward Development: Growth and Ideology Under Military Rule* (Boulder: Westview Press, 1981), 23–26.

37. Seekins, *Disorder in Order*, 93–100.

38. Union Solidarity Development Association, www.usda.org.mm/eng/, accessed July 30, 2010.

39. National League for Democracy, Gandhi Hall Declaration, 8th Waxing Day of Wagaung BE 1352, July 29, 1990, www.burmalibrary.org/docs/Gandhi_Hall _Declaration.htm, accessed July 30, 2010.

40. For further reading on recent nonviolent struggle in Burma, see Cristina Fink, *Living Silence: Burma Under Military Rule* (London: Zed, 2009); Yeshua Moser-Puangsuwan, Aurelie Andrieux, and Diane Sarosi, *Speaking Truth to Power: The Methods of Nonviolent Struggle in Burma* (Bangkok: Nonviolence International Southeast Asia, 2005), www.nonviolenceinternational.net, accessed July 30, 2010; and Yeshua Moser-Puangsuwan, "Burma—Dialogue with the Generals: The Sound of One Hand Clapping," in *People Power: Unarmed Resistance and Global Solidarity,* ed. Howard Clark (London: Pluto, 2009).

41. Chan Htun, Thakin, interviewed by the author, Rangoon, February 14, 2010.

42. Ibid.

11

Bangladesh:
Civil Resistance in the Struggle for Independence, 1948–1971

Ishtiaq Hossain

Ebarer Sangram Amader Muktir Sangram, Ebarer Sangram Amader Shadinotar Sangram (This Struggle Is for Our Freedom, This Struggle Is for Our Independence).

—Sheikh Mujibur Rahman, March 7, 1971

The Pakistani military in East Pakistan (now known as Bangladesh) surrendered to a joint command of the Mukti Bahini (Bengalis' Liberation Forces) and the Indian military in Dhaka on December 16, 1971, marking the end of a nine-month armed struggle for independence. The armed struggle had begun soon after midnight on March 25, 1971, when Pakistani forces launched Operation Searchlight against the Bengali civilian population in the major cities in East Pakistan, aiming to suppress the civil resistance launched on March 3, 1971.[1] The movement sought to force the government in Islamabad to honor the results of the first elections for the Pakistani National Assembly, held in December 1970, in which a Bengali political party, the Awami League (AL), had won an absolute majority.

When Pakistan was created as the homeland for Muslims in the Indian subcontinent, Bengalis of East Pakistan—mostly Muslims—soon learned that religion was not a sufficient basis for Pakistani unity. Instead, the West Pakistani rulers disregarded Bengali political, economic, and cultural rights. Bengalis, 55 percent of the population, were underrepresented in the military and the civil service of the country and, economically, East Pakistan became more of an "internal colony" controlled and constrained by the

West Pakistani business class. Most alarmingly for the Bengalis, their culture became the subject of political attacks, being viewed as foreign and excessively influenced by Hinduism and India. The central symbol of this was the decision that Urdu would be the sole state language of Pakistan.

Throughout Pakistan's history, Pakistani rulers regarded Bengalis' demands for autonomy with suspicion. When the AL, led by Bengali politician Sheikh Mujibur Rahman (referred to in Bangladesh as Sheikh Mujib), won an absolute majority in the National Assembly elections in 1970, Pakistani military and civilian elites refused to hand over power and declared their intention to hold on to East Pakistan at any cost and by whatever means necessary.[2] The end result was the emergence of an effective and popular Bengali guerrilla counteroffensive, which ultimately led to the establishment of a new state in South Asia. Bengalis look back at armed resistance with great admiration—no doubt a part of the romanticized view of their nation's struggle for independence.[3] "Bloody Birth of Bangladesh" proclaimed the cover of *Time* on December 20, 1971, with a photo of gun waving Mukti Bahini fighters celebrating.[4]

The armed resistance against Pakistan's military during March–December 1971 constituted a significant part of the struggle of the people of Bangladesh to achieve their independence. However, often overlooked is another critical factor—that ever since the establishment of Pakistan on August 14, 1947, time and again Bengalis had resorted to civil resistance and adopted many nonviolent methods to push for their own rights and self-rule. By taking a longer, historical view of Bengalis' struggle for independence, I focus in this chapter on the Bangla language movement and the nonviolent civil resistance movement of March 1971. Both movements were directed against a government, which repeatedly used violent means of repression against unarmed people. However, the resort to violence failed to strangulate the movements, often backfired, and ultimately proved counterproductive in the face of massive nonviolent mobilization. These two movements are viewed as important "shapers" of Bengali national identity and "enablers" of the emergence of a quasi-independent East Pakistan by the time violent struggle broke out on March 25, 1971.[5]

Glorified Resistance in Arms
and Remembrance of Fallen Heroes

In Bangladesh, armed resistance is a central focus of official and unofficial narratives of the independence struggle, which is often reinforced by national holidays that commemorate important military victories. The title of the official history of the country's independence struggle is *Muktijuddher*

Itihash (The History of the War of Liberation). A magnificent monument to honor fallen freedom fighters was erected in Savar, twelve miles from Dhaka, while in the capital itself the War of Liberation Museum attracts streams of visitors. Poems, short stories, and novels as well as school textbooks continue to depict the heroism of the Mukti Bahini. Films such as *Ora Egaro Jon* (Those Eleven) and *Arun Udayer Agni Shakhi* (Fiery Witness to the Sun Rise) are immensely popular, creating a glorified legend of armed resistance, while the musical *Payer Awaj Paoa Jai* (Footsteps Can Be Heard) has won international recognition. Literally thousands of songs have been written to honor freedom fighters. One of them is broadcast every night before the television news: "Shob Kota Janala Khule Dao Na, Ora Ashbe, Chupi, Chupi" (Open All the Windows, They Will Come, Silently, Silently). Another song that expresses the resolve of the Mukti Bahini is "Amra Ekti Phool Ke Bachate Juddho Kori" (We Fight a War in Order to Save a Flower).[6]

There are also commemorations for those who sacrificed their lives while leading nonviolent civil resistance, above all Ekushey February (February 21)—the day when a number of Bengali students who were part of the nonviolent language movement were killed by the Pakistani police and army. Ekushey February is both a national holiday and the day of celebration of Bengali culture and language. Since November 1999, this day has been observed by the UN Educational, Scientific, and Cultural Organization (UNESCO) as International Mother Language Day in tribute to the martyrs of the Bengali language movement and in universal recognition of people's ethnolinguistic rights. Every year, Dhaka University organizes literary and cultural activities centering on the Shahid Minar (Monument for the Language Martyrs), adorning the roads leading to it with beautiful alpanas (traditional Bengali decorative colorful paintings). On Ekushey February, throngs of ordinary people, barefoot and singing the Ekushey song, "Amar Bhaiyer Rokte Rangano Ekushey February, Ami Ki Bhuleti Pari" (I Will Not Forget My Brothers' Blood Soaked Ekushey February), walk to the Shahid Minar and to the graveyard of some of those massacred. The Bangla Academy, set up in 1953, each year organizes a month-long Ekushey Book Fair.

Nevertheless, despite such commemorations, there seems to be a general lack of deeper reflection on the strategic value of nonviolent resistance in which students died. There are also few serious written contributions highlighting nonviolent methods used by the Bhasha Sainiks (language soldiers)—participants in the language movement.[7] Although it is generally accepted that the Bangla language movement was successful despite violent repression, it did not lead directly to the independence of the country. Consequently, the strategic nonviolent actions that strengthened the independence struggle remain buried beneath the narratives of that struggle's final phase, the 1971 armed resistance.

The Bangla Language Movement, 1948 and 1952

The first major political movement in East Pakistan demanded that Bangla be recognized alongside Urdu as a state language in Pakistan, arguing that Bangla was the native language of more than half the people of Pakistan and Urdu of less than 5 percent (although widely understood in East and West Pakistan).[8] The language movement of 1948 and 1952 sparked the first widespread Bengali opposition to the government of Pakistan, dominated by the West Pakistan–based Muslim League party, and laid the foundation for the emergence of Bengali nationalism that played an important role in the subsequent struggles for independence.[9]

Even in the months before independence, there were signs of dispute among the West Pakistani and Bengali intellectuals as to the question of whether Urdu or Bangla should become the state language of an independent Pakistan.[10] However, after independence (in August 1947), the Pakistani government promptly began using Urdu for currency, stamps, and other official papers. Bengali intellectuals were understandably alarmed that the government intended to make Urdu the state language without any public debate. Abdul Matin, an active participant of the Bengali language movement, records that by the end of 1947, whether by word of mouth or through newspapers, whenever the common people of East Pakistan learned about the controversy over the future state language, they expressed open support for the recognition of Bangla as one of the official languages of the country. They held demonstrations and meetings in towns and villages throughout East Pakistan.[11] Historian Ahmed Karmal, who notes that the first clash between rival supporters of Bangla and Urdu languages took place in Dhaka as early as December 12, 1947, also highlights the paradox of the widespread support for the language at a time when 85 percent of the population was illiterate.[12]

Although Bengali newspaper articles and debates among intellectuals raised public awareness about the language issue, it took grassroots organizing led or supported by a number of local leaders to get a nonviolent language movement off the ground. Beginning in 1947, groups of extraordinary men and women began to organize themselves, setting up various sociocultural organizations, which together with student groups and political parties became involved in the Bengali language movement as it unfolded in 1947–1948 and 1952. One of these organizations, Tamaddun Majlish, established in Dhaka in September 1947, made particularly significant contributions to the movement.[13] At a time when the Pakistani authorities characterized the language movement as being driven by antistate and communist radicals, Tamaddun Majlish's general aim was unprovocative and noncontroversial—to "invigorate Islamic spirit and culture among the citizens of the new nation of Pakistan." However, its activities soon proved to be central in demonstrating that most Bengalis wanted Bangla to become a state language.[14]

Tamaddun Majlish published on September 15, 1947, an eighteen-page booklet, *Pakistaner Rashtra Bhasha: Bangla Na Urdu?* (Pakistan's State Language: Bangla or Urdu?), which contained three articles.[15] This booklet played a significant role in defining clear objectives for the movement: that Bangla becomes, next to Urdu, a state language and in East Pakistan the main language of education, government offices, and courts (with Urdu as a second and English as a third language). It also stated that, if Bangla was not recognized as an official language of Pakistan, the people had a right to protest and obtain their rights—and, if necessary, through secession and independence—through a mass movement.[16] Tamaddun Majlish organized meetings in schools, colleges, and throughout Dhaka in support of recognition of Bangla as a state language. The booklet gradually became an inspiration for scholars, teachers, other professionals, students, and, ultimately, the general public.

Tamaddun Majlish's prominent academics, politicians, and intellectuals—among others, Abul Kashem, Kazi Motahar Hossain, Abul Mansoor Ahmed, and Syed Nazrul Islam—played the key role in setting up the first Rashtra Bhasha Sangram Parishad (RBSP; First State Language Movement Council) in October 1947. The RBSP provided the needed organizational structure for launching the language movement in late 1947 and early 1948. In addition, during 1947–1948 a number of prominent individuals and student and public organizations joined the Bangla language movement, including Gono Azadi League (People's Independent League) established in July 1947 and Gonotantrik Jubo League (Democratic Youth League) established in August 1947.[17] Both organizations helped advance the language movement's demands by organizing various meetings and discussions.

A trigger for further mobilization was Dhirendra Nath Dutta's motion to the Constituent Assembly of Pakistan on February 25, 1948, calling for Bangla to be given equal status with Urdu as a language of the state.[18] Prime Minister Liaquat Ali Khan immediately dismissed Dutta's motion, insisting that Urdu would be the only state language of Pakistan.[19] The next day, the students at Dhaka University began to protest.

By now it became clear that Bengalis had to unite to press effectively for their demands, continuing to organize through civic activities but also building a platform of political support across party divisions. Therefore, on March 2, 1948, an All-Party Rashtra Bhasha Sangram Parishad (All-Party State Language Council of Action, or All-Party Language Council) was formed in Dhaka, calling for an East Pakistan–wide strike to be held on March 11, 1948, to protest at the rejection of Dutta's motion ahead of the impending visit of the "Father of the Pakistani Nation," Muhammad Ali Jinnah, Pakistan's first governor-general.

The main drivers behind the strike—the students and professors of Dhaka University—responded overwhelmingly to the call of the All-Party Language Council, and early in the morning on March 11, 1948, they gathered in large numbers at two of Dhaka's residential areas, Nilkhet and Plassey Barracks, to urge the government and business office-workers to join the strike. Aiming to picket government officials, student leaders stationed themselves at both gates of the Eden Buildings (commonly known as the Secretariat—the seat of the provincial government) and were indeed joined by some officials. Others donated money, which was used later to make posters and banners.[20]

Government officials from the Secretariat staged a walkout and soon were joined by workers and officials of the East Bengal Railway. When police broke up the demonstrations, a huge student protest meeting was held at Dhaka University and demonstrations spread throughout the city. Large numbers of people took up the All-Party Language Council's call to strike in Rajshahi, Jessore, Khulna, Chandpur, Jamalpur, Noakhali, Dinajpur, Pabna, and Bogra, many demonstrating on the streets of their cities in a nonviolent display of force. Demonstrators were arrested and thrown into jails. In Dhaka, key leaders like Shamsul Huq, Oli Ahad, Sheikh Mujib, and Abdul Wahed were among those imprisoned. Separate cases were filed against Shawkat Ali and Qazi Golam Mahbub for their action to stop the car carrying the inspector general of police and the police superintendent at the Secretariat's entrance gate.[21]

Under pressure from the ongoing strikes and demonstrations, Khawja Nazimuddin, the chief minister of East Pakistan, signed an eight-point agreement with the leaders of the All-Party Language Council on March 15, 1948. Its most important clauses were to submit a resolution to the next session of the East Bengal Legislative Assembly in April to make Bangla one of the state languages and the official language of the province of East Bengal (in place of English) and give Bengalis the right to use their own language in competitive exams to the state administration. As part of the agreement, all arrested demonstrators would be freed on the same day.[22]

When Jinnah arrived in Dhaka on March 18, he gave a series of speeches that proved to be of tremendous significance for the language issue—insisting that Urdu would be the only state language.[23] At his speech at Dhaka University, some students walked out while others shouted until he abandoned his speech and left the premises.[24] Having decided beforehand to meet with members of the All-Party Rashtra Bhasha Sangram Parishad, he tersely told them that he rejected the agreement "signed under duress" by Chief Minister Nazimuddin.[25] In Jinnah's view, a country as ethnically diverse as Pakistan needed a unifying language and Urdu was the appropriate choice as it was not the dominant language of any province, yet nevertheless was widely understood in both West and East Pakistan. Those in attendance argued that, if a language foreign to the majority was to be adopted, why not

accept English? They also pointed out that it was the democratic preroga-
tive of the state legislature to decide on the language issue: an edict from
the governor-general would be an undemocratic procedure. The meeting
ended without agreement.[26]

The government never implemented the March 15 agreement. Nonetheless, although the 1948 nonviolent mobilization did not achieve its main
goal of making Bangla a state language, it was an important milestone. The
mobilization demonstrated that the struggle would be long and difficult,
that people had to be ready to make supreme sacrifices to win their rights,
and also that if a movement is united and determined it cannot be crushed
or disregarded by the authorities—all of which inspired Bengalis to continue their resistance in the years to come.

During 1950–1951, Dhaka University students began to organize themselves for further actions to advance the cause of Bangla.[27] In March 1950,
they formed the Dhaka University Rashtra Bhasha Sangram Committee
(Dhaka University State Language Action Committee). The committee
raised funds from the general public and made posters informing people how
much money they had collected.[28] The decision to be transparent about the
committee's activities was strategic and helped mobilize other students.
They also decided to distribute posters and leaflets encouraging people to
commemorate the nonviolent demonstrations and strikes of March 11, 1950.

During the university break, students were asked to hold meetings in
their hometowns in support of making Bangla a state language in schools,
colleges, and libraries. The Action Committee circulated a memorandum
among members of the Pakistani Constituent Assembly, calling for Bangla
to be a state language. On reading this in the West Pakistani press, Bengalis
living in West Pakistan wrote back to the Action Committee to pledge their
support.[29]

A new chapter in the movement began in January 1952 when Nazimuddin became Pakistan's new prime minister and reaffirmed that Urdu would
be Pakistan's only official language. Immediately a new All-Party Rashtra
Bhasha Sangram Parishad was formed to organize and coordinate the protest
movement. It declared a day of action—February 21, 1952—as Bangla State
Language Day. The government, determined to thwart the protests, imposed
Section 144 (a British colonial law) banning the gatherings of more than
four people in and around the Dhaka University campus from the night of
February 20. Key members of the Dhaka University Rashtra Bhasha Sangram Committee (Dhaka University State Language Action Committee) decided that they would not violate Section 144,[30] but many students were
more defiant. Student activist Gaziul Huq recounts his experience:

> Around 3 p.m. on 20 February while we were making a list of volunteers
> at Madhu's Canteen, we heard the government making microphone an-
> nouncement declaring curfew [Emergency Act 144] for the following day

[21 February]. The students present resented the official enforcement of the Act 144 on the Bangla Language Day. Later that evening in a meeting at the Salimullah Muslim Hall [a students' dormitory] chaired by Fakir Shahabuddin it was decided that Act 144 would not be tolerated. It had to be broken. And this decision had to be passed on to the all party State Language Action Committee. Chaired by Abdul Momen another meeting was held in Fazlul Huq Hall and it was decided that Act 144 would have to be defied.[31]

All accounts of the students' meeting in front of the old Arts Faculty Building of Dhaka University on February 21 tell the story of courage and defiance by those gathered there. By noon, several thousand students assembled and shouted slogans like "Rashtra Bhasha Bangla Chai" (We Demand Bangla as the State Language). Shamsul Huq, representing the All-Party Rashtra Bhasha Sangram Parishad, spoke first and called on students to not break Section 144. However, while Abdul Matin and Gaziul Huq from the Dhaka University Action Committee were making the case for defiance, the news arrived that police had used tear gas on a group of students in the Lalbagh area of Dhaka. The agitated students began shouting, determined to disobey Section 144. Yet they did so with a concern to avoid violence. Instead of leaving en masse, they numbered off into groups of ten, believing that this would help calm police while maintaining their own nonviolent discipline. However, the peaceful nature of the protests was broken when the police began to charge with batons and fire tear gas—one tear gas canister knocked Gaziul Huq unconscious. Predictably, scuffles broke out and students began to throw stones and bricks.

The road in front of Dhaka University turned into a battlefield. Around 4 P.M., the police opened fire, killing five people—students Mohammad Salauddin, Abdul Jabbar, Abul Barkat, and two other people who had joined the protest, Raifquddin Ahmed and Abdus Salam. Scores of students were also injured. On February 22, thousands of people gathered at the Dhaka University Medical College and Engineering College for prayers before the burial of those killed in the police action. After prayers, people went to the streets to demonstrate, calling for Bangla to be a state language and for the chief minister of East Pakistan to be put on trial. Once again, police opened fire on unarmed demonstrators. An angry crowd attacked pro-government newspapers. As the situation deteriorated, the government commanded the military to restore order. Some ministers fled the city and took shelter in the Kurmitola military cantonment.

The All-Party Rashtra Bhasha Sangram Parishad called for a *hartal* (general strike) on February 25 to protest at the governmental repression while students erected a Shahid Minar at the place where Abul Barkat was shot and killed. Destroyed several times—the last time on the night of March 25, 1971—Shahid Minar became the rallying symbol for the Bengalis. On

February 24, 1952, full authority was given to the police and the military to restore order in Dhaka, leading to the arrest of almost all of the student and political leaders linked with the language movement. The following day, Dhaka University was closed for an indefinite period and students were told to leave university residences. In the face of such repressive measures, the movement lost its momentum in the capital, but it had already spread to other towns and the districts.

Chittagong—the second largest city of the province—became another important place for the mobilization of the Bangla language movement. When in January 1952 Prime Minister Nazimuddin reiterated that Urdu would be the only state language, an All-Party Rashtra Bhasha Sangram Parishad meeting was held at the office of the Chittagong Awami Muslim League where members of other political parties, people from various professions, intellectuals, and representatives of trade unions were present. On February 21, news of the killings in Dhaka reached Chittagong that evening, arousing demonstrations and strikes. Mahbubul Alam Chowdhury instantly wrote a seventeen-page poem, "Not for Tears Have I Come but I Demand—They Be Hanged," that was printed during the night. The police raided the printing press and confiscated materials, but not before 15,000 copies of the poem had already been distributed. On February 22, this poem was recited at a massive public rally at the Laldighi Maidan (Laldighi Field). People were simultaneously anguished and inspired by the words.[32] February 21 was soon to be known as Ekushey February, following Gaziul Huq's elegy, "We'll never forget, never, Ekushey February," which Altaf Mahmood (killed by Pakistani soldiers in 1971) turned into a popular song.[33]

The Action Committee formed in the town of Mymensingh expressed its determination to continue the language movement in the district in a nonviolent manner. Peaceful demonstrations and strikes were organized. But when the local authorities using the State Security Act arrested two members of the local Action Committee and students of a local college, the situation deteriorated. As the police brought students to the court, the building was surrounded by thousands of people demanding their release. The protesters dispersed only after Action Committee member Abul Mansur Ahmed, whose two sons were among those arrested, assured the crowd that he would secure the release of the jailed students.[34]

The language movement spread to many smaller towns in East Pakistan. In Barisal, for example, a five-member All-Party District Action Committee was formed in January 1952 and it organized processions and street meetings in February as well as distributed badges and posters.[35] On February 21, students from local schools and colleges formed processions that joined a mass rally at the Aswinikumar town hall. A mile-long demonstration moved from the town hall along the main roads of the town.[36] The news of the killings in Dhaka was brought in special issues of Dhaka daily newspapers that were transported 100 miles by river. Spontaneous demonstrations of outrage and anger took place throughout the night of February 21, usually with women at the front. The next morning, a rally at the town hall was joined by villagers from neighboring areas. Later in the afternoon, thousands of people attended a memorial rally in honor of those killed in Dhaka. Again on the morning of February 23, the Namaj-e-Janaza (the Islamic ritual in honor of the dead) was attended by thousands. This civic mobilization in support of the Bengali language in Barisal was marked by its nonviolent nature and not a single violent incident on the part of the demonstrators took place.

Success of the Language Movement and Its Impact on National Consciousness

The people-driven Bengali language movement was remarkably successful, particularly in light of the repressive measures used against it such as police arrests, beatings, harassment, curfews, and killings by the military. The pressure generated by the movement forced the provincial government to introduce a motion on February 22, 1952, passed unanimously in the East Bengal Legislative Assembly, recommending that Pakistan's Constituent Assembly recognize Bangla as an official language of East Pakistan. The recommendation was not immediately implemented, but this and the larger objective of making Bangla an official national language of Pakistan was soon to be gained through conventional politics.

In the wake of Ekushey February, it became easy for opposition political parties in East Pakistan to form a United Front (UF), campaigning on the promise to make Bangla a national language and a language of instruction in the East Pakistani education system. In the first East Bengal Legislative Assembly election, held in March 1954, the UF decisively defeated the ruling Muslim League. Thereafter, Bangla was spoken in the East Bengal Legislative Assembly and used officially in the province. Ultimately, it was agreed that Pakistan's 1956 Constitution would recognize both Bangla and Urdu as national languages of the country.[37] These achievements were brought about by years of nonviolent mobilization and pressure by the language movement and its hundreds of thousands of supporters.

Bangladeshi writers widely recognize that the Bangla language movement was a defining moment in Bangladesh's history and laid the foundation for the development of Bangladeshi national identity.[38] The extraordinary participation of ordinary people in the 1951–1952 language movement offered its participants experience in sustained organizing and mobilizing; setting up support structures for leading protests and demonstrations; and, no less importantly, uniting, empowering, and educating people about their right to their own language. Through their nonviolent collective actions combined with their determination and persistence in the face of violent repression, Bengalis' understanding of their own cultural separateness from the rest of Pakistan became more pronounced. Whether men or women, old or young, rich or poor, all through their participation and commitment shared the experience of struggling together, reinforced their collective desire to protect and use their own language, and formed their collective identity around Bengali language and culture.

Pakistani authorities' attempts to suppress nonviolent mobilization in support of the Bangla language backfired. Violence and repression used against the language movement increased Bengalis' emotional and psychological attachment and entitlement to the use of their mother tongue and intensified their national self-identification as distinct from being Pakistani. In that sense, the mass-based Bangla language movement established the language as a marker of Bengali nationalism and this became more important than the emphasis on Islam as the cohesive factor in Pakistani identity.

Between 1952 and 1971, many other factors, such as economic disparities between East and West Pakistan, continued discrimination in and limited access to Pakistan's civil and military services, and growing demands for expanded political autonomy further reinforced the collective consciousness of Bengalis. In aggregate, these factors contributed to a national consciousness and the desire for an independent state, which two decades later led to another unarmed insurrection in March 1971.

The Nonviolent Civil Disobedience Movement, March 1–25, 1971

Pakistan's first general election based on the principle of one person, one vote was held in Pakistan in December 1970. The Pakistan National Assembly had 313 seats, 169 of them in East Pakistan of which all but 2 were won by the Awami League, giving it an absolute majority. The AL's leader was Sheikh Mujibur Rahman. Active as a student in Calcutta in the struggle for independence from Britain, after Pakistan's independence he took part in the Bangla language movement of 1948 and 1952. For his role in that movement, he was imprisoned by the East Pakistan government. After General Ayub Khan's imposition of martial law in 1958, he served further prison terms. What now gave him heroic status, however, was a failed attempt by Ayub Khan to discredit Sheikh Mujib and thirty-four others by imprisoning them and putting them on trial for "conspiring" with India. This provoked massive protests and a wave of strikes, actions denounced by Ayub Khan as *gherao* (surrounding or besieging officials or employers) and *jalao* (burning buildings), and student protests. State violence did not quell resistance but did arouse sympathy in West Pakistan, ultimately forcing the government to drop the prosecution and release the prisoners.

Sheikh Mujib's program was based on a six-point plan that he had introduced in 1966, aiming to revive the original vision of Pakistan as a federation of autonomous Muslim states. He proposed a new federation, with considerable self-government for East Pakistan, including its own currency, but with common foreign and defense policies. The plan was popular in East Pakistan and Bengali resentment at Pakistan's inadequate response to the 1970 Bhola cyclone (which hit East Pakistan and areas of India) assured the AL of a landslide victory. Hoping that the convening of the National Assembly in Dhaka on March 3, 1971, would be followed by the formation of the federal government under the leadership of AL, Bengalis expected that long-awaited political and social change would be finally realized.

On March 1, 1971, the final day of a cricket match between Pakistan, for the first time including a Bengali, and a Commonwealth team took place at Dhaka's stadium.[39] Before the match could break for lunch, the packed stadium roared in anger and people began throwing various items onto the field. The radio had just reported that President Yahya Khan had postponed the National Assembly session. The entire crowd poured out of the stadium and started moving toward Hotel Purbani, located nearby, where the AL leaders were working on the final draft of the constitution. Soon the cricket crowd was joined by officials from the Secretariat and retailers working in nearby commercial areas. Overflowing from the space in front of the Hotel Purbani, many moved on to Paltan Maidan, which was often used for large public meetings. Their slogans included calls to arms. Offices and shops around the stadium closed and there was an expectation among the members of the crowd that Sheikh Mujib would make an important announcement after his meeting with colleagues at the Hotel Purbani.

In a crowded press conference, Sheikh Mujib declared that he could not approve President Yahya Khan's adjournment of the National Assembly session. He came out with a program of action for the next six days, which included observance of complete *hartal* in Dhaka on March 1 and a province-wide strike on March 3, the date for the National Assembly to meet. Appealing for people to remain calm and peaceful while observing the strike, he warned that if government-controlled radio, television stations, and newspapers blocked news reports about the political movement in East Pakistan, Bengali staff should refuse to obey. Sheikh Mujib further announced on March 7 at the Dhaka Race Course that he would "announce the final program."[40] This immediately raised expectations that he would make a unilateral declaration of Bangladesh's independence.

On March 1, thousands of people gathered at Paltan Maidan where student leaders announced the formation of an Action Council and vowed to establish an independent Bangladesh. This was greeted with roars of support.

Dhaka and the rest of the province were completely shut down due to strikes between March 1 and 7. Bengali employees working in key public sectors refused to cooperate with their Pakistani employers. The Bengali staff of Pakistan International Airlines at Dhaka Airport refused to handle the flights from West Pakistan bringing Pakistan military personnel to East Pakistan.[41] From March 1 onward, people went to the streets of all major cities and towns of the province, marching, chanting, and protesting. During the gathering of thousands of students in front of the western entrance to the Arts Faculty Building of Dhaka University on March 2, the protesters raised the original Bangladesh flag (a golden map of Bangladesh embedded in a crimson sun, bordered by green) and began chanting slogans such as "Joy Bangla" (Victory to Bengal), and "Bir Banglai Astro Dhoro, Bangladesh Shadin Koro" (Heroes of Bengal, Take Up Arms and Liberate Bangladesh). They pledged allegiance to the new flag while some students burned the Pakistani flag. The news of the raising of the Bangladesh flag spread quickly around the city. The military was deployed to the streets and clashes broke out between the demonstrators and the army in Dhaka, Khulna, Jessore, and elsewhere. Scores of unarmed protesters were killed between March 1 and 3 and there also were reports of army fire in Joydevpur, Chittagong, Khulna, Sylhet, and Rajshahi.

On March 3, at Paltan Maidan, Sheikh Mujib announced the launching of a nonviolent noncooperation movement in East Pakistan.[42] Following this, every day from 6 A.M. until 2 P.M., nothing would move in the province. Public and private offices were shut down completely; buses, trains, and river and air transportation stopped operating; banks and all other financial institutions remained closed. Government television and radio stations based in Dhaka came under the control of protesting Bengali employees who formed Action Councils. They repeatedly played revolutionary and patriotic songs, including Rabindranath Tagore's "Amar Sonar Bangla" (My Golden Bengal), which later became the national anthem of Bangladesh. "Jibon Theke Neya" (A Story Taken from Life), a banned film mirroring the autocratic nature of the Pakistani government, was finally shown on Dhaka television.

When the military authorities banned live broadcasting of Sheikh Mujib's March 7 speech from the Dhaka station of Radio Pakistan, Bengali radio staff shut the station down, which posed the authorities with an acute dilemma. The radio station was located next to the Hotel Intercontinental that housed most foreign journalists and was near the Dhaka Race Course. The regime wanted the world to believe that—despite the *hartals* and disruption—business as usual would soon resume. If the speech was not broadcast, and if as a result protesters tried to occupy the station, then it would be clear to foreign press corps—and to the world—just how grave the situation was. Therefore, pressured by the Bengali radio staff's noncooperation and the volatile situation, the regime allowed the speech to be broadcast live.

One of the least-mentioned actions during the period of disobedience was the spontaneous Bengali boycott of economic goods produced by West Pakistani–owned factories in East Pakistan. For example, Kohinoor Chemical products and cosmetics ceased to sell and, suddenly, Piva toothpaste and other cosmetic products produced by Bengali-owned Hena Chemicals became extremely popular. People also began using indigenously produced clothes from *khaddar* (made of cotton) material.

Awami League leaders were generally successful in maintaining the nonviolent character of the movement. They understood the strategic value of remaining nonviolent and, on a number of occasions, they showed their willingness to intervene decisively to stop violence. For example, some young AL leaders set up checkpoints at the Farm Gate area of Dhaka and searched passengers leaving for West Pakistan, hoping to find jewelry and cash. On one occasion, it led to violence. Following this incident, Sheikh Mujib ordered the checkpoints to be dismantled.

On March 5, Pakistani President Yahya Khan announced that he was convening a roundtable conference of political leaders on March 10 and a session of the National Assembly on March 25. AL leaders responded that they could not attend such events until independent investigations were conducted into the killing of civilians by the military since March 1. The entire province waited anxiously for March 7 when Sheikh Mujib was to address a public meeting at Dhaka Race Course. An estimated 3 million people attended.[43] Sheikh Mujib's eighteen-minute speech was politically shrewd. He did not declare outright independence, but made it clear that it was his ultimate aim. He laid down four conditions that had to be met before he would consider meeting with the Pakistani president: (1) withdrawing martial law; (2) returning troops to barracks; (3) investigating the killing of civilians; and (4) transferring power to the people's elected representatives, according to the results of the December 1970 elections.

The noncooperation campaign was to continue, but in a limited way so it could become more sustainable. Government offices, courts, and educational institutions were to be closed indefinitely except that, to ease hardship, workers were to collect their salaries, banks and government offices would open two hours daily to pay them, and transport would function normally "except for serving any needs of the armed forces." Money transfers outside East Pakistan were banned. "From today, until this land has been freed, no taxes will be paid to the government anymore." Sheikh Mujib warned against provocateurs, urged people to ignore the media if they failed to report the news from Bangladesh, and appealed to "brothers" in the armed forces to return to their barracks. "You are our brothers. I beseech you to not turn this country into a living hell. Will you not have to show your faces and confront your conscience some day? If we can peaceably settle our differences there is still hope that we can co-exist as brothers.

Otherwise there is no hope. . . . Give up any thoughts of enslaving this country under military rule again!" To his own people, he had a warning about how high the stakes were: "The people of this land are facing elimination, so be on guard. If need be, we will bring everything to a total standstill. . . . If the salaries are held up, if a single bullet is fired upon us henceforth, if the murder of my people does not cease, I call upon you to turn every home into a fortress against their onslaught. Use whatever you can put your hands on to confront this enemy. Every last road must be blocked."[44]

From March 7 to 25, East Pakistan was virtually governed by the provisional government of AL. The civil service, police, even the judges acknowledged the authority of its directives. The chief justice of the East Pakistan High Court refused to administer the oath of office to the Pakistani government's newly appointed governor of East Pakistan, Lieutenant General Tikka Khan. Through such acts of nonviolent noncooperation and self-organization, East Pakistan became de facto self-ruled and independent.

On March 7, 1971, the people listened to Sheikh Mujib's speech at the Dhaka Race Course in complete silence, occasionally breaking into applause. Near the end of his speech, in an emotionally choked voice, he announced, "Ebarer Sangram Amader Muktir Sangram, Ebarer Sangram Amader Shadinotar Sangram" (This Struggle Is for Our Freedom, This Struggle Is for Our Independence). The crowd roared. His rallying cry of "Joy Bangla" that followed brought even more thunderous response. At this moment, the transformation of people into a nation, not through violence but through collective acts of nonviolent resistance, was complete.

Conclusion

The common narratives around Bangladesh's independence highlight the armed struggle of the Mukti Bahini (Bengali guerrilla force) and India's decisive military intervention in December 1971. These factors were important to the outcome of the struggle. However, as I have shown in this chapter, the nonviolent civil resistance of the Bengalis for their political and cultural rights, and ultimately for their independence, was equally significant. The nonviolent language movements of 1948 and 1952 earned Bangla its due recognition as one of the state languages of Pakistan. More importantly, these movements helped unite Bengalis by defining and strengthening their national consciousness and identity. This development of linguistically and culturally based nationalism, according to a number of Bengali scholars, laid the foundation for the creation of a nation-state.[45]

The nonviolent movements, in 1948, 1952, and March 1971, were successful in part because they were not confined to the province capital of Dhaka. Civil resistance was a highly participatory form of struggle for a wide variety of Bengalis in small towns and villages all over East Pakistan; people from all walks of life, generations, and socioeconomic backgrounds were part of the nonviolent struggle.

The nonviolent movements each applied a rich selection of well-coordinated methods of nonviolent resistance, including protest and persuasion, social noncooperation and economic boycotts, tax refusal, workers' and students' strikes, walkouts, marches, and demonstrations. Protesters also established effective channels of communication with people via newspapers, radio, and later television. By mid-March 1971, the methods of nonviolent resistance delivered de facto independence to Bengalis with banks and other financial institutions, educational organizations, government offices, courts, seaports, and airports all working under the Bengali authority.

Political, economic, and cultural aspects of the nonviolent struggles influenced the entire Bengali masses by shaping their identities to extend beyond a politically limited concept of East Pakistan's province, inspiring people to think and dream about their own language and their own independent state, and, finally, helping them to survive brutal, violent assaults that ensued in the period March–December 1971.

Notes

The author would like to express his sincere gratitude to Professor Syed Sikander Mehdi of Shaheed Zulfikar Ali Bhutto Institute of Science and Technology, Karachi, Pakistan, and to reviewers for their useful comments on earlier drafts of this chapter.

1. For details of Operation Searchlight, see Siddiq Salik, *Witness to Surrender,* 2nd ed. (Karachi: Oxford University Press, 1978), 71–90.

2. Sydney H. Schanberg, "Pakistan Divided," *Foreign Affairs* 50, no. 1 (1971): 125.

3. In this chapter, "Bengalis" refers to people who at the time lived in East Pakistan or later Bangladesh and, unless otherwise specified, does not include Bengalis living in India or elsewhere.

4. "The Bloody Birth of Bangladesh," *Time,* December 20, 1971.

5. K. P. Karunakara, "East Pakistan's Non-Violent Struggle," *Economic and Political Weekly,* March 20, 1971, 650.

6. These films, songs, musicals, and stage-dramas are considered cultural icons in Bangladesh.

7. There are significant works on the movement such as Badruddin Umar's *Purba Banglar Bhasha Andolon O Totkaleen Rajniti* (East Bengal's Language Movement and Contemporary Politics) (Dhaka: Mowla Brothers, 1970); Abdul Matin's participant account *Bangali Jatir Uttso O Bhasha Andolon* (The Origin of Bengali Nation and the Language Movement) (Dhaka: Book Point, 1995); and, in English, A. M. A. Muhith's *State Language Movement in East Bengal, 1947–1956* (Dhaka: University Press, 2008). However, these are not studies about the use of nonviolent action.

8. Zillur R. Khan, *The Third World Charisma: Sheikh Mujib and the Struggle for Freedom* (Dhaka: University Press, 1996), 45; Rounaq Jahan, *Pakistan: Failure in National Integration* (New York: Columbia University Press, 1972), 12.

9. Ishtiaq Hossain and Mahmud Hasan Khan, "The Rift Within an Imagined Community: Understanding Nationalism(s) in Bangladesh," *Asian Journal of Social Science* 34, no. 2 (2006): 324–339.

10. See M. Waheeduzzaman Manik, "The Making of the Formative Phases of the Bengali Language Movement in the Early Years of Pakistan," www.global webpost.com/bangla/info/articles/manik_dhiren_early_years.htm, accessed October 10, 2010; "History of Language Day," www.nvo.com/ghosh_research/nss-folder /historyoflanguageday/, accessed October 10, 2010; and Rafiqul Islam, "The Language Movement: An Outline," www.bdsdf.org/forum/index.php?showtopic =21165, accessed October 10, 2010.

11. Matin, *Bangali Jatir Uttso,* 9.

12. Ahmed Kamal, "A People's History of the Language Movement," *New Age,* February 21, 2008, 8.

13. Umar, *Purba Banglar Bhasha,* 20–21; M. A. Barnik, "The Proclamation of the Language Movement and Early Programmes," *New Nation* (Dhaka), February 21, 2009, 10. See also Manik, "Making of the Formative Phases."

14. M. Waheeduzzaman Manik, "History of Language Day," www.nvo.com/ ghosh_research/nss-folder/historyoflanguageday/, accessed October 10, 2010.

15. The information contained in this paragraph is based on M. A. Barnik, "Proclamation of the Language Movement." Barnik commented on a booklet entitled *Pakistaner Rashtra Bhasha Bangla Na Urdu?* (Pakistan's State Language— Bangla or Urdu?) (Dhaka: Tamaddun Majlish, September 15, 1947). The three articles included in *Pakistaner Rashtra Bhasha Bangla Na Urdu?* are Abul Kasem's "Our Proposal"; Kazi Motahar Hossain's "State Language Problem of East Pakistan"; and Abul Monsur Ahmad's "Bangla Will Be Our State Language." For details see Barnik, "Proclamation of the Language Movement," 10.

16. Barnik, "Proclamation of the Language Movement."

17. Manik, "Making of the Formative Phases."

18. M. Waheeduzzaman Manik, "The Forgotten Harbinger of the Language Movement," *Daily Star* (Dhaka), February 23, 2010, 14. Dutta, a Hindu arrested in Gandhi's Quit India campaign, had opposed partition but opted to stay in Pakistan rather than move home. The first to formally demand recognition of Bangla, he later became East Pakistan's minister of health. He was arrested by Pakistani forces on March 29, 1971, tortured, and killed.

19. Rafiqul Islam, "The Language Movement: An Outline," www.bdsdf.org/ forum/index.php?showtopic=21165, accessed October 10, 2010.

20. Matin, *Bangali Jatir Uttso,* 18.

21. Ibid.

22. Islam, "The Language Movement," 2–3. The son of a language movement participant recalls that, when the authorities refused to free the leaders Shawkat Ali, Qazi Golam Mahbub, and Zakir Hossain, those activists who had already been freed returned to the prison and refused to leave until all leaders were released.

23. Philip Oldenburg, "A Place Insufficiently Imagined: Language, Belief, and the Pakistan Crisis of 1971," *Journal of Asian Studies* 44, no. 4 (1985): 716.

24. Ibid.; Matin, *Bangali Jatir Uttso,* 17. See also Quamruddin Ahmed, *Purbo Banglar Samaj O Rajniti* (East Bengal's Society and Politics), 2nd ed. (Dhaka: Inside Publishers, 1976), 107.

25. Details of the meeting between Jinnah and members of the All-Party State Language Council of Action are taken from Matin, *Bangali Jatir Uttso,* 23–24; and Ahmed, *Purbo Banglar Samaj,* 107–108.

26. For further details of the meeting between Jinnah and members of the Action Committee on March 21, 1948, see Ahmed, *Purbo Banglar Samaj,* 107–108.

27. The descriptions are based on Matin, *Bangali Jatir Uttso,* 21.

28. A fund-raising flag day involved offering donors small flags to pin on their clothes to show support for the cause of Bangla.

29. Matin, *Bengali Jatir Uttso,* 21.

30. Ibid., 23; Ahmed, *Purbo Banglar Samaj,* 120.

31. Tito Scohel, "Bangla Language Movement: 21 February, 1952," www .mukto-mona.com/new_site/mukto-mona/bengali_heritage/bangla_language _movement.htm, accessed October 15, 2010. The following account of events on February 20–21 is based on this source.

32. Hayat Mamud, "The History of Observance of Ekushey," http://21st february.org/eassy21_8.htm/, accessed October 15, 2010.

33. Mamud, "The History of Observance of Ekushey."

34. Abul Mansur Ahmed, *Amar Dekha Rajnitir Panchash Bochor* (Fifty Years of Politics, As I Observed It) (Dhaka: Nowroj Kitabstan, n.d.), 318–319.

35. Eventually, the number of committee members increased to eighty-one, including many students and a number of women. See Mamud, "The History of Observance of Ekushey."

36. The description of the language movements in Barisal and Chittagong is based on information found in ibid.

37. Although the 1956 Constitution was abrogated two years later following a military coup led by General Ayub Khan, the 1962 Constitution reconfirmed Bengali as one of the state languages of Pakistan.

38. Manik, "Making of the Formative Phases."

39. The Commonwealth, set up in 1949, is a voluntary association of countries, currently consisting of fifty-four that are mainly former British colonies and territories.

40. *The People,* March 2, 1971, reprinted in *Bangladesh Documents* (New Delhi: Ministry of External Affairs, n.d.), 190.

41. S. A. Karim, *Sheikh Mujib: Triumph and Tragedy* (Dhaka: University Press, 2006), 183.

42. Rafiqul Islam, *Ekti Phulke Bacahbo Bole* (To Save a Flower) (Dhaka: University Press, 1988), 31.

43. *Pakistan Observer,* March 8, 1971, quoted in ibid.

44. Full text of Sheikh Mujibur Rahman's March 7, 1971 speech, www.albd .org/autoalbd/index.php?option=com_content&task=view&id=117&Itemid=44, accessed January 20, 2011.

45. For example, M. Anisuzzaman, "The Identity Question and Politics," in *Bangladesh: Promise and Performance,* ed. Rounaq Jahan (Dhaka: University Press, 2002), 45–63; and Habibul Haque Khondker, "A Pendular Theory of Nationalism," Working Paper Series No. 15 (Singapore: Asian Research Institute, National University of Singapore, 2003).

12

West Papua:
Civil Resistance, Framing, and
Identity, 1910s–2012

Jason MacLeod

On June 4, 2000, the Morning Star flag, the enduring symbol of a "new Papua" and Papuan nationalism,[1] was openly displayed during a large public gathering in Imbi Square, Jayapura, and the capital of West Papua.[2] Tens of thousands of people stood solemnly, fixated as the flag was raised beside the Indonesian flag. Many participants were openly crying, expressing years of suppressed emotion. The Papuans present were civilians, all unarmed. Indonesian police stood at the back, their guns lowered. Behind the gathered Papuans was a large statue of Yos Sudarso, an Indonesian military hero, poised ready to repel unseen enemies.[3] That day the Papuans turned their backs on Sudarso's statue, intensely focusing on the Morning Star flag and their desire for a different kind of tomorrow.

Only a year earlier, security forces on Biak Island had massacred over 100 Papuans at a similar flag raising; the military had violently repressed peaceful flag-raising events across the territory. But the political climate was now more open. Indonesian president Abdurrahman Wahid extended the hand of détente. He had unbanned the Morning Star flag and helped a national gathering of Papuan independence activists organized by the Presidium Dewan Papua (Papua Presidium Council), the group that planned the June flag raising. A month later security forces would again use lethal force to prevent flag raisings.[4] But for now in the uncertain freedom of the "Papuan Spring," they watched impassively.[5]

At this flag raising, Papuans rejected their Indonesian identity and embraced a different way of being, a longing for a different kind of political community. They sang the banned national anthem "Hai Tanahku Papua," wore traditional dress, and danced traditional Papuan dances.

If in some respects the flag raising mirrored Indonesian nationalist rituals,[6] there was one vital difference. Indonesian nationalist events recount armed struggle against the Dutch and military defense of the state, thus legitimating the contemporary role of Indonesian security forces.[7] Papuans, in turning their backs on Sudarso's statue, rejected being Indonesian and part of the Unitary Republic of Indonesia[8] while implicitly opposing armed struggle as the primary means of liberation. This flag raising in Imbi Square was part of a pattern of determined civil resistance, the primary method of struggle for Papuan self-determination.

My first argument in this chapter is that Papuans overwhelmingly rely on nonviolent civil resistance to oppose Indonesian rule. My second is that civil resistance forms, frames, and reinforces Papuan national identity while, at the same time, Papuan national identity—animated by Melanesian[9] culture and Christianity—propels civil resistance.

Historical Background

While their Melanesian kin living in Papua New Guinea were colonized by the British, Australians, and Germans,[10] West Papua was the easternmost point of the Dutch East Indies. When Indonesia formally became independent in 1949, the Netherlands retained control of West Papua, arguing that it was politically and culturally distinct.[11] Belatedly, they started to create Papuan-led institutional forms of self-rule in preparation for independence. On December 1, 1961, an embryonic Papuan parliament officially raised a new flag (the Morning Star), unveiled a coat of arms, and performed West Papua's national anthem. From that time, many Papuans have observed December 1 as their national day. However, these moves toward independence triggered Indonesian plans for military invasion.

In 1962, the Dutch were persuaded to place West Papua under transitional UN rule. In less than a year, on May 1, 1963, administration was transferred to the Indonesian government on the condition that there would be an internationally supervised act of self-determination. Instead of a referendum, the Indonesian government carried out what they called the Act of Free Choice—a "consultation" restricted to just 1,022 handpicked men, less than 0.01 percent of the Papuan population.[12] The Act of Free Choice took place under conditions of extreme violence and intimidation by Indonesian security personnel toward the indigenous Papuans.[13] Despite this, the UN General Assembly in November 1969 duly "took note" and West Papua was formally integrated into Indonesia and removed from the list of territories awaiting decolonization.[14] The stage was set for protracted conflict.

Early Resistance Movements

Indigenous Papuan nations have resisted incursions from outsiders for centuries.[15] From the 1850s to 1939, the Dutch colonialists, seeking to protect the spice trade, faced no fewer than forty-two rebellions (both violent and nonviolent).[16] Religious-political movements, anthropologically sometimes labeled cargo cults, were often in reality early forms of Papuan resistance.

By 1911, Papuan resistance leaders urged followers not to pay taxes and to withhold labor.[17] These tactics were repeated in 1938 in a nonviolent movement that was unmistakably nationalistic, both in terms of geographic scope and its goals—the unity and self-determination of diverse tribes. Anggaeta Menufandu, a *konor* (indigenous prophet), articulated grievances and incited dissent through Koreri, an indigenous ideology from Biak Island that she infused with Christian symbols and rituals.

The nonviolent tactics that appeared in 1911 predominated during the Koreri uprising: mass noncooperation with Dutch orders to participate in forced labor gangs, collective tax resistance, and mass defiance of government and mission bans on *wor* (ritual singing and dancing). For Anggaeta, a commitment to nonviolent discipline was central because she taught that the shedding of blood "bars the way to *Koreri*."[18] The Dutch tricolor flag was inverted—a reversal of the colonial political order—and the Morning Star and a cross were added, symbolizing a coming Papuan kingdom. Two decades later, this flag would inspire the design of the Papuans' national flag.

The movement, which continued until 1943, aroused strong religious fervor. As Anggaeta's influence spread, pilgrims disregarded Dutch and mission bans to visit her. The Dutch sent police to torch the houses constructed by pilgrims, provoking outrage and increasing the movement's popularity. By now Anggaeta was known as Anggaeta Bin Damai (Anggaeta woman of peace). When she was arrested, Biak erupted in riots. After completing her sentence, Anggaeta returned to the island of Insumbabi where she was enthusiastically welcomed. Visiting pilgrims breached Dutch bans on performing *wor* and drinking palm wine, shed their Western clothes for traditional Biak loincloths, and followed food taboos handed down in Manarmakeri stories.[19] A Dutch administrator at the time saw this movement as "far less a religion than a self-conscious Papuan nationalism."[20]

The Japanese invasion was initially welcomed as expelling the Dutch but, after incidents of Japanese cruelty, the movement sought freedom from all foreign control. In 1942, Anggaeta was imprisoned again. Movement leadership passed to Stephanus Simiopiaref, a Biak man in jail for murder. He escaped and tried to free Anggaeta. Now the movement became more nationalistic and martial, replete with units, ranks, and wooden rifles. Stephanus proclaimed himself "General," acknowledging Anggaeta as "Queen." Previously leadership had rested with women and "peace women" even banished those "who wanted war and had shed blood" to the neighboring small island of Rani (renamed Gadara) as a way of maintaining nonviolent discipline.[21] These exiles now became warriors in Stephanus's movement.

"The core of Stephanus' message and political propaganda," writes Susanna Rizzo, "was the attainment of political independence and national unity."[22] Despite favoring armed struggle, Stephanus's analysis of power could fit in a nonviolent action manual: the source of Papuan servitude was their willingness to obey foreign orders. Building on Angganeta's reclamation of traditions, Stephanus further fused Papuan identity and Christianity into a nationalist ideology of resistance based on promoting mass withdrawal of consent and refusal to cooperate with foreign rule: "From the moment the foreigners arrived we had to obey orders and were no longer *free people in our own land*. But our time is coming; the masters will be slaves and the slaves masters."[23]

The Japanese responded ruthlessly to the call for armed resistance, eliminating resistance groups and killing leaders, including Angganeta who was executed in mid-1942. On October 10, 1943, the Japanese massacred between 600 and 2,000 Biak Islanders.[24] At this point, the violent uprising imploded. The rebels attacked not only the Japanese, but also collaborators and bystanders. The violence continued in 1944 when the United States drove the Japanese out of Biak, at the cost of thousands of lives of Japanese and islanders.

Papuan nationalism was now out of the box. After Angganeta and Stephanus's movement and a simultaneous Papuan rebellion against Dutch rule in Tanah Merah in the south, resistance movements explicitly began to promote unity and the idea of a free and independent West Papua.[25]

Papuan Core Grievances and Indonesian Policies

Five mutually reinforcing grievances animate the ongoing West Papuan resistance:[26]

1. A contested view of history. While for Indonesia the 1969 Act of Free Choice was the last stage of an internationally endorsed decolonization process, most Papuans see it as a fraud—"the Act of No Choice"—and denounce the United Nations for acquiescing in the violation of their right to self-determination.
2. State-sanctioned human rights violations in West Papua.
3. Economic injustice characterized by destructive large-scale development projects, especially mines, oil and gas projects, logging, and palm oil plantations.
4. Migration of Indonesians from other parts of the archipelago into West Papua, resulting in conflict and competition between migrant

and indigenous populations over land, resources, and economic and political opportunities.[27]

5. Institutional racism and indigenous disadvantage and marginalization in the economy, education, health sector, security forces, and bureaucracy.[28]

These grievances form a narrative of betrayal and suffering at the hands of the international community, the Indonesian state, and global capital, resulting in high levels of frustration and a near total distrust of the central government. Jakarta's legitimacy is so low that even elected Papuan politicians and senior Papuan civil servants have little commitment to the Indonesian state.[29] The overwhelming majority of Papuans, particularly the students and youth, want independence.

Since 1963, the Indonesian pattern of rule has consisted of three central strategies:

- *Modernization,* promoting large-scale development projects and in-migration that do not benefit ordinary Papuans.
- *Repression,* including the widespread use of torture, which is both targeted and indiscriminate.
- *Closing off the province from outside scrutiny:* from the Act of Free Choice in 1969 to Suharto's fall in May 1998, West Papua was a military operations area. The region remains off limits to international journalists, diplomats, and international human rights organizations. While Indonesia moves toward greater democratization elsewhere, West Papua remains semi-authoritarian, ruled by local Papuan elites and a repressive occupying military and police force.

Indonesian nationalist leaders understood the threat that Papuan nationalism posed, renaming the territory Irian Jaya and the indigenous population as Irianese. In a few short years "being Papuan" went from something promoted by the Dutch to something criminalized by the Indonesians.[30] Ever since mass civil resistance forced Suharto from power, military operations and repressive police action have continued in West Papua.

Cultural Resistance

During the 1970s, Papuan activists challenged Suharto's attempts to impose a hegemonic Indonesian identity. The cultural music group Mambesak, founded by Arnold Ap and Sam Kapissa, collected and performed songs and dances from all over West Papua, thus fashioning a pan-Papuan identity transcending tribal differences. Initially, Mambesak carefully framed their cultural action as a contribution to diversity in a unified Indonesia but, for

Papuan audiences, the implicit message of songs in their own languages, local dances, and hidden metaphors "kept a sense of alternative identities alive" that evoked pride in being Papuan.[31]

Occasionally, Mambesak were overtly political, as in 1977 when they danced naked to protest the Indonesian's bloody Operasi Koteka (Operation Penis Gourd) in the Bailem Valley.[32] Inspired by Mambesak, Papuan performance groups proliferated in the early 1980s until a new wave of repression hit them.

In November 1983 Ap was arrested and imprisoned, and in April 1984 he and another Mambesak member, Eddie Mofu, were killed, allegedly trying to escape. These murders were part of reprisals in the wake of a foiled attack by Papuan guerrillas. To draw international attention to the grave situation, some 11,000 Papuans took part in an organized mass exodus east to Papua New Guinea. Once again Papuan songs and dances were banned, and once again performing them became an act of civil resistance.

Through music and dance, Papuans came to see themselves as a distinct people with their own culture, different and separate from Indonesian culture and identity. Song commemorated suffering at the hands of the state—privations not officially taught, but remembered and passed on orally by Papuan clans and tribes.[33] As performances spread across tribal boundaries, Papuans began to see their experience under Indonesian rule as a collective injustice and Indonesian rule as intolerable. "In a dominated political environment, performing a dance of familiar local origin, to music played by local performers using *tifa* (a traditional Papuan drum) and ukulele, among people considered 'us,' was affective."[34] Teaching and spreading cultural performance was like "sharpening the blade of a knife."[35] This remains the case today when song is also used to exhort unity.[36]

The most politicized way of expressing Papuan identity is through raising the Morning Star flag—a symbol imbued with hidden, mythical Papuan understanding of the inevitability of transformation.[37] Filep Karma, a Biak civil servant and activist who at the time of this writing is in jail after being sentenced to fifteen years for raising the Morning Star flag at a nonviolent demonstration in 2004, explicitly acknowledges Koreri and Angganeta's movement as a source of inspiration for his own actions.[38] The Indonesian authorities, recognizing the power of symbols, see displaying the flag as tantamount to declaring independence. Consequently, despite the nonviolent nature of flag raisings, state security forces under Suharto and since have dealt harshly with flag raisers, be they civilians or members of the armed resistance.[39]

The Role of Church Leaders and Christianity

Christian churches are the only foreign institutions to have taken root in West Papua. They simultaneously play both a pacifying and mobilizing role, reflecting different theological traditions as well as ethnic composition. Despite this mixed history many, but not all, pro-independence activists explicitly use Christian frames to facilitate collective action. The churches as institutions have also provided an organizational base and protection for those engaged in liberation work.

Christian missionaries first arrived in Mansiram, a small island off the coast near Manokwari in 1855. Evangelism spread to the Central Highlands much later.[40] The 2000 census indicated that some 90 percent of the indigenous Papuan population is Christian.[41] Much of the theology preached in West Papua is conservative. The largest church, the Protestant Gereja Kristen Injil (GKI), has seen its role as protector of its congregation, cautioning against active resistance and even promoting the 1969 Act of Free Choice. The GKI is further constrained on the coast by the active participation of a significant proportion of migrants, including present and former Indonesian soldiers. Consequently, some Papuans view Christianity as at best irrelevant[42] and at worst as hindering or undermining resistance.[43]

Those Christian leaders working for social change have for the most part carefully eschewed political references to independence or separatism, instead invoking the gospel mandate to speak out about human rights, justice, and peace. Over time, more church leaders have become outspoken about human rights violations and the need for far-reaching justice. Some have joined pro-independence groups, called for political dialogue, taken up arms, and become active in campaigns for civil and political or economic, social, and cultural rights. Such leaders argue that the Indonesian state needs to engage politically with independence activists, whether armed or unarmed, if they want an end to conflict.

The moderator of the Kingmi Church, Benny Giay, argues that a Papuan nonviolent liberation theology is emerging organically from the Papuan people as praxis that animates action.[44] Some of its contours include

- A recognition of *memoria passionis* (the suffering of the Papuan people)[45] and an active involvement in the struggle for human rights, peace, and justice as a necessary part of being a Christian. A church that serves the people must engage itself in struggle; people need to experience God as a liberator in their own lives.[46]
- A commitment to struggle through nonviolent action in ways that are consistent with the gospel injunction to "love enemies," but are simultaneously directed toward realizing a transformed social, political, and economic order.[47]
- Pride in being Papuan. This includes a critical appraisal of those Papuan cultural values and practices that support liberation, justice, and peace, rejecting any not consistent with Christian faith.[48] It also includes incorporating Papuan cultural performances—music, dance, indigenous Papuan languages, and rituals—into church liturgies.

This practice dates back to early resistance movements, was reinvigorated by Mambesak, and has been taken up by Protestants and Catholics.[49]

- A theological justification of the need for self-government. God has made Papuans different from Indonesians and has given them their own land.[50]
- The importance of resisting illegitimate government.[51]
- A belief in the inevitability of liberation and a concomitant recognition of the need for reconciliation, including reconciling personal, tribal, and political differences within the movement. Church leaders regularly urge movement unity.

Christian identity and beliefs act as transformative frames that promote what Doug McAdam called "cognitive liberation," the belief that not only have Papuans been subject to a grave injustice but collectively they can take action to challenge and ultimately transform oppression.[52]

Papuan Resistance Since the Fall of Suharto

It is possible to map five overlapping phases of the struggle since Suharto's fall in 1998.

Phase 1: The Papuan Spring

Suharto's fall released long-repressed hopes for freedom and led to a temporary political liberalization and openness at a time when the central government and military had not yet consolidated their power. Tens of thousands of Papuans mobilized in an atmosphere of euphoria and expectation of independence. In 1999 a team of 100 Papuans met Indonesian president Bacharuddin Jusuf Habibie to demand independence. Although the meeting had no clear outcome, the Papuan struggle had exploded onto center stage and the team returned home to a hero's welcome.[53]

Mass civilian-based mobilization by Papuans led the central government to accept the Special Autonomy proposal, a compromise endorsed by Papuan moderates and their allies. This was not full independence, although the proposal developed by Papuan leaders (which was ultimately rejected in Jakarta) went a long way toward meeting many Papuan demands.[54]

Phase 2: The Collapse of Special Autonomy and Return to Repression

In 2001 after the central government had already agreed to Special Autonomy, the state jailed five Papuan independence leaders. Shortly after, in

November 2001 Kopassus (Indonesian Special Forces) assassinated Theys Eluay, chair of the Presidium Dewan Papua. Jakarta proceeded to divide the territory into two separate provinces, renewed a campaign of public acts of terror, and then failed to implement regulations essential for the acceptance of Special Autonomy by most Papuans.

Phase 3: Decline of the Overt Independence Movement and Emergence of Limited Campaigns

This phase overlapped the widespread disillusionment about Special Autonomy. As Jakarta squeezed the political space for pro-independence campaigning, more localized struggles emerged. Some were widespread, like the successful campaign that scuttled plans for a third province. Others were initially less visible such as local campaigns against logging and palm oil plantations and the Papuan women fruit and vegetable sellers' campaign for their own market place in the capital.

With the development of more localized campaigns, students demanded closure of the Freeport McMoRan/Rio Tinto gold and copper mine. The campaign against the mine, however, dissipated after a demonstration in Jayapura turned violent in March 2006 and Papuans stoned five security forces to death. Brimob (the paramilitary mobile police) retaliated, shooting up student dormitories and randomly arresting and beating Papuans. Hundreds fled to neighboring Papua New Guinea. These events set back student organizing for years.

Conditions for workers at the Freeport mine and landowners remained dire. Tongoi Papua, the first independent labor union in West Papua, was formed in 2006 by indigenous workers of the mine, uniting highlanders and islanders who had previously been separated by decades of mistrust and mutual suspicion. In April 2007, mass demonstrations and a 6,000-strong labor strike won Papuan mine workers improved conditions, including doubling the wages of the most poorly paid mine workers. Four years later, 8,000 Papuan and Indonesian workers at the mine went on strike again, over low wages, poor conditions, and the right to organize as workers. Several miners had been shot and killed by unidentifiable assailants. By November 2011 analysts estimated that the mine had forfeited a staggering US$1.3 billion in lost revenues.[55]

Phase 4: Noncooperation Spreads to State Institutions

By 2009–2010, precipitated by an emerging consensus that Special Autonomy had failed and that the religious-inspired Papua Land of Peace Campaign was ineffectual,[56] Papuan leaders felt that a more forceful approach was needed.

On June 9 and 10, 2010, the Majelis Rakyat Papua (MRP; Papuan People's Assembly), a state institution, held an open forum to evaluate Special

Autonomy. This Papuan-only senate advises the Jakarta-controlled provincial parliament on how to safeguard Papuan cultural traditions and values. The MRP concluded that Special Autonomy had failed. It promised protection and prosperity. Instead, torture and human rights violations by the security forces were worsening; migrants continued to pour in, further marginalizing indigenous Papuans; and business as usual continued for transnational companies, safe in the knowledge that the Indonesian military was keeping a repressive lid on boiling Papuan anger.

On June 18, in coordination with the newly formed Forum Demokrasi Rakyat Papua Bersatu (FORDEM; Democratic Forum of the United Papuan People), 15,000 Papuans from seven districts demanded that parliamentarians should hand back discredited Special Autonomy to Jakarta in no less than three weeks. After this deadline, 20,000 indigenous Papuans—many in traditional dress—walked and danced their way from the MRP offices to the center of Jayapura. When the protesters reached parliament, the demonstration became a two-day occupation of the building by thousands of Papuans, surrounded by fully armed police, water cannons, and armored personnel carriers. This was the largest civilian mobilization since the Papuan Spring of 1998–2000.[57]

In the past, the Papuan movement has targeted Jakarta and the international community, asking others to give them independence while their political representatives waited for the next injection of Indonesian cash. This time, it was different. Papuans targeted their own leaders, demanding a special session to return Special Autonomy to Jakarta. Papuans did not want the law revised; they wanted political negotiations and a referendum.

Phase 5: Independence Declared Again

The occupation of parliament failed to result in dialogue mediated by a third party or a referendum. Neither did it precipitate discussion about Special Autonomy. Instead, the president proposed the Unit for the Acceleration of Development in Papua (UP4B). Papuan resistance leaders saw this as further evidence that Jakarta views West Papua's crises as an economic rather than political problem.

Faced with intransigence on the part of the Indonesian government, Papuan leaders escalated tactics. On October 19, 2011, the last day of the Third Papuan People's Congress, a three-day gathering of unarmed resistance groups, Papuan leaders declared independence. The response from the security forces was swift and brutal. About an hour after the congress concluded, the security forces opened fire. Three Papuans were shot and killed. Two were fatally stabbed. Three hundred people were arrested and beaten. At the time of this writing, six of the leaders remain in jail, charged with treason. In contrast, the police who shot, stabbed, beat, and tortured people received only warning letters.

The killing of protesters at the congress relayed by phone, Facebook, YouTube, and mailing lists outraged Papuans, which led more to support independence. It divided political elites inside Indonesia, attracted more third-party support for the West Papuan cause, and revealed the ugly face of Indonesian colonial rule.

This backfire dynamic was evident a few weeks later on December 1, 2011. Despite being fired at during the congress, senior leaders organized nonviolent independence celebrations across the country. The six jailed independence leaders urged Papuans to "celebrate independence in an atmosphere of peace, safety and calm."[58] Tens of thousands of Papuans—in Jayapura, Sentani, Manokwari, Sorong, Merauke, Timika, Puncak Jaya, Paniai, Wamena, and inside Indonesia in Jogjakarta and Jakarta—waved the banned Morning Star flag and shouted "freedom." At many demonstrations inside West Papua, the October 19 Declaration of Independence was read again. Papuans had cast off their fear in a way that has not been seen before. In Sorong, for example, even Papuan government civil servants and retired Papuan military personnel joined the December 1 rally, prompting one experienced organizer to remark that this was "really different from previously."[59]

The Third Papuan People's Congress and December 1, 2011, have altered the political climate in West Papua. Papuans are less fearful, they are angrier, and they are less likely to obey bans on freedom of expression. As civil resistors simultaneously become a civilian media network, the Indonesian government's ban on the media is becoming increasingly impossible to enforce.

The following year the position of radicals on both sides of the political divide had hardened. The Komite Nasional Papua Barat (KNPB; West Papua National Committee), a nonviolent pro-independence group, continued to press for a referendum on West Papua's political status while the Indonesian military stigmatized nonviolent pro-independence groups as violent separatists who threatened the viability of the Indonesian state. Such people, the Indonesian security forces argued, forfeited their rights to protection. As KNPB protests continued to grow the country was rocked by a spate of fatal shootings followed by bomb attacks in Wamena and Jayapura. Talk of dialogue dissipated as the Indonesian police fingered KNPB as responsible for the violence. This was despite the fact that no hard evidence linked KNPB to either the shootings or the bombings. In contrast dozens of witnesses had seen members of the police shoot and kill two of the victims. KNPB chair Viktor Yeimo also consistently denied the group's involvement in violence and pressed home their nonviolent credentials but to no avail. By November 2012 the Indonesian police and military had all but "declared war" on KNPB. Detachment 88, the US- and Australian-trained and -funded counterterrorist police group, members of the Indonesian police, and the Indonesian military launched a brutal countrywide offensive, killing KNPB activists, jailing scores of others, and forcing the entire leadership underground.

Far from neutralizing dissent, repression by the Indonesian state has only galvanized Papuan's freedom dreams.

Civil Resistance and Development of Collective Identity

Civil resistance in West Papua not only expresses collective identity, but also helps form and consolidate a pan-Papuan identity. Indigenous Papuan culture and Christianity in West Papua act as markers of difference between Papuans and others—the Dutch and the Japanese in the past and Indonesian migrants in the present. However, identity is not formed only in opposition to being Indonesian, but also in relation to resistance, particularly civilian-based resistance. Nonviolent tactical choices grow out of a distinctly Papuan culture and faith. In turn, they generate and reinforce Papuan unity by emphasizing and re-creating shared identity and meaning.

The shared cultural practices in Angganeta's movement were easily replicated across clan and tribal differences, as the music and dance group Mambesak were to show. In addition to song, dance, and the Morning Star flag, food also offers scope for affirming a distinct Papuan and non-Indonesian identity. In Angganeta's day, people from Biak observed Manarmakeri's taboos. Today some Papuans who are committed to a free and independent West Papua eat sago, sweet potatoes, fish, and pig (traditional West Papuan produce) while avoiding the food of collaboration: rice, tofu, and tempe (traditional Indonesian food).

Christianity has become another marker of difference between Papuans, who are overwhelmingly Christian, and Indonesian migrants, who are overwhelmingly Muslim.[60] Culture and Christianity are entwined. Angganeta, for instance, used Christian place names to mark transformed or liberated territory and she was often called the "Golden Woman of Judea" or "Mary" and greeted her "disciples" with the refrain, "Ye-sus Christus and liberty."[61] Nowadays many Papuan activists sign off their correspondence and greet crowds with "shalom," the Hebrew expression for peace, differentiating it from the analogous Muslim greeting, "salam."

Papuan Christians use church services and prayer to support the cause of self-determination.[62] Many Papuan Christians perceive God as a liberator who gave Papuans their unique identity, their own cultural practices, and their own homeland:

> God created people to be different. Papuans are different to Javanese and different to other people too. God gave Papua to Papuans as a home, so they could eat sago and sweet potato there. God gave them a penis gourd (koteka) and loincloth (cawat) for clothes. God gave them curly hair and black skin. Papuans are Papuans. They can never be turned into Javanese or Sumatrans, or vice versa. The Javanese were given Java. Tahu (soya

bean curd) and tempe (soya bean cake) is their food. Their skin is light and their hair is straight. The real problem is that those in power in this republic have tried as best they could to make Papuans talk, think, look and behave like Javanese (or Sumatrans), and that goes against the order of God's creation. That is where the conflict comes from. How to end it? Let the Papuans and the Javanese each develop according to their own tastes and rhythms, each in their own land.[63]

Giay explains how faith enables liberation and inspires hope: "The Bible becomes a 'window' that gives people new possibilities, new dimensions to see a better world than the one they live in every day. The Bible portrays a new world, free from manipulation, intimidation, and trauma. It lifts up the eyes of those who are oppressed to a new world. Sometimes people see in this new world a New Papua, an independent West Papua."[64]

This faith-based injunction to struggle nonviolently helps to humanize Papuans to others and to ennoble Papuan views of themselves. Racist foreign discourses of Papuans as "savages" and "cannibals" are turned on their head. Through civil resistance, Papuans become dignified and "civilized" while members of Indonesian security forces—Brimob, Kostrad (infantry combat troops), and Kopassus, in particular, that use torture and barbaric killings against the Papuan people—become "devils," the signifiers of the "savage."[65]

Unlike other parts of Indonesia, Papuan national identity is not a subnational identity that complements and enriches Indonesian identity. Rather, Papuan nationalism is in competition with Indonesian identity and acts as a unifying force between diverse Papuan tribes. Papuan nationalism shaped through the process of defining Papuanness in relation to not being Indonesian also reinforces nonviolent discipline. The promotion of Papuan nationalism has not led to any widespread or regular interethnic violence between Papuans and Indonesians. Although the potential for ethnic conflict is real, incidents of interethnic violence have been extremely rare.[66]

Framing and Mobilization Around Collective Identity: A Two-Edged Sword

Mobilization around Papuan national identity works well in transcending tribal differences, but poses problems in creating networks of support as well as in its narrow strategic focus on independence—a demand less likely to resonate with potential Indonesian allies than to arouse fears that Papuans and their allies are seeking to unravel the Indonesian state.

This especially is a problem for Papuans because the Indonesian government could control Papuan land and exploit their resources even if the Papuans withhold cooperation. To maintain the occupation, Jakarta depends less on Papuans than on sustaining domestic support for a greater Indonesia.

In brief, Papuans need Indonesian allies. However, when Papuans exclusively appeal to indigenous identity and Christianity, frame their grievances around historical injustices, and communicate their aspirations in ways that emphasize independence, they unwittingly limit their ability to mobilize support from other Indonesians who are overwhelmingly nationalist and Muslim. As a result, Papuans reduce their chances of winning over a key influence on the Indonesian government: the Indonesian people.

In addition, the Indonesian state also depends on technical, economic, military, and diplomatic assistance and support from Jakarta's international allies. Therefore, a key element of any strategy of liberation requires Papuans to build broad alliances. Domestic (inside Indonesia) and international (outside Indonesia) solidarity then needs to be directed at key sources of the Indonesian government's power in order to restrain Jakarta's capability and willingness to repress Papuans.[67]

Papuan student activists complained to Neles Tebay, a Catholic priest facilitating internal dialogue between Papuan political factions and working toward dialogue with the Indonesian government, that progressive Indonesian students will support protests against the Freeport mine or for demilitarization, but will not join them in demanding a referendum for independence and do not seem to care about the historical injustices toward Papuans. Tebay responded, "psychologically it is always going to be difficult for Indonesian students to support Papuans wanting to address historical grievances. Their understanding of history is too different from Papuans and the emotional attachment to a unitary Indonesian state of even the most progressive student runs deep."[68] Instead, he counseled Papuan students first to find out what Indonesian students are passionate about. "Perhaps it is the environment, or corruption, or anti-militarism. Find this issue and then work together."

This highlights the conundrum for Papuan activists. There is a perception that working for intermediate objectives means selling out the long-term goal of independence. Yet to build Indonesian support for Papuans and put pressure on the Jakarta government require framing campaigns around intermediate objectives like freedom of expression, democracy, environmental protection, corruption, sustainable development, universal access to education and health services, accountable government, and human rights. This does not mean giving up on larger goals like independence, but views strategy and mobilizing the movement as a process of Papuans building their power through reaching out to potential allies and winning more limited campaigns that will undermine military impunity or stop ecological devastation. Such campaigns can simultaneously strengthen Indonesian democracy and build Papuans' international reputation—developments that will leave Papuans in a better position to realize larger aspirations.[69] This is a strategic challenge. Papuans need to use collective action frames that resonate with different audiences at different times, define intermediate demands, and time mobilization to achieve short-term objectives, but in ways that leave the movement in a stronger position to achieve their ultimate goal: full political freedom.

A further danger in depending primarily on a collective Papuan identity to mobilize resistance is that a new Papua is best built on an inclusive vision and a deeper articulation of the multiple meanings of *merdeka* (freedom).[70] John Rumbiak and Benny Giay urge that this vision needs to include not only diverse Papuan tribes, but also Indonesian migrants.[71] Mobilization through an exclusive Papuan identity will create a fragile unity, perhaps liable to break down under stress and certainly incapable of carrying through an agenda for democratic transformation.

A few Papuan activists have told me that independence will solve everything, "ushering in the promised land" and "a time of plenty when no one will have to work."[72] Other Papuans recognize that an independent West Papuan state could replicate the problems Papuans have with current governance or generate a new set of problems without resolving the underlying causes of injustice. For instance, resource conflict generated by mining and logging companies will not necessarily be resolved through independence. This is why civil resistance needs to be waged in ways that prefigure the kind of society Papuans want.

Conclusion

Since 1998, nonviolent means for addressing Papuan grievances and pursuing Papuan aspirations have been used more regularly and more extensively than violence or conventional political activity. Papuans recognize the futility of violent resistance against the Indonesian Army that is simply more numerous and better equipped than any armed challenge that Papuans could hope to mount. And when the Tentara Pembebasan Nasional-Papua Barat (TPN-PB; West Papuan National Liberation Army) does use violence, reprisals by the security forces exact a heavy cost on the civilian population. "Whenever there is violence there is a tendency for a violent response. That is why we need to keep our political struggle nonviolent," says former political prisoner Reverend Obed Komba.[73]

Papuan civil resistance also draws on continuous traditions of nonviolent resistance that stretch back to at least the 1850s and it relies heavily on indigenous and cultural frames as well as Christian narratives. Over many decades, civil resistance has formed and reinforced collective Papuan identity and Papuan nationalism through giving Papuans a means to defy successive colonial powers while casting the Papuan struggle as one that is civilized, dignified, and blessed by God. At the same time, this deeply rooted collective identity and nationalism has helped to strengthen civil resistance by mobilizing ordinary Papuans and forging unity among tribal groups.

Papuans have a long history of struggle against outside incursions through overt and everyday acts of resistance. Because this is so strongly based in Papuan culture and values, resistance has a strength and vitality that at times seems irrepressible. This strong collective identity is a source of empowerment for nonviolent resistance, but it can sometimes frame resistance too narrowly. An exclusive identity framed around ethnicity, Christianity, and independence restricts Papuans' ability to construct alliances with progressive Indonesians and to capitalize on decades of Papuan-led international solidarity work, thereby greatly reducing the leverage Papuans have in Jakarta. In opting for everything independence Papuans risk gaining nothing. At the same time, making demands other than independence does not necessarily mean rejecting independence; it is about building social and political power for continued struggle. In order to build alliances with progressive Indonesians, Papuans may need to consider redirecting horizontal framing around what it means to "be" Papuan to vertical framing around state and corporate abuses.

Arguably, the nonviolent and unconventional forms of civic participation and action have mobilized more people, secured more political gains, and best sustained collective Papuan identity. But civil resistance that is influenced by a relatively narrower understanding of Papuan national identity and desire for an independent state alienates progressive Indonesians and has so far failed to secure broader international support. The question remains: How can Papuans transform their civil resistance into a series of more limited campaigns waged within more broadly defined, and thus potentially more acceptable, struggles for social, economic, cultural, civic, and political rights that simultaneously build a momentum for independence?

Notes

The author thanks Maciej Bartkowski, Anne Brown, Brian Martin, Cammi Webb, Daniel Ritter, Howard Clark, Jill Prideaux, Peter King, Jim Elmslie, and Richard Chauvel for comments.

1. *New Papua* is an open term, pointing to a transformed society without prescribing its form. It was popularized in the book by Benny Giay, *Toward a New Papua*. See Benny Giay, *Menuju Papua Baru* (Jayapura: Deiyai and Elsham Papua, 2000). *Papuans* here indicates indigenous Melanesians under Indonesian rule in western New Guinea. *West Papua* and *new Papua* refer to the provinces Papua and Papua Barat.

2. This event is captured in Mark Worth's film, *Land of the Morning Star* (a Film Australia National Interest Program produced with the assistance of the Australian Broadcasting Corporation) and referred to in Richard Chauvel, "Papuan Nationalism: Christianity and Ethnicity," in *The Politics of the Periphery in Indonesia*, ed. Minako Sakai, Glenn Banks, and J. H. Walker (Singapore: NUS Press, 2009), 201.

3. Sudarso died in January 1962 in an Indonesian military operation to gain control of West Papua.

4. Human Rights Watch, "Human Rights and Pro-Independence Actions in Irian Jaya, 1999–2000" (Jakarta: Human Rights Watch, 2000), www.hrw.org/hrw/reports /2000/papua/, accessed April 2, 2007; Human Rights Watch, "Indonesia: Violence and Political Impasse in Papua" (Jakarta: Human Rights Watch, 2000).

5. The phrase "Papuan Spring" was coined by Richard Chauvel, *Constructing Papuan Nationalism: History, Ethnicity, and Adaptation* (Washington, DC: East-West Center, 2005). Since the fall of Suharto in 1998, Indonesia has had four presidents—Bacharuddin Jusuf Habibe, 1998–1999; Abdurrahman Wahid, 1999–2001; Megawati Sukarnoputri, 2001–2004; and Susilo Bambang Yudhoyono, 2004.

6. Michael Cookson, "Batik Irian: Imprints of Indonesian Papua" (PhD dissertation, Australian National University, 2008).

7. Since independence, the primary role of Indonesia's security forces has been to defend Indonesia's territorial integrity against "separatism" in Indonesia's restive peripheries: Aceh in the west, Maluku and West Papua in the east, and, prior to 1999, East Timor.

8. The English translation of the official name of the Indonesian state, Negara Kesatuan Republik Indonesia.

9. The Pacific subregion of Melanesia comprises New Guinea (Indonesian-ruled West Papua in the west and independent Papua New Guinea in the east), the Solomon Islands, New Caledonia, Vanuatu, Fiji, and the Torres Strait Islands. In the island of New Guinea (Papua New Guinea and West Papua) alone, there are some 1,200 distinct languages. In the rural areas people live in close-knit, semiautonomous, kin-based communities, with subsistence-based economies. Communally owned land connects Melanesians with an entwined past, present, and future in which the spirit realm and ancestors continue to play a central role. Melanesian political culture is based more on influence than authority, but with considerable diversity in leadership traditions. A high value is placed on dialogue, reciprocity, and exchange. See, for instance, M. Anne Brown, "Custom and Identity: Reflections on and Representations of Violence in Melanesia," in *Promoting Conflict or Peace Through Identity,* ed. Nikki Slocum-Bradley (Hampshire: Ashgate, 2008), 183–208.

10. Australia administered Papua New Guinea as a UN protectorate until independence in 1975.

11. In West Papua, unlike elsewhere in the Dutch East Indies, the Dutch chose not to operate through local rulers but established a second layer of administration run by Indonesian migrants. While this experience deepened non-Papuan Indonesians' attachment to a state that included all the former Dutch East Indies, Papuans resented the administrative role of non-Papuans, hence, their belated and marginal involvement in Indonesia's independence struggle. Chauvel, *Constructing Papuan Nationalism.*

12. Exact numbers vary but John Saltford, a leading historian of the period, argues in *The United Nations and the Indonesian Takeover of West Papua, 1962–1969: The Anatomy of Betrayal* (London: Routledge Curzon, 2003) that 1,026 people were originally selected with 1,022 (less than 0.01 percent of the population) eventually participating in the Act of Free Choice. The Act of Free Choice consisted of a series of "consultations" with a few hundred participants at a time. These staged events were held in different parts of the country over the course of a few months.

13. Saltford, *The United Nations and the Indonesian Takeover*; Pieter Drooglever, *An Act of Free Choice: Decolonisation and the Right to Self-Determination in West Papua* (Oxford: Oneworld, 2009).

14. "Take note" is the UN's lowest rank of approval. It implies that the matter in question was agreed to but with some misgivings and open to review later. Dr. Greg Poulgrain, personal communication with the author, April 2, 2006.

15. Prior to Indonesians assuming control of the territory, the Spanish, Portuguese, Dutch, Japanese, British, sultan of Tidore, and various traders and missionaries made claim to all or part of West Papua.

16. Susanna Rizzo, "From Paradise Lost to Promised Land: Christianity and the Rise of West Papuan Nationalism" (PhD dissertation, University of Wollongong, 2004); Peter Worsley, *The Trumpet Shall Sound: A Study of "Cargo" Cults in Melanesia* (London: Paladin, 1967); Freerk Kamma, *Koreri: Messianic Movements in the Biak-Numfor Culture Area* (The Hague: Koninklijk Instituut, 1972); Danilyn Rutherford, *Raiding the Land of the Foreigners: The Limits of the Nation on an Indonesian Frontier* (Princeton: Princeton University Press, 2003), 190.

17. Kamma, *Koreri*; Rizzo, "From Paradise Lost to Promised Land."

18. Kamma, *Koreri,* cited in Rutherford, *Raiding the Land of the Foreigners,* 189.

19. Angganeta prophesied that Manarmakeri would return to liberate the Papuans. Rutherford, *Raiding the Land of the Foreigners,* 151.

20. Jan Victor de Bruijn, "The Mansren Cult of Biak," *South Pacific* 5, no. 1 (1951): 10.

21. Rutherford, *Raiding the Land of the Foreigners,* 194–195.

22. Rizzo, "From Paradise Lost to Promised Land," 307; Rutherford, *Raiding the Land of the Foreigners,* 197; Kamma, *Koreri.*

23. Hugo Pos, "The Revolt of Mansren," *American Anthropologist* 52 (1960): 561–564, cited in Rizzo, "From Paradise Lost to Promised Land," 307–308 (Rizzo's emphasis).

24. Kamma cited in Rutherford, *Raiding the Land of the Foreigners,* 200.

25. Rizzo, "From Paradise Lost to Promised Land," 308.

26. See Neles Tebay, *West Papua: The Struggle for Peace and Justice* (London: Catholic Institute for International Relations, 2005); Jason MacLeod, "Self-Determination and Autonomy: The Meaning of Freedom in West Papua," in *Security and Development in the Pacific Islands: Social Resilience in Emerging States,* ed. M. Anne Brown (London: Lynne Rienner, 2007); Jason MacLeod, "The Role of Strategy in Advancing Nonviolent Resistance in West Papua," in *Building Sustainable Futures: Enacting Peace and Development,* ed. Luc Reychler, Julianne Funck Deckard, and Kevin H. R. Villanueva (Bilbao: University of Deusto, 2009). The Indonesian Institute of Sciences suggests four themes for Papuan grievances: political status and historical construction of the conflict; state violence and rights violations; failure of development; and marginalization and discrimination. See Muridan S. Widjojo et al., *Papua Road Map: Negotiating the Past, Improving the Present and Securing the Future* (Jakarta: Indonesian Institute of Sciences, 2008).

27. In many urban areas of West Papua, the indigenous populations are already a minority. In the remote interior, they make up approximately 80 percent of the population. The 2010 census details the influx of non-Papuans: Papua Province has the highest rate of Indonesian immigration (5.48 percent) in Indonesia and Papua Barat Province the fourth (3.72 percent).

28. The Indonesian government's educational policy aims to promote integration into the Unitary Republic. See Jason MacLeod, "Self-Determination and Autonomy"; and Brigham Golden, "Letter to the Editor," *Van Zorge Report,* November 30, 2000, 33–34.

29. John Braithwaite, Valerie Braithwaite, Michael Cookson, and Leah Dunn, *Anomie and Violence: Non-Truth and Reconciliation in Indonesian Peacebuilding* (Canberra: Australian National University Press, 2010), 133–134.

30. Diana Glazebrook, "Dwelling in Exile, Perceiving Return: West Papuan Refugees from Irian Jaya Living at East Awin in Western Province, Papua New Guinea" (PhD dissertation, Australian National University, 2001), 60.

31. Danilyn Rutherford, "Remembering Sam Kapissa," *Inside Indonesia* 67 (2001): 16–17, cited in Diana Glazebrook, "Teaching Performance Art Is Like Sharpening the Blade of a Knife," *Asia Pacific Journal of Anthropology* 5, no. 1 (2004): 5.

32. Glazebrook, "Teaching Performance Art," 8–9. When the Dani rebelled against this attempted ban on the penis gourd, hundreds—perhaps thousands—of them were killed. Villagers still tell stories of elders dropped from military helicopters and the Bailem River flowing red with blood.

33. Giay, *Menuju Papua Baru*; Budi Hernawan and Theo van den Broek, "Dialog Nasional Papua, sebuah kisah 'Memoria Passionis': kisah ingatan penderitaan sebangsa," *Tifa Irian* 8 (March 1999).

34. Gillian Bottomley, *From Another Place: Migration and the Politics of Culture* (Cambridge: Cambridge University Press, 1992), cited in Glazebrook, "Teaching Performance Art," 9.

35. This analogy was shared with Glazebrook ("Teaching Performance Art," 1) by a West Papuan refugee.

36. Alex Rayfield, "Singing for Life," *Inside Indonesia* 78 (2004): 7–8. The members of the contemporary Papuan music group Gejolak, for instance, refer back to reading or listening to Mambesak while chewing betel nut, which they link with resistance and liberation.

37. The Morning Star gives Manarmakeri the secret of life.

38. Rutherford, *Raiding the Land of the Foreigners*.

39. Despite President Yudhuyono's international reputation as a democrat, Indonesian Law 77/2007 contradicts the constitutional guarantes of freedom of expression and reverses Wahid's decision to allow the Morning Star flag to be displayed alongside and lower than the Indonesian flag.

40. Protestant missionaries opened posts in the Paniai region in 1938 and in Bailem Valley in 1954. Missionaries were often the first contact that highlanders had with Western society.

41. This information was not updated in the 2010 census.

42. In the mid-1990s, Benny Giay and Theo van den Broek traveled to the highlands to negotiate the release of two Belgian filmmakers held hostage by guerrillas. Giay and van den Broek were met by a group of Papuans who formally handed them their Bibles, saying that evangelical Christianity had not helped them in their struggle for independence. See Renee Kjar, "The Invisible Aristocrat: Benny Giay in Papuan History" (bachelor of arts honors thesis, Australian National University, 2002), www.papuaweb.org.au/dlib/s123/kjar/ba.pdf, accessed October 4, 2010.

43. Field notes, Jayapura, December 10, 2009. See also Reverend Willem Rumsawir: during the 1969 Act of Free Choice "people burnt their Bibles and said 'Where is the Church?' The Church is empty. Pastors talk about Emmanuel [God with us], but where is Emmanuel? God is not on our side when it comes to politics.'" Quoted in Charles E. Farhadian, *The Testimony Project Papua: A Collection of Personal Histories in West Papua* (Jayapura: Deyai, 2007), 44.

44. Farhadian, *The Testimony Project Papua,* 35.

45. Giay, *Menuju Papua Baru*; Hernawan and van den Broek, "Dialog Nasional Papua."

46. Farhadian, *The Testimony Project Papua,* 41, 44–45.

47. See Herman Awom quoted in Farhadian, *The Testimony Project Papua,* 150: "From 1965 to 1998, Papuans fought for independence using guerrilla tactics

in the forest. . . . [After 1998] Mr. Theys Eluay was the one who came up with the idea of correcting the history of Papua. After that, we realized that fighting a guerrilla war wouldn't work, because we don't have weapons like they did in Aceh. So we choose to learn the qualities of struggle from persons like Mahatma Gandhi, which is through peaceful means. Now we struggle through non-violence. We want to use dialogue, by sitting down with the government officials, and discuss democratically the future of Papua. We want an open and democratic discussion with government officials. We also follow the example of Jesus, who told us to love our enemies. That is why after Theys was killed, I told the people we cannot avenge his death. We have to be peaceful. We are going to overwhelm this country through peace."

48. This included tribal wars and cannibalism. Obed Komba quoted in Farhadian, *The Testimony Project Papua,* 52.

49. Glazebrook, "Teaching Performance Art," 6.

50. Giay, *Menuju Papua Baru.*

51. According to Willem Rumsawir, "If the government fails to fulfil its duties, then I reject them as a government. Can a government, as God's servant, kill people like here in Papua? God's servants don't kill people!" Quoted in Farhadian, *The Testimony Project Papua,* 42. Benny Giay asserts that the church "must confess its sins for supporting the government . . . [it has] not been playing its prophetic role of being the conscience of the nation." Quoted in Farhadian, *The Testimony Project Papua,* 35.

52. David Snow and Robert Benford, "Ideology, Frame Resonance and Participant Mobilization," in *From Structure to Action: Comparing Social Movement Research Across Cultures,* ed. Bert Klandermans, Hanspeter Kriesi, and Sidney Tarrow (Grenwich, CT: JAI Press, 1988), 197–217; Doug McAdam, *Political Process and the Development of Black Insurgency, 1930–1970* (Chicago: University of Chicago Press, 1999), 48–51.

53. Chauvel, *Constructing Papuan Nationalism.*

54. See Peter King, *West Papua and Indonesia Since Suharto: Independence, Autonomy or Chaos?* (Sydney: UNSW Press, 2004).

55. John McBeth, "Papua Miners' Strike: Everyone's a Loser," *Jakarta Globe,* November 22, 2011, http://www.thejakartaglobe.com/opinion/papua-miners-strike -everyones-a-loser/480053, accessed November 8, 2012.

56. In contrast to the Papuan desire to create a zone of peace, the reality came to be seen as an Indonesian-imposed zone of emergency.

57. Jason MacLeod, "Papuan Struggle Enters New Phase," *Open Democracy,* June 26, 2010, http://www.opendemocracy.net/jason-macleod/papuan-struggle -enters-new-phase, accessed November 8, 2012.

58. Alex Rayfield, "Exclusive: Detained Papuan Leaders Speak Out," *New Matilda,* November 30, 2011, http://newmatilda.com/2011/11/30/exclusive-detained -papuan-leaders-speak-out, accessed November 8, 2012.

59. Senior tribal leader in Sorong, personal correspondence with the author, December 3, 2011.

60. While some Indonesian migrants are Christians (members of the Batak tribe from Sumatra and Christian groups from Central and North Sulawesi), they practice their faith in radically different ways from Papuan Christians.

61. Kamma cited in Rutherford, *Raiding the Land of the Foreigners,* 192.

62. Papuan leaders use prayer to open mass gatherings and set the scene for discussions about liberation. At every clandestine meeting of resistance groups that I attended, daily proceedings began with prayer.

63. Agu Iwanggin quoted by Benny Giay, "Towards a New Papua," *Inside Indonesia,* July–September 2001, www.insideindonesia.org/edit67/giay.htm, accessed August 25, 2010; Giay, *Menuju Papua Baru.*

64. Giay, *Menuju Papua Baru.*

65. See, for instance, the torture and murder of a Papuan priest by Kostrad troops in April 2010, filmed and posted online in October 2010 (West Papua Media, "Indonesia's Abu Ghraib: Brutal Torture Footage Emerges from Puncak Jaya of Priest's Killing by Indonesian Security Forces," *West Papua Media,* October 18, 2010, http://westpapuamedia.info/2010/10/18/indonesias-abu-ghraib-brutal-torture-footage-emerges-from-puncak-jaya-of-priests-killing-by-indonesian-security-forces/, accessed November 8, 2012). See also Eben Kirksey, "From Cannibal to Terrorist: State Violence, Indigenous Resistance and Representation in West Papua" (master's thesis, University of Oxford, 2002).

66. There have been some episodes of interethnic violence—the most deadly being in Wamena in October 2000 when over thirty people (mostly civilian migrants) were reportedly killed after clashes between security forces and Papuans.

67. Papuan disappointment with international support has given rise to talk of the need for a "Super Santa Cruz" massacre (referring to the 1991 Dili massacre): if Papuans could provoke the security forces into overreacting, then a massacre captured on film and communicated to the outside world would trigger an international peacekeeping intervention. This strategy, however, is not widely shared. See Bilveer Singh, *Geopolitics and the Quest for Nationhood* (New Brunswick, NJ: Transaction, 2008), 191; International Crisis Group, *Radicalisation and Dialogue in Papua* (Brussels: International Crisis Group, March 11, 2010); Braithwaite et al., *Anomie and Violence,* 111.

68. Author's interview with Neles Tebay, Jayapura, December 8, 2008, and personal communication with the author, November 18, 2010.

69. There are various other constitutional options that could possibly bridge the gulf between most Papuan views and Indonesian nationalists.

70. MacLeod, "Self-Determination and Autonomy"; Braithwaite et al., *Anomie and Violence.*

71. Giay, *Menuju Papua Baru*; MacLeod, "Self-Determination and Autonomy."

72. Field notes, Wamena, November 18, 2006.

73. Farhadian, *The Testimony Project Papua,* 61.

Part 4

Nonviolent Resistance in Europe

13

Hungary: Nonviolent Resistance Against Austria, 1850s–1860s

Tamás Csapody and Thomas Weber

> *Sometimes legends make reality, and become more useful than the facts.*
> —Salman Rushdie, *Midnight's Children*[1]

The past may be in the eye of the beholder, but what the eye sees and, more importantly, what the beholder reports, is colored by the zeitgeist and their political orientation. This is abundantly true of the narrative of the civil resistance of the Hungarian population to the Austrian absolutist regime following the failed war for independence of 1848–1849. This episode was studied by and came to influence independence movements—notably in Ireland, Finland, and that of Mohandas Gandhi (Mahatma) in India. It featured prominently in the early literature on nonviolent action, despite taking place before the term was coined, and was usually described as "passive resistance."[2]

The popular history of the campaign derives from a book by the Irish nationalist Arthur Griffith, leader of Sinn Féin in its nonviolent period.[3] Griffith's was not a scholarly study, but rather was aimed to inspire emulation by presenting the still nonviolent Irish independence movement with a successful model of resistance. Griffith also highlighted the leading role of Ferenc Deák. In the 1930s, leading proponents of nonviolent action, such as Richard Gregg, Bart de Ligt, Krishnalal Shridharani, and Aldous Huxley, drew on Griffith's account.[4] Huxley's view was that "the long campaign of non-violent resistance and non-co-operation conducted by the Hungarians under Deák was crowned with complete success in 1867." Nevertheless, he continues, the name of [Lajos] Kossuth, the leader of the violent Hungarian revolution of 1848 was, and still is, far better known than that of Deák. Kossuth was an ambitious power-loving militarist, who completely failed to liberate his country. Deák refused political power and personal distinction . . . and without shedding blood compelled the Austrian government to restore the Hungarian constitution. Such is our partiality for ambition and militarism that we all remember Kossuth, in spite of the complete failure of his policy, while few of us have ever heard of Deák, in spite of the fact that he was completely successful.[5]

In this chapter, we seek to place the Hungarian nonviolent resistance in its general historical context as well as to point out its particular significance for the evolution of a history of nonviolent struggle, particularly for independence movements. We contrast the employment of the Hungarian example in the literature on nonviolent resistance with its comparative neglect in Hungarian historiography. We then draw on more recent Hungarian sources to discuss the popular character of the movement and its social context. Ultimately, we argue that such a formative experience of nonviolent resistance warrants a detailed reassessment, recognizing its achievements and clarifying its dynamics, including taking a more rounded view of the role of Deák himself.

Background

From 1526 Hungary was under Austrian rule despite several anti-Habsburg uprisings, violent and nonviolent, in the seventeenth and eighteenth centuries. In the nineteenth century, Hungarian reformers again asserted their cultural heritage and expressed their political aspirations, from the 1820s onward sometimes turning toward passive resistance. Then in 1848, a year of revolutionary ferment in Europe,[6] nationalists achieved ascendancy in parliament and passed what are known as the April Laws, ratified by Emperor Ferdinand on April 11. Mainly framed by Deák, then Hungarian minister for justice, the April Laws set the agenda for internal reform and laid the foundations for national autonomy. However, in December the old guard in Vienna, seeing such concessions as weakness, forced Ferdinand to abdicate in favor of his young nephew Franz Joseph. For Hungary, the result of the renewed imperial policy of centralization was that in August 1849 Austria crushed what had turned into armed revolt, imposed absolutist rule, and abrogated the April Laws. The disloyal nation was considered as having forfeited its constitutional rights.[7]

The new military governor of Hungary, General Julius Haynau, began a reign of terror. Military courts sentenced some 500 people to death, executed 114, including the first Hungarian head of state, Lajos Batthyány, and imprisoned 1,763. Around 50,000 former infantrymen were shanghaied into special "retribution" units and sent to fight in Italy.[8] All judicial and administrative powers were centralized under Austrian control. The civil administration was subsumed under military power and municipal administrative rights were revoked, with posts being filled exclusively by pro-Austrian members of the middle gentry. A new internal security force was formed and a campaign of Germanization ousted Hungarian as the official language.

As a result, passive resistance became a new form of opposition to authority; in fact, "citizens had no choice but to respond for the sake of their survival."[9] The vast majority of the Hungarian gentry, farmers, middle classes, and intellectuals chose survival. This meant civil resistance and noncooperation. After the defeat of armed revolt, hatred and the threat of violence remained as various groups planned armed action. However, perhaps the threat of large-scale violence hampered the consolidation of the Austrian occupation and most Hungarians understood that further violence would escalate repression. Instead, they mounted a nationwide nonviolent campaign, which, after eighteen years, resulted in the Ausgleich (Compromise) of 1867 where Hungary became an equal partner in the Austro-Hungarian Dual Monarchy. Hungary was to have full sovereignty internally and equal weight to Austria on matters of defense and foreign policy. This agreement endured until World War I ended in 1918.

The Portrayal of the Hungarian Struggle

Deák has been presented as the architect of this campaign. A military tribunal had cleared him from involvement in the uprising because he had not advocated dethronement of the monarchy or a split from Austria. He had retired from public life when, in April 1850, Austrian minister of justice Anton von Schmerling summoned him to Vienna to discuss harmonizing Hungarian and Austrian legal procedures. Deák flatly refused, writing that, "after the regrettable events of the recent past and in the prevailing circumstances, it is not possible to cooperate actively in public affairs."[10] Somehow this was leaked to the *Ostdeutsche Post* in Vienna, from where it spawned handwritten copies across Hungary. Soon the land was plastered with Deák's message of noncooperation and his statement came to define Hungary's resistance.

According to Griffith, Deák's continual declarations of loyalty to the 1848 Hungarian Constitution (which had not legally been abolished) meant his mere presence was a source of annoyance to Austria and of hope to Hungarians. Griffith presents Deák as a national voice—a figure to whom the population could turn for guidance—fanning nationalist feelings while keeping hotter heads in check. He conducted negotiations with the emperor and, when the Hungarian parliament could sit, authored its declarations.

Imperial policy fluctuated between offering concessions (for instance, when it needed Hungarian support in war) and resumed repression (when the threat of war receded). Deák's message was constant throughout: the lawful Hungarian Constitution of 1848 was still in force and, as soon as Austria recognized this and allowed Hungarians to run their own affairs in line with the constitution, they would receive Hungarian friendship and loyalty.

Naturally, the resistance had phases—reflecting both the vicissitudes of imperial policy and its own level of organization. Deák's leading English-language biographer describes the 1850s campaign as "uncoordinated and haphazard,"[11] but having gained cohesion as the years passed. When Hungarians refused to sit in the Imperial Parliament in 1861, according to Griffith, Austria was humiliated—"a butt for Europe's jests."[12] This boycott dramatized the Hungarian demand to reestablish their own parliament while denying the legitimacy of centralized Austrian rule. Griffith quotes *The Times* (London) as saying that "Passive Resistance can be so organized as to become more troublesome than armed rebellion."[13]

Richard Gregg, the West's first major popularizer of nonviolent action, begins chapter 1 of *The Power of Nonviolence* with a section on Hungary: "an outstanding successful modern example of mass, rather than individual, nonviolent resistance." Gregg follows Griffith in reporting Deák's rebuke to the moderate Hungarians who felt too weak to resist: "Your laws are violated, yet your mouths remain closed! Woe to the nation that raises no protest when its rights are outraged! It contributes to its own slavery by its silence. The nation that submits to injustice and oppression without protest is doomed."[14] Gregg recounts how Deák organized a campaign to boycott Austrian goods and set up independent Hungarian institutions while refusing to recognize Austrian ones in a spirit combining nonviolent resistance with legality: "This is safe ground on which, unarmed ourselves, we can hold our own against armed force. If suffering must be necessary, suffer with dignity." Paraphrasing Griffith, Gregg summarizes the campaign:

> When the Austrian tax collector came, the people did not beat him or even hoot him—they merely declined to pay. The Austrian police then seized their goods, but no Hungarian auctioneer would sell them. When an Austrian auctioneer was brought, he found that he would have to bring bidders from Austria. The government soon discovered that it was costing more to distrain the property than the tax was worth.
>
> The Austrians attempted to billet their soldiers upon the Hungarians. The Hungarians did not actively resist the order, but the Austrian soldiers, after trying to live in houses where everyone despised them, protested strongly against it. The Austrian government declared the boycott of Austrian goods illegal, but the Hungarians defied the decree. The jails were filled to overflowing.[15]

Although there may have been "some violence of inner attitude [the despising of the Austrians]," the Hungarian campaign "provided a remarkable example of the power of nonviolent resistance," eventually forcing Francis Joseph to grant Hungarians their full constitutional rights.[16]

Griffith describes the dénouement: in 1866, when Austria faced defeat by the Prussians at Königgrätz, a "pale and haggard" Emperor Franz Joseph sent for Deák:

> "What am I to do now, Deák?" the monarch asked of his opponent. Deák's laconic reply is celebrated in Austrian history, "Make peace, and restore Hungary her rights." "If I restore Hungary her Constitution now, will Hungary help me to carry on the war?" the Emperor inquired. The reply of Deák exhibits the fearless and uncompromising character of the great Magyar. It was in one word, "No." He would not make the restoration of his country's rights a matter of barter.[17]

By February 1867, the Austrians had to capitulate. Finally, nonviolent resistance and Deák had triumphed and the Habsburg emperor came to Pest to restore the Constitution of 1848 and to be crowned, pledging himself "as King of Hungary to defend it with his life."[18] Deák himself refused public office, but consented to serve in parliament as a simple member.

In contrast to the literature on nonviolent action, until recently histories of Hungary paid relatively little attention to and offered even less analysis of this episode. The struggle is reduced to political maneuvering by leading politicians and the impact on Austria of military defeat elsewhere. Histories of the Habsburg Empire stress its political and economic circumstances and important regional considerations.[19]

In the communist period (1948–1989), the episode was sidelined. An official history, published in English in 1975 under the auspices of the History Institute of the Hungarian Academy of Sciences, devotes much space to Lajos Kossuth, the exiled armed revolutionary, while underplaying the people's resistance. Deák is scarcely mentioned, let alone as a leader of a movement.[20] Rather, in this account, Austrian repression drove the gentry into opposition, steering them on a "middle course between the extremes of submission or conspiracy" that "entrenched itself in passive resistance." This suited them because, while rejecting "centralised absolutism," they lacked the commitment to take the national struggle further. The wealthier bourgeoisie could pursue their interests inside a military empire, but objected to the "lack of constitutional life and political security." They, along with the "patriotic plebeian masses of the towns who rebelled against autocracy," formed the basis of a national resistance.[21] By 1860–1861, it was clear to the leading strata "that passive resistance in the long run was not practical" and that "sooner or later, a situation would present itself when they would have to put aside passivity and fight or give up resistance and come to an agreement" with the majority. They preferred the latter course.[22]

There is no analysis of alternatives and passive resistance is presented as passivity rather than the active strategy described elsewhere. There is nothing about the dynamics of the resistance or how people organized. The book's biographical sketch of Deák does not mention passive resistance or Deák's leading opposition to Austrian repression, only his role in negotiating the Ausgleich. Kossuth, in contrast, is glorified as a true hero leading the armed resistance and later championing the Hungarian cause in exile.[23] The very concept of civil resistance was problematic under an internationalist communist regime that frowned on overt expressions of nationalism. Could it also be possible that a reading of history glorifying violence helped to legitimate the communists' own coming to power whereas an account such as Griffith's might have provided encouragement for opponents of Soviet-style communism?

Like all nations, Hungarians are proud of their achievements. A book celebrating their contributions to world civilization chronicles the feats of mathematicians and physicists, musicians, artists and filmmakers, linguists and philosophers, medical scientists, Nobel laureates, and, of course, athletes.[24] However, there is no mention of nonviolent resistance, which, according to the early literature on nonviolent action was perhaps one of Hungary's greatest gifts to civilization, especially given the likely influence the mid-nineteenth century movement had on Gandhi.[25] Gene Sharp, the leading modern theorist of nonviolent struggle, is more cautious about the resistance's achievements than earlier writers, yet he is clear about Deák's prescience.[26] Describing how nonviolent resistance can make the opponents' repression rebound and so undermine their power, he comments that as early as 1861 Deák already understood this mechanism.[27]

Deák and Hungarian Nonviolent Resistance

The course of Hungarian national civil resistance and Deák's personal journey intertwine and bifurcate. Teasing out Deák's actual role in the movement is difficult. At one level, he embodied civil resistance—in his character and political stature, personal code of ethics, political career and lifestyle, liberal views, and social activities. Therefore, some contemporary Hungarian historians present Deák as passive resistance personified. Another school, however, far from seeing Deák as a driver of events, equates passive resistance with broader movements that commenced after the crushing of the 1848–1849 revolution and centered on spontaneous unrest.[28]

Clearly, unlike Gandhi later, Deák did not direct campaigns. It seems unlikely that, in 1850 from his country estate, he was trying to persuade the people to follow him. Nevertheless his personal refusal to cooperate—exemplified in his reply to Schmerling (quoted above)—"became the programmatic statement of 'passive resistance,' that is noncooperation with the authorities" through refusal to billet soldiers, evading taxes, feigning ignorance of the German language, and "encumbering the life of the administrators in an environment foreign to them in all possible ways."[29]

In 1854 Deák returned to Pest, his period of total passive resistance behind him. The move had strong political undertones. Indeed, the nationalist daily *Pesti Napló* (Pest Journal) encouraged others to follow his example,[30] and the secret police compiled weekly reports of his activities.[31] Zoltán Ferenczi, Deák's most quoted Hungarian biographer, notes that in this period he became a "leader of unmatched stature in Hungarian public opinion and thinking."[32]

Without presenting a political platform, Deák became the conscience and mentor of resistance similar to his own practices. Without preaching, his statements on the constitutional situation provided a program that was simple to understand and execute: the legal situation in Hungary was that created by the April Laws. Other systems, until amended by the lawful Hungarian government, were unlawful and consequently did not have to be obeyed. Until a lawful Hungarian government was in place, Austrian oppression should be resisted nonviolently.

Deák actively promoted national pride and, more subtly, resistance through his involvement with the Hungarian Academy of Sciences, various economic and cultural organizations, and in the course of meetings in his hotel room. Deák made regular visits to the National Theatre, to the National Casino (a hub of cultural activity), to the Kisfaludy Society (the national forum of the literati), to the Society of Economists, and to the races that became a symbol of Hungarian national identity. He also supported eminent anti-Habsburg activists and, after their deaths, kept their memory alive.

Perhaps the most important single expression of resistance was his opposition to enforced official Germanization. Short of adopting a form of nationalism that would provoke the authorities, he took every opportunity to use the Hungarian language for communication in everyday life, literature, and science. His extensive correspondence illustrates this commitment. For example, in a letter to an old family friend, Deák writes, "In the midst of the great storm battering us" and "the constant attack by the powers-that-be," the only way to save the Hungarian nation is for Hungarian to remain the language of social intercourse. He continued that there must be preservation of Hungarian culture within the circle of social life and in the course of amusements, and through the maintenance of the national costume, in every place "that is beyond the reaches of our oppressor."[33] Later he insists that "we, here in Pest, have absolutely no desire to become German, and the more they pressure us the more we shall resist denying our culture. It is a natural instinct in individual people and nations alike: the instinct to survive."[34]

Addressing a women's meeting in 1858, Deák repeated this position: their nationality, Deák warned, "is being eased out of public affairs. All we can do is cultivate it and preserve it where the power of the regime does not penetrate—in the private circle of our social lives. If even there we neglect it, it will be doomed forever."[35]

The nationalist press publicized Deák's resistance. Banned from explicit political discourse, its coverage nevertheless carried unmistakably subversive undertones and, thus, it became a forum for the nation's spiritual and political renaissance.[36] Most prominent was *Pesti Napló,* edited by Zsigmond Kemény, one of Deák's best friends (and resident in the same Pest hotel). Although Deák himself rarely penned articles, through such links and visiting journalists, writers, and friends, his message was relayed widely.

Deák expected the nation to hold "the line in struggle to defend its nationality, traditions, constitution and laws."[37] The Austrian position alternated absolutist oppression and state terrorism to at least partial appeasement. One period of concessions followed Austria's military defeat in Italy in 1857. Austria's losses were partly a result of the widespread nonpayment of taxes, resistance to recruitment, and desertion among its Hungarian subjects. And by this time, both Austrians and Hungarians were growing tired of the resistance. Therefore, Vienna attempted to moderate its absolutism: Franz Joseph's "October Diploma" in 1860 granted wide autonomy to various regions of the empire. This provoked what the minister of finance, Ignaz Edler von Plener, called a state of semirevolution; tax revenue from Hungary, he declared, could be considered lost.[38] In 1861, Hungarian county councils were restored and parliament convoked. This, however, did not satisfy Hungarians and the councils soon decided to stop collecting taxes not sanctioned by the Hungarian parliament and to stop paying for the support of Austrian troops. In fact "the mood of revolt became so deep that counties and communities acted as though the absolutist regime had been abolished and, without waiting for instructions from above, elected new slates of officials."[39] During the first postrevolutionary Hungarian parliamentary session, where Deák emerged as the preeminent national leader, a conciliatory petition, which foreshadowed the Ausgleich of 1867, was issued. Austria merely renewed its repression. Deák countered with a second petition. This recognized that the time for compromise was over and prepared readers for a further round of repression. The petition concluded,

> The nation will endure the hardships if it has to, in order to preserve for future generations the freedom bequeathed to it by our ancestors. It will endure without despair, as our ancestors endured and suffered to protect the nation's rights, for what may be wrested away by main force may be

won back with time and good fortune, but what the nation voluntarily surrenders for fear of suffering may not be regained, or only with great difficulty. The nation will endure in hope for a better future and in trust in the justice of its cause.[40]

Again Deák urged a policy of nonviolent resistance. Under threat of arms, parliament was prorogued, but Deák's popularity had never been higher and he was seen as the main leader of the resistance. Furthermore, the opposition was now more organized than in the 1850s and "had an ideology in the form of the explicit and progressive petitions Deák had drafted."[41] Nevertheless, even Deák doubted how much national resistance could achieve: "Often despondent and pessimistic, he knew how weak Hungary was in comparison with the dynasty. This awareness did not raise his spirits. It was faith, not *Realpolitik,* which gave him the moral strength to persevere."[42] As it was, his policy took almost two decades to achieve his goal and depended on other pressures on the Habsburg Empire, pressures that were largely outside Hungarian control. What leverage the Hungarians practically exerted on the Habsburgs requires further research, but the character of this resistance was, despite the popular accounts, largely outside Deák's control. Although he consciously opted for passive resistance, Deák did nothing to actively lead, organize, or ideologically underpin the resistance movement. If he promoted nonviolent tactics, he never advertised his views on these and did not transform his own resistance into a cogent theory or practice. We are left not only with a vague impression of his motivational drivers, but with an equally fuzzy sense of his strategic vision.[43] This explains why it was interpreted in such different ways and appropriated to serve so many varied political agendas.[44] This is not to diminish Deák's stature or devalue his personal mission: after all, the Ausgleich, which was his life's work, was achieved. It merely places him in the context of a larger struggle that he symbolized for many, but did not actually lead.

Questions remain about the interrelationship of Deák with the movement as a whole: How spontaneous was Hungarian popular resistance? Would it have emerged without Deák? Would it have continued for so long without his presence? And would it have been less organized without his guidance? One could say that the social environment and public mood were already primed for resistance, whether arising consciously or spontaneously, and it became a central strategy for personal and national survival after the quashed revolution and the ensuing reign of terror.

Hungarian Nonviolent Resistance: The Broader Context

In fact, the resistance campaign had a long gestation period, even preceding the emergence of Deák. There was already resistance to the regime in the

1820s. Before the 1848 revolution, civil resistance was a "weapon" of those not yet able to take up arms; after 1849, it became a form of protest for the defeated and disenfranchised.

Miklós Molnár, without referring specifically to Deák, notes that resistance "became a way of life and an ethical code."[45] Taxes were avoided, as was military service.[46] Public celebrations, including the church services that gave thanks for the emperor's February 1953 escape from assassination, resulted in no-shows. Public office was eschewed, courts were boycotted, and people refused to speak German. Hungarian authors and plays were preferred to Austrian ones. The performances, selected for maximum pertinence, carried coded messages and provided a platform for patriotic affirmation. They were advertised as natives-only events where Austrians would have been persona non grata.[47] Symbolic clothing, hairstyles, and jewelry in the national colors were worn,[48] especially on significant dates (e.g., the emperor's birthday or name day and the birthdays of Kossuth and Batthyány, and dates that marked events of the revolution or commemorated the execution of its leaders) and at public functions, dances,[49] and theatrical performances.[50] When Mihály Vörösmarty, the father of Hungarian literature, died on November 18, 1855, the regime banned unannounced speeches at his funeral. The funeral drew a crowd of 20,000 silently protesting mourners.

A new and often invisible, no-holds-barred, secret war evolved "for the survival of the nation." It was "fought with arms, with the spoken and printed word, via agricultural exhibitions, pilgrimage, paintings" and "in theatres, markets, churches, at the stock exchange and in the columns of newspapers and journals in Paris, London and Hamburg."[51]

The platform of opposition, that became a way of life for a large section of the Hungarian population during the repressive 1850s, is described by Éva Somogyi as follows:

> The rich magnates and the well-to-do nobles, the intellectuals and the citizens have decided that they will not pay their taxes until the executor knocks at their doors. Only those supplies that cannot be hidden will be handed over to the military. People will deny understanding German and will everywhere demand answers to verdicts in Hungarian. Nobody will truthfully report the status of his wealth and income. If anybody is asked a question, the answer has to be—I do not know; if information is sought about a person, the answer has to be—I do not know him; if events have to be verified, the answer has to be—I have seen nothing. The slogan is: detest absolutism and ignore its servants as if they were not living amongst us.[52]

But, of course, it was not quite this simple. People's movements are not monolithic, with all the protesters acting in unison and taking their cues from one source. As with most resistance movements, here the nonviolent discipline was not complete.[53] Some cooperated with the regime; others plotted a new uprising. Most of these plotters were caught and eventually executed or sentenced to lengthy terms of imprisonment.[54]

For the study of nonviolent action, careful analysis leads to ambiguities that the early popularizers of nonviolent action did not discuss. Deák's principles resonated with Griffith, Gandhi, and later theorists, but perhaps the resistance should be seen as a more pragmatic, strategically planned and executed mass movement of people who had a goal, who knew what they were fighting for and why, and who had cohesion and self-discipline based on strong morale. Perhaps those promoting nonviolent action overstate the movement's role and downplay the importance of external factors. And further, perhaps an accumulation of evidence and folklore over several decades has allowed Griffith and others to construct Deák as a leader that he may not actually have been.

Possibly the most important question concerns what can be learned from the Hungarian example. Mass movements, especially when they are not confined to a particular class but have broad-based appeal (including support from peasants and workers), have to be located in their economic and social contexts. Class differences and economic hardships set tones of discontent. When a system is changing rapidly, whether because of new laws or changes wrought by industrialization and modernization, the distinction is blurred between resistance to change itself and resistance against the government in power at that moment. Most Hungarians were clearly opposed to the oppressive Austrian regime. Following the failed war of independence, the people lost their voice: parliament, local political autonomy, free expression, and the use of the Magyar language were replaced by foreign officials, an unfamiliar and unwelcome police system, and an expensive military police state. But, as suggested, this was far from the whole story.

At the same time as the Habsburgs were being pushed into rapprochement (by the pressure of foreign defeats and rivalries elsewhere), a capitalist boom inside Hungary, suggests Péter Hanák, by the mid-1860s brought Hungarian pressure for "normalization."[55] Class conflicts, which were submerged during the revolution, also soon reasserted themselves. Dictatorships polarize society and, always in such circumstances, there are collaborators. Sections of the aristocracy supported the crown. The gentry, too, were divided: those entitled to hold public office—the intelligentsia, the landed, and the young—usually opted for reluctant cooperation with Austria. Among the incentives for holding public office were hopes of a quick promotion and the quasi-patriotic desire for regional Hungarian hegemony over ethnic minorities.[56] However, the victorious Habsburgs managed to drive the majority of the gentry and even the Habsburg-supporting conservatives into at least nonactive resistance by ignoring their concerns.[57] The nobles withdrew from public life, eschewed public office, and "wherever they could, evaded the directives of absolutism and boycotted its representatives." They retreated to their estates, to bide their time and await a better future, perhaps "unified and intransigent" only in their determination to regain the independence taken from them.[58]

Further, the forces of industrialization were worrying the lesser nobility. As their estates dwindled and meeting their tax burdens became more difficult, they may have discovered a patriotic duty to dodge them. In the words of Paul Ignotus, "He felt he was protesting against tyranny and reaction; but in fact what hurt him most was inevitable in the process of industrializing a society."[59] Even the peasantry, struggling to obtain land and engaged in lawsuits against former landlords, hated foreign rule. Hanák notes that most "understood that the 1848 revolution had given them their liberation and land" and that the fight for independence "was alloyed in their minds with a certain amount of peasant democracy" in the same way as the "struggles of the age of absolutism were linked with national motives."[60] In other words, movements of nonviolent resistance can be spontaneous expressions of the will of the populace without top-down leadership. Inspirational actions by individuals need not be read as control or leadership of the movement.

Conclusion

Perhaps a little confusingly, László Kontler concludes that "Evidence on all sorts of collaboration uncovered by recent research suggests that the dimensions of "passive resistance" have been greatly exaggerated by national legend, but it still seems to have been the dominant type of political attitude in Hungary during neo-absolutism."[61]

Following the crushing of the 1848–1849 uprising, nonviolent resistance broke out spontaneously among the population. There was no centralized leadership. Deák provided an example as to the form and tools that could be used to conduct the struggle. However, while the struggle would probably have been sustained even without Deák, the movement in all likelihood would have been less homogeneous and sporadic local armed clashes more common. One of the strengths of being decentralized and nonhierarchical was that there was no leadership to imprison in order to decapitate the movement.

Once the armed uprising was crushed, the only possibility of protest on a wide scale was civil disobedience. But this nonviolent strategy led to victory and meant that, for some time afterward, the nation eschewed violence and warfare. Before 1848, struggles were conducted both violently and nonviolently. In 1848 violence came to the fore but, once the uprising was defeated, nonviolence characterized Hungarian politics. This was a paradigm shift and led to the freedom of the country.

Griffith's book tried to show what can be done if people are united; it was calculated to influence others to experiment with or even emulate these historical precedents. In short, he had pragmatic reasons for constructing a legend.[62] In contrast, Béla Király underplays Deák's contribution: "Deák did not originate ideas or bring mass movements to life." Nevertheless, he adds that Deák "was able to recognize political, social, and economic forces and the power balance in the Habsburg lands, and above all, to sense the moment he could harness these forces and use them to realize his goal."[63] Whatever Deák's influence in Hungary, and whatever influence this episode of resistance had on the Irish and other struggles and as an inspiration for Gandhi's campaigns, it should be better known as an important early chapter in the evolution of nonviolent resistance. Further analysis is needed to draw lessons for nonviolent struggle that do not depend on one heroic leader. As Hanák comments, while the 1848 war for independence may have created heroes, Haynau's retribution produced martyrs and fanned anti-Austrian feelings.[64]

And finally, work still needs to be done on the impact of the struggle on the Hungarian psyche. To what degree did it foster Hungarian nationalism, national collective identity, and cultural pride? Did the struggle legitimize further nonviolent action by the population? Did it influence methods of resistance to the totalitarian regime in Hungary before and after the revolution of 1956?

Not only should the nineteenth-century Hungarian resistance be better known but, as Aldous Huxley requested, it should not be overshadowed by romanticized armed uprisings. In Hungary today, Deák is a national hero and the bicentenary of his birth was widely commemorated across the country in 2003 with scores of publications, both popular and scholarly.[65] His passive resistance has been hailed as part of Hungary's national character, and he is acknowledged as A Haza Bölcse (the Sage of the Nation). Nevertheless leaders who fought with arms are better known and anniversaries of armed struggles are more enthusiastically celebrated. And in this regard, it seems that history has more recently been repeated in the region: the armed Hungarian uprising in 1956 is better remembered and more highly valued than the 1968 Czechoslovak nonviolent resistance. Yet Soviet troops crushed the Hungarian revolution in a matter of days while it took them months to regain control in Czechoslovakia.

Hungarian nonviolent resistance demonstrated 150 years ago that state terrorism can be resisted when the oppressed are sufficiently united and have a course of action that is easily understandable and simple to follow. Deeper analysis shows that the Hungarian nonviolent resistance of the 1850s and 1860s was not quite as straightforward as its foreign popularizers claimed. Nevertheless, such campaigns can achieve their goals when outside events and deeper internal economic and social drivers come together to unite the oppressed and weaken the position of the oppressor. As the Hungarian example and recent major studies of nonviolent struggle have shown, this can be achieved when the oppressed withdraw their consent to be ruled and undermine state power by targeting areas of particular vulnerability in their oppressor.[66] Ralph Summy points out that, where the oppressor needs the cooperation of the oppressed, a dependency relationship comes into existence—one that the oppressed can exploit.[67] The Prussian defeat of Austria hastened the Ausgleich, but that was merely a final chapter in a lengthy process in which noncooperation had laid the foundations for that compromise.

Notes

This chapter draws from Tamás Csapody and Thomas Weber, "Hungarian Nonviolent Resistance Against Austria and Its Place in the History of Nonviolence," *Peace and Change* 32, no.4 (2007): 499–519; and Tamás Csapody, "Secondary Forms of Passive Resistance in Hungary Between 1848 and 1865," *Central European Political Science Review* 5, no. 15 (2004): 178–189. All translations of quotes and titles from Hungarian sources are by the authors.

1. Salman Rushdie, *Midnight's Children* (New York: Avon, 1982), 253.

2. *Passive resistance* remains the term used in Hungarian and in histories of the movement. However, it would be wrong to read into the campaign the negative connotations that led Gandhi to reject this term and introduce *satyagraha* (firmly grasping truth, often translated as soul-force or truth-force).

3. Arthur Griffith, *The Resurrection of Hungary,* 3rd ed. (Dublin: Whelan and Son, 1918). First published in 1904, the 1918 edition informed the later literature on nonviolent action.

4. Richard Gregg, *The Power of Nonviolence* (Philadelphia: Lippincott, 1934), 3; Bart de Ligt, *The Conquest of Violence: An Essay on War and Revolution* (London: George Routledge, 1937), 138–139; Aldous Huxley*, Ends and Means: An Enquiry into the Nature of Ideals and into the Methods Employed for Their Realization* (London: Chatto and Windus, 1938); Krishnalal Shridharani, *War Without Violence: The Sociology of Gandhi's Satyagraha* (New York: Harcourt, Brace, 1939), 113. Clarence Marsh Case in his *Non-Violent Coercion: A Study in Methods of Social Pressure* (New York: Century, 1923), 328, also refers to the episode, but acknowledges the importance of other factors as did a later generation of researchers on nonviolent action such as William Robert Miller, *Nonviolence: A Christian Interpretation* (New York: Schocken, 1966), 242; Mulford Q. Sibley, *The Quiet Battle: Writings on the Theory and Practice of Non-Violent Resistance* (Boston: Boston Press, 1963), 131–150 (this anthology includes an excerpt from Arthur Griffith); and Gene Sharp, *The Politics of Nonviolent Action, Part 3* (Boston: Porter Sargent, 1973), 594–595.

5. Huxley, *Ends and Means,* 147.

6. Rapid economic and social transformation, as a result of the disruptions of early industrialization and the rise of nationalism and liberal political philosophies, led to violent revolutions in much of Europe (particularly in France, Prussia, and the Italian states) as well as in the Austrian Empire (particularly in Hungary).

7. On the Hungarian revolution, see Istvan Deak, *The Lawful Revolution: Louis Kossuth and the Hungarians 1848–1849* (London: Phoenix Press, 1979). It should also be noted that the April Laws, which gave the Hungarians rights vis-à-vis the Austrians, led minorities in Hungary to demand similar rights for themselves. Needless to say, Hungarians were as unsympathetic to these claims as Austrians were to Hungarian demands. This gave Austria the opportunity to pursue a policy of divide and rule.

8. Péter Gunst and Géza Závodszky, eds., *Magyar történelmi kronológia* [Chronology of Hungarian History] (Budapest: Tankönyvkiadó, 1987), 325.

9. István Nemeskürty, *Parázs a hamú alatt* [Embers Under the Ashes] (Budapest: Megvetö Könyvkiadó, 1981), 19.

10. Béla K. Király, *Ferenc Deák* (Boston: Twayne, 1975), 139.

11. Király, *Ferenc Deák,* 165.

12. Griffith, *The Resurrection of Hungary,* 33.

13. Ibid., 34.

14. Gregg, *Power of Nonviolence,* 1–3.

15. Ibid., 2–3.

16. Ibid., 3.

17. Griffith, *The Resurrection of Hungary,* 50.

18. Ibid., 63.

19. See, for example, Miklós Molnár, *A Concise History of Hungary* (Cambridge: Cambridge University Press, 2001), 206–207; and A. J. P. Taylor, *The Habsburg Monarchy 1809–1918* (Harmondsworth: Penguin, 1964).

20. Péter Hanák, "The Period of Neo-Absolutism 1849–1867," in *A History of Hungary,* ed. Ervin Pamlényi (London: Collet's, 1975), 285–320.

21. Ibid., 297–298.

22. Ibid., 312.

23. Ervin Pamlényi, ed., *A History of Hungary* (London: Collet's, 1975), 611, 619.

24. Francis S. Wagner, *Hungarian Contributions to World Civilization* (Center Square, PA: Alpha, 1977).

25. See Csapody and Weber, "Hungarian Nonviolent Resistance"; and Thomas Weber, "Claiming Credit for Gandhi," *Gandhi Marg* 27, no. 2 (2005): 165–178.

26. Conflicts, writes Sharp, "may be so complex that it is difficult to disentangle the relative roles of nonviolent action and other factors in producing the change, as for example the conclusion of the Hungarian struggle against the Austrian rule." Sharp, *Politics of Nonviolent Action,* 766–767.

27. Ibid., 594–595.

28. Even within this school, there is disagreement about the dates of resistance. Some suggest that passive resistance started in 1849 or 1850 and ended in 1857 or 1860 while others claim that it lasted until 1861 or even 1867. Further, some accounts note that various forms of passive resistance—such as tax refusal—could be observed during the so-called reform era of 1825–1848 or even earlier in the 1820s. See, for example, Kálmán Törs, ed., *Deák Ferenc emlékezete* [The Memory of Ferenc Deák] (Budapest: Deutsch M-féle Muvészeti Intézet Kiadó, 1876), 23–25; Ágnes Deák, "Társadalmi ellenállási stratégiák Magyarországon azabszolutista kormányzat ellen 1851–1852-ben" [Social Resistance Strategies in Hungary Against the Absolutist Government in 1851–1852] *AETAS* 4, vol. 10 (1995): 34.

29. László Kontler, *A History of Hungary* (Basingstoke: Palgrave, 2002), 271.

30. *Pesti Napló,* November 14, 1854, number 261-1404; *Pesti Napló,* November 21, 1854, number 267-1410.

31. Sándor Takáts, *Emlékezzünk eleinkrol* [Remember Our Ancestors] (Budapest: Genis Kiadó, 1929), 523–554.

32. Zoltán Ferenczi, *Deák élete* [Deák's Life], vol. 2 (Budapest: Magyar Tudományos Akadémia, 1904), 233.

33. Deák to Mrs. Géza Báthory, January 10, 1857, quoted in Ágnes Deák, ed., *Deák Ferenc: Válogatott politikai írások és beszédek* [Ferenc Deák: Selected Political Writings and Speeches], vol. 2 (Budapest: Osiris Kiadó, 2001), 17–18. Deák is reported to have likened the Hungarian nation to an egg: "the longer you boil it, the harder it gets." See Stephen Sisa, *The Spirit of Hungary: A Panorama of Hungarian History and Culture* (Toronto: Rákóczi Foundation, 1983), 172.

34. Deák to Mrs. Géza Báthory, February 15, 1857, quoted in Deák, *Deák Ferenc,* 18.

35. Quoted in Király, *Ferenc Deák,* 143.

36. The *Uj Magyar Múzeum* (New Hungarian Museum), a periodical published by Ferenc Toldi between 1850 and 1862, carried the Latin motto "Peragit tranquilla protestas, quea violentia nequit" (Gentle force will conquer where violence cannot).

37. Király, *Ferenc Deák,* 143.

38. Béla K. Király, "Ferenc Deák," in *Hungarian Statesmen of Destiny 1860–1960,* ed. Pál B dy (Highland Lakes, NJ: Atlantic Research and Publications, 1989), 25–26.

39. Király, *Ferenc Deák,* 26.

40. Ibid., 164.

41. Ibid., 165.

42. Ibid., 140.

43. See Péter Dávidházi, *Per passivam resistentiam: Változatok hatalom és írás témájára* [Variations on the Theme of Power and Writing] (Budapest: Argumentum Kiadó, 1998), 29–51.

44. József Pap, *Magyarország vármegyei tisztikara a reformkor végétol a kiegyezésig* [The Civil Servants of Hungary's Counties Between the End of the Age of Reform and the Compromise] (Szeged: Belvedere Meridionale, 2003), 11–38.

45. Molnár, *A Concise History,* 202.

46. The novelist Mór Jókai begins his 1862 novel *Az új földesúr* (The New Landlord) with a character who vows to give up smoking when the government introduces a tobacco monopoly, to give up drinking when a tax is imposed on wine, and to quit playing cards when stamp duty is imposed on card packs.

47. Deák, "Társadalmi ellenállási stratégiák," 39–42.

48. Ibid., 34.

49. The dance of choice was the banned *csárdás,* which in its faster movements exemplifies a "seismic frenzy of Magyar merriment." Csapody, "Secondary Forms of Passive Resistance," 185.

50. Deák, "Társadalmi ellenállási stratégiák," 33, 44.

51. Ibid., 20. The execution of Hungarian leaders and harsh repression led to international outrage, which, along with the belief that the spirit of revolution had been extinguished in Hungary, helped soften repression in mid-1850s when Haynau was replaced.

52. Quoted in Éva Somogyi, "The Age of Neoabsolutism, 1849–1867," in *A History of Hungary,* ed. Peter F. Sugar, Péter Hanák, and Tibor Frank (London: I. B. Tauris, 1990), 235–251, at 241.

53. Lajos Lukács, *Magyar függetlenségi és alkotmányos mozgalmak 1849–67* [Hungary's Independence and Constitutional Movements 1849–67] (Budapest: Muvelt Nép, 1955).

54. Csapody, "Secondary Forms of Passive Resistance," 187–188, names a range of Hungarian patriots executed or imprisoned for planning armed insurrections, or

plotting to assassinate or kidnap the emperor, including some authorized by Kossuth. In addition, armed bands, known as *betyárs,* supported the freedom fighters during the revolution and remained resolutely anti-Habsburg afterward. Their numbers were replenished by a steady supply of deserters and surviving Hungarian infantrymen on the run. Along with their most infamous representative, Sándor Rózsa, they became a symbol of resistance to the regime. See Nemeskürty, *Parázs a hamú alatt,* 82.

55. This Hungarian pressure stemmed from a desire for stability on the part of those who were benefiting from the boom, coupled with the desire to share in its proceeds by those who had not yet benefited as well as the "recurrent peasant movements and . . . the persistent claims of the nationalists, which threatened the noblenational hegemony." Hanák, "The Period of Neo-Absolutism," 312. György Szabad goes so far as to claim that, to some degree at least, the resistance movement may have had the reactionary outcome of alienating sections of the community from the rapidly changing world around them and "contributing to their falling behind" not only a rapidly developing Europe, but even a modernizing Vienna or Pest. György Szabad, *Hungarian Political Trends Between the Revolution and the Compromise (1848–1867)* (Budapest: Akadémiai Kiadó, 1977), 47.

56. Deák, *"Nemzeti egyenjogúsítás": Kormányzati memzetiségpolitika Magyarországon 1849–1860* ["National Equal Rights": The Government's Handling of Minorities in Hungary 1849–1860] (Budapest: Osiris Kiadó, 2000), 166, 169–170; Pap, *Magyarország vármegyei tisztikara,* 32.

57. Szabad, *Hungarian Political Trends,* 39–42. Paradoxically, at times people viewed by Hungarians as collaborators were seen as passive resisters by the Austrians. Hungarian public administrators were removed from office because, as Pest police chief Joseph Protmann reported, they "took every possible opportunity to backpedal and operate by the old conservative principles of passive resistance" and "slyly, by any means possible, discredit new institutions and block implementation of policies. Failing the opportunity for direct action, they employ passive resistance." According to the head of the Kassa (now Kosice) police, Hungarian civil servants fell into three categories: those who opposed all reforms; those generally opposed but "open to persuasion"; and those who appeared to cooperate but, in fact, simply paid lip service. However, their noncooperating compatriots denounced them as collaborators, "moral lepers," and "honorary traitors." Deák, *"Nemzeti egyenjogúsítás,"* 166, 171–172.

58. Hanák, "The Period of Neo-Absolutism," 297, 308.

59. Paul Ignotus, *Hungary* (London: Ernest Benn, 1972), 65.

60. Hanák, "The Period of Neo-Absolutism," 299.

61. Kontler, *A History of Hungary,* 271.

62. Steven Huxley notes that Finnish "passive resistance" entered popular mythology in a way not necessarily supported by all the evidence. For how a romanticized view of a movement can affect later theoretical positions, see Steven Duncan Huxley, *Constitutionalist Insurgency in Finland: Finnish "Passive Resistance" Against Russification as a Case of Nonmilitary Struggle in the European Resistance Tradition* (Helsinki: SHS, 1990), especially the first two chapters.

63. Király, *Ferenc Deák,* 35.

64. Hanák, "The Period of Neo-Absolutism," 289.

65. Gábor Pajkossy, "Deák-emlékév" [Deák Anniversary Year], *BUKSZ* (summer 2004): 144–157.

66. See, for example, Kurt Schock, *Unarmed Insurrections: People Power Movements in Nondemocracies* (Minneapolis: University of Minnesota Press, 2005);

Robert J. Burrowes, *The Strategy of Nonviolent Defense: A Gandhian Approach* (Albany: State University of New York Press, 1996); Peter Ackerman and Jack DuVall, *A Force More Powerful: A Century of Nonviolent Conflict* (New York: Palgrave Macmillan, 2000); and Adam Roberts and Timothy Garton Ash, eds., *Civil Resistance and Power Politics: The Experience of Non-Violent Action from Gandhi to the Present* (Oxford: Oxford University Press, 2009).

67. Ralph Summy, "Nonviolence and the Case of the Extremely Ruthless Opponent," *Pacifica Review* 6, no. 1 (1994): 1–29. The problem for the Austrians was trying to rule another nation without the consent of the population, especially when Vienna needed Hungarian taxes and soldiers. Withdrawal of consent to be ruled in such circumstances appears to be the cornerstone of successful nonviolent resistance.

14

Poland:
Forging the Polish Nation
Nonviolently, 1860s–1900s

Maciej J. Bartkowski

The third and final partition of the Polish-Lithuanian Common-wealth in 1795 brought to an end the existence of the Polish state. Partitioned between Russia, Prussia, and the Habsburg Empire, it would take more than 123 years for Poland to reemerge as an independent nation-state in 1918.

At the time of partition, no sector of society put Polish identity above class interest. Political rights had been confined to a privileged class, the szlachta, who could elect and limit the powers of kings.[1] This class had abused and exploited peasants for centuries while impeding the rise of a merchant class. Therefore, class animosities were strong, permitting the partition powers to incite events such as the 1848 "Galicia slaughter" when peasants killed more than 1,000 nobles. In 1870, it was estimated that only around a third of the Polish-speaking population considered themselves Polish.[2]

In such circumstances, the development of Polish identity and a Polish nation was by no means inevitable. Late-nineteenth-century processes such as industrialization, urbanization, and demographic growth of the Polish-speaking population do not by themselves account for the emergence of a common Polish identity and a growing demand for statehood. Social and economic changes, together with the often repressive policies of the occupying powers, helped to create a propitious environment for mass-based mobilization. But the nature of this mobilization, either subservient and passive or restive and nationalistic, was determined largely by the new way that the struggle for independence was waged: a deliberate rejection, at least for a period of time, of armed resistance in favor of novel nonviolent methods of defiance.

In this chapter, I argue that Poles developed philosophically refined and, in practice, sophisticated forms of nonviolent resistance in their struggle for national survival and independence. This nonviolent resistance took shape soon after a failed violent national uprising of 1863–1864 and, for more than five decades, it became the main weapon of defiance and a remarkably effective means of building collective identity among the Polish-speaking population. Although Poles did not end the partition by their nonviolent disobedience and confrontation—World War I did that—neither were they defeated or culturally annihilated as the partitioning powers intended. This cultural resilience in the face of severe oppression was based on ingenious mass nonviolent mobilizing, organizing, and actions, all of which instilled a deep sense of national awareness.

Eulogized Violence in Polish History and National Remembrance

General neglect of the role of nonviolent resistance does not result only from a historiographical focus on the role of political and intellectual elites, geopolitical changes, or social and economic transformations. It also is the consequence of the dramas of war, armed conflict, and dominant narratives of glorified violent resistance. Polish historians, essayists, poets, film- and opinionmakers, and politicians (mostly men) have been attracted to mesmerizing stories of militant conspiracies, plotting, army mobilizations, military campaigns, victorious battles, and heroic violent resistance, particularly against more powerful enemies, leading to unavoidable but glorious defeats. These stories have been cherished and apotheosized through collective remembrance. Valor is attached to knightly or soldierly virtues and unquestioned martyrdom for the Polish fatherland and the country's freedom. Unsurprisingly, therefore, as Adam Michnik remarks, Poles "identify most closely with the tradition of uprisings."[3] The nineteenth-century romantic literature of romanticism presents Poland as a Christ among nations, enduring injustice and persecution, and sacrificing itself on the altar of the struggle for freedom so as to rise again, regain its independence, and free other subjugated nations. In that sense, immense suffering, victimization by pernicious neighbors, immediate sacrifice, and violent heroics—symbolized by the suicidal charge of Polish cavalry against German tanks in 1939— have defined Polishness and Polish patriotism and are believed to have contributed to the nation's resilience and perseverance.

Discussion about the significance and meaning of national tragedies and sacrifices has been renewed by the crash of the presidential plane on April 10, 2010, which killed dozens of leading contemporary Polish political leaders and intellectual figures. They were flying to commemorate one of Poland's most emotive anniversaries—the 1940 Katyń massacre where Soviet secret police executed 21,000 Polish officers. In 2010, as hundreds of thousands of Poles went to the streets in an emotional outpouring of grief and solidarity, commentators reported an overwhelming sensation of patriotism and the rise of a new Polish political community: "Poles, brought together by violent death and destruction, could finally unite in pain."[4] This victimhood fuels an enduring belief that defeats, sacrifice, and martyrs are necessary to bring about greater rewards—such as independence after 123 years of unceasing struggle or a genuine community of Poles that emerged out of the April 10 tragedy. Time and again, the Polish national identity is redefined and reformed by national catastrophes—partitions, wars, and tragic accidents.

The tradition of armed resistance is ingrained in Polish culture, not least in the capital itself: Warsaw. Its numerous monuments, many erected after 1989, quintessentially represent the way Poles remember and retell their history. Monuments for fallen heroes dominate the commemorative landscape: for the brave Polish soldiers who fought and died at Monte Cassino in 1944, the decisive battle in Italy; for the 1944 Warsaw Rising; for the fallen and murdered in the East, including those executed at Katy; and the Tomb of the Unknown Soldier regularly visited by Polish notables. A conspicuous bronze figure is the Little Insurgent, a boy soldier wearing an oversized adult helmet and clenching a German Sten gun—this is near to where thirteen-year-old "Antek" was killed.

In 2005 the Warsaw Rising Museum opened, which uses modern, multimedia historical exhibitions to "recreate the atmosphere of fighting Warsaw."[5] Here, officials from the Central Anticorruption Bureau, the Internal Security Agency, and the Border Guard take their solemn oaths of office. As the spokesperson for the Internal Security Agency explained, they chose the museum because "Poles associated this place with heroism and patriotism of all those who gave their lives for the fatherland."[6] The appropriateness of linking the work of these agencies with a violent and a destined-for-defeat insurrectionary act where many children, outgunned, fought the German Army has not been questioned.

Through all these monuments, places, and commemorative rituals, Poles immortalize their heroism in armed struggles. Furthermore, in so doing, other stories of no less courageous and patriotic acts are suppressed. A participant in the nowadays forgotten nonviolent resistance during the German occupation of Warsaw recalls,

> Underground teaching on all levels of schooling was the most admirable work accomplished by Polish society [during the war]. Neither tracts [*sic*], nor violence, nor sabotages were as productive as this last manifestation of the national consciousness. It saved our society from a catastrophe equal at least to the destruction of Warsaw: the loss of five graduating

classes of engineers, architects, doctors, teachers, and students who managed to pass their baccalaureate exams [despite the German occupation and war].[7]

Historians such as Norman Davies refer to "an amazing network of clandestine classes, which eventually undertook the education of a million children."[8] Yet Warsaw has no monument to commemorate those who risked death to organize classes. Their daily heroism remained anonymous and largely forgotten.

Just as nonviolent resistance to German occupation is ignored in Polish historiography and by the public at large, so too is the role and legacy of nonviolent resistance to the partition. Adam Michnik encapsulates well how militaristic tradition eclipses the "less glamorous" achievements of nonviolent resistance:

> An attack from the battle of Samosierra [*sic*][9] is more photogenic than the tedious organization of education or the modernization of agriculture, not to mention the construction of a network of sanitary facilities. But let us remember that we would not have been able to organize our statehood had it not been for the work done in the spirit of "organicism" and "accommodation." . . . And let us remember that our grandfathers often had to pay a high price for their decision to undertake these tasks, risking moral reproach from their antagonists.[10]

Michnik also writes about Poles who see only in black and white: either one takes up arms and fights for the fatherland or one yields to the oppression and abandons the struggle entirely.[11] This binary choice excludes the option of defiance through nonviolent organizing and nonviolent direct action.

Philosophical and Historical Foundations of Nonviolent Resistance: The Birth of Organic Work

After partition, Poles engaged in armed struggle by allying with Napoleon against the partitioning powers, by conspiring and leading the violent uprising of November 1830, by joining militarily in the People's Spring of 1848, and by rising again in January 1863 to be crushed by the Russian Army. Following this violent defeat and its disastrous consequences,[12] many viewed regaining Poland's independence as unrealistic in the foreseeable future. This led to a decisive shift away from ad hoc armed revolts toward strategies of long-term constructive activism and organizing as a way to continue the struggle by other, nonviolent, means.

Nonviolent action found its context in the newly emerging social philosophy of positivism as adapted in Poland. Polish positivism offered a rational explanation for nonviolent resistance and its strategic, long-term use and eventually superseded a romantic vision of armed struggle for Poland's independence.

Influenced by their Western European counterparts, Polish positivists saw the nation as a social organism that, to survive and grow, had to be healthy and well nourished. National survival, particularly within the borders of foreign states, was endangered by continuous militant conspiracies and failed violent actions. For positivists the new strategy for reasserting national existence, vigor, and hope for eventual liberation was to accumulate intellectual, cultural, social, and economic strength. The best-educated and most intelligent, not the mightiest, would eventually survive and win. Aleksander Świętochowski, a leading Polish positivist, emphasizes the superiority of mental over physical strength: "No Krupp could make such armaments as would kill Copernicus and no Moltke could vanquish Mickiewicz or Matejko."[13] Knowledge and work became a new strategy for unity, perseverance, and resistance that were to help weave various Polish-speaking groups, most importantly peasants, into a national fabric.

This rise of positivism was paralleled with the emergence of the Cracow historical school, which argued that internal factors—weak and ineffectual government and a general economic and social malaise—rendered the country extremely vulnerable. Consequently, neighboring powers saw the opportunity for conquest and territorial expansion.

Placing the causes for Poland's downfall squarely on the domestic front meant that a remedy could also be found in internal changes and reforms. As Józef Szujski, a leader of the Cracow historical school, explained, "If the nation as a state fell, it was from its own guilt [and] if it raises, it will be from its own work, its own reason, its own spirit."[14] The school further maintained that a successful armed insurrection not only was unlikely, but it would be short-lived without a proper political, social, and economic basis. Although often criticized for religious, social, and political conservatism and loyalty toward the Habsburgs, the school helped lay down the ideational foundations for moving away from the destructive violence of armed uprisings toward constructive nonviolent strategies.

The positivist thoughts supported by the ideas of the Cracow historical school were put into effect through a new type of nonviolent defiance known as "organic work" or "work at foundations" that emphasized social and economic development, cultural learning, and preservation of language, tradition, and historical memory. It was a strategic and pragmatic choice as nonviolent methods began to look more feasible than failed armed struggles. Organic work from self-discipline and intellectual self-improvement, to national education of the masses and social, economic, and political self-organization was a nonspectacular project whose outcomes were not immediately discernible and, in contrast to insurrectionary conspiracies, often faced no immediate threat of repression. Forms of organic work were undertaken in all three parts of divided Poland, both openly and secretly, legally and illegally. The two common elements were its nonviolent character and the constructive nature of resistance. The objective was to generate solely Polish economic, social, and intellectual capital and to sustain, protect, and promote Polishness: language, culture, tradition, and history. Polish dreams of independence were now channeled through nonviolent practical tools of self-organization that would preserve, solidify, and eventually expand the cultural, ethnic, linguistic, and historical boundaries of being a Pole.

Organic Work in Austrian, German, and Russian Poland

Various initiatives in the spirit of organic work took place soon after partition, but they were not widespread nor were their scale and eventual impact comparable to developments in the 1870s and later. The failed 1863–1864 rising was a watershed. Polish society, exhausted with the armed struggles and their continuous defeats but committed to defending the core of its identity, now concentrated on harnessing its strengths internally to withstand de-Polonization. Through the creation of parallel economic, social, and educational institutions and the protection and expansion of cultural and national practices, Poles carried on their defiance throughout the partitioned country while actively seeking to awaken a unified national identity among all Polish-speaking groups.

Organic Work in Austrian Poland

Austrian Poland (Galicia) was the least economically developed territory, the most conservative in terms of social hierarchies, with strong loyalties toward the Habsburg Empire and a relatively low level of national consciousness, particularly in rural areas. The major shift toward embracing nonviolent forms of defiance occurred at the end of the 1870s, veiled in legal education activities and nonconfrontational and open forms of cultural and national festivities fostering Polish identity.

Vienna tightly controlled the education curricula in Austrian Poland, forbidding teachers to use their own materials to teach about national history and banned prepartition maps of Poland. In 1882, organicists launched the Agricultural Circle Society that quickly grew into a movement. It organized civic education and opened reading rooms while supporting self-organization among Polish-speaking villagers by opening Christian stores and credit associations.[15] The agricultural circle movement organized festivities to commemorate historic anniversaries and promoted social behavior aiming to reinforce the social and national fabric. Its strict antialcohol rules in village circle rooms were the first challenge to the dominance of taverns in village life. The agricultural circle movement's promotion of self-improvement among Galician peasants is credited with their growing identification with the Polish nation.[16] Peasants gained access to patriotic literature, history books, Polish-language newspapers, and also information on how to set up and run reading rooms.[17] Another mass education organization—the People's School Society (PSS)—was established in 1891. It grew rapidly and, by 1913, had more than 300 branches with 42,000 members. It reached out to roughly 5 million illiterate Polish-speaking peasants in Galicia, building libraries and setting up rural primary and secondary schools as well as seminaries for teachers. It incorporated the work of Polish nationalist novelists and poets in the curricula and organized national celebrations.[18] On the surface they were apolitical, but in fact self-help organizations such as the agricultural circle movement or the PSS signaled the growth of a new national consciousness.[19]

An additional participatory form of action after 1863–1864 was commemorations that brought together Poles from different social strata: intellectuals, peasants, and laborers from all parts of the divided country. The mass celebrations of national traditions, famous Polish historical and contemporary figures, mass remembrances of glorious historical events and military victories, and people's mourning during anniversaries (e.g., partitions of the Polish state or failed armed uprisings) were often accompanied by educational activities such as lectures, theatrical performances, publications of books or historical monographs, exhibitions of memorabilia, or church services. They were an alternative form of patriotic activism to counter the denationalizing and de-Polonizing policies of the partitioning powers, instead creating a sense of one community united by shared history, language, traditions, and culture. Commemorations were a "constructive, creative, yet intensely national variant of organic work—an attempt at national modernization, Polish style."[20]

It is beyond the scope of this chapter to document the myriad commemorative events, but it is worth highlighting two examples. Naturally, Austria and Germany could not object to commemorations of the bicentennial of the Relief of Vienna in 1883 by Austrian, German, and Polish forces under Polish king Jan III Sobieski. For Poles, however, celebrating this important national military victory was a reminder of their country's past glory, independence, and might that stopped Ottoman invasion of Europe. More than 12,000 peasants came to Cracow to celebrate the bicentennial, some leaving their village for the first time. They saw the Polish royal castle and heard speeches and lectures about Polish history. Both a national and a religious celebration, Polish-speaking Catholic peasants paid homage to the Polish monarch whose military genius had saved Christianity.[21]

The second example is the centennial of the failed 1794 uprising led by Tadeusz Kościuszko against Prussia and Russia. After the victorious Battle of Racławice, where a peasant battalion armed with scythes overran Russian artillery positions, Kościuszko ennobled a number of peasants, promoting Bartosz Głowacki to become the standard bearer, a symbol of the armed rising. During the centennial commemoration, numerous plays, sketches, art exhibitions, and a reenactment of the Battle of Racławice acknowledged the peasant volunteers' readiness to sacrifice for the Polish nation. Thousands of Polish-speaking peasants visited Cracow to take part. In Lviv, under the cover of an exposition of technological advances and agricultural developments in Austrian Poland, the organizers displayed a national trope: Wojciech Kossak and Jan Styka's enormous painting, *The Racławice Panorama,* showing peasants with scythes leading the charge against the Russian cannons. In four months, more than a million people visited the exposition and an estimated 200,000 people viewed *The Racławice Panorama.*[22] The PSS organized peasant group visits, including funding the trips of more than 6,000 schoolchildren. During one of many pilgrimages to *The Racławice Panorama,* 3,000 peasants passed a resolution demanding universal and direct voting rights—a year later the Polish Peasant Party was established.

This tactic of mass commemoration required the adroit use of nationally significant anniversaries that would influence peasants and other social groups to identify as Polish citizens, cognizant of their national identity, duties, and political rights, while doing so in a low-risk, nonviolent way that reduced the likelihood of repression. Commemorations were a pedagogical tool for Polish speakers who previously did not identify with the nation. The strength of this newly acquired national identity came into clear display during World War I when peasants constituted the majority of Polish volunteers.[23]

Organic Work in German Poland

In German Poland, the nonviolent resistance was similarly advanced through building a number of civic institutions independent from the authorities and thus countering Germanization policies known as *Kulturkampf* (the struggle for land and minds) and strengthening national awareness among the Polish population.

In 1872, organicists founded the Society for Peasant Education with the goals of offering alternative education and increasing national awareness of Polish language, history, and culture. It established nearly 120 libraries all over German Poland, distributed books and other reading materials, and set up day nurseries. The German authorities dissolved this organization, leading Polish organicists in 1880 to found the Society for Folk Reading Rooms, whose activities conformed to German legal restrictions. Within three years, this society had set up almost 400 rural and 85 urban libraries and supplied them with 79,000 Polish-language cultural, literary, and religious books. By 1890, almost 1,000 libraries were established with the society's help. In addition to the society's work, organicists set up more than 100 reading circles in German Poland.[24]

In 1886, German chancellor Otto von Bismarck allocated 100 million marks to buy out indebted Polish landowners in German Poland and replace them with Germans. In response, Polish organicists made plans to buy back the lands for Poles. Thanks to parcelation institutions, beginning with the Polish Land Bank in 1888, within a decade Poles were able to acquire more land than the Germans. A famous example of resistance to the German land grab is the story of the Polish peasant Michał Drzymała. In 1904, German authorities refused to allow him to build a permanent residence on his new property. Therefore, Drzymała turned his caravan-trailer into his home and, to abide by German law, moved it a few centimeters each day to show that it was not permanent and, therefore, did not require a permit. The resulting legal battle lasted for more than four years and ended when Drzymała sold the land and purchased another with an already built house that did not require a building permission. By then, British, French, and US newspapers made a mockery of the German institutionalized and legalized land discrimination policy against Poles while Drzymała and his caravan became a symbol of creative nonviolent resistance to the German expansionist policies.

Various Polish economic and financial institutions were created in rural areas to counteract German economic expansion. The number of Polish credit cooperatives rose from 25 in 1868 to 76 in 1891, reaching 204 by 1913 with close to 126,000 members—almost half of them peasants.[25] They offered Poles more favorable interest rates than German banks and so helped modernize and expand both the rural and urban economy in German Poland.[26] Organicists pushed for the establishment of Polish industrial societies with both political and national objectives to strengthen the middle-class economic basis in order to compete effectively with German entrepreneurs. The industrial societies proliferated and, by 1914, there were almost 170 societies in the region of Poznań alone with almost 11,000 members.[27]

The number of peasant agricultural circles increased from 45 in 1875 to 60 with 10,000 members in 1900, reaching 310 with 17,000 members by 1910, some 40 percent of all Polish-speaking rural landowners—the new social cadre of peasant activists.[28] Next to facilitating information exchange about crop-growing and agricultural trade, including selling agricultural products and delivering fertilizer, coal, and seeds to the Polish farmers, the circles also advanced knowledge about legal, credit, tax, and inheritance issues that aimed at countervailing German administrative, juridical, and economic efforts to uproot Polish-speaking peasants from their land. In addition,

6,000 dairy cooperatives and 6,000 credit banks were set up to support the cultural, social, and economic development of the Polish village.[29]

Concurrent with the growth of Polish economic, social, and educational institutions, the Polish-language press also grew and its total annual print in German Poland doubled in the first decade of the twentieth century to 400,000 copies per year.[30] Evidence of the impact of increasingly muscular nationalist press could be clearly seen in the school strikes in 1901–1907 (discussed below).

By 1914, an estimated one in four adults belonged to a Polish economic, social, cultural, or political institution in the largest region of German Poland, Wielkopolska.[31] Overall by 1913, Polish organic institutions reached 140,000 members of the adult population of Wielkopolska—although the total number of Poles influenced by such institutions was higher since younger Poles were exposed to organic education without being counted as members.[32] Through these activities, the organizers and their beneficiaries "learned that they could attain specific economic, cultural, and social goals through a group effort that relied on legal, practical actions rather than . . . revolutionary violence."[33]

School Strikes in German Poland

The school strikes that broke out in German Poland beginning in 1901 were the largest form of coercive nonviolent defiance in the partitioned lands. The years of 1906–1907 were the peak of the strike, with more than 93,000 children staying away from school.

This resistance to Germanization had been built through decades of less confrontational mobilization. As far back as 1871, 110,000 people signed a petition against German plans for schools while 160,000 signed a petition in support of Polish language in elementary schools. When in 1885 the government ordered all subjects to be taught in German, including religion and Polish-language classes, 60,000 people signed a petition that demanded church (rather than state) oversight of religion classes and teaching of the Polish language. These petitions, together with open public meetings to discuss education policies, were lessons in citizens' self-organization to defend the rights to their own language. They generated greater awareness among Polish speakers of the necessity to defend Polish education and were an important prelude to the school strikes. The conflict was further intensified as the Polish Catholic Church was drawn into the dispute to defend the use of Polish in religious instruction. Poles became ready to replace legal methods of petition with more disruptive, illegal, nonviolent resistance through school strikes.

The first major strike in 1901 took place in the town of Września. First, parents refused to buy the German-language religious texts. When school officials bought them, pupils refused to use the books or answer questions in German. The defiant pupils prayed in Polish instead of German and "refused to attend the ceremonies commemorating the German victory over France at Sedan."[34] German teachers and Poles loyal to the German authorities punished the children, including with corporal punishment. During a mass caning, when townspeople heard the children's screams, about 1,000 people, mainly women, entered the schoolyard and protested. German police forced the crowd to leave, and later twenty-one protesters, including seven women and three teenagers, were sentenced to prison terms and financial penalties.

Far from subduing the public, these harsh sentences backfired, converting the Września affair into a national symbol of the Polish resistance and sacrifice in defense of the Polish language. Soon, celebrated poems and essays about children's heroism were published[35] while donations came from Poland, Europe, and the United States to cover legal fees, provide support for the prisoners' families, and gifts for the beaten pupils—an example of solidarity across partitioned borders.[36] Pro-Września protests took place in other parts of Poland, including at the German consulates in Warsaw and Lviv. The international public also noticed the brutality of the German oppression through press coverage in France, Britain, the Netherlands, Denmark, Belgium, Italy, Argentina, and the Vatican. This in turn contributed to an increase in international support for Poles' right to self-determination.

Despite the backlash, the German authorities remained inflexible, thus paving the way to a much larger wave of school strikes in 1906–1907. The first strike began in October 1906 and involved an estimated 70,000 pupils from 950 state schools, including 20,000 in Pomerania and 47,000 in Wielkopolska (more than half of those pupils were required to study religion in German).[37] Eventually, 93,000 children from over 1,600 schools in German Poland joined the school strikes.[38] The fruits of more than a half century of organic work among the peasant population were reflected in the strikers' class background. Close to 90 percent of the striking pupils came from families of peasants and agrarian workers while around 10 percent from families of craft and industrial workers.[39]

The Polish-language press in German Poland played an important role in preparing the ground for general school strikes and sustaining the mobilization. In 1906 they printed sample petitions for parents to use in protest at German religion classes, then published a call for a general organizational meeting of all provinces in German Poland to discuss new forms of resistance—a meeting ultimately attended by more than 2,000 people despite police stopping many participants en route. Once the strikes broke out, the Polish press published regular reports on the ongoing protests in different parts of German Poland. Because schools often demanded proof of parents' acquiescence to their children's strike, newspapers printed examples of parental consent notes for pupils to give to teachers. The press praised striking pupils and encouraged others to follow their example while also urging nonviolent discipline and calmness in pursuing the strike and unity and resolve in recognizing that only with broad participation could it succeed.

Despite the size and scope of participation, the authorities stood firm. Various Polish politicians were skeptical about the success of the school strikes, recognizing neither their value nor power. Meanwhile, German repression was taking its toll. Some parents lost custody of striking pupils, some pupils were expelled, and many were denied school diplomas. Newspapers faced huge fines, which undermined them financially. By late spring 1907, the strikes were dying out.

It took the Germans more than a year to tame this wave of strikes and only by deploying a set of extraordinary measures. The Polish press presented the eventual end not as a defeat, but as the moment when the Polish public had fulfilled its patriotic obligation. Indeed, for many strikers the struggle was no longer about the means to reach a specific objective, but an end in itself with great symbolic value. In that sense, the strikers achieved a moral victory.[40] This also had serious tangible consequences. The Polish language became a unifying force as never before. No armed insurrection had mobilized such a diverse group of people: young and old, girls and boys, women and men from villages and towns across the region. The protest against the German religion classes became a movement for preserving Polish identity and politicized a swathe of the Polish-speaking population.[41]

These strikes serve as a yardstick of much deeper changes at work in Polish society through organic work and in defense of Polish culture and identity. They were followed by a new surge of social and cultural activities, including the growth of Polish sports, religious, and clandestine education associations that were to be the backbone of the reborn Polish society after World War I.

Organic Work in Russian Poland

The policies of czarist Russia after the failed 1863–1864 uprising aimed at either preventing the emergence of Polish national identity or uprooting it altogether. In order to win over Polish-speaking peasants and weaken the Polish landowning class (the most nationally aware group), Russia abolished serfdom in Russian Poland in 1864. Pressing forward with the Russification of its western lands, in 1866 the government made Russian the mandatory language of instruction in state and private schools for selected subjects. A year later it extended this requirement to all subjects except Polish language and religion. Finally, in 1885, all types of schools were required to teach everything except religion in Russian. Polish not only was banned in school corridors and yards, but in all public places. Polish shop signs had to be removed, and Polish newspapers and libraries were closed.[42]

In Russian Poland, underground, illegal classes secretly offered teaching in Polish language, history, and literature, thus becoming the centerpiece of the organic work and nonviolent resistance. In 1894 a woman activist, Cecylia Śniegocka, set up the Association of the Secret Teaching. Within ten years, 2,000 children were taking secret classes in Warsaw that constituted half of all pupils in government-controlled primary schools in the city.[43] By 1901, according to Russian government sources, a third of the Polish population in Russian Poland at some point had received secret teaching that enabled them to read and write in Polish.[44]

A prominent form of secret higher education was the "flying university" that developed in the mid-1870s. Academics offered lessons in private premises on both science and humanities with emphasis on Polish history, culture, and language. More than 5,000 men and women passed through the flying university in Russian Poland in the 1880s, including the future Nobel Prize winner Marie Curie-Skłodowska.[45]

Russian Poland's tradition of resistance through clandestine organizing and teaching, self-education circles, and mutual assistance organizations laid the ground for the 1905 movement to boycott the state school system. More than 20,000 students, mostly young women and girls, actively joined the boycott.[46] They demanded restoration of Polish as a language of instruction and a representative, democratic, and participatory system of education with societal rather than governmental control. Urban civil resistance spilled over to rural areas where thousands of new village schools were created through the initiative of Polish-controlled local and communal municipalities. Literate peasants began to offer secret instruction in Polish grammar and religion. Confronted with growing social unrest, in October 1905 the czarist government permitted the establishment of private schools with Polish as the language of instruction for all subjects except Russian language, history, and geography. Unable to win further concessions, the movement faced brutal antistrike measures—martial law and curfews that closed down higher education institutions, dismissal of 142 teachers, mass expulsion of students, and severe movement restrictions imposed on students who remained enrolled under the threat of large financial penalties or prison sentences.[47] Consequently, the movement switched to using the existing legal system to create a network of Polish private schools as an alternative to the Russified state system.

In 1906 drawing on both the experience and tradition of the flying university, Polish Motherland Schools (PMS) were launched to establish Polish private schooling in Russian Poland. By the start of the school year, the PMS boasted 680 registered schools and 70,000 enrolled students.[48] Soon these numbers increased to almost 800 schools and nearly 120,000 pupils, and the next year a further 450 private schools requested registration. Then, the Russian government cracked down and closed the PMS themselves. In response, Polish organicists began the establishment of parallel underground schools. Despite the arrest of hundreds of teachers, repressive government policies failed to crush this movement. Poles saw the state school system as a tool for Russification, thus parents often continued their boycott of the state schools by sending their children to private elementary and middle schools and commerce schools. By 1914, 18 percent of all elementary school pupils (70,000 children) attended more than 800 private schools.[49] At the same time, private middle schools enrolled 38,000 pupils, more than 60 percent of the total in Russian Poland.[50]

Even in the oppressive environment of Russification, Russian Poland nevertheless organized its commemoration movement, albeit more limited than in Austrian Poland. The 1898 celebration of the centenary of Adam Mickiewicz's birth and the idea of honoring this national bard with a bronze statue aroused public enthusiasm. In just two months, over 100,000 people donated 200,000 rubles for the statue; more than 80 percent of these donations were from private individuals from mainly the middle class and peasantry.[51] This monument was built not only to celebrate Mickiewicz's poetry, but also to honor a national symbol of freedom and resistance. The dedication itself, with plays and speeches, evoked national pride among peasants and workers.[52] The czarist government had been obstructive about the event—imposing censorship, limiting the tickets available, and cordoning off the celebration area—yet more than 12,000 people attended the official ceremony. The self-organization of the citizens' committee to build the monument, the fund-raising drive, and the dedication ceremony were seen by a contemporary commentator as

> the most wonderful, sublime and invigorating signs of collective existence, . . . one of the great victories in the unceasing . . . battle for the existence of the Polish nation. Under the oppression of the strictest police surveillance . . . , under the oppression of censorship . . . , this miraculous plebiscite took place with lighting speed, in the face of which the mighty state stood amazed, helpless, and lacking courage to prevent and suppress.[53]

Women and Organic Work

Organic work and particularly overt and secret education activities gave women a much more prominent presence in the Polish nonviolent resistance than during the romanticized period of armed insurrections.

Women and girls played a leading role in Polish underground education in Russian Poland and during the school strikes under the German and Russian partitions. Women led an estimated 40 percent of the education movement's activities associated with the education movement in Russian

Poland. Because in the household women were largely responsible for educating children, they were now active in generating, distributing, and using elementary education materials and leading parent self-help organizations.

The emphasis of positivism on constructive nonviolent organizing through economic, social, and intellectual development highlighted a role for women that went beyond maternity or the tragic archetype of the Mother-Pole (Matka Polka) whose son sacrifices his life to fight oppression. The positivist Mother-Pole was an educator of her own children as well as a social activist, teacher, organizer, and writer who educated others, particularly illiterate peasants—a role that placed women in direct confrontation with the partitioning empires and their de-Polonization policies.[54]

Conclusion

Vast parts of the Polish-speaking population with little or no Polish national identity might have been assimilated among the three empires that divided their country. That this did not happen was largely the result of a mass nonviolent constructive program that became the main strategy of defense and resistance when armed uprisings proved futile against militarily superior enemies.

The nonviolent strategy of organic work ensured national and cultural survival and successfully politicized masses in all three parts of Poland. Under the harshest conditions in Russian Poland where the onslaught of Russification covered all spheres of public life, the organicists carried out their work mainly through underground, secretive, and illegal institutions and activities. In German Poland, the constitutional and economic parameters of the system allowed organicists to build legally permitted social and economic institutions to counter German de-Polonization policies. Germans often harassed Polish organizations and, while permitting Polish entrepreneurship, waged a total cultural war against Polishness and banned all Polish educational initiatives. Nonetheless, Germanization of education failed to diminish the rising wave of Polish national sentiment or stop open resistance in Polish schools. Finally, in Austrian Poland—the most liberal of the partitions where Poles seemingly had some loyalty to their occupier—Polish conservatives used nonviolent organic work to prevent open violent confrontation. Eventually, the organic work in Austrian Poland did more to turn Poles, particularly peasants, into a nation than all of the previous armed risings.

Nevertheless, eulogized violence in Polish tradition and history have reinforced the perception of organic work as a form of "less assertive patriotism,"[55] as a tool of loyalist accommodation with the foreign power, and even as a betrayal of the generations of Poles who joined armed resistance and gave their lives in national risings. The continuing glorification of military resistance paradoxically enough can be attributed to the successes and achievements of nonviolent movement that after all relied on cultural forms of resistance (e.g., commemorations) and parallel institution building (e.g., patriotic education). These both often shaped and propagated the attitudes of admiration for the tradition of armed resistance that further romanticized past violent struggles and inadvertently helped overshadow its nonviolent popularizers.

A critical attitude toward organic work is particularly perplexing given the extent to which the nineteenth-century nonviolent resistance and its constructive program of creating and running parallel institutions served as an inspiration for future generations of Poles faced with oppression.[56] The conspiratorial experience of organizing and running secret education became ingrained in the collective memory of the national resistance. It was recalled during traumatic events such as the German occupation of 1939–1945 and during communist rule, particularly during the 1970s and 1980s when widespread illegal education (including the reestablishment of the flying university) ensured the truthful reading of national history, culture, and tradition. In fact, working at the base of society became the imperative nonviolent strategy of the anticommunist opposition. Solidarity leaders drew parallels between their nonviolent efforts to liberate the society from the control of the communist government and the nonviolent strategies of nineteenth-century organicists to undermine the authority of the partitioning powers.[57]

Bohdan Cywiński's influential *Genealogy of the Defiant* (1971) studied the fin-de-siecle (defiant ones) and made parallels between their nonviolent defiant attitude and practice against the czarist government and the then contemporary resistance to communism.[58] That book inspired thousands of Poles and showed clearly how a century-old tradition of nonviolent resistance—although generally underappreciated in the national annals—could play a vital role in shaping the thinking, and determining the strategies and actions, of a new generation of unarmed resisters struggling with no less oppressive autocratic rulers than their indomitable predecessors who lived under partitions.

Without nonviolent resistance, Poles could not have taken charge of their national destiny after World War I or changed the geopolitical situation in their favor during the 1980s. It would have been equally implausible to integrate partitioned lands after 1918 and establish statehood so swiftly without the base of social, economic, and cultural development constructed through organic work. Although nonviolent resistance has been widely used by different generations of Poles against both external occupation and domestic dictatorship, this form of struggle is still awaiting much-deserved recognition of its role in not only defending, but essentially reimagining, the Polish nation.

Notes

1. The szlachta, comprising landowning gentry and nobility, was estimated at 10 percent of the Polish-speaking population in the sixteenth and seventeenth centuries, several times higher the politically active population in other parts of Europe.

2. Tadeusz Lepkowski, *Poland: The Birth of the Modern Nation, 1764–1870,* quoted in Patrice M. Dabrowski, *Commemorations and the Shaping of Modern Poland* (Bloomington: Indiana University Press, 2004), 12.

3. Adam Michnik, *Letters from Prison and Other Essays* (Berkeley: University of California Press, 1987), 173. Michnik, as well as being an intellectual leader of Solidarność, is a conscientious student of nineteenth-century Polish history.

4. "Polaków łaczy tylko ból" [Only Pain Unites Poles], interview with the literary critic and historian Stefan Chwin, *Gazeta Wyborcza,* May 2, 2010, http://wyborcza.pl/duzyformat/1,127291,7830585,Polakow_laczy_tylko_bol.html, accessed May 3, 2010.

5. From the website of the Warsaw Raising Museum, http://www.1944.pl/en.

6. Dominika Olszewska, *Gazeta Wyborcza,* February 6, 2010. http://wyborcza.pl/1,75248,7533860,Konspiracyjne_przysiegi_w_muzeum.html, accessed February 6, 2010. This practice had previously been secret.

7. Quoted in Jacques Semelin, *Unarmed Against Hitler: Civilian Resistance in Europe, 1939–1943* (Westport, CT: Praeger, 1993), 80.

8. Norman Davies, *God's Playground: 1795 to the Present. A History of Poland,* vol. 2 (New York: Columbia University Press, 2005), 345.

9. In the 1808 Battle of Somosierra, Napoleon sacrificed his Polish cavalry in a charge on Spanish cannon. This charge is immortalized in various Polish paintings and history books.

10. Michnik, *Letters from Prison,* 174.

11. Adam Michnik, *Polskie Pytania* (Paris: Cahiers Litteraires, 1987), 183.

12. During the 1863 uprising, several thousand Poles were killed, a further 1,000 were executed, close to 40,000 were sent for penal servitude to Siberia, and more than 10,000 chose immigration. This was on top of massive material destruction, property expropriation, and land confiscation. See Lech Trzeciakowski, "Ziemie polskie pod panowaniem państw zaborczych (1815–1918)" in *Dzieje Polski,* ed. Jerzy Topolski (Warsaw: Polskie Wydawnictwo Naukowe, 1975), 446–611; and Stefan Kieniewicz, *Historia Polski 1795–1918* (Warsaw: Polskie Wydawnictwo Naukowe, 1983), 267.

13. Aleksander Świętochowski quoted in Brian Porter, *When Nationalism Began to Hate* (Oxford: Oxford University Press, 2000), 72. The German arms manufacturer and the Prussian army commander cannot compare with a great Polish scientist, poet, and painter.

14. Porter, *When Nationalism Began to Hate,* 54.

15. The number of Christian stores set up reached 149 in 1847, 525 in 1891, and 911 in 1898. Keely Stauter-Halsted, *The Nation in the Village: The Genesis of Peasant National Identity in Austrian Poland 1848–1914* (Ithaca: Cornell University Press, 2001). Between 1901 and 1913, agricultural circles almost doubled to 2,000 while their membership grew from 41,000 to 85,000 Polish-speaking peasants. Andrzej Zakrzewski, *Od Stojałowskiego do Witosa* (Warsaw: KAW, 1988), 49.

16. Dabrowski, *Commemorations,* 108–109.

17. By 1914, the agriculture circle movement had almost 2,000 village reading rooms. Kieniewicz, *Historia Polski,* 404.

18. In 1903 the People's School Society arranged 145 celebrations, and more than 1,000 by 1913, all having borne some sort of national symbols and subtext. See Dabrowski, *Commemorations,* 109.

19. Norman Davies refers to the memoirs of Galician peasant Jan Słomka, *Pamiętniki włościanina, Od pańszczyzny do dni dzisiejszych* (Towarzystwo Szkoły Ludowej, 1929 [1912]) in order to illustrate the process of national awakening among Galician peasants. In Słomka's youth, "only the gentlemen were regarded as Poles. On learning to read, however, and by participating in the work of the Peasant Movement in Galicia, Słomka became enthusiastically aware of his own Polish identity. He became a pioneer of rural education, and ended his life as the respected mayor of his village. . . . When he was born (in 1842), only a small minority of the population of the Polish lands would have consciously belonged to the Polish nation; when he died (in 1929), the great majority would have done so." See Davies, *God's Playground*, 220–221.

20. Dabrowski, *Commemorations*, 15.

21. Ibid., 61.

22. Ibid., 118.

23. Zakrzewski, *Od Stojałowskiego*, 61.

24. Stauter-Halsted, *The Nation in the Village*, 117, n. 3.

25. Zakrzewski, *Od Stojałowskiego*, 47.

26. Stanislaus A. Blejwas, *Realism in Polish Politics: Warsaw Positivism and National Survival in Nineteenth Century Poland* (New Haven: Slavica Publishers, 1984), 49.

27. Kieniewicz, *Historia Polski*, 406; Blejwas, *Realism in Polish Politics*, 48–49.

28. Stefan Kieniewicz, *Dramat Trzeźwych Entuzjastów: O Ludziach Pracy Organicznej* (Warsaw: Wiedza Powszechna, 1964), 163; Kieniewicz, *Historia Polski*, 406.

29. Stauter-Halsted, *The Nation in the Village*, 117, n. 3.

30. Ibid., 407.

31. Ibid., 406.

32. Witold Jakóbczyk, *Przetrwać nad Wartą* (Warsaw: KAW, 1989), 74.

33. John Kulczycki, *School Strikes in Prussian Poland, 1901–1907: The Struggle over Bilingual Education* (New York: Columbia University Press, 1981), 23.

34. At the height of the protest in Września, more than 120 twelve- to fourteen-year-old pupils refused to use German in the religious class. Ibid., 52.

35. See Maria Konopnicka, "O Września" (About Września) and *Władysław Reymont "W pruskiej szkole"* (In a Prussian School), quoted in Kulczycki, *School Strikes*, 67.

36. Some of this money was also used to smuggle three convicted people out of German Poland to Austria-Hungary. Ibid., 62–63.

37. Ibid.

38. Kormanowej and W. Najdus, eds., *Historia Polski 1900–1914*, vol. 3, part 2 (Warsaw: Polska Akademia Nauk, 1972), 555.

39. Ibid., 557; Jakóbczyk, *Przetrwać nad Wartą*, 67.

40. For the German authorities, this was in any case a "Pyrrhic victory" without formally changing policy; in practice further efforts to displace the Polish language in schools ceased because of pupils' lack of progress using German materials. Consequently, a considerable number of pupils in lower grades continued to receive religious instruction in their native language. See Kulczycki, *School Strikes*, 218.

41. According to Kulczycki, the school resistance "proved a hothouse for the growth of Polish nationalism [and gave] the emotional warmth of concreteness to abstract membership in the Polish nation." Ibid., xvi, 82.

42. Porter, *When Nationalism Began to Hate*, 81.

43. Edmund Staszyński, *Polityka Oświatowa Caratu w Królestwie Polskim: Od Powstania Styczniowego do I Wojny Światowej* (Warsaw: PZWS, 1968), 197.

44. Henryk Wereszycki, *Historia Polityczna Polski 1864–1918* (Warsaw: Ossolineum, 1990), 91. Government statistics are probably an underestimate as czarist officials were often bribed to ignore illegal activities. In reality, secret self-education circles existed in most state schools in Russian Poland.

45. Ibid., 85.

46. Robert E. Blobaum, *Rewolucja: Russian Poland, 1904–1907* (Ithaca: Cornell University Press, 1995), 169.

47. Ibid., 177.

48. Staszyński, *Polityka Oświatowa*, 202.

49. Ibid., 207.

50. Ibid., 209; Blobaum, *Rewolucja*, 169.

51. Kieniewicz, *Historia Polski*, 394; Edward Strzelecki, "Sprawa Pomnika Adama Mickiewicza w Warszawie," in *Z Dziejów Książki i Bibliotek w Warszawie*, ed. Stanisław Tazbir (Warsaw: PIW, 1961), 436.

52. Porter, *When Nationalism Began to Hate*, 100.

53. Witkiewicz, Polish artist and art critic, quoted in Dabrowski, *Commemorations*, 149.

54. Stauter-Halsted, *The Nation in the Village*, 43.

55. Porter, *When Nationalism Began to Hate*, 53.

56. Michnik, *Polskie Pytania*, 126.

57. Ibid., 83–84; Michnik, *Letters from Prison*. See also Adam Bromke, *The Meaning and Uses of Polish History* (New York: Columbia University Press, 1987), 54, fn., where he recalls a conversation he had in 1978 with one of the leaders of the opposition movement who linked their choice of nonviolent defiance against the communist government with the nonviolent, organic strategies of the nineteenth-century positivists in Russian Poland.

58. Bohdan Cywiński, *Rodowody Niepokornych* (Warsaw: Biblioteka Wiezi, 1971).

15

Kosovo:
Civil Resistance in
Defense of the Nation, 1990s

Howard Clark

Each year on March 5–7, Kosovo celebrates the Epopee of the Kosova Liberation Army (KLA)—the anniversary of the 1998 gun battle in the village of Donji Prekaz where Adem Jashari, a founder of the KLA, and more than fifty of his family members were killed. The Jashari home is now a shrine. The Epopee includes the Night of Flames when fifty fires are lit and a gathering in Prekaz of Kosovo's leading dignitaries and the uniformed successors of the KLA (at one time the Kosovo Protection Corps, now the Kosovo Security Force). The main speeches in 2010 were made by the prime minister and president—at that time Hashim Thaçi, a founder of the KLA, and Fatmir Sejdiu, a founder and leader of the Democratic League of Kosova (LDK), the party most associated with the nonviolent struggle. Sejdiu began,

> On March 5, 1998 . . . the legendary Commander of the Kosovo Liberation Army, Adem Jashari, and his father Shaban and his brother Hamëz, fell on the altar of freedom. That day, besides these three martyrs, many other children and members of Jashari family were deprived of their lives. But, by virtue of their matchless sacrifice, they were decorated with the most precious and gilded crown in the history of our long-lasting war for freedom and independence and turned into an incomparable symbol of sublime self-sacrifice for the homeland.[1]

Sejdiu's conclusion, however, invoked the memory of Kosovo's first president, Ibrahim Rugova, the figurehead of the nonviolent struggle and the person credited with first raising the demand for independence, praising his "Euro-Atlantic" vision.

Rugova and Jashari are contrasting figures. The urbane Rugova (Tirana denounced his "decadent modernism") gained an image among Albanians as "the U.S.'s chosen one" as early as April 1990, addressing the US

279

Congressional Human Rights Caucus. He never lost this image, despite changes in US attitudes.[2] At the time of his death, despite everything that might have destroyed his credibility, Rugova was Kosovo's president and most trusted politician.[3] Furthermore, the memory of nonviolent resistance remains largely identified with him.

Jashari, on the other hand, was a rural icon in the *kaçak* tradition, as indicated by his nephew Murat:

> Each nation has a saint and story that is the foundation that forms the society, its basis. My family's story is the link of a chain . . . that goes back to the Albanian flag, Azem Galica, Shaban Palluzha and others. Albanians have always been under an oppressive foreign power, whether Turkey, Austria, Serbia, and there have been many moments of fighting for freedom: this is the Albanian national question in the Balkans.[4]

Jashari's status as a legendary warrior hero, contend Anna Di Lellio and Stephanie Schwandner-Sievers, provides a "hegemonic discourse" beyond public debate that sidelines Kosovo's experience of civil resistance and, in particular, the role women played in nonviolent struggle and the "parallel structures."[5]

Jashari was never convinced by the nonviolent strategy, but he himself had to flee Kosovo in winter 1991–1992. At that time people with his views could do little inside Kosovo except recognize that the nonviolent struggle was "the only game in town," as did Jakup Krasniqi—the friend who hid Jashari from the police.[6] Although in mid-1998 Krasniqi emerged as the KLA's first field spokesperson, until that year he had been a leading activist in his local LDK, and was even voted onto the Kosovo-wide presidency of the LDK.

In this chapter, my account of civil resistance concentrates on the period until 1994—the time of maximum unity in resistance. After that, the struggle entered a phase of stagnation—the LDK was dominant and undemocratic, Rugova was remote and passive, and the horrors of war in Bosnia made all parties in the Kosovo conflict (including Belgrade) wary of escalation. I also discuss the period after the Dayton Accords on Bosnia-Herzegovina (November 1995), a time of increasing frustration in Kosovo, and how in 1997 eventually the active nonviolence of Prishtina students demonstrated some of the possibilities that a more assertive alternative strategy might have offered. The Drenica massacres of February–March 1998—not only the Jashari siege, but the slaughter of unarmed families who followed the counsel to stay nonviolent—marked the end of the nonviolent struggle in Kosovo.

The Context

Invaded by Serbia in 1912 and again after World War I, Kosovo was once more forcibly incorporated into Yugoslavia under Josip Broz Tito after

World War II. The largest non-Slavic group in Yugoslavia (Albanians) was subjected to discrimination, denial of rights, and periodic attempts to "transfer" them, especially to Turkey during the 1950s.[7]

The position of Albanians improved dramatically after 1966, when Tito's League of Communists of Yugoslavia (LCY) opted for a Yugoslav-wide policy of decentralization. For Kosovo Albanians, this heralded a cultural renaissance, with the provision of university education and expansion of publishing and broadcasting in Albanian. Politically, the province gained an autonomy, confirmed in the 1974 Constitution that made it a quasi-republic, with its own system of self-government, even a territorial defense force, and participation in the federal presidency on an equal basis with the republics.[8] However, this brought two fundamental problems. First, while Kosovo Albanian expectations were rising, the economic gap between Kosovo, the poorest unit in Yugoslavia, and the rest of Yugoslavia was also growing. Second, Serbs in Kosovo—although still more likely to be employed, to be higher paid, and to hold management jobs—felt aggrieved at their loss of privilege and increasingly beleaguered as the minority population in Kosovo.

What distinguished Kosovo from the republics was that it lacked the right to secede. In March 1981—a year after Tito's death—a wave of protest rocked Kosovo, spontaneous mainly student-led demonstrations, which often raised the demand for Kosovo to become a republic. Federal troops were sent to crush the rising, perhaps killing as many as 300 in the next two months.[9] Subsequently, the whole Albanian population of Kosovo was under suspicion and the federation required the Albanian leadership of the provincial LCY—who had believed that Kosovo was progressing toward gaining republic status—to repress "irredentism." After this, the great majority of Yugoslav political prisoners were Kosovo Albanians.[10]

The 1981 riots offered an opportunity for Serb nationalists to alert Yugoslavia, especially other Serbs, that Kosovo Albanians were preparing the way for secession by harassing Serbs to leave Kosovo and simply by breeding. From 1981 the ethnic polarization sharpened, especially with Serbian accusations of "cultural genocide" in Kosovo, and from the mid-1980s onward every wild allegation against Kosovo Albanians was repeated or amplified in the Serbian press.[11] Slobodan Milošević seized control of the Serbian LCY, presenting himself as the champion of suffering Serbs throughout Yugoslavia, but especially as symbolized in Kosovo. In 1988, he used rent-a-mob tactics to end Vojvodina's autonomy and bring Montenegro into line. However, in revoking Kosovo's autonomy, he met stouter resistance not from the Kosovo LCY, but from the miners.

In the first snows of winter during November 1988, 3,000 miners marched forty-five kilometers (twenty-eight miles) from the pithead in Trepça to Prishtina in defense of the constitution and autonomy. The miners were joined throughout Kosovo by perhaps another 300,000 people—20 percent of the population. With self-discipline and dignity, and without any violence, they faced down the police. Their extraordinary protest provided powerful images that were broadcast throughout the federation.

The situation escalated. Milošević appointed new provincial leaders. In February 1989, when the Serbian Assembly was due to annul Kosovo's autonomy, the miners began a stay-in strike, many of them deep underground, some on hunger strikes. A general strike spread throughout Kosovo while in Slovenia and Croatia there were massive solidarity demonstrations. On the sixth day, the provincial LCY announced the resignation of Milošević's appointees, and the next day the miners emerged into daylight apparently victorious. They had, however, been tricked. Belgrade rejected the resignations, imposed a state of emergency, and began a wave of arrests. The strikes resumed until all strikers received a letter telling them to return to work or be fired (or arrested).

Contemporary reports of the miners' actions were optimistic about the organized power of workers withholding cooperation and paralyzing production in Kosovo's industries.[12] However, a strike's main power is usually that the opponent needs the workers' product; the Milošević regime was soon to demonstrate that it had no such dependence.

If the miners' steadfastness prefigured—and partly inspired—the later turn toward nonviolent resistance, it was in sharp contrast with both the timidity of Kosovo's official representatives and the undisciplined protests that then erupted. On March 23, 1989, the Kosovo Assembly—surrounded by armored cars, with helicopters overhead, and with Serbian security forces actually inside the chamber—voted to annul Kosovo's autonomy. During the next six days, there were clashes around Kosovo; Amnesty International reported an estimate of 140 dead.[13]

Belgrade now tried to "decapitate" the resistance through wholesale detentions. Instantly, the mainly Albanian provincial LCY crumbled and new organizational initiatives took shape. The "early risers" were groups connected with what can be broadly identified as the "Kosova Alternative," concerned less with independence than with democratization and often in touch with pan-Yugoslav civil society networks. These Prishtina activists tended to stay outside the LDK, although two of them—Youth Parliament leaders Blerim Shala and Veton Surroi—years later became members of Kosovo's negotiating team.

A Chronicle of Nonviolent Resistance

Building Organization

Two organizations central to mass nonviolent resistance were founded in December 1989. The Council for the Defense of Human Rights and Freedoms (CDHRF) became the main monitoring and data center on human rights violations and police maltreatment. It set out to ensure that regime brutality would backfire. An all-party group, it involved many former political prisoners and became heavily identified with Adem Demaçi, its chair from his release from prison in 1990 until he entered party politics in 1997. A few days later, LDK was founded—the force that was to dominate Albanian politics in Kosovo. Within weeks, it had hundreds of thousands of members, including both recent defectors from the LCY and those whom the LCY had repressed since 1981.

The LDK founders considered taking up arms. When instead they issued calls for restraint, at first they were ignored: in January and February 1990, there were violent incidents throughout Kosovo, including protesters using firearms. Police killed at least thirty-two people. Increasingly Kosovo Albanians became convinced that Milošević wanted to provoke war. The most extreme provocation occurred in March 1990—the "poisoning" of schoolchildren.[14] Furious mobs of Albanians immediately looked to take reprisals on Serbs: fifty personal attacks were reported. The recently formed organizations—the CDHRF, the LDK, and the Youth Parliament—intervened to prevent lynching and eventually calmed the situation. By now, it was becoming clear how high the stakes were. Somehow, in the frequently repeated words of Shkëlzen Maliqi, soon to be leader of the Social Democratic Party, "nonviolence imposed itself."[15]

The pragmatic case against armed struggle at this time was overpowering. However, the early period of nonviolent struggle is remarkable for its idealism—most visible in an identity shift, instigated by civil society groups, but taken up at large. After the fall of the Berlin Wall, many Kosovo Albanians aspired to become modern Europeans. Rather than hark back to nationalist traditions, in this moment of crisis they campaigned to reform their own society. Civil society leaders such as Surroi and Maliqi were well aware that ethnonationalism was waiting in the wings, but saw the opportunity to call for a new democratic culture. Others addressed unacceptable features in Albanian society—notably the blood feud, high illiteracy, and the position of women—so building a solidarity that could withstand the Serbian onslaught. At times, these modernizing elements faced rejection—Maliqi and Surroi for their desire to find allies among the Serbian opposition[16] or the volunteers in a women's literacy program for seeming to threaten the patriarchal order—but in this early phase they projected a vision of social transformation.

This identity shift went much further than the Euro-Atlanticism today attributed to Rugova, which can be reduced to the political calculation that Kosovo Albanians needed to look for support from the West.[17]

Naming the Violence

Surroi originated one of the most important organizing tools for establishing a nonviolent policy, the petition. Titled "For Democracy, Against Violence," it gathered 400,000 signatures (most of the adult population) before Surroi and Rugova presented it at the United Nations in June 1990. Its commitment "to make each death a public act" meant, first, reporting, and, second, organizing homages such as five-minute work stoppages or sounding factory sirens or car horns at set times. Avoiding street confrontation, the idea was to use what little space existed to organize low-risk actions strengthening popular morale and unity. Curfew was marked by lighting candles and making noise.[18]

The practice evolved that, whenever there was a violent incident, someone from the LDK or CDHRF would go to the scene to calm the situation, to record what had happened, and to explain the strategy of nonviolent action. The documentation of police brutality would then be presented internationally so that regime violence would backfire against Belgrade.

The very act of documenting violence could change a victim's attitude. Police aimed to humiliate Albanians but then, as social psychologist Anton Berishaj found in his own experience, being interviewed by activists and posing for photos "somehow made us proud. . . . To some extent, media exposure provided an alternative to traditional vengeance."[19]

Mass Dismissals

In April 1990, mass dismissals began: first Albanian police were dismissed; in July staff at Radio and TV Prishtina were locked out; and in August the medical faculty was purged (partly for lending credibility to the accusations of poisoning). Milošević soon showed that he cared little about Kosovo's economic resources, devastating the territory's productive capacity. He imposed emergency management, often bringing in new Serbian bosses while requiring Albanian workers to sign an oath of loyalty to Serbia. Refusing this oath became a common pretext for dismissal. At many workplaces, managers locked out workers and then posted lists of who could return. In April 1990, the founders of Kosovo's first free trade union federation—the BSPK (Bashkimi i Sindikatave të Pavarura të Kosovës; the Union of Independent Trade Unions)—little realized that their main task would be to document dismissals: their final estimate was that 146,025 (83 percent) of the 164,210 employed Albanians in 1990 lost their jobs.

The Defense of Education

The best-known feature of the nonviolent struggle in Kosovo is the construction of parallel institutions, especially the schools and university, which were backed up by a system of voluntary taxes levied inside Kosovo and also in the diaspora. Education was a central issue partly because of the youth of the population, partly Yugoslavia's long history of denial of the right to education in Albanian, and partly because Belgrade viewed institutions such as the University of Prishtina as "a nest of nationalism."

In August 1990, Belgrade imposed a uniform curriculum throughout Serbia (including Kosovo and Vojvodina). Albanian teachers decided to work on without compliance, teaching the curriculum agreed upon before Milošević annulled Kosovo's autonomy. First, Belgrade refused to pay their wages, and by August 1991 it had dismissed 6,000 secondary teachers. At the start of the 1991–1992 school year, Belgrade moved to exclude Albanians from all schools. When Albanian children, teachers, and parents arrived at schools on September 2, they found armed police blocking their entry. In many places, there were beatings and arrests. This was repeated daily, highlighting the need for a shift in strategy. The teachers' union compiled an inventory of premises where teaching could continue; in January 1992 the parallel schools opened, using a mixture of private premises and the buildings of primary schools (as the Yugoslav Constitution guaranteed the right to primary education).

From 1992–1998, this school system played a vital role in maintaining the Albanian community in Kosovo despite some decline in pupil numbers and a loss of qualified teachers (many went into exile, needing paid work to support families). Most teachers believed this was an emergency measure that would be needed for only perhaps two years. They also faced police harassment—and, in 1995 and 1996, the CDHRF made a special point of reporting the number of people maltreated by police during educational activities.

The prime organizers of the education system were teachers themselves through their unions and with the support of fired educational administrators and local parent groups. The full system involved more than 325,000 school pupils, 18,000 school teachers, and nearly 14,000 university students. The voluntary taxation system had 1,000 volunteer tax collectors inside Kosovo (mostly tax collectors dismissed for refusing to sign loyalty oaths).

In her authoritative study of the parallel education system, Denisa Kostovicova remarks on its role in heightening solidarity: "[Albanians] believed that, by closing Albanian schools and the university, the Serbs actually intended to incite an Albanian violent insurrection. . . . The totality of the Serbian encroachment in education was to have a mobilizing rather than demoralizing effect on the Albanian community. In the process, the Albanian school emerged as an epitome of its peaceful resistance."[20] Nevertheless, she also criticizes the history taught for strengthening traditional "victim" nationalism that was ambivalent about nonviolent resistance. The truth is that once the system was established, it did not develop into a base for further activity or teach pupils to think for themselves and to develop civic values. In general, the educational methods were as moribund as those in

Serbia, with the added disadvantage that classrooms were overcrowded, facilities poor, the dropout rate rising (especially among girls), and teachers' pay continually in arrears. For these reasons, despite being a major achievement, in the collective memory there is little love for the parallel education system. For young people in their formative years, this protracted experience could only deepen their hostility toward Serbs.

Grassroots Initiatives to Reform Kosovo Albanian Society

Social anthropologist Janet Reineck devoted much of her doctoral thesis to "explaining the profound allegiance to tradition held by many Albanians prior to the events of 1989."[21] However, the Serbian threat spurred a different type of activism. "Topics of conversation once taboo are now openly expressed. People are able to consider their own vision of the future. . . . While the masses await liberation,' others have seized the moment, concentrating on what they can do during the interim. Convinced that democracy must start at home, they have initiated grass-roots movements to right the social wrongs embedded in the Albanian social system."[22] She went on to refer to two specific initiatives: Motrat Qiriazi, a women's literacy program with the slogan "To Europe with a Pencil!" and the campaign for the reconciliation of blood feuds. Nobody disputes Motrat Qiriazi's nonviolent character. However, some people have offered a traditional interpretation of blood feud reconciliation, suggesting that Albanians seek to reconcile blood feuds in order to unify in preparation for war.[23]

The Campaign to Reconcile Blood Feuds is mainly associated with Anton Çetta (1920–1995), a noted folklorist but also a polyglot, social reformer, and board member of the CDHRF. He took up this issue after being approached by students from Peja. Fifteen people, including some students, had been killed in blood feuds in 1989 and, for their own safety, several thousand were confined to their family homes. In a campaign from 1990 to 1992, some 500 students volunteered to tour villages trying to locate blood feuds. Then, elders such as Çetta and his coleader, the Catholic priest Don Lush Gjergj, visited not only to talk with the male head of the family, but also to encourage women to exert their influence. Eventually, there were public ceremonies of reconciliation, the biggest on May 1, 1990, attended by hundreds of thousands of people. Behind this, a network of local reconciliation committees was set up to address disputes without turning to Serbian courts.

Blood feud reconciliation was indeed part of the national struggle—people offered the hand of forgiveness "in the name of the people, youth and the flag." However, as Mirie Rushani explains, this was a call "to unite in a general resistance without arms, with the awareness that nonviolent resistance could carry enormous suffering and a high price."[24] Çetta offered a nonviolent reinterpretation of traditional Kosovo Albanian values, in the manner of Mohandas Gandhi's nonviolent reading of the Bhagavad Gita. Interviews with Çetta and eyewitness reports present him as consciously giving an impulse to nonviolent struggle, to social solidarity, and to self-organization. Gjergj has remained a consistently nonviolent voice, repeating his message to oppose postwar vengeance: "revenge is fratricide which is the same as suicide."[25] It was no coincidence that these two leaders also headed the Mother Teresa Association, the humanitarian network whose achievements include establishing a network of health clinics. A fuller flavor of their campaign can be gleaned from an article in the *New York Times*:

> "When women took off the veil it was difficult, but now they sit among us," Mr. Çetta said to the families of one village. "Now it is difficult to make the gift of blood [make a truce], but later it will be normal. We must swear that we will not kill each other any more. We hope to enter the European Community, and we should go in without these old burdens from the ancient past," he said. "There are many things we have to become more civilized about. We will be more civilized when a grandmother says to her grandson, 'Bring me the newspaper.' We will be civilized when grandmothers know how to read and care about what is happening in the world."[26]

Popular Unity

Two massive demonstrations of popular unity were the self-organized referendum in September 1991 when 87 percent of the total electorate voted and 99.87 percent favored a declaration of independence, and then the May 1992 elections for a parliament and president of the Republic of Kosova. The election turnout was almost as high as that of the referendum. With twenty-four parties taking part, the LDK won 76 percent of the vote while Rugova was elected president with 99.5 percent. The sheer numbers involved in these displays of unity established the legitimacy of the political leadership. But the organizers also took care to show continuity from structures abolished by Milošević: the referendum was called by a special meeting of most delegates to the dissolved assembly.

The referendum and the elections were organized in the name of the Coordinating Council of Political Parties—a platform that included small parties (such as the Youth Parliament and the Social Democratic Party). However, not only did this cease to function after the elections, but Maliqi and Surroi as leaders of small parties were marginalized.

Kosovo Albanians experienced the period from 1990 onward as an occupation, in which their very way of life was under attack—their jobs, their education system, and their physical safety—in the face of repeated police beatings and attacks. However, their conscious nonviolent strategy denied Milošević a casus belli. Maliqi often described Kosovo as a situation of "neither war nor peace," sometimes adding "but closer to war."[27] And increasingly, looking north to Bosnia, they could see what a war option would mean.

Internationalizing the Question of Kosovo

In view of their comparative weakness (numerically, militarily, and economically) against Serbia, Kosovo Albanians knew they had to look for alliances. Internationalizing the issue was vital, especially as Kosovo Albanians were cut off from former allies in Yugoslavia and had few hopes of (and, mostly, took little interest in) finding powerful allies in Serbia.

Initially, for a population of 2 million, they were remarkably successful—not only in organizing their own diaspora, but also in entering international networks and gaining attention for Serbia's human rights abuses, including Demaçi's winning the European Parliament's Sakharov Prize (human rights) in 1991. A huge success came in December 1992 when the outgoing George H. W. Bush administration threatened to bomb if Serbia escalated human rights violations, a warning reiterated by the William J. Clinton administration in February 1993. However, by that time, the European Badinter Commission had already ruled that only Yugoslav republics, not provinces, had the right to self-determination. This set the pattern combining international complaints about human rights violations in Kosovo with insistence that it remain in rump Yugoslavia (Serbia and Montenegro), a stalemate in desperate need of some intermediate objectives.

During Milan Panić's brief premiership of rump Yugoslavia (July 1992–February 1993), the Conference on Security and Cooperation in Europe (CSCE), later the Organization for Security and Cooperation in Europe (OSCE), made a futile attempt to mediate negotiations over education, lecturing Albanians on "sacrificing their children in a cause they couldn't win." At the same time, those in control in Serbia (not Panić) treated the negotiations with contempt, failing to show up at meetings while mildly harassing the Kosovo Albanian negotiators. In 1992 the CSCE also established a small observer mission to Kosovo, the Sandzak, and Vojvodina, a welcome if token international presence to restrain Serbian excesses. But this had to be withdrawn in 1993 when rump Yugoslavia was suspended from the CSCE.[28]

The chief Kosovo Albanian negotiator, LDK vice-president Fehmi Agani, was clear that negotiations could bring gains other than independence such as an interim UN administration but equally clear that it would be folly to abandon the demand for independence before negotiations even began. Increasingly, however, as wars raged elsewhere in the former Yugoslavia, the West's key goal over Kosovo was merely to contain the situation. From 1990 until 1999, Western governments were firm that Kosovo would not gain more than an enhanced autonomy within Serbia. They sympathized that human rights were being abused, and they commended Rugova's nonviolent policy while wishing he was a little less obdurate. Otherwise their priorities lay elsewhere.

It is not clear what role international influence had in the decision of Kosovo Albanians to suspend protests. When Panić visited Kosovo in October 1992, perhaps half the population was mobilized to protest about education despite the police brutality. Subsequently, Kosovo Albanians declared a moratorium on protests. "They cost more than we can gain through them."[29] The parliament, voted in by almost the entire Albanian population in a resounding act of self-assertion, was not convened ostensibly because it would be too "provocative." If the elections of May 1992 were empowering, this failure to convene parliament was the reverse. Thus missed was the opportunity to present Milošević with an acute dilemma: "let our parliament function, or show the world how you deny democracy" while pressing home the message internationally that Albanians would never resign themselves to living under Serbia.

In the coming three years, criticism mounted that the LDK was seeking to "monopolize" political space while its organs behaved less and less democratically and Rugova relied increasingly on a small inner circle of advisers.

In November 1995, the Dayton Accords ended the war in Bosnia, also marking the beginning of the end of Rugova's monopoly on political leadership in Kosovo. His lack of progress in winning international support stood exposed. The Dayton Accords ended all but an outer wall of the sanctions on Serbia. The opening of the US Information Office in Prishtina (locally called "the US embassy") was some symbolic compensation. The European Union (EU), however, failed to keep its promise to do likewise.

In September 1996, Italian mediators brokered an agreement for the "normalization" of education that was signed by Milošević and Rugova. However, a year passed without further progress, thereby emboldening the (Albanian) Students Union (UPSUP) to defy Rugova and end the post-1992 moratorium on demonstrations by calling a nonviolent march to reclaim the university buildings at the start of the new academic year, October 1, 1997.[30]

Rugova summoned the UPSUP leaders to explain why they should postpone the march. They, however, insisted that students had the right to demonstrate for their own education. As a test of support, UPSUP asked students to join the evening promenades on the main street in Prishtina and were delighted at the popular response. Diplomats, in contrast, were alarmed: the most powerful diplomatic delegation ever to visit Kosovo—twelve ambassadors, headed by the ambassadors of the United States, Britain, and the Netherlands (at the time, the Netherlands held the presidency of the EU)—came from Belgrade to beseech the UPSUP leaders not to risk this provocation. Rugova had heeded this kind of advice before by not pursuing potentially provocative initiatives. For UPSUP, however, the delegation merely confirmed that action was the best way to attract attention. The students proceeded to prepare their march, taking care to ensure a nonviolent discipline as, for the first time in Kosovo, protesters actually courted physical violence to dramatize the underlying violence of the regime. When police blocked their way, the marchers stood their UPSUP leaders at the front, prepared to be beaten, as indeed they were.[31]

Since 1994 Rugova's critics had often urged active nonviolence, but this was the only time that anyone had given it substance by planning a nonviolent confrontation. Rugova had little choice but to praise UPSUP while Western diplomats condemned police brutality and feted the protesters that they had previously tried to restrain. Through invoking the universal right to education, UPSUP had solid ground not only to defy Rugova in the name of its members, but also to gain support internationally and even from Belgrade students—a rare instance of Serbian solidarity with Kosovo Albanians.

UPSUP planned further protests—and two more demonstrations took place in 1997—but the movement was soon overshadowed by the first public appearance of the KLA on November 28, 1997 (Albanian National Day) and the increasing number of skirmishes prior to the police offensive of February– March 1998 and the Drenica massacres. No doubt, there was new energy and international support for implementing the education agreement but, once the fighting had started, education no longer was such a central issue.

Finally, having neither helped community-level organizing nor maintained a serious international presence in Kosovo when it would have made a difference, international powers decided to take a stand when the armed strife was imminent.

The Place of Civil Resistance in History

Civil resistance in Kosovo is widely perceived as a failure. I view it as a limited success, a means of survival without surrender against an oppressor who wished to provoke war. In particular, it attained three vital objectives:

1. *Maintaining the Albanian community and way of life in Kosovo*. Despite rafts of anti-Albanian measures, the devastation of Kosovo's economy, and the onslaught on education, Albanians stayed even though many family breadwinners went abroad.
2. *Preventing war when it was most dangerous*. By the time war came to Kosovo, world leaders understood, from Bosnia as well as Kosovo, the criminal nature of the Serbian nationalist project.
3. *Winning international condemnation of the regime* (if not yet support for independence).

In extremely difficult conditions for any kind of resistance, civil resistance should at least be respected as a vital phase when armed struggle would have been catastrophic.

The nonviolent struggle identified two complementary objectives in the phase of civil resistance that were equally valid for later: (1) to convince states that Kosovo Albanians should not be expected to live under Serbia; and (2) to demonstrate that the Serbian minority in Kosovo could survive and enjoy full rights without the protection of Serbia.

There remains a strong case that the criminal character of Serbian rule, and in particular the ethnic cleansing of 1999, meant that Serbia should have forfeited any claim to Kosovo. However, this argument has been weakened by skepticism about the guarantees of the safety and freedom of movement of the remaining Serbian population. In the early 1990s, Kosovo Albanians were eager to demonstrate that they would uphold the rights of all—reserving vacant seats in the parallel parliament for Kosovo Serbs, demonstrating the ecumenism of the movement by observing Christian festivals, and explaining repeatedly that Kosovo Albanians had traditionally protected the sacred sites of all religions. However, such values have been betrayed. In addition to wartime incidents including the KLA's kidnapping and murder of Serbian civilians, since the war ended in June 1999 the Kosovo Albanian population has not successfully restrained the elements that would drive Serbs out of Kosovo or defile Orthodox churches.

Furthermore, the proposition that "armed struggle succeeded where civil resistance failed" needs to take account of the price of "liberation war" and the unsatisfactory nature of what now passes for "independence."

The War Record

The price of war was predictable: killing, rape, destruction of homes and displacement—13,421 deaths in the conflict from January 1998 to December 2000, including 10,533 Albanians, 2,278 Serbs and Montenegrins, plus a further 1,886 missing.[32] Many might respond that it was "a price worth paying for freedom" and invoke "the will of the people," but the KLA modus operandi in 1998 was to provoke reprisals against unarmed civilians. The villagers who suffered these reprisals were not consulted about their willingness to be sacrificed and woe to those who objected that the KLA could provoke but not protect.[33] For all of today's pilgrimages to the Jashari shrine, little attention is paid to the families of the missing. Kosovo parliamentarians and the Prishtina political elite were acutely embarrassed to be reminded of this when, in 2004, the Kosova Action Network hung laminated photos of missing people on the parliament railings.[34]

Furthermore, arguing that the KLA fought a just war against a criminal opponent, many Albanians believe that KLA soldiers should enjoy impunity from war crimes investigations. The International Criminal Tribunal for the

Former Yugoslavia (ICTY) has found that the KLA was responsible for "cruel treatment, torture, rape and murder," but—partly because of witness intimidation—has lacked evidence to convict more than a few named KLA fighters.[35] The majority of Serbs killed from 1998 to 2000 were civilians, including 309 women—perhaps a fraction of the numbers of Albanian civilians and women killed by Serbian forces and paramilitaries. But if there is to be any process of restorative justice, this part of the truth needs acknowledging.

The KLA had a particular responsibility for the immediate postwar violence: it was the only armed force capable of restraining it, yet some members were leading perpetrators.[36] In general, having been victims of Serbs for so long, many Albanians were slow to react when compatriots also violated human rights. After all, these crimes did not match the enormity of those committed by Serbian forces and paramilitaries, they were not orchestrated by a regime, and there were mitigating circumstances (perhaps collective trauma). Many Serbs fled Kosovo even before North Atlantic Treaty Organization (NATO) troops entered. However, what this also means is that those Serbs subsequently driven out from mixed areas were those who planned to stay, the ones most willing to adapt to being an ethnic minority in Kosovo.

World leaders mouthed glib phrases about building a multiethnic democracy in Kosovo, understanding little of the process of ethnic polarization since 1981. Among those who still stood for human rights, it was common to hear remarks such as Adem Demaçi's, "I know of a great number of cases where Serbs protected Albanian homes, but I also know of even more cases where Serbs looted Albanian homes."[37] Subsequently, however, Demaçi and others who work for coexistence have been disappointed that so few Albanians have been willing to take personal risks to protect Serbs. In the opinion of UN officials, Rugova was the political leader least "helpful on minority issues."[38]

The now-disbanded Kosovo Protection Corps was also a problem. Created to channel KLA veterans into a civil emergency force, its officers repeatedly fell under suspicion for acts of armed violence, including against fellow Albanians and in neighboring territories.[39]

Compromised Independence

While Kosovo Albanians have been celebrating independence since 2008, this is not the independent Kosovo people volunteered for in 1990 but one riddled with corruption and organized crime, where power struggles are lethal, and without the brief-lived social solidarity celebrated by Reineck (as described above).[40] Forget UN Security Council Resolution 1235 that called for involvement of women in negotiating processes—Kosovo's postwar negotiating teams have been all male. Independent Kosova is a disappointment compared with the hopes of 1990–1992.

Postwar events have also strengthened Serbia's hand in campaigning for partition. The formation of Serbian enclaves has established on-the-ground conditions for partition while the municipal reorganization currently under way as part of the international plan furthers this possibility by enhancing the powers of Serbian majority municipalities able to form a horizontal federation (with each other inside Kosovo) and to link vertically to Belgrade.

Conclusion

In view of Kosovo's significance in the history of humanitarian military intervention and the development of the doctrine of Responsibility to Protect (R2P), it is necessary to discuss the international failure to prevent war. The R2P doctrine maintains that, when a state cannot protect its citizens from human rights violations or is itself an active violator (as was Serbia), then that protection becomes an international responsibility.[41] This is what eventually happened in Kosovo. However, R2P misses the key lesson of failure of prevention. Urging states to respond to early warnings, including through support to civil society, the doctrine fails to mention civil resistance. If states are ultimately prepared to intervene militarily against criminal regimes, surely they should help those citizens who nonviolently challenge that regime's legitimacy. The states that now promote Kosovo's independence—and that in 1999 reconciled themselves to allying with an armed group recently considered terrorist (the KLA)—spent most of the 1990s urging Kosovo Albanians to relinquish the goal of self-determination and to further soften their already nonprovocative nonviolent strategy. Only at Rambouillet, in February 1999, did international powers admit the possibility of the separation of Kosovo from Serbia.

This failure to respond adequately to civil resistance campaigns is likely to be repeated elsewhere until international powers are prepared to act on the recognition that nonviolent struggle—even with secessionist goals—is an appropriate reaction to persecution and is far more desirable than armed struggle and the negative consequences that flow from it.

Notes

1. *The President's Activities, No. 12, March 2010* (Prishtina: Republic of Kosovo—Office of the President) at www.president-ksgov.net, accessed April 5, 2010.

2. The activities of the US Information Office in Prishtina (established in 1996) sought to end Rugova's monopoly on leadership, including by promoting the leaders of the 1997 student protests, while in 1998 the KLA, previously listed as terrorists, received US training.

3. A short list includes the widening discrepancy in the 1990s between what was said in Rugova's meetings with diplomats and what he reported at home; his denial of the existence of the KLA and subsequent political paralysis; his craven appearance on television shaking hands with Milošević in Belgrade during the 1999 NATO bombings; his ineffectual postwar leadership; and collusion with the corruption that has infected Kosovo.

4. Anna Di Lellio and Stephanie Schwandner-Sievers, "The Legendary Commander: The Construction of an Albanian Master-Narrative in Post-War Kosovo," *Nations and Nationalism* 12, no. 3 (2006): 513–529. Kaçak is a general term for rural bandits, but also refers specifically to the Kaçak rebellions after 1918 that were led by Azem and Shota Galica. Shaban Palluzha became the leader of post–World War II resistance to pacification after his Yugoslav Partisan unit refused to be posted outside Kosovo.

5. A step toward including women in the historical narrative has been taken with the publication of Nicole Farnsworth, ed., *History Is Herstory Too—The History of Women in Civil Society in Kosovo, 1980–2004* (Prishtina: Kosovo Gender Studies Center, 2008).

6. Jakup Krasniqi, interviewed by the author, Prishtina, October 21, 1999. Jashari's firing at police provoked a raid on Donji Prekaz on December 31, 1991.

7. Under Minister of the Interior Ranković, Yugoslav Albanians were so terrorized that 195,000 were convinced to accept repatriation to Turkey in 1954–1957. Miranda Vickers, *Between Serb and Albania: A History of Kosovo* (London: Christopher Hurst; New York: Columbia University, 1998), 157. The demographic balance in Kosovo was a permanent problem for Serbs. The only time in the twentieth century that census figures indicate the Serb-Montenegrin population of Kosovo reached 30 percent was in 1939 after a concerted settlement drive.

8. Rather anomalously Kosovo and the other autonomous province, Vojvodina, also remained represented in Serbian institutions. Yet together their votes on the presidency could outweigh Serbia.

9. The official death toll was 11, but Amnesty International cited an internal LCY report suggesting that more than 300 Albanians were killed. Hugh Poulton, *The Balkans: Minorities and States in Conflict* (London: Minority Rights Group, 1991), 60.

10. See Howard Clark, *Civil Resistance in Kosovo* (London: Pluto Press, 2000), for a more detailed survey of this history.

11. The most authoritative study addressing the controversies of 1974–1989 is Mom ilo Pavlović, "Kosovo Under Autonomy, 1974–1990," in *Confronting the Yugoslav Controversies: A Scholars' Initiative,* ed. Charles Ingrao and Thomas A. Emmert (West Lafayette, IN: Purdue University Press, 2009).

12. See Branka Magaš, *The Destruction of Yugoslavia* (London: Verso, 1993).

13. Amnesty International, *Yugoslavia: Police Violence in Kosovo Province—The Victims,* EUR 70/16/94 (London: Amnesty International, September 1994), 4.

14. This is the fourth and final of the "myths and truths" examined in detail by Julie Mertus, *Kosovo: How Myths and Truths Started a War* (Berkeley: University of California Press, 1999), 187–198. In the period March 18–23, 7,600 pupils in thirteen places complained of symptoms of neurointoxication, perhaps caused by a chemical agent such as Sarin (manufactured by the Yugoslav People's Army). Serbian officials tended to dismiss this as "politically-induced mass hysteria."

15. Shkëlzen Maliqi, *Kosova: Separate Worlds—Reflections and Analyses* (Prishtina/Peja: MM Society and Dukagjini, 1998), 101.

16. I first met Surroi and Maliqi on December 25, 1991, when they visited Belgrade to appeal to the "democratic opposition." Surroi looked at my War Resisters'

International broken rifle badge and said, "I'm a war resister too." He had just arranged for conscripts from Kosovo to find shelter in Croatia while Maliqi referred to Kosovo Albanians as "the biggest peace movement in Europe."

17. The Slovenian and Croatian treaties of secession from Yugoslavia included a commitment to noninterference in Yugoslav affairs (including Kosovo).

18. See chapter 3, "The Turn to Nonviolence," in Clark, *Civil Resistance in Kosovo.*

19. Anton Berishaj, "Violence Following Violence," *Psychosocial Notebook— Archives of Memory: Supporting Traumatized Communities Through Narration and Remembrance,* vol. 2 (Geneva: International Organization for Migration, October 2001), 79–86.

20. Denisa Kostovicova, *Kosovo: The Politics of Identity and Space* (Abingdon: Routledge, 2005), 90–91.

21. Janet Reineck, "The Past as Refuge: Gender, Migration, and Ideology Among the Kosova Albanians" (PhD dissertation, University of California at Berkeley, 1991), 201. Also, "Seizing the Past, Forging the Present: Changing Visions of Self and Nation Among the Kosova Albanians," *Anthropology of East Europe Review* 11, nos. 1–2 (1993), 100–109.

22. Reineck, "Past as Refuge," 202.

23. Tanya Mangalakova, *The Kanun in Present-Day Albania, Kosovo, and Montenegro* (Sofia, International Centre for Minority Studies and Intercultural Relations, 2004).

24. Mirie Rushani, "La vendetta e il perdon, nella tradizione consuetudinaria albanese," *Religioni ee Società,* no. 29 (1997): 150.

25. Nexhat Buzuku, "Attacks Harm Those Who Carry Them Out," *Koha Ditore,* August 20, 2000.

26. Chuck Sudetic, "Prishtina Journal; Albanians' New Way: Feuds Without Blood," *New York Times,* April 7, 1990.

27. Shkëlzen Maliqi's invaluable commentaries were collated in *Kosova: Separate Worlds—Reflections and Analyses 1989–1998* (Peja: MM Society, 1998). His postwar article, "Why the Peaceful Movement in Kosova Failed," was published in Robert Hudson and Glenn Bowman, eds., *After Yugoslavia: Identities and Politics Within Successor States* (New York: Palgrave Macmillan, 2011), 43–76.

28. See chapter 4, "Two Sovereignties," in Clark, *Civil Resistance in Kosovo.*

29. Teachers' union leader Agim Hyseni, interviewed by the author, Prishtina, February 7, 1993.

30. Women in Prishtina had defied the LDK leadership in 1996 to protest the killing of a student by a Serbian sniper.

31. For a fuller discussion of the student move, see Clark, *Civil Resistance in Kosovo,* 151–157.

32. Humanitarian Law Center press release, "Belgrade Presentation of the Interim Results of the List of Killed, Dead and Missing Serbs, Roma, Bosniaks, Montenegrins and Other Non-Albanians in Kosovo," October 7, 2009, http://hlc-rdc.org /Saopstenja/1799.en.html, accessed October 6, 2010.

33. One documented example was in the early "KLA stronghold," Malisheva. When Serbian forces overran Malisheva in July 1998, the KLA "lost much territory but few fighters." James Pettifer, *Kosova Express* (London: Hurst, 2005), 190. When they returned, some villagers objected. A Statement of KLA Military Police Directorate, November 1, 1998, announced the "arrest" of two local LDK activists later released—for spreading anti-KLA propaganda and for "colluding" with two "collaborationists," now "executed." (The full statement is included in the transcript of the ICTY open session of the trial of Fatmir Limaj on February 14, 2005,

3396–3397, at www.icty-org/x/cases/Limaj/trans/en/050214IT.htm, accessed November 5, 2012.

34. Kathryn Harakal, *Haunted by Images: Photography as Witness and Evidence: Kosovo's Missing Persons* (Berlin: Irmgard Coninx Stiftung, 2009), http://www.irmgard-coninx-stiftung.de/fileadmin/user_upload/pdf/Memory_Politics/Workshop_1/Harakal_Essay.pdf, accessed April 5, 2010.

35. For instance, when the ICTY Appeals Chamber upheld the acquittals of Fatmir Limaj and Isak Musliu, it also noted that the Trial Chamber's "factual findings . . . show that KLA soldiers systematically committed cruel treatment and torture in the camp." ICTY Appeals Chamber press release, The Hague, September 27, 2007, reference CVO/MOW/ PR1184e, www.icty.org/sid/8841, accessed November 5, 2012.

36. Belgrade's Humanitarian Law Center reports instances where Albanian human rights activists, including KLA officers, intervened to end the abduction. Humanitarian Law Center, *Abductions and Disappearances of Non-Albanians in Kosovo,* Spotlight Report No. 30 (Belgrade: Humanitarian Law Center, 2001).

37. Quoted in Shkëlzen Gashi, *Adem Demaçi, a Century of Kosova's History Through One Man's Life,* trans. Elizabeth Gowing (Prishtina: Rrokulia, 2010), 186. One of the most consistent promoters of coexistence in Kosovo has been Igballa Rogova, cofounder of Motrat Qiriazi and now director of the Kosova Women's Network. Her sense of betrayal by Serbian neighbors is expressed in Igballa Rogova, "I Am Alive!" in *Women's Side of War,* ed. Lina Vušković and Zorica Trifunović (Belgrade: Women in Black, 2008), 347–355.

38. Iain King and Whit Mason, *Peace at Any Price: How the World Failed Kosovo* (London: Hurst, 2005), 207.

39. The KPC was finally dissolved on the recommendation of UN envoy Martti Ahtisaari. Many senior officers were accused and some convicted of offenses, including murder, kidnapping, intimidating witnesses and judges, gun-running, and various forms of corruption. See Naser Miftari and David Quin, "Policing the Protectors," in Institute for War and Peace Reporting, *Balkan Crisis Report* 440, June 30, 2003.

40. Avni Zogiani, the head of Çohu! (Wake Up!), Kosovo's coalition against corruption, suggests that the three largest political parties all "have had their parallel structures and intelligence services: gangsters basically, who control part of the economic resources in Kosovo," and that at one time the strongest of these was the LDK. See John Rosenthal, "Corruption and Organized Crime in Kosovo: An Interview with Avni Zogiani," *World Politics Review,* February 2, 2008, www.worldpoliticsreview.com/articles/print/1559, accessed November 5, 2012. International institutions in Kosovo have also been corrupt: the most egregious act of embezzlement was by UN official Joseph Trutschler who stole €3.9 million from the Kosovo Electric Company.

41. International Commission on Intervention and State Sovereignty, *The Responsibility to Protect* (Ottawa: International Development Research Centre, 2001).

Part 5

Nonviolent Resistance in the Americas

16

The United States: Reconsidering the Struggle for Independence, 1765–1775

Walter H. Conser Jr.

Stories of national origin provide conceptions of national identity for the people who share them. They celebrate the charter events of a people, enshrine particular historical episodes, and privilege specific historical interpretations. People in the United States, by eulogizing stories of violence in their national origin, have effaced or oversimplified important nonviolent parts of their country's early history. This may be due both to fascination with violence and to ignorance about nonviolent conflict, including the lack of an analytical framework to identify its strategic successes.

From invocations of "the shot heard round the world," to exclamations of "don't shoot until you see the whites of their eyes," literature and legend teach that armed resistance achieved US independence from Britain. Movies such as Mel Gibson's *The Patriot* (2000) going back to Disney's *Johnny Tremain* (1957) show that American men fought valiantly and violently to achieve their national freedom.[1]

This is compelling narrative and imagery: a discourse of national origins replete with dramatic violence, courageous patriots, and linear outcomes. It locates itself in easily identified actions, discrete male leaders, heroic rhetorical statements, and emotional commemorations of those who gave their lives for liberty.

But consider an alternative scenario, one that extends longer in time, includes more than only men, and reaches into the political, economic, and cultural reality of American life. "A history of military operations . . . is not a history of the American Revolution," warned John Adams in 1815. "The revolution was in the minds and hearts of the people, and in the union of the colonies; both of which were substantially effected before hostilities commenced." Thus, the real revolution was in the united actions of the colonies in campaigns of resistance to British authority that took place before the war.[2]

John Adams's evaluation can be substantiated in the October 1774 Continental Association—a program of nonimportation, nonconsumption, and nonexportation combined with provisions for enforcement that utilized social ostracism and economic boycott. This was adopted by the First Continental Congress, which encouraged the formation of other extralegal committees that effectively assumed functions of government throughout the colonies. Nonimportation caused the collapse of British imports in 1774–1775: in New England their value dropped from £562,476 in 1774 to £71,625 in 1775, in Virginia and Maryland from £528,738 to £1,921, and in the Carolinas from £378,116 to £6,245. Even in New York, a Loyalist center, imports fell. By early 1775, Americans had established hundreds of committees to enforce the Continental Association in direct opposition to British authority. The balance of power shifted so that the provincial conventions and committees now in fact governed most colonies. In reality, political independence from Britain was evident before the Battles of Lexington and Concord in April 1775.[3]

This independence had its roots in the decade of nonviolent struggle from 1765 to 1775, notably in three specific campaigns: against the Stamp Act of 1765, the Townshend Acts of 1767, and the Coercive Acts of 1774. These resistance campaigns used such nonviolent means as extraordinary petitions, protest marches, demonstrations, boycotts, and refusals to work. When the British Crown levied taxes on certain imports, Americans organized campaigns to refuse to purchase them.

Other methods were also devised. Colonial merchants were ostracized if they continued to import boycotted goods. Additionally, colonial activists sometimes conducted regular business in violation of British law, by using documents without tax stamps, by settling legal disputes without courts, and by sending protest petitions to Britain without permission from the royal governor. They also formed local, county, and provincial committees to support, extend, and enforce resistance. In 1774 and 1775, many such bodies assumed governmental powers, acting as extralegal authorities with powers greater than the remnants of colonial royal government.

A Decade of Nonviolent Resistance

Until the 1774 Continental Congress, colonial nonviolent action was mainly improvised. Colonists frequently did not have a clear idea of what was involved in waging effective nonviolent struggle. They were at times confused about which steps to take if a particular method was losing impact and often found it difficult to judge a campaign's relative effectiveness. Yet they were acutely aware that some methods were more effective than others and acted on that. A review of the three campaigns of resistance between 1765 and 1775 provides a basis for assessing the nonviolent tactics and strategies used by the resistance movement.

The Campaign Against the Stamp Act, 1765–1766

The Stamp Act, enacted in March 1765 and due to come into force in November, introduced direct taxation—a stamp duty on all legal documents and various other printed materials. This provoked an open resistance campaign that marked the beginning of the movement toward colonial self-government. Previously, complaints against British policies were voiced in petitions to Parliament from the colonial legislatures and approved by the royal governor. After the Stamp Act, opposition widened, including not only petitions without executive approval for repeal of the law but colonial refusal to pay the taxes, social and consumer boycotts against supporters of the act, and nonimportation and nonconsumption of British goods.

The Massachusetts and Virginia legislatures passed resolutions against the act while popular protests pressured Crown-appointed tax agents to resign—crowds hanged effigies of tax agents and confronted them at home. During August 1765, actions against tax officials took place in Massachusetts, Connecticut, New York, Rhode Island, and Maryland. Philadelphia merchant Charles Thompson informed his London friends that stamp officials throughout the thirteen colonies had resigned their offices.

Meanwhile several colonies were preparing the Stamp Act Congress for October 1765. This innovative step in intercolonial cooperation produced a statement of colonial rights and the proper limits of parliamentary authority. Copies of the congressional proceedings were sent to every colony plus one set to Britain as the united appeal of the American colonies.

By the time the Stamp Act went into effect on November 1, 1765, colonial resistance was well under way. The Stamp Act Congress was meeting. Newspapers, such as the *Maryland Gazette,* the *Pennsylvania Gazette,* and the *South Carolina Gazette,* announced they would cease publication rather than be boycotted for using stamps. Other papers, such as the *New London Gazette,* the *Connecticut Gazette,* and the *Boston Gazette,* defied the Crown by continuing to publish without stamps. The *Newport Gazette, Boston Post-Boy,* and *Pennsylvania Journal* appeared anonymously without the editor or printer identified. Newspapers that remained open reported resistance activities and, thereby, provided support for opposition to the act.

In parallel fashion, many courts were closed because lawyers would not use stamps and judges would not proceed without them. Similarly, shipping permits were supposed to be stamped. However, if no one would distribute or use the stamps, then ports would either have to close completely or open and operate in defiance of the law.

Actions such as these effectively nullified the Stamp Act, but without bringing about its repeal. That was achieved through nonimportation pacts agreed by merchants in the three major port cities: Boston, New York, and Philadelphia. On October 31, 1765, New York merchants pledged refusal to import British goods until the tax was repealed. Philadelphia merchants followed on November 7 and Boston on December 9. British merchants, alarmed by these pacts, petitioned Parliament to repeal the Stamp Act.

While Parliament had expected Stamp Act revenues to yield £60,000 a year, the total levied did not cover even half the expenses of printing: a mere £3,292 in early 1766. Even before its repeal in March 1766, the Stamp Act was a dead letter in the colonies. The people had discovered, in the words of Governor Francis Bernard of Massachusetts, that "they have it in their power to choose whether they will submit to this act or not." Numerous ports had reopened without using stamps while various local courts conducted business in violation of British law. Repeal brought a degree of calm to North America, but the colonists had experienced the power of non-cooperation.[4]

The Campaign Against the Townshend Acts, 1767–1768

When Parliament passed the Townshend Acts in 1767, imposing duties on imports such as glass, paint, paper, and tea, colonial activists again turned to the weapon of nonimportation. For example, in Providence, Rhode Island, a nonconsumption pact listed imports to be boycotted. Anyone disregarding this was to be "discountenanced, in the most effectual, but decent and lawful Manner." Similarly in Newport, Rhode Island, local tailors charged less for work on American-made cloth but extra for imported cloth.[5]

Initially, resistance was sporadic and, unlike the Stamp Act, the Townshend Acts went into effect on November 20, 1767, with no attempt to prevent their enforcement until the following month when an essay by John Dickinson galvanized a new campaign. In January 1768, the Massachusetts House of Representatives petitioned the king for repeal of the Townshend Acts and distributed a Circular Letter to all colonial assemblies hoping they would back this call. These hopes were fulfilled. By the end of 1768, every colonial assembly had petitioned the king challenging Parliament's right to levy taxes on the colonies.

While colonial assemblies acted on the Massachusetts letter, a movement for nonimportation began. Planning commenced in Boston in March 1768, but no accord was reached until August 1. Later that month, New York merchants signed a similar pact, adding that merchants who violated it or refused to enroll should be boycotted and labeled "Enemies of Their

Country." Philadelphia merchants hesitated until February 1769, after which a number of smaller ports followed. George Washington applauded the prospect of a nonimportation campaign in Virginia. He told George Mason that "we have already . . . proved the inefficacy of the addresses to the throne and remonstrances to Parliament. How far, then, their attention to our rights and privileges is to be awakened or alarmed, by starving their trade and manufactures, remains to be tried." Mason agreed on the potential impact of nonimportation and suggested a related tactic: "It may not be amiss to let the ministry understand that, until we obtain a redress of grievances, we will withhold from them our commodities, and particularly refrain from making tobacco, by which the revenue would lose fifty times more than all their oppression could raise here."[6]

The Townshend Acts, except the duty on tea, were repealed in April 1770. When this news reached the American colonies, New York merchants reduced the requirements of their nonimportation agreement and those of Philadelphia and Boston followed suit, so ending the second major campaign of resistance to British authority. Due to uneven and late implementation, it had been more limited than the Stamp Act campaign. Yet the nonimportation agreements succeeded in sharply reducing trade with Britain and the lessons learned, such as the need for unified action to strengthen colonial leverage, were applied to the later nonintercourse agreements of 1774–1775.

The Committees of Correspondence

In the period between 1770 and 1774, one vital development was the formation of Committees of Correspondence for sharing information between the colonies. By the end of December 1772, at the suggestion of the Boston town meeting, such committees had been formed throughout Massachusetts. In March 1773, the Virginia House of Burgesses elected a standing Committee of Correspondence and requested other colonial assemblies to do likewise. An expanded network of correspondence committees throughout the colonies was firmly in place by early 1774.

In May 1773 Parliament passed the Tea Act. Aiming to reassert British imperial authority, this act essentially granted the East India Company a monopoly on tea imports. Colonists planned to nullify the act by convincing tea agents to resign. Some resisters, however, took more direct action—resulting in the Boston Tea Party of December 16, 1773—dumping dutied tea into Boston harbor.

British reaction was swift and harsh. To punish the people of Massachusetts for ten years of flaunting imperial authority, Parliament enacted a series of measures known as the Coercive Acts. News of these reached the colonies in May 1774 and immediately prompted resistance. A meeting of the Virginia House of Burgesses, which convened in defiance of the governor's orders, called for an intercolonial congress. The Massachusetts House proposed this should take place in September in Philadelphia. By the end of August, every colony except Georgia had elected delegates, some in extralegal sessions prohibited by Crown-appointed governors.

As the congress neared, plans were readied in several colonies to reinstitute commercial sanctions. Support grew for economic resistance and various localities enacted their own nonintercourse agreements. Resistance organizations ranged from local through provincial to the intercolonial level.

The First Continental Congress met in Philadelphia from September 5 through October 22, 1774, with delegates from every colony except Georgia. It passed a series of resolutions articulating the colonies' rights and grievances and, on October 20, adopted the Continental Association, which it called the "most speedy, effectual, and peaceable" measure. It was decided that all imports from Britain, Ireland, and the West Indies should stop on December 1, 1774, and they should be replaced with American-made items. Additionally, should nonimportation not gain redress of grievances, colonists would adopt what many felt was the most forceful commercial weapon available—the nonexportation of items such as lumber, naval stores, tobacco, and other raw materials. If needed, nonexportation would begin on September 10, 1775.

The Continental Association did not simply call for economic resistance, but also designed means to organize and enforce it. These provisions were quickly implemented throughout the colonies, ostracizing those who violated the association.

Colonial noncooperation throughout the resistance to the Coercive Acts was not limited to a refusal to buy British goods, but extended to all royal laws. Courts were closed, taxes refused, governors openly defied. Throughout the colonies, extralegal provincial congresses were convened in 1774 and early 1775 to oversee enforcement of the Continental Association. These "illegal" assemblies at the local, county, and provincial levels often assumed legislative and judicial functions in executing the wishes of the Continental Congress. As the conservative *Rivington's New York Gazetteer* wrote in February 1775, the association took "Government out of the hands of the Governor, Council, and General Assembly; and the execution of laws out of the hands of the Civil Magistrates and Juries."[7]

Naturally, the Crown tried to counter. On November 18, 1774, George III told Prime Minister Lord North that "the New England Governments are in a State of Rebellion; blows must decide whether they are to be subject to this Country or independent."[8] The issue for Parliament and George III was no longer redress of grievances; the colonists had demonstrated the eclipse of British authority and the Crown needed to restore its power. Consequently, in

January 1775, Colonial Secretary Lord Dartmouth directed General Thomas Gage to quell the heretofore nonviolent rebellion by arresting and imprisoning leaders in Massachusetts. Gage took the offensive by attempting to seize military stores at Concord where he clashed with colonists on April 19, 1775.

Organizations throughout the colonies were immediately confronted with a decision: whether to follow the Massachusetts example and shift strategy from nonviolent resistance to military force. Only seven colonies—New Hampshire, Massachusetts, Rhode Island, and Connecticut in the north; Virginia, Maryland, and South Carolina in the south—had authorized the organization of local militias prior to Lexington and Concord. And at that, these militia groups were poorly trained and equipped and seen more as protection against Indians and escaped slaves than as a defense against the British. Nevertheless, in May 1775 the Second Continental Congress assumed direction of the quickly developing military struggle, appointing George Washington as commander in chief of the newly created Continental Army and requisitioning military supplies. Nonviolent methods were superseded by violence as the primary means of struggle and the colonists embarked on a military war that would last eight years.

Dynamics of the Nonviolent Struggle

In identifying the emergence and assessing the tactics and strategies of resistance prior to May 1775, attention must be given to the movement's political and social dynamics. The gradual transformation of British North America from colonies to an independent state involved five factors:

1. The collective expression of American political differences with Britain and a concomitant sense of American identity;
2. The growth of organizations and institutions that articulated colonial interests and argued against new British powers and controls;
3. Open resistance to specific acts of the British government;
4. Mass political and economic noncooperation with British authority; and
5. The development of parallel institutions, particularly institutions of government.[9]

Each of these factors was essential for effective opposition to the Crown and instrumental in the revolutionary break from Britain. Collectively, they also contributed to the development of the eventual governing structures in the new United States. All of the components existed simultaneously throughout the decade of resistance, though each developed to varying degrees at different times. All five could be seen in the resistance to the Stamp Act, for example, yet they were not fully maintained after that campaign. The growth of organizations expressing American interests and the formation of new parallel institutions was not rapid until after 1770. Thus, the constituent parts of the process leading to independence were themselves developed and transformed in successive struggles, just as they contributed to the final achievement of independence. Space only allows for illustrative examples.

Political awareness of differences with Britain was crucial for the independence movement. Colonists with diverse personal interests and backgrounds slowly found themselves developing similar attitudes about the governance of their colony and the larger relationship of the American colonies to Britain. Common grievances and goals were identified in the Stamp Act and later the Townshend Acts campaign, as British taxation was considered an attack on colonial rights. In both cases, it was believed that members of Parliament had either been duped by bad advice or were using their powers improperly. Colonial Americans had no direct representatives in Parliament, hence, the slogan "No taxation without representation." By 1774–1775 colonial experience with parallel American institutions and increasing suspicion about the depth of British opposition moved many colonial Americans from seeking reform of British laws to seeking complete independence. This experience shaped their identities as Americans who shared common traditions with the British but, through their involvement in a decade of nonviolent resistance, had learned that they were a separate nation.

The second factor, institutions and organizations expressing colonial grievances, was critical in gaining independence and building democratic power-sharing governance structures. Colonial resistance was largely improvised, with new leaders who emerged that were capable of expressing grievances while successfully organizing protest actions. Intercolonial organizations sporadically arose, as with the Stamp Act Congress or the merchants' boycott agreements against the Townshend Acts. Not until the First Continental Congress in 1774 did measures materialize that were strategically conscious, applied throughout the colonies, and equipped with political and economic sanctions for noncompliance.

Popular resistance to British authority, the third factor, could take many forms. For example, methods of protest and persuasion included demonstrations and parades on behalf of a resistance campaign, the development of political symbols such as the Liberty Tree, and the publication of papers naming supporters or opponents of the resistance. A mock funeral in Wilmington, North Carolina, in October 1765 illustrated many of these methods. The *North Carolina Gazette* reported that some 500 Wilmingtonians (out of a total population of 800–1,000) met to protest against the Stamp Act. They paraded an effigy of Liberty, symbolizing the rights of colonists under attack by the British Parliament. The crowd put the effigy "into a Coffin, and marched in solemn procession with it to the Church-yard, a Drum in Mourning beating before them, and the Town Bells muffled ringing a doleful Knell at the same time." Just before the crowd interred the coffin, they checked the pulse of Liberty, and discovering she was still alive, "concluded the Evening with great Rejoicings, on finding that Liberty still had an Existence in the Colonies." The newspaper account observes "not the least Injury was offered to any Person." Here religious ritual, political protest, and mass action were conjoined within a nonviolent method of resistance. Urban political theater, such as this mock funeral, dramatized resistance issues, enlisted participation, and pressured royal officials. For onlookers, it raised awareness of the controversy and identified their neighbors and friends as supporters of the resistance. It encouraged all to support the resistance goals in a context that was not particularly threatening for the participants and witnesses, though the meaning of the episode was clear.[10]

Allied to popular resistance was the fourth factor—noncooperation. The varied methods of noncooperation all involved refusing to do what was ordered or expected, thereby breaking the habits of obedience and the bonds of cooperation. Social boycotts of individuals opposed to resistance are well documented. For example, the freemen of Essex, New Jersey, met in October 1765 to declare the Stamp Act unconstitutional and assert that they would

> detest, abhor, and hold in utmost contempt, all and every person or persons who shall meanly accept of any employment or office relating to the said Stamp Act, or shall take any shelter or advantage from the same . . . and they will have no communication with any such persons, nor to speak to them on any occasion, unless it be to inform them of their vileness.[11]

Similarly, a number of women in Providence and Bristol, Rhode Island, agreed not to accept the addresses of any man who favored the Stamp Act. Clearly, social boycotts exerted pressure on individuals, yet any offender who mended their ways was quickly restored to the good graces of the community.[12]

Economic forms of noncooperation provided more powerful sanctions. Organized campaigns of nonimportation of British goods imposed an economic cost on the British. Between October 31 and December 8, 1765, most merchants along the eastern seaboard cities boycotted British goods.

Nonconsumption of British goods also involved promotion of American-made items. In 1766 Thomas Hutchison, lieutenant-governor of Massachusetts, had to admit,

> When I first saw the proposals for lessening the consumption of English manufactures, I took them to be mere puffs. The scheme for laying aside

mourning [English funeral wear] succeeded to my surprise, and scare any-body would now dare to wear black for the nearest relative . . . the humour for being clothed in homespun spreads every day not so much for econ-omy as to convince the people of England how beneficial the Colonies have been to them.

In 1769 the students and president of the Baptist Rhode Island College (later Brown University) appeared at commencement dressed in American homespun, not imported English, formal gowns. So too, the colonialists ex-panded production of scythes, spades, wallpaper, and liquor rather than pur-chasing them from British merchants. Thus, even if the campaign's primary impact was political, another consequence was a fledgling move toward economic self-reliance.[13]

In 1769 an account in the *Boston Newsletter* described seventy-seven young women assembling at the house of the Reverend John Cleveland with their spinning wheels to make homespun yarn. When they finished, Cleveland observed how the women might recover to this country the full and free "enjoyment of all our rights, properties, and privileges . . . by liv-ing upon, as far as possible, only the produce of this country; and to be sure to lay aside the use of all foreign teas. Also by wearing as far as possible, only clothing of this country's manufacturing." Similarly, in Newport, Rhode Island, Congregational minister Ezra Stiles hosted ninety-two "Daughters of Liberty" who spent the day spinning yarn as their contribution to the resistance.[14]

A variation on these nonconsumption actions took place in Edenton, North Carolina, in October 1774 when fifty-one women signed this decla-ration: "We the Ladys of Edenton do hereby Solemnly Engage not to Con-form to that Pernicious Custom of Drinking Tea, & that we the aforesaid Ladys will not promote ye wear of any Manufacture from England until such time that all Acts which tend to Enslave this our Native Country shall be Repealed." Even children got involved. When Susan Boudinot, the nine-year-old daughter of a New Jersey patriot, was offered a cup of tea while visiting the royal governor, she curtsied, raised the cup to her lips, and tossed the tea out the window.[15]

These various actions point to the significant involvement of women in civil resistance. The nature of the civil resistance created a gendered space for various forms of participation by women. This space could be private—the decision not to consume British goods in the household. It could also be public space—participating in spinning at a church or openly protesting British policy. Sometimes, as in Edenton, women were lampooned in the British press for supposedly stepping outside their prescribed gender roles. However, such a parody itself suggests that British observers took women's actions seriously.

Although absolute numbers are unknown, women played an essential role in many local campaigns. Within their culturally prescribed domestic spheres, women made the decisions about household and family purchases, therefore bringing about the success of boycott campaigns. When women ventured into the public arena—a move that contemporary gender conventions did not endorse—their actions not only expressed open approval for the goals of resistance, but also had the unintended consequences of subverting gender conventions. Nevertheless, women could justify actions such as spinning wool as remaining within their domestic sphere while choosing domestic over imported goods as simply shopping frugally. Participation in various aspects of the colonial resistance increased these women's awareness of the relevant political issues; it involved them with wider assemblages of fellow citizens and unintentionally challenged the prevailing gender conventions.

In addition to shunning British goods and substituting American-made counterparts, a late form of colonial noncooperation involved the refusal to export American raw materials such as lumber and naval stores. This plan was mandated by the Continental Association, but went into effect only after the war had started (September 1775) and thus was not tested in its own right.

Here then was the real work of civil resistance: it was carried out in villages and towns, in the countryside as well as the city, by forgotten patriots, female and male. These now nameless men and women spun, wove, and wore homespun cloth; united in the boycott of British goods; and encouraged their neighbors to join them and stand firm. Many came together in crowd actions and mass meetings to protest and served on or supported local resistance committees. They refused to obey the statutes and officers of the British Crown, which so recently had been the law of the land. It was these acts of resistance and noncooperation that struck most openly at the Crown's authority.

The fifth factor, development of parallel institutions, began with the refusal to use existing royal political, judicial, and legislative institutions as well as refusing to dissolve colonial assemblies or intercolonial bodies such as the Continental Congress. It could also involve settling legal cases in courts or clearing incoming or outgoing ships without the required stamps as in the Stamp Act campaign. Ultimately, it involved the creation of new political institutions, such as the Stamp Act Congress (1765), the Committees of Correspondence (1772–1775), and the First Continental Congress (1774–1775). These extralegal political bodies corresponded to extralegal judicial and legislative colonial organizations that also developed during the decade of resistance. If the Stamp Act Congress was ad hoc and dissolved itself, gradually these institutions became continuous and self-sustaining—with the standing committees of correspondence and then later the First Continental Congress being recognized by colonists as fully functional American replacements for organs of British authority. Taken together, these new colonial political institutions embodied the parallel government that emerged most forcefully and visibly in 1774 and 1775.

This new American government, parallel in function to the British government, provided the basis for de facto independence and formed the foundation for new government once the country finally became independent. In fundamental ways, the decade of resistance contributed to this foundation through the politicization of American society. Politicization meant the increased recognition by merchants, lawyers, and others to increase their political participation. John Adams, Samuel Adams, Benjamin Franklin, John Hancock, Patrick Henry, Thomas Jefferson, and George Washington all supported the resistance campaigns and went on to serve the new United States. Politicization also meant the growing awareness that this political sphere extended in crucial ways to London as much as it included America.

The ability of the American colonies to dispense with royal direction of their political institutions and, simultaneously, to develop replacement institutions to fulfill the functions of government represented a major political accomplishment of civil resistance and the beginning of American independence. Self-government in the colonies was not gained by the war, as is so often assumed; it was actually established much earlier. Nonviolent methods probed specific British imperial vulnerabilities. They challenged Britain on ideological grounds, proclaiming to an American, British, and international audience that the British were suppressing American liberty. They leveraged their particular economic power through campaigns of nonconsumption, nonimportation, and nonexportation directed at the British mercantile establishment. Finally, they undermined the social and political foundations of the imperial system in America by withdrawing cooperation from British institutions and authorities and replacing them with parallel American institutions.

A Shift in Strategy

Although Americans achieved substantial political accomplishments during their nonviolent struggle, these gains were eventually defended by military force. Examination of this shift in strategy, if only on a preliminary basis, sheds light on important issues. Some might argue that violence was used throughout the resistance campaign, and that the shift to military means was necessary if not inevitable. However, could it be that many American colonists understood what they had achieved by this point, but did not understand what could have been further achieved through continued nonviolent resistance?

During this decade of resistance, American colonists used many types of resistance. These did include violent actions, but they have been greatly overemphasized and were of questionable value in altering parliamentary policy between 1765 and 1775. The 1773 Boston Tea Party did not endanger physical safety. However, its destruction of property may have been counterproductive: if some people found it symbolically or emotionally satisfying, without doubt it infuriated the British government, which introduced the Coercive Acts. Tarring and feathering of opponents is often cited as an example of the colonial use of violence against persons. Yet fewer than a dozen cases of this actually occurred between 1765 and April 1775, usually involving customs informers and being seen as private grudges rather than elements of political resistance. In 1769 several Sons of Liberty protected the Loyalist James Murray from an angry Boston crowd: they called out "No violence, or you'll hurt the cause." Even Samuel Adams, often considered an advocate of violence, warned in 1774, "Nothing can ruin us but our violence." Consequently, it is clear that the civil resistance movement was overwhelmingly nonviolent. Examples of property destruction and still less personal violence played no important role in the three resistance campaigns.[16]

Did the colonists understand that they were employing a specific type of resistance, namely, nonviolent action? Certainly, they did not use a twenty-first-century vocabulary. Yet in 1767 John Dickinson realized that boycotts meant "withholding from Great Britain all the advantages she has been used to receiving from us,"[17] and many other historical records document conscious support for the programs of social, economic, and political noncooperation. One thing is clear—colonial leaders did not adopt this technique in order to remain morally pure or because they had a principled objection to the use of violence. Rather their commitment was to resist Crown authority effectively and their choice of technique was based on a strategic judgment of the most effective means of resistance. That they did not have a thorough understanding of the nature, dynamics, and scope of this technique is clear. So too is that they underestimated or misunderstood the gains that the nonviolent resistance had achieved.

Likewise, there was little or no strategic consideration given to the implications of the shift from nonviolent action to military force. For example, from 1765 to 1775, British merchants had often supported campaign goals of overturning various British taxes and duties. Indeed, it was a measure of success of noncooperation campaigns that British merchants used their influence on Parliament. A strategic strength of the American colonies was their economic importance to Britain, both as a market for goods and as a source of raw materials. The choice of nonviolent means facilitated accommodation to, if not acceptance of, colonial demands by significant elements in the British mercantile and political communities much more than violent colonial opposition would have allowed. The widespread effectiveness of the nonimportation and nonconsumption movements during the Stamp Act campaign decreased British profits so much that these influential merchants complained to their parliamentary representatives and demanded policy change. With profits down, British workers were laid off, thus raising the specter of additional social and political trouble. In this context, Parliament's repeal of the Stamp Act is clearly attributable to these campaigns of American civil resistance, notwithstanding any face-saving statements to the contrary by British politicians.

Parallel attempts during the Townshend and Coercive Acts resistance campaigns also sought to pressure British merchants to influence Parliament. In each campaign other groups, such as Protestant Dissenters (non-Anglican Protestants), were also lobbied for their support. In such ways, the nonviolent resisters exerted important pressure on third parties.

Once military hostilities broke out, these efforts at third-party persuasion ceased to be effective. British mercantile encouragement eroded quickly once supporting the colonists became tantamount to sedition. Even in the early 1780s, when France had sided with the Americans and the British Army had suffered defeats, British calls for an end to the war aimed to cut their country's losses, not to concede the justice of the American cause. Moreover, the Second Continental Congress actively recruited several Europeans—Marquis de Lafayette, Johann DeKalb, Casimir Pulaski, Thaddeus Kosciusko, and Friedrich von Steuben—who drew on their experience to forge a military strategy. None of them were familiar with the decade of nonviolent resistance and its accomplishments; instead all had training in armed struggle. Their military appointments helped reinforce the shift from civil resistance to military action.

On the domestic front too, the shift in strategy had several implications. For example, when the Second Continental Congress decided to form an army, political decisionmaking moved from the popular assemblies and broad-based committees in each colony to a command structure more responsive to military exigencies. This realignment away from more popularly based decisionmaking certainly played a role in the conflicts over democracy in the postwar early American republic. Women, so vital to the success of boycott and other resistance campaigns, were now relegated to secondary roles of support for all-male armies. Finally, opponents of the colonial cause were treated differently. During the previous decade, colonists who disagreed with civil resistance were boycotted. While some were threatened, few were actually attacked. After the Battles of Lexington and Concord, fear of Loyalist opposition grew and some committees proposed violence against Loyalists to intimidate them into submission.

Also worthy of consideration are the effects of strategy shift on mobilization of the people. By its very nature civil resistance aims to enlist the participation of a large proportion of the population, people willing to act even under the threat of repression. As already noted, this participation included men, women, and even children. Moreover, it was not only widespread, but also well organized. All the colonies involved in the First Continental Congress endorsed the provisions of the Continental Association with the exception of New York and, even there, local committees enforced nonimportation. Except in Georgia and the occupied city of Boston, David Ammerman notes, "purchases from Great Britain stopped entirely. The most outspoken critics of the measure [the Continental Association's call for noncooperation] were forced to admit that the boycott had the force of law throughout the colonies." Ammerman concludes that, because enforcement of the association was placed in the hands of local groups rather than provincial assemblies or congresses, "these committees became the regulatory agencies of the First Continental Congress." Lessons about organizing campaigns so as to maximize unity, increase participation, and reinforce timing had been learned from earlier campaigns. Here in the Continental Association, comprehensive and coordinated strategies of nonimportation and nonexportation carried out by dedicated, disciplined, and united men and women were widely and effectively enforced.[18]

Levels of participation dropped or changed dramatically once the strategy shifted to violence. Women and older men, having no place in armies, became tangential sources of support. The various strategic levels of resistance from individual through local committees and provincial congresses, up to the Continental Congress, were fundamentally weakened in favor of the military's demands. Once the war began, Robert Calhoon observes, approximately 50 percent of the colonists of European ancestry (including the Loyalist contingent) tried to avoid any involvement in the conflict or supported the British. Perhaps only 40 percent to 45 percent of the white populace actively supported the patriot cause, Calhoon concludes. Beyond that, while critics of civil resistance claim that some merchants did not observe the nonimportation agreements, Don Higginbotham's estimate of the desertion rate from the Continental Army at 20 percent suggests that armed resistance was more polarizing and weakened American social unity. Consequently, despite the nostalgic rhetoric about the minutemen and the Continental Army, surprisingly large numbers avoided and opposed participation or deserted once the strategy shifted to military struggle.[19]

To be sure, had the resistance remained nonviolent, further sacrifices would have been exacted. Though by 1775 morale was high and the resistance movement was well organized with competent leadership in colony and modes of communication between the colonies in place, confronting the British Army would have been daunting. At the same time, protracted occupation in the face of active nonviolent resistance would have been extremely costly for the Crown. Furthermore, it is doubtful that casualties from nonviolent resistance would have reached 4,435, the number of American military deaths in the War for Independence. In short, the shift to military strategy had many disadvantages, both domestically and internationally. It had not been thought out strategically but rather reflected the emotions of the moment.[20]

Perhaps US citizens and others looking back at their national origins should ponder this alternative to the familiar narrative of military struggle. The result of the decade of American nonviolent resistance between 1765 and 1775 was de facto independence. Allegiances had shifted and the functions of government passed from royal to colonial institutions—and all this before the Battles of Lexington and Concord. Indeed, regarding the development of political and social institutions, one could even claim that the war achieved little that had not already been gained by the parallel governments.

These campaigns of civil resistance spanning ten years displayed impressive self-discipline, used largely improvised strategies until the very end, and achieved serious gains. They cultivated third-party support in Britain as well as neutralized domestic opponents without shedding blood. Their broadly democratic nature was matched by new extralegal political institutions that wrested control out of the hands of British authorities. Making legislative policy, enforcing judicial decisions, even collecting taxes in some cases was carried out by colonists on their own and outside the imperial orbit. Beyond that, although the campaigns were largely improvised, the colonists showed in the implementation of nonimportation and nonexportation as part of the Continental Association a conscious level of strategic planning. In hindsight, perhaps they were mistaken to delay the implementation of nonexportation; nevertheless, the very fact of deliberate strategic decisionmaking is significant. Finally, the tactics of the resistance campaign and the enforcement of their policies were carried out nonviolently—not as a matter of principled opposition to violence, but rather as a pragmatic response to the need to resist perceived injustice. That the participants in these successful nonviolent campaigns had so little prior training, that their leaders knew little of strategic precedents, and that their applications of nonviolent struggle were so often improvised make their accomplishments all the more remarkable.

Reasons for the Lack of Attention to Civil Resistance

In 2009 crowds celebrated the fiftieth anniversary of the Minute Man National Historical Park in Concord, Massachusetts, witnessing the reenactment of the Battles of Lexington and Concord, events described by the National Park Service as "the opening battle of the American Revolution."[21]

Why are these events of the war celebrated and the sacrifices of its participants eulogized while the decade of civil resistance is largely ignored? What is the relation of history to memory in this case? Americans are not an innately violent people, despite the alarming levels of violence in American society, both historical and contemporary. Rather, it is because of cultural influences, social factors, and historical experience. Consequently, while scholarly debate shows no signs of achieving unanimity, several factors provide grounds for suggestive speculation.[22]

One reason for the lack of attention to the decade of civil resistance is simply ignorance. Thousands of school children in the United States are drilled on the sacrifices of soldiers. Few learn of the defeat of the Stamp Act by nonviolent resistance, the effects of the Continental Association, or the achievement of de facto political independence before the outbreak of the war.

Another more psychosocial factor is the emotional ethos associated with the dramatized, glamorized, and often antisepticized image of war versus the view that nonviolent resistance is submissive and passive. Put simplistically, soldiers fight and do things; nonviolent resisters just refuse to do things. US culture celebrates a connection between male honor and violence. But while the bandit, cowboy, and detective often employ violence, it usually is for a good cause and therefore is legitimated, just as going to war is sanctioned by supposedly legitimate ends. Gaining national independence is routinely taken as justifying violence and those involved in it regarded as heroic patriots. If Americans have a penchant for identifying the war for independence with the achievement of independence, John Adams's statement at the beginning of this chapter reminds us that not all narratives arrive at this conclusion.

Finally, there is the well-established use of violence in US history, and its subsequent cultural familiarity and acceptance—from white-Indian and white-black through agrarian and urban to vigilante violence. Add to this that nearly 200 million Americans today own firearms and it is clear that many Americans view violence as a crucial and appropriate means for securing their lives and property.

In such a situation, eulogizing past armed struggle and commemorating its participants becomes an all-too-familiar expression of US social logic. It is a construct, however, that can and needs to be challenged by a fuller appreciation of the historical record: not erasing the stories of nonviolent civil resistance from US collective memory, but recognizing their existence, significance, and power.

Notes

1. *The Patriot,* directed by Roland Emmerich (Culver City, CA: Columbia Pictures, 2000); *Johnny Tremain,* directed by Robert Stevenson (Burbank, CA: Walt Disney Productions, 1957).

2. John Adams to Dr. Jedediah Morse, November 29, 1815, *The Works of John Adams,* vol. 10, ed. Charles F. Adams (Boston: Little Brown, 1850–1856), 182. When not otherwise cited, this chapter draws on material documented in Walter H. Conser Jr., Ronald M. McCarthy, David J. Toscano, and Gene Sharp, eds., *Resistance, Politics, and the American Struggle for Independence, 1765–1775* (Boulder: Lynne Rienner, 1986).

3. David Macpherson, *Annals of Commerce, Manufacturing, Fishing, and Navigation,* vol. 3 (London: Nicols and Sons, 1805), 564–585. By the beginning of the Second Continental Congress in 1775, even Georgia had overcome its misgivings and sent delegates to this interprovincial extralegal assembly.

4. This figure for income includes colonies that did not become part of the United States and where cooperation was greater (e.g., Grenada, the West Indies, Quebec, and Nova Scotia). See Lawrence Gipson, *British Empire Before the Revolution,* vol. 10 (New York: Knopf, 1961), 328, 391; Francis Bernard to Richard Jackson, August 23, 1765, "Bernard Papers," vol. 4, The Houghton Library, Harvard University, 19.

5. *Pennsylvania Gazette,* December 24, 1767; *Pennsylvania Gazette,* March 24, 1768.

6. George Washington to George Mason, April 5, 1769, in Kate Mason Rowland, *Life of George Mason, 1725–1792,* vol. 1 (New York: G. P. Putnam's Sons, 1892), 139; George Mason to George Washington, April 5, 1769, in ibid., 141–142.

7. *Rivington's New York Gazetteer,* February 18, 1775.

8. Sir John Fortescue, ed., *The Correspondence of King George the Third,* vol. 3 (London: Macmillan, 1927–1928), 153.

9. See Crane Brinton, *The Anatomy of Revolution* (New York: Vintage, 1965); and Charles Tilly, *From Mobilization to Revolution* (Reading, MA: Addison-Wesley, 1979).

10. William L. Saunders, ed., *Colonial and State Records of North Carolina,* vol. 7 (Raleigh: Trustees of the Public Libraries, 1886), 124.

11. *Newport Mercury,* November 18, 1765.

12. Arthur M. Schlesinger, *The Colonial Merchants and the American Revolution, 1763–1775* (New York: Atheneum, 1968), 77.

13. Thomas Hutchinson to Thomas Pownall, March 8, 1766, "Hutchison Correspondence," vol. 26, The Houghton Library, Harvard University, 200–206; Reuben A. Guild, *Early History of Brown University Including the Life, Times, and Correspondence of President Manning, 1756–1791* (Providence: Snow and Farnum, 1897), 82–87.

14. *Boston Newsletter,* July 6, 1769; Linda K. Kerber, *Women of the Republic* (New York: Norton, 1986), 38.

15. Kerber, *Women of the Republic,* 39–41.

16. Bernhard Knollenberg, *The Growth of the American Revolution, 1765–1775* (New York: Free Press, 1975), 361, n. 64; Samuel Adams to James Warren, May 21, 1774, "Warren-Adams Letters," Massachusetts Historical Society Collections, vol. 7 (1917); Nina Moore Tiffany, ed., *The Letters of James Murray, Loyalist,* reprint ed. (Boston: Gregg Press, 1972 [1901]), 159–160.

17. John Dickinson, *Letters from a Farmer in Pennsylvania to the Inhabitants of the British Colonies* (New York: Outlook, 1903 [1767–1768]), 29–30.

18. See David Ammerman, "The Continental Association," in *Resistance, Politics, and the American Struggle for Independence, 1765–1775,* ed., Walter H. Conser Jr., Ronald M. McCarthy, David J. Toscano, and Gene Sharp (Boulder: Lynne Rienner, 1986), 246–247.

19. See Robert M. Calhoon, "Loyalism and Neutrality," in *The Blackwell Encyclopedia of the American Revolution,* ed. Jack P. Greene and J. R. Pole (Cambridge: Blackwell, 1991), 247; Don Higginbotham, "The War for Independence, After Saratoga," in *The Blackwell Encyclopedia of the American Revolution,* ed. Jack P. Greene and J. R. Pole (Cambridge: Blackwell, 1991), 317.

20. Ann Leeland and Maria-Jones Oboroceanu, *American War and Military Operations, Casualties: Lists and Statistics* (Washington, DC: Congressional Research Service, 2009), 2.

21. See the Minute Man National Historical Park website, www.nps.gov/mima, accessed July 28, 2010.

22. For the following discussion I have drawn on several sources, notably Robert B. Toplin, *Unchallenged Violence: An American Ordeal* (Westport, CT: Greenwood Press, 1975); Michael Kimmel, *Manhood in America: A History* (New York: Free Press, 1996); David Courtwright, *Violent Land* (Cambridge: Harvard University, 1996); Richard Maxwell Brown, *Strain of Violence* (New York: Oxford University Press, 1975); Hugh Graham and Ted Roberts Gurr, eds., *Violence in America,* rev. ed. (London: Sage, 1979); Philip Cook and Jens Ludwig, "Guns in America: National Survey on Private Ownership and Use of Firearms," National Institute of Justice and US Department of Justice Research in Brief (Washington, DC: National Institute of Justice; US Department of Justice, May 1979).

17

Cuba:
Nonviolent Strategies for
Autonomy and Independence,
1810s–1902

Alfonso W. Quiroz

Traditional views of nineteenth-century nationalist struggles worldwide have emphasized the violent means necessary to achieve patriotic goals. Violent heroic feats are seen as confirming that nations are forged with the blood of patriots in armed struggle against foreign oppression. Interpretations of Cuban efforts to achieve independence from Spain are no exception. Indeed, the cult of national heroes and racial freedom fighters, such as martyred "Apostle" José Martí and "Bronze Titan" General Antonio Maceo, killed in action during the insurrection of 1895–1898, remains today a dominant theme in political praxis, education, identity, culture, and history writing in Cuba.[1]

If in contrast we study more widely the historical record of Cuban struggles for self-determination led by civilian-based political and civic movements during the Spanish control of the island, countless yet unsung nonviolent efforts can be found. These were defiant struggles to oppose colonialist restrictions and abuses, and to achieve full constitutional rights and political autonomy without armed conflict. As the insurrectionist General Máximo Gómez recognized in 1891, Cuban civilian leaders engaged in nonviolent resistance "do not believe it's necessary to use brute force ever. They are right in part because when triumph is obtained with that force the road ahead is plagued with disasters."[2] A strengthening native civilian collective firmly rooted in the island's constrained socioeconomic realities had promising chances of leading a nonviolent transition toward independence and a resilient postindependence democracy in Cuba. This promise was substantially realized despite the ascendancy of violent separatist groups and US military intervention.

After 1826, the only remaining Spanish American colonies were Cuba and Puerto Rico. Cuba's strategic importance and rising colonial revenues extracted from a booming sugar, coffee, and tobacco export economy reliant on slave and peasant labor made the island indispensable to Spain. In consequence, political and military events in Cuba and Spain became even more intimately intertwined. Cuba's elite remained collaborative while the Madrid government granted tax and customs concessions. However, following the death of King Ferdinand VII in 1833, successive Spanish captain-generals (colonial governors in charge of the Spanish colonial administration in Cuba) in Havana reinforced military despotism and harmful commercial and fiscal policies. Madrid hardened colonial discrimination against those born in Cuba. Successive waves of Spaniards arrived in Cuba—particularly after the 1840s—to bolster the regular army, colonial bureaucracy, and urban service sector, thereby displacing Creole (Cuban born of European descent) and free black inhabitants from their former positions. Simultaneously the slave population in Cuba increased dramatically and free black groups lost some of their traditional rights.[3] Colonialist use of abusive force and a divide and rule policy to control Cuban society and exploit the stark divisions between free and enslaved people, and Creole- and Spanish-born inhabitants, sparked the organization of the first reformist and separatist movements.

Two distinct historical strategies developed among divided groups of Cuban reformists and separatists. One strategy was based on nonviolent, gradualist traditions that pressed for colonial reform, attainment of constitutional and civil rights already recognized in Spain, a distinctive Cuban education, and autonomous self-government. The other strategy relied on violent conspiracies, rebel naval expeditions, and armed insurrection that eventually triggered two destructive wars for independence—the Ten Years' War (1868–1878) and the War of 1895–1898. Violent military action and reaction and, ultimately, US military intervention in 1898, weakened the political standing and leadership of nonviolent strategists. However, by building a grassroots core through unifying civilian-national identity and an autonomous civil society clearly differentiated from the colonialist state's divisive social designs, the contributions of nonviolent organization and action toward an independent Cuba were irreversible.

Radical nationalist stances—inspired by insurrectionist leader Martí and his views on revolutionary violence—have considered crucial nonviolent actions as being antipatriotic and pro-colonial because they did not contribute to armed struggle for independence.[4] With a similar political logic, nonviolent dissent in Cuba today is persistently declared reactionary and pro-imperialist. What is remarkable is that, despite violent colonialist reaction, nonviolent strategies and goals remained consistent and received wide popular support and recognition among Cubans throughout the nineteenth century. It is therefore important to set the record straight concerning civilian-based non-violent movements in Cuba through the assessment of their preindependence scope and influence as well as their successes, failures, legacies, and lessons for future nonviolent transitions.

Socioeconomic and Political Developments in Nineteenth-Century Cuba

The strategic importance of Cuba in the Atlantic placed it at the center stage of historical imperial disputes and geopolitics. After the British invasion of Havana in 1762, the Spanish empire reinforced its defenses, enhancing fortifications, building up the navy, and militarizing Cuban society by reorganizing the regular army and local militias.[5] Cuban business and landholding elites linked the advancement of their interests with Spanish colonialist authorities, Spanish transatlantic networks of trade in goods and slaves, and monopolist and protectionist interests in Spain.

The massive influx of slaves to Cuba after the Haiti slave rebellion (1791–1804) and British prohibition of slave trade (1807) was accompanied by the introduction of new machinery and economic reforms leading to a sugar boom. Initially, Creole landholders dominated sugar production, Francisco Arango y Parreño (1765–1837) being credited with its modernization,[6] while Spanish merchants controlled trade. The demographic and ethnic changes resulting from the slave influx intensified divisions that were reinforced and manipulated by the increasingly despotic and militaristic Spanish rulers who reasserted colonialism in the island. The island thus faced a transformation that endangered its condition as a settler society and reinforced elements of a colonial plantation society and captive market benefiting mainly Spanish trading interests.

The swift independence of most Spanish American colonies had been attained in the period 1810–1826 at a time of instability and a crisis of power in Spain itself. Cuban Creoles noted the turmoil in the newly independent Latin American republics and, in general, remained loyal to the Spanish crown. In the 1820s thousands of defeated Spanish soldiers and loyalist immigrants from former colonies resettled in Cuba,[7] which increasingly was run by a centralized military and official bureaucracy that privileged Spanish officers and left little space for local self-government or municipal authority. The growing Creole middle and professional classes were displaced from their previous positions of influence. Under the Spanish constitution of 1812, Spaniards "in both hemispheres" were recognized as citizens, Creoles of Spanish descent being entitled to vote and to be represented in the Cortes in Spain.[8] However, subsequent revisions were to disenfranchise them. Under the growing tyranny of the captain-general, buttressed by the island's emboldened Spanish "party" (slave-trafficking interests), and immigration of Spanish soldiers and civil servants, Cuba became the milk cow that provided strategic fiscal revenues to a needy Spanish monarchy. In Spain, Regent María Cristina and her daughter Isabel II—in alliance with the colonialist Moderate Party, ambitious military leaders, and protectionist agricultural and manufacturing interests in Spain—made use of colonial revenues to fight off Don Carlos, the archconservative pretender to the throne.

Nonviolent Resistance and Formation of a Cuban Identity

Two basic strategies were soon obvious to Cuban civilian leaders and movements from the 1830s to 1850s—a time period of colonialist reassertion and authoritarian military rule in Cuba. The first strategy was to support separatist conspiracies that organized violent uprisings in Cuba as well as "filibustering" expeditions, mainly from the United States, that landed in Cuba and incited armed insurrection. The major filibustering expeditions were led by insurrectionary militarist leaders and supported by elite proslavery Cuban exiles, allied to southern US interests seeking US annexation of Cuba. In 1851 the defeat and execution of the annexationist filibuster Narciso López, a disgruntled former military officer, was an important lesson: armed insurrection might appease injured military and patriotic honor, but it had little chance of overcoming the strongest Spanish military establishment outside Spain. Moreover, such violent actions raised dangers of dictatorial caudillo ambition as well as intervention by other foreign powers, especially the United States. Despite these obvious pitfalls and recurrent defeats and repression affecting the island's entire population, separatist violence repeatedly broke out in the following decades.

The second strategy involved continuing and enhancing the liberal, nonviolent economic and political efforts initiated by Creoles of Arango's generation. This strategy eventually encompassed actions to demand and obtain constitutional rights, increased institutional autonomy, free press, and autonomous association in voluntary cultural, educational, professional, and self-help societies and clubs.

As early as the first decade of the nineteenth century, the press organs linked to patriotic societies—voluntary associations formed mainly by Creole elites and professionals—cultivated a sense of the island's economic and distinctive cultural identity in the pages of the newspapers *Papel Periódico* (Periodic Paper) and *Aurora* (Dawn) of Havana. This occurred despite the limits on press freedom imposed by captain-generals and provincial governors. During the first constitutional period of 1812–1814, private and independent pamphlets and periodicals, such as Havana's *Diario Cívico*

(Civic Daily) and *El Patriota Americano* (American Patriot) and Santiago de Cuba's *La Sabatina* (Saturday's), advocated administrative reform and full extension of constitutional rights of free press and association, despite being subject to official censorship and stern vigilance. Associational autonomy was also sought more actively. In 1813, daring members of the Havana Patriotic Society challenged the legality of the captain-general's political interference in the society's internal affairs. Other early cultural and ethnic associations included black societies that preserved Afro-Cuban identities and literary lyceums and philharmonic societies, cultivating artistic and literary contributions to a distinct Cuban culture and collective selfhood. Cuban-born inhabitants of the island could thus rely on an alternative social fabric and polis that contrasted and competed with the rigid colonial social establishment.

A renewed constitutional cycle in 1820–1823 consolidated the liberal constitutionalist character of a new generation of Creole civilian intellectuals who published in the independent newspapers *Revisor Político y Literario* (Political and Literary Examiner) and *Observador Habanero* (Habana's Observer). In these newspapers the articles of influential authors and educators Félix Varela and José Agustín Caballero, the first proponents of Cuba's political autonomy and independence, and their younger disciples urged constitutional changes that implied a thorough colonial reform and increased administrative autonomy. This constitutionalist-reformist spirit spread to provincial patriotic societies and cultural associations that published periodicals such as *La Aurora de Matanzas* (Dawn of Matanzas) between 1828 and 1856 and the *Revista Bimestre Cubana* (Cuban Bimester Review) founded in 1832. Other cultural periodicals included *La Siempre Viva* (Always Alive) and *La Moda* (Fashion). These publications reaffirmed Cuban literary and cultural identity by promoting Cuban authors such as the Afro-Cuban poet Plácido and Cirilo Villaverde, author of *Cecilia Valdés* (1839).

In 1836, a palace revolt in Spain led to the reinstatement of the 1812 constitution, which was immediately adopted by the Spanish governor of Santiago de Cuba, Manuel Lorenzo, who called elections without waiting for authorization from Madrid or Captain-General Miguel Tacón in Havana. Tacón sent troops to Santiago and prominent supporters of Lorenzo's in the Santiago Patriotic Society, including educator Juan Bautista Sagarra, were punished with a period in exile.[9] Other important leaders with island-wide popularity advocating nonviolent strategies at the time were the liberal constitutionalists and gradualist abolitionists José Antonio Saco and Domingo del Monte who engaged in active unofficial and official opposition in the press and associations, organized networks of Creole intellectuals in *tertulias* (soirées), and encouraged black authors to publish. These activities, too, brought persecution by the Spanish authorities and periods in exile.[10]

Underlying patriotic associational and independent press efforts, a conscious emphasis on spreading grassroots education since the early nineteenth century contributed to the formation of a wider Cuban identity. Sociedades Económicas in the most important cities and towns of the island financed and established hundreds of free, nonreligious primary schools for thousands of white and black, male and female students. With practically no official subsidy, Havana's Sociedad Económica funded more than forty free schools with nearly 1,000 students in 1846. Various "model schools" were established, including private high schools run by revered liberal educators such as José de la Luz y Caballero, the defiant director of Sociedad Económica in the 1840s, and Juan Bautista Sagarra who founded the Colegio de Santiago de Cuba on his return from exile. In higher education, too, innovative alternatives were established and reformist Cuban-born professors and medical doctors formed a majority among the island's higher education faculty.

Generations of Cuban children and young people were educated in these schools with up-to-date textbooks by Cuban authors critical of traditional Spanish methods of instruction and historical interpretation. Educational authorities in Spain censored Cuban textbooks for their irreverent views of Spanish religious fanaticism and violent conquest. Furthermore, Spanish political authorities on the island were wary of the challenge posed by Cuban primary and higher education to colonial control and thus redoubled efforts to "assimilate" the island's population to Spanish culture. In 1847, the Spanish colonial state took over the administration of primary schools formerly funded by local Sociedades Económicas. The ensuing centralized administration of education by the Spanish colonial state was perennially underfunded. Despite continued anti-Cuban education policies and bureaucratic harassment, Cuban-born teachers in public schools and the surviving private schools contributed to increasing literacy levels and, with this, to raising the political and national awareness of the Cuban population.[11]

The Springtime of Civilian Colonial Reformism

In the 1860s, political change in Spain led to a reformist interlude in Cuba that nonviolent civilian strategists were able to exploit to advance the goal of Cuban autonomy. In Spain a wave of reinvigorated associational impetus was sweeping the main cities, bringing to life civil, reform-minded, liberal economic, social, and cultural groups and lobbies that opposed tariff protection and advocated the abolition of slavery in Spanish colonies.

In Cuba, a broadening reform movement also pressed for enhanced fiscal and political autonomy, constitutional and electoral rights, compliance with international treaties banning the slave trade (formally prohibited in

1820), and freer press and association. A more autonomous civil society emerged with the innovation of mutual aid associations, part of a growing international mutualist movement. Mutualism facilitated the self-financing of popular groups such as artisans and workers who were now able to pool resources together. The first labor unions among urban tobacco and other manufacturing and service artisans and workers were formed in Cuba on the basis of mutual aid associations. The first successful tobacco workers strike was organized in August 1865 to demand the right of collective bargaining and higher salaries. In March 1866, slaves of the largest sugar plantations in Matanzas refused to work any longer as slaves and demanded payment for their work. This unprecedented slave strike, however, was soon quashed by government troops.

The establishment of secret, previously outlawed Masonic lodges by returning Cuban émigrés was officially tolerated by Spanish authorities. The Cuban-dominated associations of leisure and culture, such as casinos, centers, and circles, harbored a membership stirred by ideas of political reform and autonomy.[12] Worker, Masonic, and cultural associational leadership was closely linked in this period to reformist political, educational, and cultural activities. The reformist newspaper *El Siglo* (Century) (1862–1868), and the pro-worker *Aurora* (1865–1868), rallied increasing public support for the political club (parties were still outlawed) known as the Círculo Reformista. Successful electoral campaigns resulted in the election of leaders like José Antonio Saco to represent Santiago de Cuba in an official colonial policy forum, the Junta de Información (1866–1867) set up in Madrid. Reformist representatives from Cuba and Puerto Rico aspired to use this official assembly on colonial affairs to introduce economic and civil reforms.

Public performances in theaters, cultural associations, and public spaces accentuated Cuban nonviolent demonstrations of solidarity and civic demands. Critical and satirical pieces of Cuban Bufo theater attracted full audiences of Cuban spectators like those who filled Havana's Teatro Villanueva during a tragic night in 1869 when colonialist fanatics fired at the crowd for cheering Cuba's freedom.

In 1862 and 1866, at the funerals first of educator José de la Luz y Caballero and then of cultural and reformist-separatist icon Gaspar Betancourt Cisneros, thousands of citizens gathered in peaceful public processions. These politically charged gatherings symbolized the reality of the past decade—that since the mid-1850s, nonviolent civilian-based organizing and mobilization had advanced the cause of obtaining important civil rights for Cubans as well as a sharp reduction in illicit slave trading into Cuba. A firmly independent civil society had become an important bulwark defying colonial despotism. What came after 1867, however, violently suppressed advances accumulated through open and arduous nonviolent struggle.

War Reversals, 1868–1878

The Spanish government in Madrid turned to the right and closed the Junta de Información in 1867, thus dealing a hard blow to Cuban aspirations of colonial reform. A new captain-general was appointed to undo all reforms advanced during the past few years in Cuba and raise taxes. Reactionary Spaniards and loyalists in Cuba, organized in so-called volunteer militias, worked to eradicate the reformist civilian spaces and associations. However, when in Spain La Gloriosa Revolución deposed Isabel II in 1868, Carlos Manuel de Céspedes—a landowner in eastern Cuba—seized the opportunity to launch an armed insurrection for independence. This led to the Ten Years' War (1868–1878). Brutal warfare in rural areas included the forced relocation of rural populations—later known as the deadly *reconcentración.* Spanish repression of the urban population practically annihilated civil society. Almost all associations with majority Creole membership as well as black societies were forcibly closed or could not withstand political persecution and economic hardship. Thousands of civilians were imprisoned or forced into exile. The war's total death toll among the Cuban population was estimated at 200,000 people, around 14 percent of the total population. Most of the persecuted civilians did not actively support the separatist insurrection. Many of those imprisoned or exiled were nonviolent reformists or ordinary civilians. Internal war supplanted civic engagement and the reformist nonviolent movement dwindled as it got caught in the middle of two violent factions.[13]

The separatist insurrectionary movement in central and eastern Cuba initially emphasized civilian over military leadership, appointing Céspedes head of a separatist government subject to rebel parliamentary control. Soon, however, the military pro-caudillo factions prevailed and deposed Céspedes. The new separatist government pursued diplomatic campaigns through their representatives in New York who unsuccessfully lobbied the US government for recognition. Several waves of Cuban exiles to the United States over the previous decades were joined by 30,000 or more emigrés due to post-1869 political persecution. They formed a militant, though divided, Cuban community in exile. Old annexationist and reformist leaders in exile were opposed by intransigent and radical revolutionaries who rejected any negotiation with the US government or the slightest possibility of a diplomatic settlement with Spain through US mediation or "purchase" of Cuba. Revolutionaries favored instead support to filibustering expeditions and the escalation of military insurrectionary actions into the wealthy western region of Cuba to increase the economic costs of the Spanish war efforts.[14] Despite the costs inflicted on the Spanish government in Cuba, however, the insurrection never managed to succeed militarily or to gain wide support in major urban centers. The protracted, languishing guerrilla fighting prolonged the conflict and led to a massive Spanish counteroffensive that delayed a nonviolent rebuilding of the cultural, political, and civil basis for an independent Cuba.

The wider international and geopolitical context was not favorable for armed insurrection. Despite expansionist and annexationist pressures, the long-term US diplomatic approach preferred a stable Cuba under Spanish reformed rule to war and instability. Despite their abolitionist pressures, British and other European foreign policies also favored Spanish rule over a US takeover. Once Spain abandoned the attempt to reimpose itself militarily in several former colonies, Latin American governments were mostly indifferent to the Cuban separatist cause during the Ten Years' War, lacked geopolitical weight, or mainly worried about a possible US intervention in Cuba.

A negotiated solution to the conflict and reform in Cuba thus gained momentum by 1876. In circumstances of war, nonviolent movements for expanded rights and autonomy had floundered. A few underground, nonviolent actions ended in the harshest of Spanish loyalist repression and reprisal. In 1871, under suspicion of having desecrated the tomb of a colonialist propagandist, eight medical students were summarily tried and executed and thirty-one others imprisoned. Students had previously protested the captain-general's abolition of Havana University's doctoral degree. Many nonviolent reformist leaders had been persecuted, expropriated, exiled, and imprisoned during the first years of the war. Once released from prison or returned from exile, however, these leaders formed movements to try to end the war. To reach a transitional political compromise with both nonviolent and defeated violent factions, the Spanish authorities promised major constitutional and abolitionist reforms that the nonviolent reformist movement of the early 1860s had previously demanded and supported during the war.[15]

Renewed Nonviolent Civic Movements

Slavery was, of course, a central issue. Over time, more slaves came to Cuba than the rest of Spanish America combined. By the mid-nineteenth century, around half of them were working on sugar plantations that supplied a third or more of the world's sugarcane.[16] A powerful lobby supported slavery: Hispano-Cuban slave traders, planters, colonial officials, and colonialist protectionist interests in Spain. The Creole abolitionists, such as José Antonio Saco, generally took a gradualist stance, afraid of the violence that abolition might trigger. The slave trade, illegal since 1820, was finally ended in 1867 shortly after the US decision to abolish slavery, but slavery itself was not abolished until 1886.

During the Ten Years' War, both sides promised to abolish slavery and to free slaves who enlisted militarily in their ranks. At the same time, Spain itself—the last European country to condone slavery—began to change. Spain's Moret Law (1870) freed children born of slaves and slaves over age sixty. In 1873, slavery was completely abolished in Puerto Rico (with compensation to slave owners). When Alfonso XII appointed the reformist Arsenio Martínez Campos as captain-general, Martínez Campos not only signed the Treaty of Zanjón to end the war (and to emancipate those slaves who had fought), but also expanded Cuba's autonomy and civil and political rights, including the right to organize political parties. However, the antislavery law passed in 1880, after Martínez's return to Spain, was based on a concept of Patronato—slaves still had to serve a period of eight years as indentured laborers before they would be free. The Liberal Autonomist Party and the Democratic Party, founded in 1881, campaigned against the Patronato system, as did the Abolitionist Society in Spain. And finally, slavery was abolished by royal decree in 1886.[17] A major nonviolent demonstration in celebration of the end of slavery was held in Havana in January 1887, supported by a wide range of black societies and unions, thus building momentum for further campaigns against racial discrimination and full integration into a freer society.

The major concessions offered by Martínez Campos were achieved fundamentally because of the nonviolent struggles by liberal reformists in previous decades. Those rebels unwilling to sign the Treaty of Zanjón were thoroughly defeated in the Guerra Chiquita (1879–1880). Nonetheless, historians of Cuba generally follow the tradition of exalting patriotic violence and, therefore, argue that such reformist laws were mainly the result of sustained pressure by armed struggle. However, history shows that long- and short-term nonviolent efforts at liberal constitutional solutions to Cuba's colonial oppression from the 1860s throughout the 1880s and 1890s need to be understood as an alternative strategy to armed struggle. These proved to be successful at achieving reformist progress and laying a viable institutional foundation for the future Cuban nation.

After 1879 Cuban subjects enjoyed—although with certain conditions and exceptions—the rights guaranteed by the Spanish Constitution of 1876 and a restricted electoral system. Within that political framework, liberal reformists organized in the Liberal Autonomist Party. Led by middle- and lower-middle-class professionals, and with wide popular support among urban and rural sectors and Creole and black groups, the party pressed for the extension of full rights and political autonomy within the Spanish constitutional monarchy. Despite the opposition and occasional backlash of authorities in Havana and Madrid, the Autonomists struggled persistently for a decentralized autonomous government and parliament similar to that negotiated by the British in Canada.[18] In the political process of the period

(1878–1895) the Autonomists became a massive party, the legal political representative of the Cuban born striving for increased Cuban self-government.

By initiative of the Autonomists and their allies among the business class, several civic movements and lobbies were formed including two—the Junta Magna (1883–1884) and the Movimiento Económico (1890–1892)—that demanded fiscal liberalization and lowering of export taxes during periods of acute economic problems exacerbated by Spanish protectionist measures. These movements united important sectors of the formerly opposed liberal and conservative factions of Cuban producers to achieve national economic goals. Despite an active campaign to advance their demands and intense negotiation with the Spanish authorities, these so-called economic movements failed to maintain a unified front to carry on economic boycott and increase their leverage over government economic policies. The alarmed Spanish military authorities were convinced that such nonviolent movements could bring about Spain's complete loss of Cuba if allowed to grow. Under heightened pressure from the island's government that exploited the divisions among the coalition members of Creole and Spanish origin, several factions withdrew from the movement, effectively ending its activities. However, nonviolent movements for other reforms and rights persisted.

By 1890, there was more space for Cuban civil society than previously and many associations, particularly labor unions and cultural associations, became increasingly racially integrated over the decade. Firmly rooted in this burgeoning civil society, various nonviolent civilian-based movements led by reformists and Autonomists aimed to unify into a larger movement seeking full autonomy. To this end, the now unbanned Masonic lodges, unified in the Grand Lodge of the Island of Cuba, gathered thousands of members in every city. Many Masonic leaders were also Autonomists. Likewise, labor unions continued to multiply and formed leagues encompassing island-wide labor groups with increasing bargaining power and political direction. Unions continued to demand the right to organize, freely associate, and bargain salaries at pressing economic times. Black societies, boosted by the abolition of slavery, organized a Directorio Central de las Sociedades de Color that led important lawsuits and petitions to eradicate segregation and racism. Reformist lawyers, organized through the Liberal Autonomist Party and including members of the Grand Lodge, collaborated both with labor and black societies' leaders and movements to provide legal advice in successfully litigated cases to grant Afro-Cubans access to restricted private and public spaces and to municipal education.[19] These legal victories bolstered constitutional rights and provisions against racial discrimination in the island.

Additional victories by nonviolent movements during the decade include the successful student strike in March 1892, which finally restored doctoral degrees at Havana's university.[20] In another instance, labor unions organized strikes that were successful in achieving higher salaries for workers and more powerful labor organizations and press organs. Civil society organizations and nonviolent movements also increasingly used available political space to spread their message, as when leaders of the Directorio Central voiced its political ideas of independence and separatism peacefully through its main newspapers.

The Liberal Autonomist Party repeatedly demanded electoral reform, especially abolishing property tax qualifications. By the mid-1880s, growing from earlier nonviolent initiatives, the party was Cuba's largest. The Autonomists held mass support in all the provinces and cities and represented Cuban provinces at the Cortes of Spain. However, a conservative-dominated legislature in Madrid increased property tax requirements for voters, thus unduly benefiting higher-income, conservative Spanish candidates in Cuba. This led to a movement of electoral retraction in 1891 aimed at raising political opposition and electoral boycott. This nonviolent tactic, at least temporarily, had a negative impact on the Liberal Autonomist Party, as the recourse to electoral boycott translated into a decline in its popular following.

The nonviolent movements also faced other challenges. One of the structural issues of the nonviolent movements headed by the Autonomists was an unwillingness or inability to amplify the economic and political struggle and turn it into overt, nonviolent conflict with widespread civil disobedience. Despite their increasing popular appeal, Cuban Liberal Autonomists did not amplify their struggle to include more disruptive actions. Mohandas Gandhi (Mahatma) had not yet demonstrated the effectiveness of massive disobedience.[21] Liberal Autonomist Party leaders had learned, however, that popular, civilian-based nonviolent pressure for reform could ultimately lead to full civil liberties for all Cubans. The Spanish constitutional regime would likely have yielded expanded freedoms and autonomy in Cuba if only more pressure had been exercised. However, in a volatile international situation, nonviolent strategies and methods during the struggle for Cuban independence were still evolving and had not reached the necessary organizational level to launch more unified, disciplined, and effective nonviolent actions. General strikes and mass demonstrations in the streets to attain electoral and autonomy goals required an unprecedented scaling up of social mobilization. Also other, more radical, legal groups such as those led by journalist and politician Juan Gualberto Gómez, an active organizer within black and labor societies and the press in Havana, opted to conspire in support of radical violent separatism instead of nonviolent struggle.

The Perils of Violent Insurrection

The 1895 violent insurrection had been prepared for years by a growing number of Cuban exiles. Separatist military leaders collected funds from militant exiled communities in the United States, mainly in Florida. However, the anarchist-inclined Florida tobacco workers then began to question how much current nationalist thinking reflected their socioeconomic vision. This led to Martí's recognition of the need to appeal for social and racial unity in a struggle where national independence would lead to social transformation. Martí therefore formed the Partido Revolucionario Cubano (PRC) in 1892, building on Cuban political clubs in New York, Florida, and Mexico.

Detached from the changing realities of Cuba, pro-independence groups in exile were more excited by revolutionary solutions than the nonviolent reformism. The pro–Cuban independence political groups outside Cuba followed a political stance different from that of the nonviolent reformist struggles in the island. Two or three generations of political exiles and dissatisfied workers had brewed support for a violent, republican, and revolutionary solution to the quest of Cuban independence. Major insurrectionist leaders became idols and heroes in the minds of those exiled communities, often out of touch with changes in Cuba. The level of organization of exiled groups and their support for the insurrectionary path further complicated an already problematic geopolitics around the question of Cuba's independence.

Martí designed the PRC with a highly centralized top leadership. Its policy was complete rejection of negotiation, instead engaging in an all-encompassing nationalistic rhetoric geared to unify Cubans of different social and racial backgrounds behind the goal of a republican Cuba. The means to achieve this ideal was armed struggle, hence making the PRC the heir of the historical uprisings and military caudillos who emerged during the Ten Years' War and the Guerra Chiquita.[22]

Martí was killed in action shortly after the beginning of the insurrection in 1895. In the aftermath, civilian and military circles vied to apply the military lessons learned from previous insurrectionist warfare in Cuba. The militarist generals Máximo Gómez and Maceo took charge and extended destruction by fire and dynamite to the wealthiest western region of Cuba, bringing its sugar output and trade to a temporary but alarming halt. The Spanish brutal counteroffensive was devastating for the mostly innocent general population and, particularly, the now famished and ill rural inhabitants who were forcibly reconcentrated in urban centers to decrease popular support for the insurrectionists.

As with the Ten Years' War, the separatist insurrection was not powerful enough to achieve military victory. The Spanish Army contained and then reversed insurrectionist penetration into the western part of the island. Maceo was killed in action and Gómez lost support. The insurrection had been unable to gain support in cities from independent civil society: autonomous associations were weary of the violent militarist means. However, faced by a standstill, the Spanish government decided to seek a negotiated solution.

This time, a major political transformation to Cuba's colonial status was introduced. An Autonomous government was formed in 1898 led by Cuban Autonomist and nonviolent leaders. This marked the achievement of an important goal of past nonviolent movements: political autonomy. With autonomy, universal male suffrage was also extended to Cuba. The new government took swift measures to restore rights and freedoms and to advance toward the end of the war, reconstruction, and economic recovery. However, this political transition came in the context of civil war and of immense domestic and foreign pressure. Several historians have argued that autonomist change had arrived too late to give the new government an opportunity to consolidate itself and implement its espoused policies.[23] But the Autonomist government's measures proved initially highly effective and nonviolent parties again offered, as in 1879, viable solutions to the thorny political issues of internal war.

Insurrectionist leaders, unable to achieve a clear military victory, were adamantly opposed to any negotiated solution with the new Cuban government. Despite incessant diplomatic efforts in Washington, DC, and Mexico City, separatist leaders could not obtain official recognition of their belligerent status against Spain. Their public campaigns advocating a solution to the Cuban question through a negotiated annexation of the island to Mexico failed when the Mexican government reaffirmed its neutrality. Mexico, like other Latin American countries, expected a US intervention in Cuba and, therefore, withheld outright support to the separatist insurrection as they awaited a decisive US move.

What would have happened in Cuba if the explosion of the US battleship *Maine* in Havana harbor on February 15, 1898, and the ensuing war between the United States and Spain had not occurred? The War of 1898 changed completely Cuba's internal political evolution. US military engagement in Cuba defeated not only Spain, but also the nonviolent alternative to the ongoing civil war in Cuba. The Autonomist government was replaced by a US military government. The insurrectionists themselves felt betrayed and had to disarm under US pressure. Peace was enforced at a high cost in terms of national autonomy and injured patriotic pride. For example, the Cuban Republican Constitution of 1901, drafted by a group of former Autonomist and separatist statesmen, included the foreign-imposed Platt Amendment allowing US intervention in any future danger of instability in Cuba. However, the constitution also guaranteed basic civil rights, including universal male suffrage and the establishment of other national institutions of Cuban self-government.

After the withdrawal of US troops from Cuba in 1902, Cuba became an independent republic. No immediate resistance (violent or nonviolent) to the US presence developed in Cuba as the promises of military and political withdrawal were kept and important groundwork in infrastructure, sanitation, and education was accomplished in 1898–1902. However, the political establishment in Cuba after 1902 was thoroughly divided, unable to reconcile feuding factions under a unified and legitimate authority as well as out of step with a resilient and autonomous civil society. The recourse to violence in Cuban domestic political affairs became ingrained in Cuban politics thereafter and evolved on the basis of a cult of nineteenth-century intransigent, separatist heroes. Reformist nonviolent leaders remained active in opposing postindependence constitutional and political transgressions, but were organizationally and politically sidelined. In the first decades after independence, political parties and groups appeared to be dominated by veteran separatist caudillos.

Conclusion

In the long struggle to reform and end the oppressive and divisive socioeconomic and political system of colonialism in Cuba, a distinct cultural and national identity developed in the island. The foundations of this rising collective consciousness were laid by successive waves of innovative nonviolent organizations and actions seeking recognition of autonomous, self-reliant associations and constitutional equality. Distinctly Cuban cultural associations and publications, and self-financed educational drives and liberal policy projects, bolstered growing civil resistance against old-fashioned colonial education and rigid monopolies and protectionism. The long-standing opposition to the slave trade and slavery through tenacious, nonviolent abolitionist campaigns obtained a belated but complete abolition of slavery. Together with the boost and transformation of preexisting free black and labor associations, nonviolent resistance contributed greatly to the integration of former slaves into the emerging Cuban civil society in search of greater racial equality and expanded democratic rights.

Radical nationalist historical accounts have predictably downplayed the important role of reformist nonviolent efforts to build a Cuban national consensus and generate pressure for change to solve Cuba's colonial issues. Cuba's liberal constitutional traditions and the nonviolent organizing and mobilization that accompanied them represented a rational and calculated stance against overwhelming military oppression and menacing foreign ambitions. The growth of autonomy of civil society was achieved in large part through constitutionalist-reformist, nonviolent struggles for basic civil rights, national education, electoral representation, and demands for further socioeconomic autonomy and political independence from Spain. The promising road toward racial and ethnic equality—a fundamental tenet in defeating colonialism and building a unified and more just Cuban nation—had also been opened through nonviolent campaigns and leadership. These were all irreversible grassroots attainments that formed the foundation of the Cuban postindependence social and political fabric.

What were the lessons and legacies of the nonviolent civilian-based movements and struggles to achieve more democratic autonomy and independence in Cuba? While the strategic nonviolent course was remarkably consistent and fruitful in the long run, nonviolent tactics of defiant conflict, boycott, and civil disobedience did not develop to the level necessary to ultimately supersede the bold radical violent tactics and populist memory of radical revolutionaries. The pro-independence violent alternative developed mostly outside the island and captured the nationalistic narrative of heroism, courageous self-sacrifice, and racial and popular unrest. Violent militaristic separatism soon introduced undemocratic and dictatorial problems and opened the gates for a different kind of foreign intervention.

The gradual, but effective, nonviolent approach to national autonomy produced a stronger postindependence democratic base. Reinforced by evolving twentieth-century nonviolent strategies, the civilian leadership might have enjoyed better conditions within an effective system of checks and balances against undue military influence, violent political militancy, and looming foreign influence. Radical separatism and foreign intervention in 1898 prevented this from fully happening. The legacy of civilian-based nonviolent tradition, however, continued to live on despite end-of-the-century violence and subsequent political setbacks.

Although the Liberal Autonomist Party was dissolved after 1898, other political organizations carried on the struggle for upholding constitutional rights against despotic infringements. Civil society continued to enjoy rights of free association that facilitated the use of public spaces to resist political and governmental intervention. After 1902, civil society in Cuba developed further despite occasional efforts to exert militant or military pressure on its autonomy. The inherent legitimate and nonviolent nature of civil society made it an important bulwark and base for further development of a broad-based, pluralistic democracy. Important civic, nonviolent movements in the twentieth century developed on the basis of civil society and exercised considerable influence in the advancement of socioeconomic improvements and the opposition to dictatorships such as those of former generals Gerardo Machado (1925–1933) and Fulgencio Batista (1952–1958). However, shortly thereafter in 1960–1961, civil society was effectively banned with the imposition of radical revolutionary political imperatives. This drastic curtailment left practically no civilian space for legal dissidence and seemingly insurmountable obstacles for organized, civilian-based nonviolent protest and disobedience. Nonetheless, nonviolent resistance has persisted and its modern forms—such as those developed by the Proyecto Varela constitutional reform movement, and recent struggles for the liberation of political prisoners through hunger strikes and public demonstrations by the Damas de Blanco movement—are heirs of the nonviolent strategies of the nineteenth century and continue the Cuban tradition of civic organizing for reform, rights, and an open society.

Notes

1. Jorge Mañach, *Martí, el apóstol* (Havana: Editorial de Ciencias Sociales, 1990 [1933]); John M. Kirk, *José Martí: Mentor of the Cuban Nation* (Tampa: University Presses of Florida, 1983); Philip S. Foner, *Antonio Maceo: The "Bronze Titan" of the Cuban Struggle for Independence* (New York: Monthly Review Press, 1977).

2. Gómez's correspondence cited in Marta Bizcarrondo and Antonio Elorza, *Cuba/España: El dilema autonomista, 1878–1898* (Madrid: Editorial Colibrí, 2001), 14.

3. The 1841 census recorded a population of 1,007,624, 42 percent white (divided between about 380,000 Cuban born and 38,000 Spanish born), 43 percent slaves, and 15 percent free persons of color. The original indigenous (Indian) population of the island dwindled radically and was absorbed by the white and black population after the Spanish conquest in the sixteenth century.

4. Mildred de la Torre, "Los nuevos autonomistas y la historia oficial" (May 2005), http://www.areitodigital.net/los_nuevos_autonomistas_y_la_his.htm, accessed November 12, 2012. For a more nuanced stance regarding nonviolent organizing and resistance in nineteenth-century Cuba, see María del Carmen Barcia et al., *La turbulencia del reposo: Cuba, 1878–1895* (Havana: Editorial de Ciencias Sociales, 1998), 109–111.

5. Allan J. Kuethe, *Cuba, 1753–1815: Crown, Military, and Society* (Knoxville: University of Tennessee Press, 1986).

6. Initially a spokesperson for the planter elite, Arango contributed to Cuba's dependence on slavery, although later he was to advocate its gradual abolition.

7. Manuel Moreno Fraginals and José Moreno Masó, *Guerra, migración y muerte: El ejército español en Cuba como vía migratoria* (Oviedo: Ediciones Júcar, 1993), 46–48.

8. The 1812 Cadiz Constitution was repealed in 1814, but returned to force in 1820–1823 and again in 1836–1837.

9. In 1837, the Spanish Cortes again voted to exclude colonial deputies to contain Cuban demands.

10. Larry Jensen, *Children of Colonial Despotism: Press, Politics, and Culture in Cuba, 1790–1840* (Tampa: University Presses of Florida, 1988), 17–18, 43–46, 61.

11. Alfonso Quiroz, "La reforma educacional en Cuba, 1898–1909: Cambio y continuidad," in *Culturas encontradas: Cuba y los Estados Unidos,* ed. J. Coatsworth and R. Hernández (Cambridge, MA: Rockefeller Center, Harvard University; Havana: Centro Juan Marinello, 2001), 113–125.

12. Joan Casanovas, *Bread or Bullets! Urban Labor and Spanish Colonialism in Cuba, 1850–1898* (Pittsburgh: Pittsburgh University Press, 1998), 76–77.

13. Alfonso Quiroz, "Loyalist Overkill: The Socioeconomic Costs of 'Repressing' the Separatist Insurrection in Cuba, 1868–1878," *Hispanic American Historical Review* 78, no. 2 (1998): 265–305.

14. Gerald E. Poyo, *"With All, and for the Good of All": The Emergence of Popular Nationalism in the Cuban Communities of the United States, 1848–1898* (Durham, NC: Duke University Press, 1989).

15. Earl R. Beck, "The Martínez Campos Government of 1879: Spain's Last Chance in Cuba," *Hispanic American Historical Review* 56, no. 2 (1976): 268–289.

16. For figures see Christopher Schmidt-Nowara, *Empire and Antislavery: Spain, Cuba, and Puerto Rico, 1833–1874* (Pittsburgh: University of Pittsburgh Press, 1999), 4.

17. Ibid.; Jim Powell, *Greatest Emancipations: How the West Abolished Slavery* (New York: Palgrave Macmillan, 2008).

18. J. C. M. Ogelsby, "The Cuban Autonomist Movement's Perception of Canada, 1865–1898: Its Implications," *The Americas* 48, no. 4 (1992): 445–461.

19. Aline Helg, *Our Rightful Share: The Afro-Cuban Struggle for Equality, 1886–1912* (Chapel Hill: University of North Carolina Press, 1995), 37–38.

20. Renate Simpson, *La educación superior en Cuba bajo el colonialismo español* (Havana: Editorial de Ciencias Sociales, 1984), 283–290. I thank Rafael Tarragó for alerting me about this case and reference.

21. Peter Ackerman and Jack DuVall, *A Force More Powerful: A Century of Nonviolent Conflict* (New York: Palgrave Macmillan, 2000), 65.

22. Antoni Kapcia, "*Lucha* and *Cubanía:* The (Re)Construction of a Cuban Historical Identity Through the Idea of (Revolutionary) Struggle," in *Political Violence and the Construction of National Identity in Latin America,* ed. W. Fowler and P. Lambert (New York: Palgrave Macmillan, 2006), 55–72. Compare to Rafael E. Tarragó, "'Rights Are Taken, Not Pleaded': José Martí and the Cult to the Recourse of Violence in Cuba," in *The Cuban Republic and José Martí: Reception and Use of a National Symbol,* ed. M. Font and A. Quiroz (Lanham, MD: Lexington Books, 2006), 53–70.

23. See, for example, Mildred de la Torre, *El autonomismo en Cuba 1878–1898* (Havana: Editorial de Ciencias Sociales 1997), 199–205.

Part 6

Conclusion

18

Insights into
Nonviolent Liberation Struggles

Maciej J. Bartkowski

> *Revolution reveals in a flash how civil obedience—to laws, to rulers, to institutions—is but the outward manifestation of [people's] support and consent.*
>
> —Hannah Arendt, *On Violence*

Throughout this book, the authors have noted that civil resistance often remains unexamined by researchers and historians because the ordinary people who engage in civil resistance are seen as weak and lacking political power, particularly in relation to oppressive state structures and unfavorable conditions. State power is material and predicated on its monopoly of violence. When the state uses its superior means of violent coercion against unarmed populations, the expected outcome is either subordination or annihilation (genocide or politicide) of any nonmilitary and, thus, powerless party.[1] The prevailing view is that those struggling for independence can face oppression and reduce the asymmetry of force only if they take up arms. Resisting an opponent or occupier violently is seen as the sole option for the downtrodden, short of surrender or inaction.

This default thinking about material power often overlooks the fact that ordinary people have historically been able to strategize and plan effective individual and group actions that turn their perceived weaknesses into strengths. Far from choosing violence as the only or even last available option, self-actuating people can be a contending force precisely because they are capable of identifying and agreeing together to pursue strategically the best available options to seek their goals through nonviolent engagement. This ability to choose unarmed confrontation (political over military) against an oppressive adversary presupposes not desperation but a recognition of opportunities, not martyrdom and physical destruction but a drive for self-preservation, self-organization, institution building, and skills development.

This choice requires that people not be seduced by romanticized violence, the idea that young, able-bodied men must be the prime actors in the struggle (as is so often the case in guerrilla warfare). Rather, people opting for civil resistance understand that coordinated participation and purposeful actions by all civilian resisters—women, men, children, youth, adults, elders, and people from diverse sectors of society—are necessary in order for a movement to wield sufficient power. Once the seemingly powerless are recognized as being capable of initiative, an important cognitive recognition takes place so that people can choose outside of two deep-seated polar opposite choices: violence or passivity. Then, they can mount an alternative means of waging conflict through withdrawal of consent and mass-based nonviolent mobilization.

The fervent nationalist and triumphalist approach to historiography (to borrow from Chapter 5 on Mozambique), together with political factions burnishing historical legacies of their victorious armed struggles (Algeria, Burma, Kosovo) as a way to justify and consolidate their power, and combined with a popular view of people as a disempowered collective, have all led to reductionist thinking about independence struggles and movements that gives more weight to the potential of violence and violent actors than they actually deserve. This view in turn has reinforced the message that force of arms alone creates change, thereby discouraging those who want to challenge the new regime with means other than violence, and that this change can take place only through an elite vanguard and not ordinary people.

Furthermore, by incorporating into the study of popular liberation struggles the analytical lenses of civil resistance, this book goes beyond the Great Man theory of political change—or the idea that charismatic individuals shape history. The study of civil resistance with its focus on the role of shared agency helps contextualize the role of leaders. Most of the analyzed movements were in fact leaderless but, in those cases (e.g., in Hungary, Zambia, Ghana, and Egypt in 1919) where single individuals played an important role, it was also clear that the leaders were responding to people's views that equally empowered and constrained the leaders' actions.

This volume discounts the sole importance of structural or state-centric conditions as determinants of political change and gives weight to the role of conscientious and autonomous agency epitomized by the independent actions of ordinary people. This departure is quite significant given the prevalence of structuralist and process-oriented approaches in the studies of revolutionary changes.[2] The book's historical lens helps discover and show the origin, paths of development, and resilience of civil resistance despite constraining or oppressive conditions and structures that seemingly favored either armed rebellion or general passivity and surrender. As such, the chapters are very much in line with the view that "structural conditions might define the possibilities for revolutionary insurrections . . . but they do not explain how specific groups or individuals act, what options they pursue (and how), or what possibilities they may realize."[3] In fact, many chapters demonstrate how common people, far from being resigned and passive in the face of seemingly insurmountable obstacles, resorted to a variety of forms of nonviolent individual and collective resistance. By doing so, they not only influenced trajectories of important socioeconomic and political changes, but in essence made them happen.

Armed Resistance Cloaked in the Archetype of Masculinity

Changing entrenched views about the effectiveness of armed resistance is particularly hard as they are usually rooted in a warrior psychology that is shaped by violent masculinity and patriarchy. Struggles for independence typically have privileged male leadership. As a consequence, conspiracies of belligerent men plotting in small, secretive circles in an atmosphere that congratulates violent bravery and rewards machismo, leave little room for recognizing the importance of nonviolent alternatives or the contributions of women or non-fighting-age young men to the struggle. In fact, the discourse of hegemonic victors tends to conform to a masculinist construct that, as Jean Bethke Elshtain maintains, from antiquity through to the present has divided society into "just warriors" (male fighters and protectors) and "beautiful souls" (female victims and noncombatants).[4] The circle of just warriors is also limited as it would normally exclude men who wanted to play other roles (i.e., gays) or their virility did not conform to the prevailing warrior archetype. Furthermore, teaching history, including the rise of nations, formation of state institutions, conduct of state politics, and development and implementation of public policies, shapes a nation's commemorative landscape and punctuates it with stories of military battles, patriotic risings, wars, and violent defeats—all dominated by men, be they soldiers, scholars, politicians, or other elite actors. This has inhibited people from remembering, acknowledging, and understanding the presence and efficacy of civil resistance, including the central place of women at the forefront of nonviolent actions during nationalist struggles—a role that is highlighted in most of the chapters in this book. Here, we see women engaged in writing and distributing petitions; organizing and leading demonstrations and protests; setting up and running autonomous associations and educational institutions; and supporting and participating in social and economic boycotts, strikes, and sit-ins.

Masculinity and Civil Resistance

While armed struggle and violent masculinity are almost symbiotically joined in the historical imagination, the question of systemic male domination in civil resistance is more complex and ambiguous. Foreign occupation and colonization has frequently been based on economic exploitation and has often involved cultural genocide or extreme forms of coercion such as slavery, forced migration, resettlement, and conscription. Often a systematic part of foreign domination has been sexual exploitation of women and (as mentioned in Chapter 7 on Egypt) humiliation of indigenous men.[5] In conditions where a foreign colonizer's racist stereotypes affected both a symbolic and real emasculation, the oppressed population—particularly its men—often saw "regaining manhood" as a basic element of independence equivalent to self-respect or dignity. Becoming men is thus a common theme to be found in both armed and nonviolent anticolonial struggles, as indeed in other struggles against other kinds of oppression.[6]

A further common feature in many independence movements and not only in armed struggles is that after liberation women activists retreat—either voluntarily or under social pressure—to the private sphere and men resume their traditional dominance in public life. Women have been at the forefront of grassroots organizing, movement building, and waging nonviolent struggles for independence, and not only when male activists were in prison or exile. However, revolutionary struggles for statehood, with perceived high stakes for power in newly emerging nations, defined resistance in existential terms and forced women to subordinate their gender-specific demands to overriding national priorities such as state building, territorial integrity, and defense of the ethnonational community. Little if any room was left to consider the lingering problems of discrimination of women and their unequal representation or to acknowledge the historical role of women in the civic part of the struggle. For example, in Poland, the role of women as social activists, teachers, organizers, and writers during the resistance was rarely extended beyond that of a silent, supporting cast whose nonviolent activism was first and foremost needed for national liberation rather than gender emancipation. In Kosovo, women were at the heart of the opening phase of the nonviolent struggle and feminist questioning of patriarchal traditions broadened the vision of change. This, however, was eventually subordinated to more militant nationalist and militaristic themes.

Finally, it has to be acknowledged that on the theme of gender, Étienne de la Boétie, Henry David Thoreau, Leo Tolstoy, and the pioneering nonviolent action researcher Gene Sharp, all of whom have shaped the conceptual framework of nonviolent resistance, have also been men of their time who replaced the heroism of male physicality with the heroism of the wise counselor or strategist who was usually assumed to be a man. Mohandas Gandhi (Mahatma)—while campaigning for the uplift of women (expanding their rights) and stressing the importance of their contribution to the struggle—has been criticized not only for his own behavior that depended on a supportive, obedient wife, but also his exaltation of self-sacrifice seen as part of a manly conduct. The predominantly masculinist views and writings of the forebears of strategic nonviolent resistance are now seen as having suppressed alternative discourses, including the recognition of women's agency.[7]

Transnational Dimensions of Nonviolent Struggles

The extent to which foreign occupiers depend on domestic consent of the occupied population varies (e.g., the British in the American colonies or Burma relied more on the indigenous authorities and population than is the case for the Indonesian government in West Papua).

However, in general, struggles for independence and self-rule waged against unduly foreign influence, domination, or occupation are often hard to win because the foreign hegemon or occupier usually draws substantial resources and support from its own capital and society. Therefore, these foreign masters may not necessarily depend in full on the ongoing cooperation and obedience of the subjugated population, often ruled by a small, domestic political elite submissive to the wishes of those masters (e.g., Chapter 8 on Iran).

Furthermore, in contrast to domestic antiauthoritarian movements, struggles for independence and self-rule do not usually threaten to sweep the occupier's ruling class out of power or put their lives directly in danger since the challengers are either militarily weaker, geographically distant, or both. Much less pronounced in the situation of the domestic authoritarian regimes that face internal revolt, a considerable social distance between occupier and occupied population not only makes physical or political elimination of the occupying foreign elites rather unlikely, but it plays a large role in ensuring that the loyalty of the foreign troops—the main force that carries out repressive orders—remains with their home country or government. Because it is not very probable that the indigenous population will be able to shift the allegiance of occupying troops, foreign rulers can maintain their readiness and capability to use extreme brutality in case their control seems to be in jeopardy.

This is not to say that the populations of occupied societies cannot exercise any direct leverage over the occupiers, particularly if the occupier's goals are to introduce settlements (as in Palestine); integrate or assimilate the local population with the culture, society, territory, or polity of the colonizers (as in Algeria and Poland); profit from extraction of resources or water pathways (as in West Papua and Egypt); or enlist the colonized population in cheap labor and use its local market for profitable manufacturing and trade (as in Britain's American colonies). In such circumstances, the occupiers rely on at least some degree of cooperation or acquiescence from parts of the controlled society in order to maintain a semblance of stability and ensure that transportation and communication routes remain open, that trade in goods and money is unimpeded, and that colonial structures are not jeopardized by the indigenous population. Generally, however, the wide distance between a foreign government and a subjugated population limits the latter's influence over the occupier and makes it necessary for the population to create external leverage by taking its cause to an international audience and to the society of the occupying forces. In doing so, a nonviolent posture is more likely to attract potential allies abroad and gain the support of groups within the occupier's society while a violent response is more likely to dismay international state and nonstate actors and solidify the support of the occupier's society for repressive tactics against the occupied population.

External actors do not always have a substantial impact on nonviolent movements[8] and successful civil resistance relies on the decisive agency of local people, not foreign forces. But the cases of the United States, Zambia, Mozambique, Poland, West Papua, Algeria, Egypt, and Palestine, among others, show that in some circumstances there are clear benefits to enlisting international sympathy, winning over external allies or, at least, neutralizing traditional supporters of the adversaries. In all of these cases, civil resisters were cognizant of the importance of cultivating international support to further their cause.

With regard to the question of how such support is cultivated, Gene Sharp suggests that appealing vaguely to "world opinion" is not enough since "a determined opponent can ignore hostile opinion."[9] What an outside third party is unlikely to disregard, however, is when the civil resisters are effective in disrupting the opponent's existing power relations, and increasing the costs of maintaining control that, in turn, often leads to a disproportionate use of violent force by the agents of the regime—the actions that are likely to backfire on domestic and international levels. Sharp explains the linkage between grassroots actions and external help in the following words:

> It is in the nature of the nonviolent technique that the main brunt of the struggle must be borne not by third parties but by the grievance group immediately affected by an opponent's policies. For third-party opinion and actions to be most effective . . . they must . . . play the auxiliary role of backing up the main struggle. . . . Overconfidence in the potential of aid

from others may distract resistance efforts from their own most important tasks. In fact, third-party support is more likely to be forthcoming when nonviolent struggle by the grievance group is being waged effectively.[10]

Thus, the strategy for undermining the immediate control of the adversary is central to successful civil resistance, as various episodes in this book describe. This is seen as far back as the eighteenth century, when the American campaigns of nonconsumption, nonimportation, and nonexportation convinced the British mercantile establishment to pressure their own government to reduce colonial taxation. Another element of successful civil resistance—highlighted in the work of Sayyed Jamal al-Din Asadabadi (el-Afghani) in nineteenth-century Iran and through various figures in the twentieth-century pan-African movement—is the development of strategic skills, training of activists, and establishment of publications in places abroad that are out of the reach of domestic forces of repression. In addition, diaspora communities have often played an important role in giving voice to a domestic movement, as with Poland in the nineteenth century, or in raising funds among Kosovo Albanians to support their movement for independence. The Cuban example cautions that a diaspora can give impetus to armed resistance instead of nonviolent actions.

Johan Galtung refers to the strategy of reaching out to potential third-party allies as "the great chain of nonviolence" that, by extending nonviolent resistance beyond the domestic battlefield, reduces the social distance between the occupied and the occupier's society.[11] This in turn increases the chances to influence the domestic base of the occupying regime. The strategy involves looking for potential links in the chain, with the idea that they will lead to further links with other external groups that can become potential allies of the nonviolent movement. Some opportunities for making these links might seem obvious, for instance, when students from colonies studied at universities of colonial powers—in Britain, France, Portugal, and Indonesia—and connected with opinion leaders of the colonial societies through fellow students and local citizens. Other instances—such as the transformation of missionaries from agents of cultural imperialism to critics of foreign domination and advocates for the rights of the subjugated—suggest new potential alliances across borders and among foreign and local groups and institutions within the colonized or occupied country. The effect of such alliances and solidarity might not be immediately decisive to the outcome of the struggle, but questioning within the dominant society—for example, by some policymakers, intellectuals, business elites, or functionaries that are asked to carry out repressive orders—can have a cumulative impact by eroding belief in the legitimacy of foreign domination or the will to pay the price of maintaining it.

Over time, the scope for transnational action can expand, as other examples in this book indicate. One such form of expanded activities is transnational support for domestic nonviolent movements through international nonviolent interventions, as was done with the World Peace Brigade in Zambia—the organization established in 1961 to furnish small teams of peace activists to intervene nonviolently in conflicts. Another form is seen in the Bangladesh freedom struggle, which featured considerable diaspora mobilization for lobbying and funds as well as a nonviolent contestation of the West Pakistani blockade. Known as Operation Omega, this unarmed confrontation involved an international group of activists trying to deliver humanitarian aid to Bangladesh. Additionally, the first pop solidarity mega-concert organized by George Harrison and Ravi Shankar in 1971 was attended by 40,000 people, but reached many more through the movie and best-selling album that helped raise international awareness about the plight of Bangladeshi refugees and collect funds.[12]

In many ways, these actions were forerunners to contemporary "chains" of transnational solidarity to support the Palestinians such as the international boycott of products from Israeli settlements and the Freedom Flotillas to challenge Israel's blockade of Gaza.[13] Through the conscious use of nonviolent actions, Palestinians and their allies, which included some Israelis, have mounted these solidarity campaigns. Activists from other countries and from Israel have also joined Palestinians in repeated protests against the Segregation Wall in the West Bank.

Diffusion of the Civil Resistance Know-How

There has been a noticeable spread of civil resistance over recent decades, even in the struggles ravaged by the most acute conflicts: for example, against dictatorship, occupation, or for self-determination—from eight instances that are known to have taken place between 1899 and 1950, to sixty-five between 1951 and 2000, and already to fifty within the first and second decade of the twenty-first century (including the 2011 nonviolent insurrections of the Arab Spring).[14] This trend, among others, has been facilitated by the increasing success rate that civil resistance movements have had in achieving their objectives.[15]

With each victory—and failure—popular resisters learn from experiences of their own as well as those of others while international institutions, scholars, and trainers have transnationalized the knowledge of strategic nonviolent conflict through publications, workshops, and other educational initiatives. The role and impact of these international actors is important, though it bears mention that it has always been the inventiveness and resourcefulness of the population itself that has driven civil resistance.[16]

Dissemination of the knowledge of nonviolent resistance, combined with its skillful application to indigenous conditions, has been historically notable as a factor in the proliferation of civil resistance movements and subsequent academic studies and research. Gandhi learned, among others, from the Hungarian civil resistance of the 1850s–1860s and the Russian Revolution of 1905.[17] Also the Hungarian nonviolent struggle was an inspiration for Arthur Griffith, the leader of the Irish nationalist movement Sinn Féin, and the Finnish constitutionalists who resisted czarist Russia. The Russian revolution of 1905 created ripple effects of largely nonviolent popular uprisings in Russia's near and far abroad. As described in Chapter 8, at the end of 1905, unarmed Iranians took to the streets and built citizens' committees to press for constitutional changes, including a democratically elected parliament. At the same time, as highlighted in Chapter 14, the Russian part of partitioned Poland, awakened by the events in Russia proper, was soon engulfed in waves of workers' and school strikes, demonstrations, and citizens' antiregime activities that came with rising demands for social, political, and national rights, including the use of the Polish language in schools and public offices.

The process of transnationalization of civil resistance practice and knowledge has continued during decolonization struggles in Africa where, among others, Ghanaian and Zambian leaders—see Chapters 3 and 4, respectively—read Gandhi's work and drew lessons from the Indian resistance against the British, including Gandhi's idea to devise and lead their own independence campaigns. Decades later, sharing civil resistance experience across borders has been especially visible, first with the so-called color revolutions (Serbia, 2000; Georgia, 2003; Ukraine, 2004) and later with the Arab Spring. The transnational diffusion of civil resistance has also included specific methods adopted from the tactical repertoire of past victorious nonviolent struggles in other, more contemporary, conflicts with the goal of emulating earlier successes. In November 2011, for example, the Palestinian freedom riders, without required permits, boarded an Israeli public bus headed to Jerusalem and were subsequently arrested before being able to reach the city.[18] By establishing a transnational and timeless linkage between their struggle and the famous freedom riders' campaigns of the US civil rights movement against segregated buses, Palestinians sought to dramatize the discriminatory policies they face on a daily basis. Through the adoption of what are now considered legendary tactics from another historical struggle, Palestinians attempted to appeal to the conscience of the American public and strike an emotional chord with potential supporters in the United States, Israel, and other countries.

Tactical Dynamics of Civil Resistance

As a means of waging struggle, one of the strengths of civil resistance is that it sets a low threshold for individual and collective participation and, thus, offers opportunities for many groups to join. These people and groups would have been unlikely to enlist en masse in armed struggle, much less lead it. Therefore, nonviolent nationalist movements allowed thousands of children, elders, and women, many of whom would have had at most marginal involvement in an armed struggle, to be at the vanguard of nonviolent defiance (see Chapters 3, 4, 6, 7, 11, 14, and 16 on Ghana, Zambia, Algeria, Egypt, Bangladesh, Poland, and the United States).

Furthermore, regimes often see their repression of civil resistance backfiring on them. This can bend the willingness or capacity of the authorities to carry out repressive policies, which in turn paves the way for concessions. In Poland, the Russian authorities' initial repression against school strikers in 1905 only increased resistance and social protests, forcing the czarist government to concede the right to Polish-language education. In Egypt in 1919, the British deported the main nationalist leaders and tried to crush their supporters. But by 1920–1921, faced with a growing popular resistance, the British offered political dialogue. Backlash against violent government actions has often been magnified by word-of-mouth about committed atrocities (Bangladesh), by communication tools such as telegraph and newspapers (Iran, Egypt, Poland), or by the Internet and social media (West Papua, Palestine). All of these have been used to increase both domestic mobilization and international sympathy for the liberation cause.

The empirical studies described in this book provide a plethora of information on the methods of civil resistance. The volume relies in part on Gene Sharp's categories of nonviolent actions (see Table 18.1)—protest and persuasion; social, political, and economic noncooperation; and disruptive and creative nonviolent interventions—to study the extent to which nonviolent resistance and its strategic dimension were present in nationalist struggles.

Instances of civil resistance in the empirical studies were classified according to the categories shown in Table 18.1 in order to develop conflict summary tables that are included in the Appendix. These tables in the Appendix list a wide range of nonviolent methods used by a given movement and provide information about the participation, length, and direct or immediate impact of individual tactics as well as the long-term, cumulative influence of a set of tactics (referred to in the tables as a "campaign"). This information is intended to offer a quick tactical snapshot of each struggle, show the relationship between campaigns and tactics, and provide a framework for a systematic analysis of tactical impact. This can help readers to better analyze and understand the trajectory of a struggle, where nonviolent methods used in one place and time influence the evolving situational context that iteratively sets the stage for the subsequent development of the struggle. The Appendix also offers a useful reference for discussing tactical innovation and the sequencing of methods that can prove essential for a movement to maintain its momentum.[19] Finally, the Appendix illustrates the degree to which this volume supplements (through the descriptions of

Table 18.1 Methods of Nonviolent Action

	Noncooperation			Nonviolent Intervention	
Protest and Persuasion	Social	Political	Economic	Disruptive	Creative
Symbolic acts of expression of grievances toward a status quo or in support of desired change.	Acts of limiting or refusal of engagement in typical performance of duties, obedience to and following of established sociocultural conventions and practices.	Acts of suspending or refusing to carry on usual forms of political and civic participation.	Acts of suspending or refusing to carry on economic relationships as expected.	Acts designed to directly interject into a normalcy of a given state of affairs by disrupting or preventing established patterns of behavior, institutions, policies, and relationships.	Acts designed to interject into a normalcy of a given state of affairs by embarking on resource- or relationship-creating activities that generate new patterns of behavior, institutions, policies, or practices.

Source: Based on Gene Sharp, *The Politics of Nonviolent Action*, part 2: *The Methods of Nonviolent Action* (Boston: Porter Sargent, 1973).

immediate and long-term outcomes of nonviolent methods and campaigns) and enriches (through the emphasis on indirect, more subtle forms of resistance) Sharp's list of 198 methods of nonviolent action.[20]

The empirical cases included in this volume fortify and expand Sharp's taxonomy of unarmed methods of struggle in a strongly heuristic manner. The development of knowledge about nonviolent methods has in fact been driven by people's creativity and their push to develop and master effective operations—often through trial and error—to overcome specific injustices. This epistemology of tactical dynamism of civil resistance in liberation struggles is partly being developed inductively—through case studies presented in this book—and is then reflected in the conflict summaries in the Appendix, and through quantitative research that identifies crucial movement-centric variables—nonviolent discipline, self-sustaining collective organizing, coalition building, unity, and resilience, among others—in order to explain the trajectories of nonviolent resistance as well as to lead to greater understanding of the immediate and possible long-term outcomes of civil resistance struggles.

The Enduring Impact of Civil Resistance

Though more research is required, civil resistance can create and leave behind a legacy of defiance in the form of sociocultural practices, political tradition, generational stories, and individual or collective memories that a population may unconsciously and instinctively draw from during future crises. This attests to the continued importance and relevance that civil resistance may have in other, yet to come, pivotal moments of a nation's quest for freedom. It therefore is not a coincidence that Poles who lived under the communist oppression during the twentieth century looked to their nineteenth-century progenitors of nonviolent actions to develop their own effective, but also surprisingly similar, repertoires of nonviolent methods of resistance. Likewise, Burmese and Algerians at the end of the 1980s and during the 2000s, and Egyptians in 2011, have deployed an arsenal of nonviolent strategies and tactics startlingly reminiscent of the resistance activities that their predecessors relied on during their nationalist struggles decades ago.

A careful analysis of nonviolent tactics, particularly those categorized as nonviolent creative intervention that involve parallel institution building, can offer useful insights into the longer-term impact of civil resistance on political change. As some chapters indicated, the tactics that developed civic, cultural, and political organizations and institutions during quieter resistance phases—if not undermined or destroyed by an armed conflict—might have helped with state building and generated a more tranquil post-independence political order.

While stopping short of making the general claim that civil resistance leads to more peaceful societies in the postconflict period, a number of cases in this book do point to the practice of nonviolent contestation as creating a more propitious and peaceful environment for state formation. In these examples, civil resistance contributed or led to the emergence of a more inclusive, participatory, and less violent postindependence political and constitutional order than likely would have been the case had violent resistance been used. This argument suggests that civil resistance can be "an incubator of democracy."[21] Recent quantitative findings reinforce this view by showing that political transitions brought about through bottom-up, nonviolent mobilization have better prospects for leading to the establishment of freer societies and more durable democracies than do transitions that come about through armed struggle, international military intervention, or change of power among powerholders.[22] This is because armed struggle usually requires martial values as well as hierarchical, secretive, and elitist leadership combined with skills in destroying, maiming, or killing an adversary. Victorious rebel leaders tend to bring all of these virtues and modi operandi into the new regime. At the same time, nonviolent movements generally require building broad coalitions across various segments of society and mastering skills of negotiation, rational deliberation, compromise, and moderation—the features that are propitious for and constitute an important harbinger of a democratic governance.

Consequently, not only does civil resistance provide a population with the means to wage a struggle or lay the foundation for the emergence of nascent state institutions, it also summons and engenders a psychologically constructive power that can create, shape, and strengthen a population's national identity to guard its cultural or societal fabric against foreign domination, assimilation, or annihilation.

Civil Resistance Studies as an Emerging Academic Discipline

Perhaps to a greater degree than in other social science disciplines, scholarship on civil resistance is an applied form of study that is necessarily derived from real events. In fact, civil resistance is gaining further credibility as a field of serious academic analysis because of spectacular outcomes exemplified by those regarded as powerless who are effectively challenging ostensibly invincible rulers, most recently in the Arab world. Even though there is yet no formally established academic discipline of civil resistance studies or advanced degrees offered in this subject, civil resistance as an organized interdisciplinary field of scholarship and research has been advancing since the 1950s. And a number of doctoral dissertations about strategic nonviolent conflict and nonviolent campaigns and movements have been written at leading universities in recent decades.

A self-standing graduate specialization in civil resistance and the first endowed chair "in the study of nonviolent direct action and civil resistance" have been established.[23] These reflect an important, though still limited, shift in academia to provide more permanent, structured, and multidisciplinary frameworks and repositories for specialized knowledge on civil resistance, including an institutional home for a growing number of academic courses solely focused on strategic nonviolent conflict.

Since knowledge about nonviolent strategies is constantly tested and validated by the testimony of practitioners and by ongoing events, it ensures that civil resistance research—its hypotheses, findings, and recommendations directed to various audiences of academics, present and future action takers, journalists, policy experts, nongovernmental organization professionals—stays relevant and adequately explanatory. Because of the remarkable outcomes achieved by civil resistance (the shifting of power structures that governments and regional experts had tended to treat as permanent), there has been an accelerating interest on the part of universities, research centers, governments, democracy-promotion organizations, and international institutions in the means of civil resistance and the possibilities that it offers.

All above, this portends that civil resistance is on the cusp of becoming a self-standing scholarly discipline equivalent in importance to peace, conflict resolution, or security studies, which a few decades ago had no serious institutional presence in academia. Current events repeatedly indict past neglect of nonviolent struggle by larger political and social disciplines and call out for further research. This volume—by highlighting historical episodes where the role of civil resistance has been eclipsed—both serves as another contribution to the expanding analytical and empirical landscape on the subject and underlines the need for a stronger presence of this growing field in the academic institutions and beyond.

Notes

1. Charles Tilly, *The Politics of Collective Violence* (New York: Cambridge University Press, 2003), 57, 104.

2. See Alex de Tocqueville, *The Old Regime and the French Revolution* (New York: Doubleday Anchor Books, 1983); Jeff Goodwin, *No Other Way Out: States and Revolutionary Movements, 1945–1991* (Cambridge: Cambridge University Press, 2001); Patrick Van Inwegen, *Understanding Revolution* (London: Lynne Rienner, 2011); Jack A. Goldstone, *Revolutions: Theoretical, Comparative, and Historical Studies* (Belmont, CA: Wadsworth, 2008); Eric Selbin, *Revolution, Rebellion, Resistance: The Power of Story* (London: Zed Books, 2010); Fred Halliday, *Revolution and World Politics: The Rise and Fall of the Sixth Great Power* (Durham: Duke University Press, 1999).

3. Eric Selbin, "Agency and Culture in Revolutions," in *Revolutions: Theoretical, Comparative, and Historical Studies,* ed. Jack A. Goldstone (Belmont CA: Wadsworth, 2008), 78–79.

4. Roland Bleiker, *Popular Dissent, Human Agency and Global Politics* (Cambridge: Cambridge University Press, 2000), 151.

5. R. W. Connell, "Globalization, Imperialism, and Masculinities" in *Handbook of Studies on Men and Masculinities,* ed. Michael S. Kimmel, Jeff Hearns, and R. W. Connell (Thousand Oaks, CA: Sage, 2005), 73.

6. I thank Howard Clark for the suggestion and clarification regarding this point.

7. For a feminist critique of nonviolent practitioners and scholars, see, among others, Bleiker, *Popular Dissent,* 151–154; Feminism and Nonviolence Study Group, *Piecing It Together: Feminism and Nonviolence* (London: Feminism and Nonviolence Study Group; War Resisters' International, 1983), www.wri-irg.org/pubs/Feminism_and_Nonviolence; Kate McGuinness, "Gene Sharp's Theory of Power: A Feminist Critique of Consent," *Journal of Peace Research* 30, no. 1 (1993): 101–115; Thomas Weber, "Gandhian Nonviolence and Its Critics," *Gandhi Marg* 28, no. 3 (2006): 269–283; Pam McAllister, ed., *Reweaving the Web of Life: Feminism and Nonviolence* (Philadelphia: New Society, 1982).

8. For example, Erica Chenoweth and Maria Stephan, "Why Civil Resistance Works: The Strategic Logic of Nonviolent Conflict," *International Security* 33, no. 1 (Summer 2008): 7–44; Erica Chenoweth and Maria Stephan, *How Civil Resistance Works* (New York: Columbia University Press, 2011); and Sharon Erickson Nepstad, *Nonviolent Revolutions: Civil Resistance in the Late 20th Century* (Oxford: Oxford University Press, 2011).

9. Gene Sharp, *The Politics of Nonviolent Action,* part three: *The Dynamics of Nonviolent Action* (Boston: Porter Sargent, 1973), 662.

10. Ibid., 662–663.

11. Johan Galtung, *Nonviolence and Israel/Palestine* (Honolulu: University of Hawaii Institute for Peace, 1989).

12. See Chapter 9 on Palestine and Paul Hare and Herb Blumberg, eds., *Liberation Without Violence: A Third-Party Approach* (London: Rex Collings, 1977).

13. See more about the international nonviolent mobilization against Pakistan and its actions in East Pakistan in Richard K. Taylor, *Blockade: A Guide to Nonviolent Intervention* (Maryknoll, NY: Orbis Books, 1977).

14. See the NAVCO 1.0 dataset that includes nonviolent resistance campaigns from 1899 to 2006, http://echenoweth.faculty.wesleyan.edu/research-and-data; and the Global Nonviolent Action Database for more contemporary civil resistance struggles, http://nvdatabase.swarthmore.edu/.

15. Chenoweth and Stephan, *How Civil Resistance Works,* 7–9.

16. Gene Sharp, who heads the Albert Einstein Institute and has been rediscovered by the mainstream media transfixed by the 2011 Arab Spring, is careful not to overestimate the role of third parties, including his own, in nonviolent insurrections. For example, during an interview about the 2011 revolution in Egypt, Sharp was explicit about who in his view was really driving the January 25 nonviolent rising: "The people of Egypt did that—not me," he said. See "Times Topics: Gene Sharp," *New York Times,* February 17, 2011, http://topics.nytimes.com/top/reference/times topics/people/s/gene_sharp/index.html, accessed February 17, 2011.

17. Mary E. King, *A Quiet Revolution: The First Palestinian Intifada and Nonviolent Resistance* (New York: Nation Books, 2007), 22–23.

18. Jillian Kestler-D'Amours, "Israel Arrests 'Freedom Riders' Challenging Apartheid Road System," *The Electronic Intifada,* Jerusalem, November 15, 2011,

http://electronicintifada.net/content/israel-arrests-freedom-riders-challenging
-apartheid-road-system/10595#.TsU_gz0r27t, accessed November 16, 2011.

19. I thank Hardy Merriman for his insights on the summary tables, Suravi Bhandary for her incredibly meticulous work on creating the draft tables, and Consuelo Amat for additional table reviews.

20. See Sharp, *The Politics of Nonviolent Action*. A compact version of Sharp's 198 methods is available online at www.aeinstein.org/organizations103a.html, accessed June 10, 2011.

21. Peter Ackerman and Jack DuVall, *A Force More Powerful: A Century of Nonviolent Conflict* (New York: Palgrave Macmillan, 2000). According to Jack DuVall various "emerging properties" of civil resistance—including popular representation, collective voluntary consent, moderation, and the use of reason—help nonviolent movements practice democracy under repression before such democracies "are formally open for business." Jack DuVall, discussions at the International Center on Nonviolent Conflict, August 25–26, 2011.

22. Peter Ackerman and Adrian Karatnicky, eds., *How Freedom Is Won: From Civic Mobilization to Durable Democracy* (Washington, DC: Freedom House, 2005); Chenoweth and Stephan, *How Civil Resistance Works*. The latter study shows, for example, that the states that experienced nonviolent campaigns are ten times more likely to have stable and peaceful order five years after the end of the conflict than are the countries with a history of violent insurrections. And, the likelihood that the country will relapse to civil war within ten years after the end of the conflict is almost two times lower for nonviolent resistance than it is for violent struggle. See Chenoweth and Stephan, *How Civil Resistance Works,* particularly 60 and 201–219.

23. A graduate program on civil resistance is currently being offered at Rutgers University, www.ncas.rutgers.edu/program-civil-resistance; and the endowed chair on the study of nonviolent direct actions and civil resistance has been set up at the University of Massachusetts.

Appendix:
Conflict Summaries

This appendix has been compiled by the book's editor, Maciej Bartkowski, based on the information presented in the corresponding chapters of the book. Cases are arranged alphabetically. (Any omissions in the tables are either of the editor's own making or the information was not available.)

Key

Method and Type of Nonviolent Action
Nonviolent intervention
    Disruptive
    Creative
Noncooperation
    Political
    Economic
    Social
Protest and persuasion

Length of the Campaign
Short: 1 day up to 4 weeks
Medium: 1 month up to 1 year
Long: More than 1 year

Level of Participation of People
Low: 1–100 people or less than 20 percent of the population
Medium: 100–1,000 people or between 20 percent and 50 percent of
    the population
High: More than 1,000 people or more than 50 percent of the population

Algeria

Main Campaigns	Action	Method/*Type*	Date	Length
	Mass emigration	Noncooperation/ *Social*	1830 onward	Long
	Women rejected French settlements and refused to stay in these new places	Noncooperation/ *Social*		
Rejection and boycotts	Local population refused to adopt medical services provided by the French Army	Noncooperation/ *Social*		
	Boycott of French schools	Noncooperation/ *Social*		
Withdrawal	Internal *hijra*, a personal withdrawal to protect a private space (family, home, religious or spiritual life)	Noncooperation		
Young Algerians movement	Setting up and printing various periodicals and newspapers that demanded full citizenship rights	Nonviolent intervention/ *Creative*; Protest and persuasion	end of 19th century to 1920s	
	Opening cultural and fraternal clubs, including literature, music, geography, and sports associations	Nonviolent intervention/ *Creative*		
	Political rallies were organized	Protest and persuasion		
Ulama movement	Building a nationwide network of schools and associations to promote Arabic language and reinvigorate collective identity through the return to a salafi form of Islam	Nonviolent intervention/ *Creative*	1930s	Long
	Setting up and workings of cultural and children's associations	Nonviolent intervention/ *Creative*	1930s	
	Theater performances, music, and religious celebrations	Protest and persuasion	1930s	
	Establishing political parties and their affiliated newspapers	Nonviolent intervention/ *Creative*	second half of 1940s to 1962	Long
	Holding party rallies and conferences, leading inscription campaigns, distributing leaflets	Protest and persuasion		Long

Level of Participation	Direct Impact	Long-Term/Overall Impact of Civil Resistance
High	Emigration threatened French-imposed security in Algeria as hostile Algerian populations concentrated on the Moroccan and Tunisian borders	
	Exodus of local tribes contributed to the breakdown of public order in Algeria such that the French had to address and expend resources	
	Because of emigration, loss of the labor force for the emerging French economy in Algeria was critical	
	Some schools had to close because of lack of pupils	
Medium	Women's practices such as their behavior, clothing, and role in the family became symbols of cultural resistance to European domination	
	Demands of full French citizenship rights were met with restrictive policies	Young Algerians movement laid foundations for the emergence of political organizations
		Cultural associations became a tool to involve the population in forming and consolidating their collective identities and practices separate from the French
High	Arabic language and history were popularized	Developed a culture of nationalism and what it meant to be Algerian
	Algerianness and popularized nationalist discourse were reinforced	
	A new form of cultural resistance was promoted: nationalist figures and historic dates commemorated; Arab and Islamic history popularized	
	Algerian flags were invented and displayed	
	Patriotic songs and plays were performed	
	Inscription "Algérie libre" (free Algeria) written visibly on the cities' walls	
	Police surveillance and repression, censorship of newspapers	

(continues)

Algeria (Cont.)

Main Campaigns	Action	Method/*Type*	Date	Length
	Making security arrangements and deploying them to protect party meetings, preventing police informants from entering, checking membership cards, blocking the doors, warning party members of police presence	Nonviolent intervention/ *Creative*	1940–1962	Long
	Algerian workers joined the campaign to stop shipment of weapons to Indochina	Noncooperation/ *Economic*	first half of 1950	Long
	General strike and stay-ins at home combined with a day of mourning in solidarity with Tunisians killed by the French	Noncooperation/ *Social, Economic*; Protest and persuasion	April 25, 1952	Short
	Permanent student strike	Noncooperation/ *Social*	May 1956	
	Eight-day strike	Noncooperation/ *Economic*	January 28, 1957	Short

Bangladesh

Main Campaigns	Action	Method/*Type*	Date	Length
Bangla language movement, 1948–1952	Setting up sociocultural organizations	Nonviolent intervention/ *Creative*	1947–1948	Long
	An 18-page booklet "Pakistan's State Language: Bangla or Urdu?" was published	Protest and persuasion	September 15, 1947	Short
	Demonstrations	Protest and persuasion	1947	Short
	Strikes	Noncooperation/ *Economic*	1947	Medium
	Protests after the eight-point agreement was rejected	Protest and persuasion	February 25, 1948	Short
	All-Party State Language Council of Action formed in Dhaka	Nonviolent intervention/ *Creative*	March 2, 1948	Long
	Strike	Noncooperation/ *Economic*	March 11, 1948	Short
	Government officials from the provincial government staged a walkout	Noncooperation/ *Political*	March 1948	Short

Level of Participation	Direct Impact	Long-Term/Overall Impact of Civil Resistance
	Developing conspiratorial and underground skills	Developed a culture of nationalism and what it meant to be Algerian
High	Actions of Algerian workers were coordinated with and reinforced strikes in France against transportation of weapons to Indochina	Nonviolent actions were captured by and reinforced violent struggle
High	Strikes not only politicized, but also radicalized swathes of the Algerian population Strikes were used by the violent pro-independence group, the National Liberation Front (FLN), to increase its membership and furnish support for armed resistance	
High		

Level of Participation	Direct Impact	Long-Term/Overall Impact of Civil Resistance
Medium	They offered an organizational structure for the language movement and mobilized Bengalis in their struggle for Bangla to become a state language	Nonviolent struggles influenced the entire Bengali population by shaping its national identity beyond a politically limited idea of East Pakistan's province, inspired people to think and dream about their own language and to long for their own independent state
	The booklet defined objectives for the Bangla movement and became an inspiration for Bengalis	
High	Under popular pressure, the chief minister of East Pakistan signed an eight-point agreement, including a clause on a resolution to make Bangla one of the state languages and the official language of East Bengal Province	
High		
High	Maintaining momentum of the language movement	
	Building a platform of political support across various parties and political groups The Council called for an East Pakistan–wide strike on March 11, 1948	
High	Students and faculty of Dhaka University joined the strike, picketed the provincial government, and urged government workers and businesspeople to join the strike Strikers collected money, which was used later in making posters and banners	
High	Government officials were joined by workers of the East Bengal Railway Police tried to break up demonstrations that spread throughout the city	

(continues)

Bangladesh (Cont.)

Main Campaigns	Action	Method/*Type*	Date	Length
Bangla language movement, 1948–1952	Dhaka University State Language Action Committee set up	Nonviolent intervention/ *Creative*	March 1950	Medium
	New All-Party State Language Council of Action formed	Nonviolent intervention/ *Creative*	January 1952	Medium
	Student protests	Protest and persuasion	February 21, 1952	Short
	Funeral homage for killed protesters	Protest and persuasion	February 22, 1952	Short
	Students erected Shahid Minar (Monument for the Language Martyrs)	Protest and persuasion; Nonviolent intervention/ *Creative*	February 1952	Short
	General strike	Noncooperation/ *Economic*	February 25, 1952	
Nonviolent civil disobedience movement, March 1–25, 1971	Public demonstrations followed after Awami League was denied its national electoral victory	Protest and persuasion	March 1, 1971	Short
	Announcement of *hartal*	Protest and persuasion	March 1, 1971	Short
	Province-wide strike	Noncooperation/ *Political*	March 3, 1971	Short
	Flag raising	Protest and persuasion	March 2, 1971	Short
	Formation of Action Councils	Nonviolent intervention/ *Creative*	March 1 and 3, 1971	Short
	Boycott of economic goods produced by West Pakistani–owned factories in East Pakistan; shutdown of public and private offices, buses, trains, river and air transportation, banks and all other financial institutions; and refusal by television and radio stations to follow censor's orders	Noncooperation/ *Political, Economic, Social*	March 3, 1971	Short
	Three million people attended public gathering at the Dhaka Race Course	Protest and persuasion	March 7, 1971	Short

Level of Participation	Direct Impact	Long-Term/Overall Impact of Civil Resistance
	The committee mobilized students, raised public funds, and distributed posters and leaflets encouraging people to commemorate March 11 and circulated a memorandum demanding Bangla as a state language	Nonviolent struggles influenced the entire Bengali population by shaping its national identity beyond a politically limited idea of East Pakistan's province, inspired people to think and dream about their own language and to long for their own independent state
High	Coordinated protests and called for demonstrations on February 21	
High	Police opened fire, killing five people, and injuring many others Thousands gathered and prayed at the university campuses for those killed in demonstrations	
High	Police again opened fire Ongoing protests forced the provincial government to introduce a motion calling for the recognition of Bangla as an official language of East Pakistan	
High	Shahid Minar became a powerful rallying symbol for Bengalis	
	Police detained student and political leaders of the language movement Dhaka University was closed by the authorities Protests and demonstrations spread to other towns	
High	Military deployed, attacking and killing demonstrators Bengalis began calling openly for independence	
High		
High		
High		
High		
High	As a result of the boycott, cosmetic products produced by Bengali-owned Hena Chemicals became extremely popular People began using indigenously produced clothes from *khaddar* (hand-loomed cotton) Through acts of noncooperation, East Pakistan became de facto self-ruled and independent before the armed invasion by West Pakistan	
High	Articulation of the demands and visualization of the national movement	

Burma

Action	Method/*Type*	Date	Length	Level of Participation
Founding of Young Men's Buddhist Association (YMBA)	Nonviolent intervention/ *Creative*	1906	Long	High
Setting up General Conference of Buddhist Associations	Nonviolent intervention/ *Creative*		Long	
YMBA organized public meetings around issues of discontent	Protest and persuasion	1915–1917	Long	High
National campaign against wearing footwear in Buddhist shrines	Protest and persuasion	1915–1917	Long	High
First student strike to broaden educational opportunities for Burmese	Noncooperation/ *Social*	1920		Medium
Setting up and workings of Burmese parallel educational institutions	Nonviolent intervention/ *Creative*	1920		Medium
Boycott of British goods	Noncooperation/ *Economic*	1920s	Long	High
Setting up Wunthanu associations	Nonviolent intervention/ *Creative*		Long	
Displaying Wunthanu signboards in support of homemade goods	Protest and persuasion	1920s	Long	High
Wearing *pinni* (the native homespun cloth)	Nonviolent intervention/ *Creative*	1920s	Long	High
Singing patriotic songs (the Dobama song) at the opening of any social event	Protest and persuasion	1930s–1940s	Long	High
Printing and distributing political pamphlets	Protest and persuasion	1930s	Long	Medium
Formation of the Dobama Asiayone (Our Burma Association)	Nonviolent intervention/ *Creative*	early 1930s		
Boycott of colonial titles	Noncooperation/ *Social*	1930s		
Student strikes	Noncooperation/ *Social*	1936	Long	High
Public funeral of a student activist	Protest and persuasion	1938	Short	High
Labor strike	Noncooperation/ *Economic*	1935–1938	Long	High

Direct Impact	Long-Term/Overall Impact of Civil Resistance
Raised popular support for an independent political platform Led to the establishment of a national organization	Civil resistance propelled by student activism fed the growing nationalist leadership and was the birthplace of almost all major civil and political leaders of pre-independence Burma
Laid groundwork for launching anticolonial campaigns	
Forced Buddhist holidays onto the official register of colonial holidays Buddhist temples won exemption from colonial land tax	
Offered lessons for political organizing	
Taught unity	
Empowered people	
Established parallel educational institutions	
Instilled anticolonial and pro-independence values	
Boycott had noticeable impact on the colonial economy	
Helped launch Burmese-made products and boycott British goods campaigns	
Wearing *pinni* remains a symbol of opposition's resistance today	
The Dobama song became the national anthem after Burma's independence	
The Dobama Asiayone spearheaded Thakin movement and students' strikes	
Instilled dignity in the people	
The Dobama Asiayone gained national recognition and its chapters began to be organized across the country	
Display of people's defiance against emergency laws	
Workers organized themselves into strikers' parliament Greater appreciation of people's political power	

Cuba

Main Campaigns	Action	Method/*Type*	Date	Length
Nonviolent social and political reformism	Formation of patriotic societies, including cultural, artistic, and ethnic associations	Nonviolent intervention/ *Creative*	1812–1814	Long
	Issuing pamphlets and publishing periodicals and independent newspapers	Protest and persuasion	1820–1823	Long
	Networks of Creole intellectuals were organized independently from authorities		1830s	
	Spreading grassroots education with model schools and private high schools	Nonviolent intervention/ *Creative*	Mid-19th century	Long
	Growth of mutualist movement with setting up and workings of mutual aid associations	Nonviolent intervention/ *Creative*	1860s	Long
	Tobacco workers' strike	Noncooperation/ *Economic*	1865	Short
	Slave strike	Noncooperation/ *Economic*	1866	Short
	Formation of Masonic lodges and Cuban-dominated associations of leisure	Nonviolent intervention/ *Creative*	1860s	
	Plays and performances in theaters, cultural associations, and public spaces	Protest and persuasion	1860s	Long
	Mass patriotic gatherings at funerals	Protest and persuasion	1862 and 1866	Short
	Student protested against captain-general's abolition of doctoral degree at Havana University	Protest and persuasion	1870–1871	Short
	Students desecrated the tomb of a colonialist propagandist	Nonviolent intervention/ *Disruptive*	1871	Short
	Formation of the Liberal Autonomist Party	Nonviolent intervention/ *Creative*	1878–1895	Long

Level of Participation	Direct Impact	Long-Term/Overall Impact of Civil Resistance
Low	Built a parallel social structure to colonial social establishment	Constitutionalist-reformist, nonviolent struggle laid foundations for the growth of autonomous civil society and a stronger call for political independence from Spain
	Cultivated a sense of the island's economic and cultural identity and collective selfhood	
	Advocated freedom of the press and association despite being subject to censorship	
	Promotion of constitutionalist-reformist approach to political change	Nonviolent campaigns for racial and ethnic equality were crucial for defeating colonialism and helped to build a racially diverse and more unified Cuban nation
	Urged constitutional changes, including administrative autonomy	
	Reaffirmation of Cuban cultural identity	
	Prosecutions and forced exiles followed	
Medium	Cuban textbooks were censored and the Spanish authorities strengthened their assimilation efforts to Spanish culture	
	Literacy level increased and with it political and national awareness and identity of the Cuban population	
High	Promoted self-financing of artist and worker groups	
	Facilitated formation of first labor unions	
High		
High	Quashed by government troops	
	Reinforced ideas of political reform and autonomy	
	Often through satire, Cubans voiced their opposition toward Spanish authorities and called for political freedoms	
High	They symbolized people's mobilization for rights of all Cubans	
Low		
	Eight students were tried and executed	
	By the mid-1880s, the Liberal Autonomist Party became the largest political grouping in Cuba	

(continues)

Cuba (Cont.)

Main Campaigns	Action	Method/*Type*	Date	Length
Nonviolent social and political reformism	Organizing economic movements that demanded fiscal liberalization and lowering of export taxes	Nonviolent intervention/ *Creative*	1883–1892	Long
	Masonic lodges unified in the Grand Lodge of the Island of Cuba	Nonviolent intervention/ *Creative*	1890s	Long
	Labor unions grew in membership and formed leagues	Nonviolent intervention/ *Creative*	1890s	Long
	Black societies led petitions and lawsuits to eradicate segregation and racism	Protest and persuasion	1890s	Long
	Student strike	Noncooperation/ *Social*	March 1892	Short

Egypt

May 1805 revolution	Public appeal to the Wali Ahmad Khurshid Pasha to meet the demands of the people	Protest and persuasion	1804–1805	Medium
	Masses went out on the streets, protesting, beating drums, and shouting	Protest and persuasion	1804–1805	Short
	Women protested by putting mud on their hands and hair as a visual form of dismay and disapproval of the wali and his policies	Protest and persuasion	1804–1805	Short
	Religious scholars issued a fatwa to highlight that people have a right to change an unjust ruler	Protest and persuasion	1804–1805	
	40,000 Egyptians together with the Albanian troops surrounded Khurshid's citadel and laid nonviolent siege	Nonviolent intervention/ *Creative*	1804–1805	Medium
Orabi movement of 1881	Officers protest against a new law preventing peasants from becoming army officers	Protest and persuasion		Short
	Building a broad coalition: political and urban establishment, local mayors, landlords, government employees, intellectuals, peasants, and the army	Nonviolent intervention/ *Creative*		

Level of Participation	Direct Impact	Long-Term/Overall Impact of Civil Resistance
Low	United liberal and conservative factions of Cuban producers to achieve national economic goals Failed to maintain a unified front to carry on economic boycott and increase their leverage over government economic policies Eventually, under the pressure of the Spanish authorities, the movement split and ended its activities	Constitutionalist-reformist, nonviolent struggle laid foundations for the growth of autonomous civil society and a stronger call for political independence from Spain Nonviolent campaigns for racial and ethnic equality were crucial for defeating colonialism and helped to build a racially diverse and more unified Cuban nation
High		
High	Unions became increasingly political, demanding the right to organize, freely associate, and bargain salaries	
High	Legal victories bolstered constitutional and civil rights activists	
High	Granting of doctoral degrees at Havana University was restored	

Medium	The plea was rejected and that exacerbated the situation and galvanized the resistance	The 1805 revolution marks the first people's intervention in political affairs of their state and the beginning of the rise of a modern Egyptian national identity
High	The soldiers on the streets empathized with people's grievances	
High		
	The wali did not resign, and the opposition pushed for his impeachment	
High	Under pressure, the Ottoman sultan withdrew Khurshid and appointed Muhammad Ali as a new wali	
Low	Dismissal of the war minister Osman Rifki and annulment of the law Demands to include constitutional reforms widened	After military invasion and defeat of the Egyptian armed resistance in 1882, Britain established colonial rule over Egypt, which set the stage for further largely nonviolent resistance
Low	Uniting various groups against khedive (viceroy) Pasha Tawfik	

(continues)

Egypt (Cont.)

Main Campaigns	Action	Method/*Type*	Date	Length
Orabi movement of 1881	Civilian-military demonstration in front of Abdin Palace	Protest and persuasion	September 9, 1881	Short
Nonviolent resistance against British occupation	Formation of pro-independence parties and launching of nationalist and pro-constitutionalist newspapers	Nonviolent intervention/ *Creative*	1906 onward	Long
	Petitions and protests against press censorship	Protest and persuasion	March and April 1909	Short
	Newspapers found foreign owners and editors to circumvent the laws and some publications went underground	Nonviolent intervention/ *Creative*	1900s onward	Long
	Setting up Egyptian consumer cooperatives and trade unions and opening schools	Nonviolent intervention/ *Creative*	1906 onward	
	Mass nationalist gathering of some 250,000 people at the funeral of Mustafa Kamil	Protest and persuasion	1908	Short
1919 revolution for independence	Massive protests after the arrest of the Wafd delegation that requested British authorities' permission to join the Versailles Peace Conference	Protest and persuasion	November 13, 1918	Short
	Signature collection campaign in support of full independence for Egypt through peaceful means	Protest and persuasion	1919	Medium
	Public statements by professional groups condemning British violent repressions	Protest and persuasion	1919	Medium
	Student strikes	Noncooperation/ *Social*	March–May 1919	Medium
	Workers' and peasants' strikes	Noncooperation/ *Economic*	March 1919	Medium
	Infrastructure sabotage that cut railway lines and disrupted communication lines	Nonviolent intervention/ *Disruptive*		
	Formation of national police	Nonviolent intervention/ *Creative*	1919	Medium

Level of Participation	Direct Impact	Long-Term/Overall Impact of Civil Resistance
High	Tawfik yielded to the demands to expand the powers of the representative assembly	British colonial rule over Egypt set the stage for further largely nonviolent resistance
	British decided to invade militarily in summer 1882 to protect its interest in Egypt and established a direct colonial rule after the defeat of the Egyptian armed resistance	
Medium	Growing politicization and nurturing of a greater sense of national identity	Led to a collective national awakening
	Fearing freedom of the press, the British authorities revived censorship laws	
High		
	Circumvention of British censorship	
Medium		
High	Ordinary Egyptians visualized a nationalist movement	
Low	The British government was forced to release leaders of the Wafd delegation, but the movement had already gathered momentum	Under pressure of nonviolent resistance, Britain unilaterally declared the end of Egypt's protectorate and its formal independence on February 28, 1922
High	The authorities prohibited and confiscated the petition. Petitions were printed and distributed secretly until 100,000 signatures had been collected	Women's activism in the pro-independence movement built up a momentum for their later public participation in various political and social activities
High		Demonstrations involved both Muslims and Christians, which illustrated and strengthened a sense of common, national identity among Egyptians despite religious differences
High	Schools closed and students left for home bringing revolutionary fervor to the countryside and other cities	
High	Strikes showed that the movement now involved a coalition of different social groups	
	British authorities relied heavily on transportation and communication lines in Egypt and their crippling weakened British colonial control over the country	
High	National police helped organize effective demonstrations and kept them peaceful	

(continues)

Egypt (Cont.)

Main Campaigns	Action	Method/*Type*	Date	Length
1919 revolution for independence	Protesters took refuge in a sacred place and delivered public speeches in its sanctuary	Protest and persuasion; Noncooperation/ *Social*	1919	Medium
	Women demonstrated and wore veils in protest	Protest and persuasion	March 1919 onward	
	Flyers about the protests and pamphlets with nationalist demands distributed secretly to homes	Protest and persuasion	1919	
	Demonstrations at public funerals	Protest and persuasion	1919	Short
	Arranging food delivery and assistance to those who sabotaged the railway lines and communications in Upper Egypt	Nonviolent intervention/ *Creative*	1919	
	Boycotts of British goods	Noncooperation/ *Economic*	1919	
	Boycotts of British political mission to Egypt	Noncooperation/ *Political*	1919	Medium
	Day of mass prayer for independence	Protest and persuasion	May 1920	Short
	Displaying a symbolic unity flag with the cross and crescent on a green background	Protest and persuasion	1919	Short
	Use of plays, music, and literature advocating resistance	Protest and persuasion	1919	

Ghana

Main Campaigns	Action	Method/*Type*	Date	Length
Protest against direct taxation	Women in Accra marched to Government House and protested against British direct taxation	Protest and persuasion	1896	Short
	Women sent a petition to the colonial secretary in London to protest direct taxation	Protest and persuasion		
Campaign against bill ceding control of "all waste and unoccupied lands" to colonial authorities	Establishment of the Aborigines Rights Protection Society (ARPS) to campaign against a bill that would establish British control over unoccupied lands	Nonviolent intervention/ *Creative*	1897	Long
	Growth of voluntary associations and benevolent societies, including charitable organizations; professional associations; trade unions; youth, women's, and farmers' groups; cooperatives; and political parties	Nonviolent intervention/ *Creative*	1902 onward	Long

Level of Participation	Direct Impact	Long-Term/Overall Impact of Civil Resistance
High	Speeches boosted people's morale and informed the public about decisions relevant to the conduct of protests and strikes	Under pressure of nonviolent resistance, Britain unilaterally declared the end of Egypt's protectorate and its formal independence on February 28, 1922
	Women's protests created a dilemma for the British who would use force to stop demonstrations	
High		Women's activism in the pro-independence movement built up a momentum for their later public participation in various political and social activities
		Demonstrations involved both Muslims and Christians, which illustrated and strengthened a sense of common, national identity among Egyptians despite religious differences
High		
High	Mass prayer made the whole nation feel part of the struggle	
High	Strengthened Muslim and Christian unity in the struggle	
High	A number of patriotic songs were considered so inflammatory by the British that they forbade their performance	

High	The nonviolent actions did not change British policy, but mobilized indigenous elites	Nonviolent resistance showed that withdrawing cooperation leaves colonial forces powerless while cooperation reinforces colonial control
		Nonviolent resistance facilitated the process of nation building
High	Strengthened unity among the colony's chiefs and local educated elite	
	In 1898, under the pressure of local nonviolent mobilization the bill was withdrawn	
High	The organizations became a force against the colonial status quo and for nationalist mobilization	
	They spread political awareness that encouraged resistance against colonial authorities	

(continues)

Ghana (Cont.)

Main Campaigns	Action	Method/*Type*	Date	Length
Campaign against Waterworks Bill and Ordinance 21	Delegations sent to London to petition British government to annul the Waterworks Bill and Ordinance 21 that curbed freedom of the press	Protest and persuasion	1934	Short
	Farmers and traders refused to sell cocoa and boycotted imported goods in opposition to the European cartel's price-fixing	Noncooperation/ *Economic*	1930–1931	Medium
1937 cocoa boycott	Coalition of local brokers, market women, and chiefs organized boycott of European goods and refused to sell cocoa	Noncooperation/ *Economic*	1937	Medium
	Native tribunals did not press cases against farmers for repayment of debts	Noncooperation/ *Political, Economic*	1937	Medium
	Truck drivers refused to deliver goods and fishermen refused to fish	Noncooperation/ *Economic*	1937	Medium
	Protests of ex-servicemen motivated equally by economic grievances and desire for an independent country	Protest and persuasion	February 28, 1948	Short
Positive action campaign	Convention People's Party (CPP) was set up and youth political movement was formed	Nonviolent intervention/ *Creative*	1949–1950	Long
	Newspaper and education campaigns launched	Protest and persuasion	1949–1951	Long
	Establishment of independent schools and colleges	Nonviolent intervention/ *Creative*	1949–1951	Long
	Rally and Kwame Nkrumah's speech	Protest and persuasion	January 8, 1950	Short
	March to Christiansburg	Protest and persuasion	January 17, 1950	Short
	Economic boycotts, closing of stores, sit-downs at home, strikes	Noncooperation/ *Economic*	1950	Long

Level of Participation	Direct Impact	Long-Term/Overall Impact of Civil Resistance
	Local mobilization and organization skills were tested and developed	Nonviolent resistance showed that withdrawing cooperation leaves colonial forces powerless while cooperation reinforces colonial control
	Precursor to boycotts in the future	Nonviolent resistance facilitated the process of nation building
High	Under the pressure of the indigenously led noncooperation, the British governor refused to follow London's orders to protect the European cartel and convinced the government to appoint a Commission of Inquiry to defuse the tensions	
High	The cocoa boycott was seen as a major inspirational event in the political history of nonviolent resistance in Ghana	
High		
High	Police opened fire and riots broke out	
	Telegrams were sent to the United Nations, and the world press said the riots showed that the British could no longer rule the country effectively	
	Nationalist leaders, including Nkrumah, urged nonviolent discipline that for the most part was maintained throughout the independence struggle	
	Arrest of the nationalist leaders backfired, raising their popularity	
	Spread of the nationalist message and fostering of unity	
	Newspaper editors arrested	
High	Call for nonviolent mobilization and noncooperation	
High	Police provoked violence	
	British arrested Nkrumah	
High	British control over the country was shaken	

(continues)

Ghana (Cont.)

Main Campaigns	Action	Method/*Type*	Date	Length
	CPP built its organizational capacities and established its branches in all parts of the country	Nonviolent intervention/ *Creative*	1951	
	Political compromise	Nonviolent intervention/ *Creative*	1952–1956	Long

Hungary

Action	Method/*Type*	Date	Length	Level of Participation
Hungarians refused to sit in the Imperial Parliament	Noncooperation/ *Political*	1861	Medium	Low
Wearing symbolic clothing, hairstyles, and jewelry in the national colors, especially on significant dates for Hungarians	Protest and persuasion	1850s–1860s	Long	High
Setting up Hungarian institutions	Nonviolent intervention/ *Creative*	1850s–1860s	Long	High
Ferenc Deák writes petitions to Austrians	Protest and persuasion	Early 1860s	Short	Low
Refusal of military service	Noncooperation/ *Social, Political*	1850s–1860s	Long	
Resistance to Germanization, including refusal to speak German socially, preference for Hungarian authors and plays over Austrian ones, public performances with coded nationalist messages	Protest and persuasion	1850s–1860s	Long	High
Boycott of government celebrations, including church services	Noncooperation/ *Political*	1850s–1860s		High
Refusal to provide board and lodging for Austrian soldiers	Noncooperation/ *Social, Political*	1850s–1860s	Long	High
Boycott of courts	Noncooperation/ *Social, Political*	1850s–1860s	Long	High
Withholding tax payments to the Austrian government and boycotting government auctions of seized goods	Noncooperation/ *Economic*	1850s–1860s	Long	High
Campaign to boycott Austrian goods	Noncooperation/ *Economic*	1850s–1860s	Long	High

Level of Participation	Direct Impact	Long-Term/Overall Impact of Civil Resistance
	CPP election campaigns used the skills and experience of innovative organizing and mobilization learned from past nonviolent actions	Nonviolent resistance showed that withdrawing cooperation leaves colonial forces powerless while cooperation reinforces colonial control
	CPP victories in municipal and parliamentary elections	
	Nkrumah released from prison	Nonviolent resistance facilitated the process of nation building
High	A new constitution was adopted; Nkrumah became a prime minister; main focus was on economic reforms and development of infrastructure	Ghana gained its independence on March 6, 1957

Direct Impact	Long-Term/Overall Impact of Civil Resistance
Dramatized Hungarians' demand to reestablish their own parliament and denied the legitimacy of centralized Austrian rule	Hungarian nonviolent resistance served as an inspiration for the Irish nationalist leader Arthur Griffith and for Mohandas Gandhi
Demonstrated both opposition and a national pride	Hungarians' noncooperation laid down foundations for winning political concessions from Austrians in the form of compromise that established dual Austro-Hungarian monarchy in 1867
Helped continue nonviolent resistance	
A platform for patriotic and national affirmation	
Resulted in no shows	
After trying to live in houses where everyone despised them, Austrian soldiers protested strongly to their superiors against staying with the Hungarian hosts	
The government discovered it was costing more to distrain the property than the tax was worth	

(continues)

Hungary (Cont.)

Action	Method/*Type*	Date	Length	Level of Participation
Funeral ceremony of Mihály Vörösmarty attended by 20,000 people. It was a silent protest since the regime banned unannounced speeches during this ceremony	Protest and persuasion	1855		High

Iran

Main Campaigns	Action	Method/*Type*	Date	Length
	Petitions by merchants and craftspeople against economic privileges granted to foreign importers	Protest and persuasion	1830 onward	Long
	Articles and treaties advocating representative government and the rule of law and denouncing foreign concessions	Protest and persuasion	Prior to 1891	
	Protests often involving women and minorities	Protest and persuasion		
	Taking *bast* (inviolable refuge) in shrines, mosques, and foreign legations	Noncooperation/ *Social, Political*		
	Closing of bazaars	Noncooperation/ *Economic*		
	Boycotting of foreign goods	Noncooperation/ *Economic*		
Tobacco movement 1891–1892	A leading cleric in Shiraz preached noncompliance with the order to sell tobacco to the foreign company	Protest and persuasion	1891	Medium
	Protests in Shiraz, Isfahan, Teheran, and several other cities and appeals for the top ulama's support against concessions	Protest and persuasion	1891	Medium
	The Iranian leader of all members of the Shia sect issued fatwa saying that all use of and commerce in tobacco, so long as the concession existed, was against the will of the Hidden Imam	Protest and persuasion	1891–1892	Medium
	Boycott of tobacco	Noncooperation/ *Economic*	1891–1892	Medium
	Massive nonviolent demonstrations in Teheran	Protest and persuasion		Short

Direct Impact	Long-Term/Overall Impact of Civil Resistance
Show of unity, nonviolent resistance, and national inspiration	Hungarian nonviolent resistance served as an inspiration for the Irish nationalist leader Arthur Griffith and for Mohandas Gandhi

Level of Participation	Direct Impact	Long-Term/Overall Impact of Civil Resistance
Medium	Petitions failed. Given its long-term treaties with foreign governments, there was little the government could do, short of risking war	
Medium	Forced the dismissal of the prime minister Led to the cancellation of the economic concession to a British subject, Julius de Reuter	Contributed to making Iranians believe that resistance, including nonviolent resistance, against autocratic rulers and foreign domination might be effective
Medium		
Medium		
Medium		
High	Galvanized people to protest The movement's main religious leader exiled	A tactical and strategic alliance was formed between modernizers and merchants that played an important role in the 1905–1911 revolution
High		The tobacco movement pioneered tactics that were used again during the constitutional revolution
High	Fatwa ensured the widening of civil disobedience and a growing popular boycott of tobacco use and selling that was also observed by the shah's wives	
High		
High	Several people were killed, which backfired on the government and led to more nonviolent protests Protests and boycott forced the government to cancel the entire tobacco concession	

(continues)

Iran (Cont.)

Main Campaigns	Action	Method/*Type*	Date	Length
	Formation of secret societies, the Society of Learning, National Library, and schools	Nonviolent intervention/ *Creative*	Between 1892 and 1905	
	Plays, essays, treatises, and newspaper articles critical of Iran's misgovernance, corrupt clergymen, and the mistreatment of women	Protest and persuasion	Between 1892 and 1905	
	Antigovernment leaflets known as "night letters" distributed	Protest and persuasion	1902–1903	
Constitutional Revolution, 1905–1906	A large group of *mollas* and *bazaaris* took *bast* in Tehran's royal mosque to avoid government repression	Noncooperation/ *Social, Political*	1905	
	Bastis refused to disperse	Noncooperation/ *Political*	1905	
	Popular nonviolent demonstrations	Protest and persuasion	1905	
	Bazaar strikes	Noncooperation/ *Economic*	1905	Medium
	Protesters took mass *bast* in Qom	Noncooperation/ *Social, Political*	March 1905	Medium
	Protesters took mass *bast* in the British legation	Noncooperation/ *Social, Political*		
	General strike	Noncooperation/ *Economic*	1906	Medium
	Mass participation of guild members, students, and radical intellectuals of the secret societies	Protest and persuasion	1906	Medium
	Mass protests	Protest and persuasion	1906	Medium

Level of Participation	Direct Impact	Long-Term/Overall Impact of Civil Resistance
	These institutions educated their members and others by reading and disseminating critical literature	
Medium		
High	When government violated their sanctuary, they went to another shrine and formulated the demand for a representative *adalakhaneh* (house of justice)	The resistance movements of 1890–1911 led to the growth of Iranian nationalist ideas, increased Iranians' national awareness and collective identification, though impact of civil resistance on subsequent nationalist strategies is less clear
High	The shah dismissed the governor of Tehran	
	The shah did not establish an *adalakhaneh*, which	
High	led to further protests	
High	*Bast* was used to educate people about constitutional government and human rights	
High	Thousands of supportive women demonstrated outside the Legation	
High	Business was brought to a standstill	
High	Formulation of new demands: dismissal of the prime minister and the establishment of a *majles* (representative parliament)	
High	Failure of efforts by the shah to buy off conservative supporters	
	Defections within the government	
	Shah dismissed the premier and accepted the *majles*	

Kosovo

Main Campaigns	Action	Method/*Type*	Date	Length
	Miners march in defense of the constitution and autonomy	Protest and persuasion; Noncooperation/ *Political*	November 1988	Medium
	Miners went on hunger strike and used stay-in strike underground	Nonviolent intervention/ *Disruptive*; Noncooperation/ *Political, Economic*	February 1989	Medium
	General strike	Noncooperation/ *Economic*	February 1989	Short
	Solidarity demonstrations in Slovenia and Croatia	Protest and persuasion	February 1989	Short
	Founding of Democratic League of Kosova (LDK)	Nonviolent intervention/ *Creative*	December 1989 onward	Long
	Establishment of the Council for the Defense of Human Rights and Freedoms (CDHRF)	Nonviolent intervention/ *Creative*	December 1989 onward	Long
"For Democracy Against Violence"	Petition with a commitment to make each death a public act	Protest and persuasion	1990	
	Homage to those who were tortured and killed with five-minute work stoppages	Protest and persuasion; Noncooperation/ *Economic*	1990	
	At set times, factory whistles or car horns sounded	Protest and persuasion	1990	
	Lighting candles or making noise at the time of curfew	Protest and persuasion	1990	
	Photos of bruised and beaten people handed to foreign visitors at the CDHRF offices and distributed internationally	Protest and persuasion	1990	
	CDHRF and LDK went to the scenes of committed atrocities to mitigate violent responses to repression and explain the need for nonviolent discipline	Protest and persuasion	1990	

Level of Participation	Direct Impact	Long-Term/Overall Impact of Civil Resistance
High	An estimated 300,000 people—20% of Kosovo's population—joined the miners Their peaceful protest was broadcast throughout the Yugoslav federation	Helped maintain the Albanian community and way of life in Kosovo Prevented war when it was most dangerous
High	Resignation of Slobodan Milošević's appointees, but the government in Belgrade did not accept it	Won international condemnation of the Serbian regime
High		Helped convince the international community that Kosovo Albanians should not be expected to live under Serbia
High	State of emergency introduced and a wave of intimidation and arrests of strikers followed	Ensured that the Serbian minority in Kosovo could survive and enjoy full rights without the protection of Serbia
High	Hundreds of thousands of people joined LDK that dominated politics in Kosovo in the following years Mitigated violent response to repression and explained the need for strategic nonviolent resistance	
	Made brutality of the regime backfire by presenting documentation about torture and killings of Kosovars to foreign media and officials Mitigated violent response to repression and explained the need for strategic nonviolent resistance	
High	Ensured that the regime's brutality backfired on it	
High	Strengthened popular morale and unity of the resisting population Avoided vengeance by publicizing through media and international officials the crimes committed on Kosovars	
High		
High		
Medium		
Medium		

(continues)

Kosovo (Cont.)

Main Campaigns	Action	Method/*Type*	Date	Length
	Self-organized referendum	Nonviolent intervention/ *Creative*	September 1991	Medium
	Self-organized elections for a parliament and president of the Republic of Kosova	Nonviolent intervention/ *Creative*	May 1992	Medium
Reconciling blood feuds	Volunteers toured villages to locate blood feuds for respected elders to intervene and for public ceremonies of reconciliation to be arranged	Nonviolent intervention/ *Creative*	1990–1992	Long
Education	Protests by teachers and parents against Belgrade-imposed curriculum in the schools	Protest and persuasion	1991–1992	Medium
	Formation of parallel education institutions, schools and university, supported by a system of voluntary taxes in Kosovo and among the diaspora members	Nonviolent intervention/ *Creative*	January 1992–1998	Long
	Launching a women's literacy campaign with slogan "To Europe with a Pencil!"	Protest and persuasion		
	Massive protests organized by teachers' union during the visit of the Yugoslavian/Serbian prime minister	Protest and persuasion	October 1992	Short
	Nonviolent march organized by students at the University of Prishtina	Protest and persuasion	October 1997	Short

Mozambique

Action	Method/*Type*	Date	Length	Level of Participation
Singing, dancing, and carving caricatures of the colonizers with distorted features	Protest and persuasion	Late 1920s and early 1930s	Long	High
Forming mutual aid societies to provide scholarships for students and apprentices	Nonviolent intervention/ *Creative*	Late 1920s and early 1930s	Long	High
Setting up newspapers and magazines critical of colonial rule and European domination	Nonviolent intervention/ *Creative*	Late 1920s and early 1930s	Long	High
Writings and paintings with anticolonial themes	Protest and persuasion	1940s–1960	Long	Low

Level of Participation	Direct Impact	Long-Term/Overall Impact of Civil Resistance
High	87 percent of the total electorate voted, 99.87 percent in favor of a declaration of independence	Helped maintain the Albanian community and way of life in Kosovo
High	LDK gained 76 percent of the vote and Ibrahim Rugova was almost unanimously elected president Such displays of unity established the legitimacy of the political leadership	Prevented war when it was most dangerous Won international condemnation of the Serbian regime
High	Gave an impulse to social solidarity, to self-organization, and to a feeling of being a European	Helped convince the international community that Kosovo Albanians should not be expected to live under Serbia
Medium	Led to the creation of parallel education institutions	Ensured that the Serbian minority in Kosovo could survive and enjoy full rights without the protection of Serbia
High	Played a vital role in maintaining the Albanian community in Kosovo Strengthened a "victim" nationalism	
High	Brutal repression by police Kosovars introduced a moratorium on protests	
High	Brutal repression of the nonviolent protesters by the regime Helped internationalize the student struggle; Western diplomats condemned police brutality and invited protesters to visit their countries	

Direct Impact	Long-Term/Overall Impact of Civil Resistance
Delegitimizing colonial rule	Civil resistance of the 1940s–1960s influenced and consolidated collective understandings of common identity (and shared a destiny as one nation) among the majority of Mozambicans
Cross-ethnic and regional coalition building	
	The collective consciousness of resistance and reconciliation can now be seen in contemporary adherence to popular democratic electoral participation, continued high levels of involvement in community-based grassroots organizations, and an openness to an internationalism that defies traditional North-South or East-West dynamics

(continues)

Mozambique (Cont.)

Action	Method/*Type*	Date	Length	Level of Participation
Setting up a student group, Nucleo dos Estudantes Africanos Secundarios de Mocambique (NESAM)	Nonviolent intervention/ *Creative*	1949	Long	
Urban workers' and farmers' strikes	Noncooperation/ *Economic*	With iteration from 1947 until early 1960s	Long	High
Rural resistance in a form of noncompliance with quotas	Noncooperation/ *Economic*	1940s–1960s	Long	High
Production boycotts	Noncooperation/ *Economic*	1955 and 1958	Long	Medium
Organizing community-based, indigenous farming cooperatives	Nonviolent intervention/ *Creative*		Long	High
Mozambique Liberation Front (FRELIMO) built parallel civic and nonmilitary alternative institutions	Nonviolent intervention/ *Creative*	Second half of 1960s until 1970s	Long	High
Acts of sabotage: cutting of transmission line cables and destruction of unstaffed transmission towers against Cabora Bassa hydroelectric project	Nonviolent intervention/ *Disruptive*	1970s	Short	
Sending captured Portuguese soldiers back home	Protest and persuasion	1970s	Short	

Palestine

Main Campaigns	Action	Method/*Type*	Date	Length
Palestinian resistance in the 1920s and early 1930s	Assemblies, deputations, entreaties, manifestos, processions, protests, and formal statements	Protest and persuasion	1920s	Long
	Demonstrations, marches, and petitions	Protest and persuasion	1920s	Long
	Printing black mourning bands on the front pages of Palestinian newspapers	Protest and persuasion	1920s	Medium
	Election boycotts	Noncooperation/ *Political*	1920s	Medium
	Resignation from jobs in the British colonial administration	Nonviolent intervention/ *Disruptive*	1920s	Long

	Long-Term/Overall Impact
Direct Impact	of Civil Resistance
Helped spur coalition building among colonized groups and across wide geographical areas Facilitated civic networking structure	Civil resistance of the 1940s–1960s influenced and consolidated collective understandings of common identity (and shared a
Offered self-organizing experience for workers	destiny as one nation) among the majority of Mozambicans The collective consciousness of resistance and reconciliation can
Demanded increased wages and greater control over the land	now be seen in contemporary adherence to popular democratic
Cotton-picking wages were increased	electoral participation, continued high levels of involvement in
Membership expanded by thousands Production increased Inspiration for local farmers to intensify their efforts at earning a living wage and proving their effectiveness as workers and traders Negotiated exemptions from forced labor with local authorities	community-based grassroots organizations, and an openness to an internationalism that defies traditional North-South or East-West dynamics
Institutions transformed into local engines of a people's democracy after independence One of FRELIMO's institutions, the Organization of Mozambican Women, is today one of Africa's most dynamic and successful civic organizations	
Drained the colonial powers' fiscal and physical resources, making the project more expensive	
Many Portuguese soldiers refused military service in protest against their own government's colonial policies	

Level of Participation	Direct Impact	Long-Term/Overall Impact of Civil Resistance
High	The British opted for collective punishments: detentions, imposing fines, conducting mass arrests, and demolishing homes	Instilled relentless persistence in rejecting the Israeli occupation
High	The 1920s and 1930s nonviolent actions failed to influence the British, which split the Arab	
High	movement between moderates and those who considered violence as the most effective weapon	
High		
High		

(continues)

Main Campaigns	Action	Method/*Type*	Date	Length
Palestinian resistance in the 1920s and early 1930s	General strikes	Noncooperation/ *Economic*	1920s	Long
	Village *mukhtars* refused to cooperate with government commissioners	Noncooperation/ *Political*	1920s	Long
	Excommunication of those who had sold land to Zionist brokers or middlemen	Noncooperation/ *Social*	1920s	Long
	Women protested against eviction of the peasantry from farmland	Protest and persuasion	1920s	Long
	Women organized a silent procession, submitted statements to diplomatic consulates, and telegrammed protest petitions to Queen Mary	Protest and persuasion	1920s	Long
	One-day strike: all the Arab shops closed	Noncooperation/ *Economic*	1925	Short
	Political parties evolved	Nonviolent intervention/ *Creative*	1930s	Long
	Local and national committees formed to coordinate and lead strikes	Nonviolent intervention/ *Creative*	1936	
	General strikes	Noncooperation/ *Economic*	1936	Long
	Several hundred veiled women marched in Gaza	Protest and persuasion	April 25, 1936	Medium
	Development of *sumud*, a philosophy of persistence in doing everyday activities and thus staying on the land	Protest and persuasion; Nonviolent intervention/ *Creative*	Second half of 1960s	Long
	Emergence of student and faculty unions, community-based networks, professional associations, and youth and women's clubs	Nonviolent intervention/ *Creative*	1970s	Long
Intifada of 1987	Activist scholars produced and translated writings on nonviolent resistance	Protest and persuasion	1980s	Long

Level of Participation	Direct Impact	Long-Term/Overall Impact of Civil Resistance
High	The British opted for collective punishments: detentions, imposing fines, conducting mass arrests, and demolishing homes	Instilled relentless persistence in rejecting the Israeli occupation
Medium	The 1920s and 1930s nonviolent actions failed to influence the British and Zionists, which split the Arab movement between moderates and those who considered violence as the most effective weapon	
High		
Medium		
Medium		
High		
High		
High		
High		
	Offered the "third way" between passivity in the face of military occupation and armed struggle	Helped Palestinians develop resilience and self-reliance
High	Helped to create a nascent independent civil society Helped to promote new ideas about how to struggle for rights and facilitated a reassertion of nonviolent methods	The intifada's achievements include the 1991 Madrid peace conference and the opening of political space for the 1993 Oslo Accords
Low	Popularized political tools as more realistic than armed struggle Spread awareness that the Israeli military occupation persisted in part because of Palestinians' obedience, which could be withdrawn	Acceptance by the Palestine Liberation Organization (PLO) of the concept of a Palestinian state side by side with Israel Nonviolent resistance did more for coining a model of authentic democratic governance in the Arab world than any other force to date Nonviolent strategies shifted a discourse from independence to liberation and framed it around human rights

(continues)

Palestine (Cont.)

Main Campaigns	Action	Method/*Type*	Date	Length
Intifada of 1987	Organization of joint Israeli-Palestinian committees against the occupation	Nonviolent intervention/ *Creative*	1980–1990	Long
	The joint committees used banners, documentation, denunciation, news releases, speeches, picketing, leaflets, and vigils	Protest and persuasion		Long
	Biweekly leaflets issued by the leadership command	Protest and persuasion		Long
	Fasting	Nonviolent intervention/ *Disruptive*		
	General and local strikes, resigning from jobs, and boycotts	Noncooperation/ *Economic*		
	Public prayers	Protest and persuasion		Long
	Renaming of streets and schools	Protest and persuasion		
	Ringing of church bells	Protest and persuasion		
	Unfurling of flags	Protest and persuasion		Long
	Setting up clandestine leadership command that did not lead, but coordinated nonviolent actions	Nonviolent intervention/ *Creative*		
Intifada of the wall	Protests and demonstrations in villages directly affected by Israel's separation barrier, called "the wall"	Protest and persuasion	2000s–2010s	Long
Cultural resistance	Freedom Theatre at the Jenin refugee camp; songs, drama performances, use of giant puppets, driving a Freedom Bus from village to village	Nonviolent intervention/ *Creative*	2010s	Long
"Empty Stomach" campaign	Hunger strikes of Palestinian political prisoners in Israeli prisons	Nonviolent intervention/ *Disruptive*		Long
Boycott Divestment Sanctions campaign	Coalition of the Palestinian civic organizations and international solidarity groups working to promote tertiary sanctions against Israel	Noncooperation/ *Economic, Social, Political*	2005 onward	Long
Gaza flotilla	Ships with international activists attempt to break the Israeli blockade of Gaza Strip	Nonviolent intervention/ *Disruptive*	2010 onward	Long

Level of Participation	Direct Impact	Long-Term/Overall Impact of Civil Resistance
Medium	Solidarity network developed between Palestinian and Israeli groups Divisions within Israeli society	The intifada's achievements include the 1991 Madrid peace conference and the opening of political space for the 1993 Oslo Accords
	Served as an important information and deliberation tool about direction of the uprising, including an 18-month-long debate on adopting total civil disobedience	Acceptance by the Palestine Liberation Organization (PLO) of the concept of a Palestinian state side by side with Israel
	Israel introduced curfews in the West Bank and Gaza, arrested and exiled scholar activists School and university closings helped to spread ideas about nonviolent struggle as 14,500 students and professors were sent home to their villages and refugee camps where they planned the next nonviolent actions against the occupation	Nonviolent resistance did more for coining a model of authentic democratic governance in the Arab world than any other force to date Nonviolent strategies shifted a discourse from independence to liberation and framed it around human rights
Medium	Israeli Supreme Court rulings in favor of the protesters' demands The Israeli Defense Forces often disregard these rulings Alternative media, including Palestinian and Israeli, cover the intifada of the wall though international media largely ignore it	Increased international solidarity
		Popularized nonviolent resistance and the plight of Palestinians living under occupation
High	Popularized demands of imprisoned Palestinians Conditions in Israeli prisons improved	
High	Became a globally decentralized international campaign Led to third-party sanctions, including corporate disinvestment and cultural, social and economic boycotts	
	Internationalized Palestinian nonviolent struggle against Israel's occupation	

Poland

Main Campaigns	Action	Method/*Type*	Date	Length
Education campaign in Austrian Poland	Forming of the Agricultural Circle Society	Nonviolent intervention/ *Creative*	1882	Long
	Opening Christian stores and credit associations	Protest and persuasion	1882 onward	Long
	Establishment of People's School Society	Nonviolent intervention/ *Creative*	1891	Long
Commemorations campaign in Austrian Poland	Mass celebrations of national anniversaries, military victories, and famous Polish historical and contemporary figures	Protest and persuasion	1880 onward	
	Mass mourning during anniversaries of Poland's partitions or failed armed uprisings	Protest and persuasion	1880 onward	
	Educational activities during commemorations, including lectures, theatrical performances, exhibitions, and church services	Protest and persuasion	1880 onward	
	Formation of the Society for Peasant Education	Nonviolent intervention/ *Creative*	1872	
Campaign for indigenous, grassroots-led socioeconomic development in German Poland	Establishment of Society for Folk Reading Rooms	Nonviolent intervention/ *Creative*	1880	Long
	Setting up Polish economic and financial institutions in rural areas to counteract German economic expansion	Nonviolent intervention/ *Creative*	1885 onward	Long

Level of Participation	Direct Impact	Long-Term/Overall Impact of Civil Resistance
High	Launching patriotic education movement in rural areas Civic education offered to Polish-speaking villagers Promoted social behavior that reinforced the social and national fabric Organized festivities to commemorate historic anniversaries	The strength of the newly acquired national identity was displayed during World War I when peasants constituted the majority of Polish Army volunteers Experience of organizing and running secret education became part of Polish collective memory of the national resistance and
High		was used during the German occupation of 1939–1945 and
High	Reached out to 5 million illiterate Polish-speaking peasants Built libraries and rural primary and secondary schools Incorporated the work of Polish nationalist novelists and poets in the curricula Organized national celebrations	during communist rule Cultural forms of resistance as well as patriotic education further romanticized past violent struggles and inadvertently overshadowed Polish tradition and the practice of nonviolent resistance
High	Brought together Poles from different social strata (intellectuals, peasants, workers) and instilled in them emotional attachment to Polish history, tradition, and culture	
High		
High		
High	Established nearly 120 libraries, distributed books and other reading materials, and set up day nurseries German authorities eventually dissolved the organization	
High	Within three years, the society had set up close to 400 rural and 85 urban libraries and supplied them with 79,000 Polish-language cultural, literary, and religious books By 1890, almost 1,000 libraries were established More than 100 reading circles were opened	
High	Polish credit cooperatives rose from 25 in 1868 to 76 in 1891, reaching 204 by 1913 with close to 126,000 members—almost half of them peasants Helped modernize and expand both the rural and urban economy in German Poland Within a decade, Poles were able to acquire more land than Germans	

(continues)

Poland (Cont.)

Main Campaigns	Action	Method/*Type*	Date	Length
	Establishment of Polish industrial societies	Nonviolent intervention/ *Creative*		Long
	Establishment of Peasant Agricultural Circle	Nonviolent intervention/ *Creative*	1875 onward	Long
	Growth of Polish-language press	Nonviolent intervention/ *Creative*		Long
School strikes in German Poland	Gathering signatures and preparing petitions against Germanization of schools	Protest and persuasion	1871 onward	Long
	Września strike where school children refused to use books, answer questions, and speak German during prayers and religion classes, and commemorate the German victory over France at Sedan	Noncooperation/ *Social*	1901	Medium
	Student strikes	Noncooperation/ *Social*	1906–1907	Medium
	Work of the Polish press to publicize and inform about school strike	Protest and persuasion	1906	Medium
Commemoration movement in Russian Poland	Erecting a bronze statue for a national bard, Adam Mickiewicz	Protest and persuasion; Nonviolent intervention/ *Creative*	1898	Short

Level of Participation	Direct Impact	Long-Term/Overall Impact of Civil Resistance
High		The strength of the newly acquired national identity was displayed during World War I when peasants constituted the majority of Polish Army volunteers
High	Teaching legal, credit, tax, and inheritance issues to countervail German administrative, juridical, and economic efforts to uproot Polish-speaking peasants from their land Peasant agriculture circles increased from 45 in 1875 to 60 with 10,000 members in 1900, and reached 310 with 17,000 members by 1910	Experience of organizing and running secret education became part of Polish collective memory of the national resistance and was used during the German occupation of 1939–1945 and during communist rule
High	Influenced school strikes in 1901–1907	
High	Petitions were lessons in citizens' self-organization They generated greater awareness among the Polish-speaking population of the necessity to defend Polish education and built up a momentum for the school strikes	Cultural forms of resistance as well as patriotic education further romanticized past violent struggles and inadvertently overshadowed Polish tradition and the practice of nonviolent resistance
High	Children were punished with mass beatings Thousands gathered near the school when they heard children screaming and later twenty-one protesters were sentenced to prison terms and financial penalties The punishment of children and harsh sentences backfired and Września became a national symbol of the Polish resistance in defense of the Polish language Increased international support for Poles' right to self-determination Inflexibility of German authorities paved the way to a larger wave of school strikes	
High	93,000 children from over 1,600 schools in German Poland were on strike	
High	Printed sample petitions for parents to use in protest against German religion classes Printed examples of parental consent notes for pupils attending a strike to give to their teachers Published regular reports on the ongoing protests in different parts of German Poland Praised striking pupils and encouraged others to join	
High	In two months, more than 100,000 people donated money for the statue 12,000 people attended the official ceremony despite police restrictions	

(continues)

Poland (Cont.)

Main Campaigns	Action	Method/*Type*	Date	Length
Resisting Russification in Russian Poland	Offering illegal classes in Polish language, history, and literature	Nonviolent intervention/ *Creative*	1885 onward	Long
	Creation of the Association of the Secret Teaching	Nonviolent intervention/ *Creative*	1894	Long
	Development of the flying university	Nonviolent intervention/ *Creative*	1870s onward	Long
	Boycott of the state school system	Noncooperation/ *Social*	1905	
	Polish Motherland Schools (PMS) launched	Nonviolent intervention/ *Creative*	1906	

United States

Campaign against the Stamp Act, 1765–1766	People hanged effigies of tax agents and confronted them at home	Protest and persuasion	1765–1766	Medium
	Colonial legislatures' petitions against Stamp Act	Protest and persuasion	1765–1766	Medium
	Mock funeral of effigy of Liberty	Protest and persuasion	October 1765	Short
	Social and consumer boycotts against supporters of the act	Noncooperation/ *Social, Economic*	1765–1766	Medium
	Tax refusal	Noncooperation/ *Economic*	1765–1766	Medium
	Nonconsumption of British goods	Noncooperation/ *Economic*	1765–1766	Medium

Level of Participation	Direct Impact	Long-Term/Overall Impact of Civil Resistance
High	By 1901, according to Russian government sources, a third of the Polish population in Russian Poland at some point had received secret teaching	The strength of the newly acquired national identity was displayed during World War I when peasants constituted the majority of Polish Army volunteers
High		
High	More than 5,000 men and women passed through the flying university in Russian Poland in the 1880s, including the future Nobel Prize winner Marie Curie-Skłodowska	Experience of organizing and running secret education became part of Polish collective memory of the national resistance and was used during the German occupation of 1939–1945 and during communist rule
		Cultural forms of resistance as well as patriotic education further romanticized past violent struggles and inadvertently overshadowed Polish tradition and the practice of nonviolent resistance
High	Thousands of new village schools under the Polish-controlled local municipalities were set up	
	Czarist government in October 1905 permitted the establishment of private schools with Polish as the language of instruction except Russian language, history, and geography	
	By 1914 more than 100,000 primary and secondary school children attended private schools, continuing the boycott of Russian-controlled state schools	
High	Russian government cracked down on and closed PMS	
	Polish organicists built parallel underground schools in response to the Russian government crackdown	

High	Stamp officials throughout the 13 colonies had resigned their office	Collective expression of differences with Britain raised the political awareness of Americans
	Articulated colonial grievances	Through civil resistance, people learned that they were a separate nation
Medium	Dramatized resistance	
	Enlisted participation	Civil resistance formed a sense of American identity
	Pressured royal officials	
	Raised awareness and identified people as supporters of the resistance	Development of parallel institutions to the British government led to a de facto independence and laid the foundation for a new government of the United States
High	Widened opposition beyond legislative actions	
High	Broke habits of obedience to British authority	
High	Promotion of American-made goods and economic self-reliance	

(continues)

Main Campaigns	Action	Method/*Type*	Date	Length
Campaign against the Stamp Act, 1765–1766	Nonimportation by merchants in Boston, New York, and Philadelphia	Noncooperation/ *Economic*	1765–1766	Medium
	Newspapers ceased publication or defied the British Crown by continuing to publish without stamps	Noncooperation/ *Political*	1765–1766	Medium
	Lawyers did not use stamps while judges did not proceed without them	Noncooperation/ *Political*	1765–1766	Medium
	Setting up and workings of Stamp Act Congress	Nonviolent intervention/ *Creative*	1765–1766	Medium
Campaign against the Townshend Acts, 1767–1768	Massachusetts House of Representatives distributed a Circular Letter to all colonial assemblies to petition the king for repeal of the Townshend Acts	Protest and persuasion	1767–1768	Medium
	Social boycott of those who did not participate in the nonconsumption campaign of British goods	Noncooperation/ *Social*	1767–1768	Medium
	Local tailors charged less for work on American-made cloth, but extra for imported cloth	Nonviolent intervention/ *Creative, Disruptive*	1767–1768	Medium
	Nonimportation agreement among merchants	Noncooperation/ *Economic*	1767–1768	Medium
	Setting up of Committees of Correspondence	Nonviolent intervention/ *Creative*	1770–1774	Long
Campaign against the Coercive Acts of 1774	The Boston Tea Party, dumping dutied tea into Boston harbor in defiance of the 1773 Tea Act	Nonviolent intervention/ *Disruptive*	December 16, 1773	Short
	Resolutions articulating the colonies' rights and grievances	Protest and persuasion	September–October 1774	Long
	Nonimportation of British, Irish, and West Indian goods	Noncooperation/ *Economic*	October 20, 1774	Medium
	Formation and workings of the First Continental Congress	Nonviolent intervention/ *Creative*	September–October 1774	
	Threat of nonexportation of items such as lumber, naval stores, tobacco, and other raw materials	Protest and persuasion	October 1774	

Level of Participation	Direct Impact	Long-Term/Overall Impact of Civil Resistance
Medium	Stamp Act was to yield £60,000 a year, but it generated only £3,292 in early 1766, not even covering the cost of printing	Collective expression of differences with Britain raised the political awareness of Americans
Low	Effectively nullified the Stamp Act, but without bringing about its repeal	Through civil resistance, people learned that they were a separate nation
Medium		Civil resistance formed a sense of American identity
High	Coordinated intercolonial cooperation

Helped produce a statement of colonial rights and limits of parliamentary authority

Leveraged pressure on British merchants who insisted on repeal by British politicians

Stamp Act repealed | Development of parallel institutions to the British government led to a de facto independence and laid the foundation for a new government of the United States before the war broke out |
Medium	By the end of 1768, every colonial assembly had petitioned the king challenging Parliament's right to levy taxes on the colonies	
High	Renewed collective civil resistance to British authority	
	Illustrated local expression of wider American resistance	
	Merchants who violated it or refused to enroll were boycotted and labeled as enemies of the country

Townshend Acts, except the duty on tea, were repealed in April 1770 | |
	They became fully functional American replacements for organs of British authority and embodied the parallel government	
Medium	Britain enacted a series of measures known as the Coercive Acts, but they backfired and immediately prompted resistance	
High	Stated the shared issues and expressed a growing common identity of Americans	
High	Promotion of American-made goods and economic self-reliance	
	Adopted resolutions articulating the colonies' rights and grievances

Enacted decision to stop imports from Britain, Ireland, and the West Indies | |
| | To be in force by September 10, 1775

Demonstrated other methods of resistance and potential for additional pressure on the British | |

(continues)

United States (Cont.)

Main Campaigns	Action	Method/*Type*	Date	Length
Campaign against the Coercive Acts of 1774	Convening extralegal provincial congresses	Nonviolent intervention/ *Creative*	1774 and 1775	Medium
	Colonial noncooperation extended to all royal laws	Noncooperation/ *Political*	1775	Medium

West Papua

Anti-Dutch struggle	Refusal to pay taxes and labor withholding	Noncooperation/ *Economic, Political*	1911	Medium
	Wearing traditional Biak loincloths	Protest and persuasion		
	People defied Dutch orders that banned visits to Angganeta Menufandu, a *konor* (indigenous prophet)	Noncooperation/ *Social, Political*	1911	Medium
	Designed a flag with inverted Dutch tricolor flag, Morning Star, and a cross as a symbol of the future Papuan kingdom	Protest and persuasion	1911	Long
	Mass defiance of bans on *wor* (ritual singing and dancing) and drinking palm wine	Noncooperation/ *Social*	1911–1943	Long
Anti-Indonesian struggle	People defied bans on Papuan songs and dances while the music group Mambesak performed songs in indigenous languages and local dances that included hidden identity-defining metaphors	Noncooperation/ *Social, Political*; Protest and persuasion	1970s and 1980s	Long
	Organized mass exodus of Papuans east to Papua New Guinea	Noncooperation/ *Political*	1984	Medium
	Church leaders called for active engagement in campaigns for civil and political or economic, social, and cultural rights	Protest and persuasion		
The Papuan Spring	Creation of a parallel government with a 500-member panel and parallel civil society, including formation of human rights organizations	Nonviolent intervention/ *Creative*	1999	Long
	Mass civilian-based protests and demonstrations	Protest and persuasion	1999 onward	Long

Level of Participation	Direct Impact	Long-Term/Overall Impact of Civil Resistance
Medium	Provincial congresses often assumed legislative and judicial functions in executing orders of the Continental Congress	Development of parallel institutions to the British government led to a de facto independence and laid the foundation for a new government of the United States before the war broke out
High	Courts were closed Colonists refused to pay taxes Governors defied royal laws	

High	The Dutch harassed the pilgrims that came to see Angganeta, which increased the anti-Dutch sentiment and the movement's popularity The arrest of Angganeta led to further protests	Over many decades, civil resistance has formed and reinforced collective Papuan identity and Papuan nationalism Civil resistance is framed narrowly around ethnicity, Christianity, and independence that limits Papuans' ability to form alliances with progressive Indonesians
	The flag inspired the design of the Papuans' national flag	
High		
	Evoked pride in being Papuan and fashioned a pan-Papuan identity distinct from Indonesia. It transcended tribal differences Inspired other Papuan cultural groups that proliferated in the early 1980s Exhorted unity	
High		
	Emergence of the Papuan nonviolent liberation theology for rights and self-determination Instilling of the need and obligation to resist illegitimate government A recognition of the need for reconciling personal, tribal, and political differences within the movement	
Medium		
Low	Led to the establishment of the Special Autonomy (it collapsed in 2001 and repression returned)	

(continues)

West Papua (Cont.)

Main Campaigns	Action	Method/*Type*	Date	Length
The Papuan Spring	Local campaigns, including protests against logging and palm oil plantations, mobilization of the Papuan women market sellers to win their own marketplace in the capital, protests against third province	Protest and persuasion	2001 onward	Medium
	Raising the Morning Star flag	Protest and persuasion	2000 and 2004	Long
Anti-Indonesian struggle	Formation of first independent labor union of gold and copper mine workers in West Papua	Nonviolent intervention/ *Creative*	2006	
	Labor strike	Noncooperation/ *Economic*	April 2007	Short
	Formation of FORDEM	Nonviolent intervention/ *Creative*	2010	
	Petition delivered to the provincial parliament by 15,000 people	Protest and persuasion	June 18, 2010	Short
	March of 20,000 Papuans to the provincial parliament	Protest and persuasion	August 2010	Short
	Two-day occupation (sit-in) of the provincial parliament	Protest and persuasion	August 2010	Short
	Third Papuan People's Congress, a three-day gathering of unarmed resistance groups	Nonviolent intervention/ *Creative*	October 2011	Short
	Independence celebrations: waving the Morning Star flag; shouting "freedom"; reading in public the October 2011 Declaration of Independence	Protest and persuasion	December 2011	Short

Level of Participation	Direct Impact	Long-Term/Overall Impact of Civil Resistance
Medium/ Low	Growth of student movement	Over many decades, civil resistance has formed and reinforced collective Papuan identity and Papuan nationalism
High	Symbolic rejection of being part of Indonesia Filep Karma, a Biak civil servant and activist, was sentenced to fifteen years for raising the Morning Star flag	Civil resistance is framed narrowly around ethnicity, Christianity, and independence that limits Papuans' ability to form alliances with progressive Indonesians
	Helped breach differences and facilitated workers' unity and organization in preparation for strike	
High	Papuan mine workers won improved conditions, including doubling of their wages	
	Prepared a petition	
High		
High	When the protesters reached parliament, they began an occupation of the building	
High	Parliamentarians did not heed protesters' demands	
High	During the last day of the event Papuan leaders declared independence Security forces opened fire, killing three Papuans, two were stabbed, hundreds were arrested Violence backfired Increased support for independence among Papuans who pressed forward with organizing pro-independence celebrations Led to divisions within political elites inside Indonesia Generated more outside attention and support for the West Papuan cause	
High	Many Papuans cast off their fear of expressing their pro-independence views Wide segments of the Papuan society mobilized, including Papuan civil servant and retired military Hardened pro-independence stance among Papuans who press for national referendum on political status of the region Repression by the Indonesian military	

Zambia

Action	Method/Type	Date	Length	Level of Participation
Refusal to pay tax, provide forced labor, and recognize colonial authority	Noncooperation/ *Economic, Political*	1890 onward		Medium
African-led churches called for equality of blacks and whites and rejection of both colonial and traditional chiefly authority	Protest and persuasion	1918 onward	Long	Low
Workers' strikes in Copperbelt towns	Noncooperation/ *Economic*	1935 and 1940	Medium	High
Labor unions representing various professional groups were formed	Nonviolent intervention/ *Creative*	late 1940s	Long	High
Setting up welfare associations	Nonviolent intervention/ *Creative*	1920 onward	Long	High
Welfare associations led awareness-raising campaigns, protested against racial discrimination, demanded better schools and infrastructure	Protest and persuasion	1920 onward	Long	High
Formation of political groupings and parties with nationalist goals	Nonviolent intervention/ *Creative*	From late 1930s until late 1950s	Long	High
Sending delegations to London to pressure the colonial and British government to reject the idea of a Federation with white-dominated Southern Rhodesia	Protest and persuasion	1950 onward	Long	High
Protest meetings held throughout the territory to mobilize African opinion against the British. Harry Nkumbula, leader of African National Congress, symbolically burned the government white paper announcing a Federation	Protest and persuasion	1950 onward	Long	High

Direct Impact	Long-Term/Overall Impact of Civil Resistance
Most of the resistance was unsuccessful as taxes were levied, land seized, forced labor exacted Some resistance succeeded in persuading the colonial administration to reverse its decisions to abolish a system of shifting cultivation and allow for its use next to a settled agricultural system	
Thousands were influenced by the teaching of the churches The colonial government arrested "seditious" preachers and banned Watchtower	Strengthened development of a sense of African identity and a feeling of empowerment
Strikes emphasized unity in diversity of the African labor force Advocacy of nonviolent action was present during strikes and helped engender moderation and nonviolent (though militant) behavior as part of the postwar nationalist resistance	
Unions' pressure forced the colonial government to reverse its policy on short-term labor migrants and accept that Africans would remain in the towns as permanent workers	Facilitated development of a politicized multiethnic urban proletariat that in turn helped the growth of a sense of national identity Labor unions became the source of a militant support for nationalist parties as their economic struggles had strong anticolonial overtones
The welfare associations often achieved local objectives. Under their public pressure in Ndola, government among others set up a new school, improved sanitary conditions, opened a township market, and distributed land for garden plots	The associations developed political awareness, including strengthening African unity beyond tribal differences, and taught democratic organization and decisionmaking The welfare associations were a harbinger of the first territory-wide nationalist party
Colonial authorities at first denied registration Taught political organization, participation, and mobilization skills Provided forums for Africans to articulate their political opinions	
The delegation did not succeed	

(continues)

Zambia (Cont.)

Action	Method/*Type*	Date	Length	Level of Participation
National strike	Noncooperation/ *Economic*	April 1953	Short	Low
Refusal to feed touring government officials	Noncooperation/ *Political*			
Campaigns of noncooperation with government: refusal to store grain and inoculate cattle, ignoring regulations for compulsory communal storage of kaffir corn and cassava	Noncooperation/ *Political, Economic*	1959		
Boycotts of Asian and European shops that practiced segregation, including butcher shops, beer halls, tearooms, and hotels	Noncooperation/ *Economic, Social, Political*	1950s		
Women marched, bare breasted, against the color bar	Protest and persuasion			
Women in Luapula Province helped hide political prisoners	Noncooperation/ *Political*	1950s		
Public burnings of the ID passes that all Africans were required to carry	Protest and persuasion	1959		
Boycott of elections	Noncooperation/ *Political*	1958		
Launching the cha cha cha campaign that aimed at damaging property and infrastructure to make the territory ungovernable	Nonviolent intervention/ *Disruptive*	1961	Short	High

Direct Impact	Long-Term/Overall Impact of Civil Resistance
The response to a call for a strike was not widespread. It was observed in two Copperbelt towns and in Lusaka The ANC failed to organize a broad coalition in support of its anti-federation strike	Resort to nonviolent actions made Zambians more inclined to seek political change through political parties and movements rather than through violence. Zambia's postcolonial history has been largely peaceful and politically less violent than many of its neighbors
Boycotts had an economic impact Resistance actions motivated people by showing the unity and strength of the movement Increased government repression Political leaders, including Kenneth Kaunda, were arrested Harsh measures backfired, fueling support for resistance and nationalist parties	
From July 15 to October 31, 146 roads were either destroyed or blocked, 64 bridges destroyed, 64 schools destroyed, 77 other public buildings destroyed, and 69 motor vehicles burned or destroyed—making the territory ungovernable for the British Twenty African protesters killed by the police The campaign prompted the British government to accept that Zambia should gain independence	

Acronyms

ACOA	American Committee on Africa
AL	Awami League
ALN	National Liberation Army
ANC	African National Congress
ARC	African Representative Council
ARPS	Aborigines Rights Protection Society
BDS	Boycott Divestment Sanctions
BSPK	Union of Independent Trade Unions
CDHRF	Council for the Defense of Human Rights and Freedoms
CGT	Confédération générale du travail
CPP	Convention People's Party
CSCE	Conference on Security and Cooperation in Europe
CYO	Committee of Youth Organizations
EU	European Union
Fateh	Harakat al-Tahrir al-Filistiniyya or Palestine Liberation Movement
FLN	National Liberation Front
FORDEM	Forum Demokrasi Rakyat Papua Bersatu
FRELIMO	Mozambique Liberation Front
GCBA	General Conference of Burmese Associations
GKI	Gereja Kristen Injil
ICNC	International Center on Nonviolent Conflict
ICTY	International Criminal Tribunal for the Former Yugoslavia
IDF	Israel Defense Forces
ILO	International Labour Organization
INC	Indian National Congress
KLA	Kosovo Liberation Army

KNPB	Komite Nasional Papua Barat
LCY	League of Communists of Yugoslavia
LDK	Democratic League of Kosova
MRP	Majelis Rakyat Papua
MTLD	Mouvement pour le Triomphe des Libertés Démocratiques
NATO	North Atlantic Treaty Organization
NCBWA	National Congress of British West Africa
NESAM	Nucleo dos Estudantes Africanos Secundarios de Mocambique
NLM	National Liberation Movement
OJM	Organization of Mozambican Youth
OMM	Organization of Mozambican Women
OSCE	Organization for Security and Cooperation in Europe
PA	Palestinian Authority
PCA	Algerian Communist Party
PCP	Palestinian Communist Party
PLO	Palestine Liberation Organization
PMS	Polish Motherland Schools
PPA	Parti du Peuple Algérien
PRC	Partido Revolucionario Cubano
PSS	People's School Society
R2P	Responsibility to Protect
RBSP	Rashtra Bhasha Sangram Parishad
RENAMO	Mozambican National Resistance
TPN-PB	Tentara Pembebasan Nasional-Papua Barat
TUC	Trades Union Congress
UDMA	Union Démocratique du Manifeste Algérien
UF	United Front
UGCC	United Gold Coast Convention
UGTA	Union général des travailleurs algériens
UNESCO	UN Educational, Scientific, and Cultural Organization
UNIP	United National Independence Party
UP4B	Unit for the Acceleration of Development in Papua
UPSUP	Students Union
USDA	Union Solidarity and Development Association
YMBA	Young Men's Buddhist Association
YMCA	Young Men's Christian Association
ZANC	Zambia African National Congress

Bibliography

Ackerman, Peter. "Have Faith in People Power." *Washington Post,* March 18, 2005.

Ackerman, Peter. "Iran's Future? Watch the Streets." *International Herald Tribune,* January 5, 2006.

Ackerman, Peter. "Skills or Conditions: What Key Factors Shape the Success or Failure of Civil Resistance." Paper presented at the Conference on Civil Resistance and Power Politics, Oxford, March 2007.

Ackerman, Peter, and Jack DuVall. *A Force More Powerful: A Century of Nonviolent Conflict.* New York: Palgrave Macmillan, 2000.

Ackerman, Peter, and Jack DuVall. "People Power Primed: Civilian Resistance and Democratization." *Harvard International Review* 27, no. 2 (summer 2005): 42–47.

Ackerman, Peter, and Jack DuVall. *Strategic Nonviolent Conflict: Lessons from the Past, Ideas for the Future.* Special Report. Washington, DC: United States Institute of Peace, May 1, 2002.

Ackerman, Peter, and Michael Glennon. "The Right Side of the Law." *American Interest,* September–October 2007.

Ackerman, Peter, and Adrian Karatnicky, eds. *How Freedom Is Won: From Civic Mobilization to Durable Democracy.* Washington, DC: Freedom House, 2005.

Ackerman, Peter, and Christopher Kruegler. *Strategic Nonviolent Conflict: The Dynamics of People Power in the Twentieth Century.* Westport, CT: Praeger, 1994.

Aday, Sean, Henry Farrell, Marc Lynch, John Sides, John Kelly, and Ethan Zuckerman. "Blogs to Bullets: New Media in Contentious Politics." *Peaceworks,* September 2010. www.usip.org/publications/blogs-and-bullets-new-media-in contentious-politics. Accessed on May 12, 2011.

Arendt, Hannah. *On Revolution.* New York: Viking Press, 1963.

Arendt, Hannah. "A Special Supplement: Reflections on Violence." *New York Review of Books,* February 27, 1969.

Bartkowski, Maciej, and Annyssa Bellal. "A Human Right to Resist." *Open Democracy,* May 3, 2011. www.opendemocracy.net/maciej-bartkowski-annyssa-bellal/ human-right-to resist. Accessed on May 15, 2011.

Bartkowski, Maciej, and Lester R. Kurtz. "Egypt: How to Negotiate the Transition. Lessons from Poland and China." *Open Democracy,* February 4, 2011. www

.opendemocracy.net/maciej-bartkowski-lester-r-kurtz/egypt-how-to-negotiate transition-lessons-from-poland-and-china. Accessed on February 5, 2011.

Beyerle, Shaazka. "Courage, Creativity, and Capacity in Iran: Mobilizing for Women's Rights and Gender Equality." *Georgetown Journal of International Affairs* 9, no. 2 (2008): 41–49.

Binnendijk, Anika, and Ivan Marovic. "Power and Persuasion: Nonviolent Strategies to Influence State Security Forces in Serbia (2000) and Ukraine (2004)." *Communist and Post-Communist Studies* 39 (2006): 411–429.

Bleiker Roland. *Popular Dissent, Human Agency and Global Politics.* Cambridge: Cambridge University Press, 2000.

Boaz, Cynthia. "Red Lenses on a Rainbow of Revolutions." *Open Democracy,* November 17, 2010. www.opendemocracy.net/cynthia-boaz/red-lenses-on-rainbow-of revolutions. Accessed on December 1, 2010.

Boaz, Cynthia, and Jack DuVall. "Defying Violence with Democracy: Why Grassroots Civil Society Is Key to the Future of Iraq." *Sojourners,* September–October 2006.

Bond, Douglas, Christopher Kruegler, Roger S. Powers, and William B. Vogele. *Protest, Power, and Change: An Encyclopedia of Nonviolent Action from ACT-UP to Women's Suffrage.* New York: Routledge, 1997.

Boserup, Anders, and Andrew Mack. *War Without Weapons: Non-Violence in National Defense.* Berlin: Schocken Books, 1975.

Brett, Roddy. *Social Movements, Indigenous Politics and Democratization in Guatemala, 1985–1996.* Leiden: Brill, 2008.

Burrowes, Robert J. *The Strategy of Nonviolent Defense: A Gandhian Approach.* Albany: SUNY Press, 1996.

Carter, April. *Direct Action and Democracy Today.* Cambridge: Polity Press, 2005.

Carter, April. *People Power and Political Change: Key Issues and Concepts.* New York: Routledge, 2011.

Carter, April, Howard Clark, and Michael Randle, eds. *People Power and Protest Since 1945: A Bibliography of Nonviolent Action.* London: Housmans, 2006.

Chenoweth, Erica. "People Power." *Sojourners,* May 2011.

Chenoweth, Erica. "Why Security Studies Should Take Nonviolent Conflict Seriously." *The Monkey Cage,* March 1, 2011. http://themonkeycage.org/blog/2011/03/01/why_security_studies_should_ta. Accessed on March 5, 2011.

Chenoweth, Erica, and Maria Stephan. *How Civil Resistance Works.* New York: Columbia University Press, 2011.

Chenoweth, Erica, and Maria J. Stephan. "Why Civil Resistance Works: The Strategic Logic of Nonviolent Conflict." *International Security* 33, no. 1 (summer 2008): 7–44.

Clark, Howard. *Civil Resistance in Kosovo.* London: Pluto Press, 2000.

Clark, Howard, ed. *People Power: Unarmed Resistance and Global Solidarity.* London: Pluto Press, 2009.

Colburn, Forrest D., ed. *Everyday Forms of Peasant Resistance.* London: M. E. Sharpe, 1989.

Conser, Walter H., Jr., Ronald M. McCarthy, David J. Toscano, and Gene Sharp, eds. *Resistance, Politics, and the American Struggle for Independence, 1765–1775.* Boulder: Lynne Rienner, 1986.

Cortright, David. *Gandhi and Beyond: Nonviolence for an Age of Terrorism.* Boulder: Paradigm, 2006.

Crawshaw, Steve, and John Jackson. *Small Acts of Resistance: How Courage, Tenacity, and Ingenuity Can Change the World.* New York: Union Square Press, 2010.

Crist, John, Harriet Hentges, and Daniel Serwer. "Strategic Nonviolent Conflict: Lessons from the Past, Ideas for the Future." Special Report No. 87. Washington, DC: United States Institute of Peace, May 1, 2002. www.usip.org/publications/strategic-nonviolent-conflict-lessons-past-ideas-future. Accessed on November 10, 2011.

Crow, Ralph, Philip Grant, and Saad Ibrahim. *Arab Nonviolent Political Struggle in the Middle East.* Boulder: Lynne Rienner, 1990.

Dalton, Dennis. *Mahatma Gandhi: Nonviolent Power in Action.* New York: Columbia University Press, 1993.

Davenport, Christian, Hank Johnston, and Carol Mueller, eds. *Repression and Mobilization.* Minneapolis: University of Minnesota Press, 2005.

de Ligt, Bart. *The Conquest of Violence: An Essay on War and Revolution.* London: George Routledge, 1937.

"A Diplomat's Handbook for Democracy Development Support." Council for a Community of Democracies, 2010. www.diplomatshandbook.org/.

Dudouet, Véronique, and Howard Clark. *Nonviolent Civic Action in Support of Human Rights and Democracy.* Brussels: Directorate-General for External Policies, European Parliament, 2009. www.nonviolent-conflict.org/images/stories/pdfs/est25679.pdf. Accessed on December 5, 2010.

DuVall, Jack. "Civil Resistance and Alternatives to Violent Struggle." London: International Centre for the Study of Radicalization and Political Violence (ICSR), 2008. www.nonviolent-conflict.org/index.php/learning-and-resources/resources-on nonviolent-conflict?bTask=bDetails&catid=8&bId=74. Accessed on April 20, 2010.

DuVall, Jack. "Civil Resistance and the Language of Power." *Open Democracy,* November 19, 2010. www.opendemocracy.net/jack-duvall/civil-resistance-and-language-of power. Accessed on November 20, 2010.

DuVall, Jack. "Democratic Views Akin to Lincoln's." *Financial Times,* June 29, 2005.

DuVall, Jack. "The Power of Plenty." *New Republic,* June 20, 2009.

DuVall, Jack. "Regime Reversal." *Sunday Times* (London), April 23, 2006.

Ford, Peter. "The Twilight of the Tyrants." *Christian Science Monitor,* December 19, 2003.

Gamson, William A., and Gadi Wolfsfeld. "Movements and Media as Interacting Systems." *Annals of the American Academy of Political and Social Science* 528, no. 1 (1993): 114–125.

Gandhi, Mahatma. *The Mind of Mahatma Gandhi.* Comp. R. K. Prabhu and U. R. Rao. Ahmadabad: Navajivan Press, 1967.

Giugni, Marco, Doug McAdam, and Charles Tilly, eds. *How Social Movements Matter.* Minneapolis: University of Minnesota Press, 1999.

Gregg, Richard. *The Power of Nonviolence.* Philadelphia: Lippincott, 1934.

Hastings, Tom H. *Nonviolent Responses to Terrorism.* Jefferson, NC: McFarland and Company, 2004.

Havel, Vaclav. *Disturbing the Peace.* New York: Vintage Books, 1991.

Havel, Vaclav. *The Power of the Powerless.* New York: M. E. Sharpe, 1990.

Helvey, Robert L. *On Strategic Nonviolent Conflict: Thinking About the Fundamentals.* Boston: Albert Einstein Institution, 2004.

Hess, David, and Brian Martin. "Repression, Backfire, and the Theory of Transformative Events." *Mobilization* 11, no. 1 (2006): 249–267.

Holmes, Robert L., and Barry L. Gan, eds. *Nonviolence in Theory and Practice,* 2nd ed. Long Grove: Waveland Press, 2005.

Kamphoefner, Kathy. "Best Practices in Egypt." *Sojourners,* May 2011.

Karatnycky, Adrian. "Zigging and Zagging Toward Democracy." *Washington Post,* November 15, 2005.

Karatnycky, Adrian, and Peter Ackerman. "How Freedom Is Won: From Civic Resistance to Durable Democracy." New York: Freedom House, May 24, 2005. www.freedomhouse.org/template.cfm?page=383&report=29. Accessed on May 30, 2010.

King, Mary E. "Nonviolent Struggle in Africa: Essentials of Knowledge and Teaching." *Africa Peace and Conflict Journal* 1, no. 1 (2008): 19–44.

King, Mary E. *A Quiet Revolution: The First Palestinian Intifada and Nonviolent Resistance.* New York: Nation Books, 2007.

Krauss, Leah. "Is Nonviolent Change More Effective?" United Press International, May 20, 2004.

Kumar, Mahendra, and Peter Low, eds. *Legacy and Future of Nonviolence.* New Delhi: Gandhi Peace Foundation, 1996.

Kurtz, Lester R., ed. *Encyclopedia of Violence, Peace, and Conflict.* Amsterdam: Elsevier, 2008.

Kurtz, Lester R. "Repression's Paradox in China." *Open Democracy,* November 17, 2010. http://www.opendemocracy.net/lester-r-kurtz/repression's-paradox-in-china. Accessed on November 20, 2010.

Lakey, George. *Powerful Peacemaking: Strategy for a Living Revolution.* Philadelphia: New Society, 1987.

Loeb, Paul Rogat, ed. *The Impossible Will Take a Little While: A Citizen's Guide to Hope in a Time of Fear.* New York: Basic Books, 2004.

Maney, Gregory M., Rachel Kutz-Flmenbaum, Deana R. Rohlinger, and Jeff Goodwin. *Strategy in Action: Movements and Social Change.* Minneapolis: University of Minnesota Press, 2012.

Martin, Brian. "Gene Sharp's Theory of Power." *Journal of Peace Research* 26, no. 2 (1989): 213–222.

Martin, Brian. *Justice Ignited: The Dynamics of Backfire.* Lanham: Rowman and Littlefield, 2007.

McAdam, Doug. *Freedom Summer.* New York: Oxford University Press, 1988.

McAdam, Doug, and Sidney Tarrow. "Nonviolence as Contentious Interaction." *Political Science and Politics* 33, no. 2 (2000): 149–154.

McAdam, Doug, Sidney Tarrow, and Charles Tilly. *Dynamics of Contention.* New York: Cambridge University Press, 2001.

McCarthy, John D., and Mayer N. Zald. "Resource Mobilization and Social Movements: A Partial Theory." *American Journal of Sociology* 82, no. 6 (1977): 1212–1241.

McCarthy, Ronald M., and Gene Sharp. *Nonviolent Action: A Research Guide.* New York: Garland, 1997.

McManus, Philip. *Relentless Persistence.* Philadelphia: New Society, 1990.

Merriman, Hardy. "The Trifecta of Civil Resistance: Unity, Planning, Nonviolent Discipline." *Open Democracy,* November 19, 2010. www.opendemocracy.net/hardy-merriman/trifecta-of-civil-resistance-unity-planning-discipline. Accessed on November 19, 2010.

Merriman, Hardy, and Jack DuVall. "Dissolving Terrorism at Its Roots." In Senthil Ram and Ralph Summy (eds.), *Nonviolence: An Alternative for Defeating Global Terror(ism).* New York: Nova Science, 2007, chap. 13.

Moser-Puangsuwan, Yeshua, and Thomas Weber, eds. *Nonviolent Intervention Across Borders.* Honolulu: University of Hawaii Press, 2000.

Moyer, Bill, JoAnn McAllister, Mary Lou Finley, and Steven Soifer. *Doing Democracy: The MAP Model for Organizing Social Movements.* Gabriola Island, British Columbia: New Society, 2001.

Nagler, Michael. *Is There No Other Way? The Search for a Nonviolent Future.* Berkeley: Berkeley Hills Books, 2001.

Nepstad, Sharon Erickson. *Nonviolent Revolutions: Civil Resistance in the Late 20th Century.* Oxford: Oxford University Press, 2011.

O'Brien, Kevin J., and Lianjiang Li. *Rightful Resistance in Rural China.* Cambridge: Cambridge University Press, 2006.

Palmer, Mark. *Breaking the Real Axis of Evil: How to Oust the World's Last Dictators by 2025.* Lanham, MD: Rowman and Littlefield, 2003.

Popovic, Srdja, Slobodan Djinovic, Andrej Milivojevic, Hardy Merriman, and Ivan Marovic. *Canvas Core Curriculum: A Guide to Effective Nonviolent Struggle Students Book.* Belgrade: Centre for Applied Nonviolent Action and Strategies, 2007. www.canvasopedia.org/legacy/content/special/core.htm. Accessed on September 15, 2009.

Press, Robert M. *Peaceful Resistance: Advancing Human Rights and Democratic Freedoms.* Burlington, VT: Ashgate, 2006.

Randle, Michael. *Civil Resistance.* London: Fontana Press, 1994.

Rigby, Andrew. *Living the Intifada.* London: Zed Books, 1991.

Roberts, Adam, ed. *Civilian Resistance as a National Defense: Nonviolent Action Against Aggression.* Harrisburg, PA: Stackpole Books, 1968.

Roberts, Adam, and Timothy Garton Ash, eds. *Civil Resistance and Power Politics: The Experience of Non-Violent Action from Gandhi to the Present.* Oxford: Oxford University Press, 2009.

Schaeffer-Duffy, Claire. "Regime Change Without Bloodshed." *National Catholic Reporter Online,* November 15, 2002. http://www.natcath.org/NCR_Online/archives/111502/111502g.htm. Accessed on February 10, 2010.

Schell, Jonathan. *The Unconquerable World: Power, Nonviolence, and the Will of the People.* New York: Henry Holt, 2003.

Schock, Kurt. "Nonviolent Action and Its Misconceptions: Insights for Social Scientists." *PS: Political Science and Politics* 36, no. 4 (2003): 705–712.

Schock, Kurt. *Unarmed Insurrections: People Power Movements in Nondemocracies.* Minneapolis: University of Minnesota Press, 2005.

Scott, James C. *The Art of Not Being Governed: An Anarchist History of Upland Southeast Asia.* New Haven: Yale University Press, 2009.

Scott, James C. *Domination and the Arts of Resistance: Hidden Transcripts.* New Haven: Yale University Press, 1992.

Secor, Laura. "War by Other Means." *Boston Globe,* May 29, 2005. www.boston.com/news/globe/ideas/articles/2005/05/29/war_by_other_means/. Accessed on October 17, 2009.

Semelin, Jacques. *Unarmed Against Hitler: Civilian Resistance in Europe, 1939–1943.* Westport, CT: Praeger, 1993.

Sharp, Gene. *From Dictatorship to Democracy: A Conceptual Framework for Liberation,* 4th ed. Boston: Albert Einstein Institution, 2010.

Sharp, Gene. *The Politics of Nonviolent Action,* part 1: *Power and Struggle.* Boston: Porter Sargent, 1973.

Sharp, Gene. *The Politics of Nonviolent Action,* part 2: *The Methods of Nonviolent Action.* Boston: Porter Sargent, 1973.

Sharp, Gene. *The Politics of Nonviolent Action,* part 3: *The Dynamics of Nonviolent Action.* Boston: Porter Sargent, 1973.

Sharp, Gene. *There Are Realistic Alternatives*. Boston: Albert Einstein Institution, 2003.

Sharp, Gene, ed. *Waging Nonviolent Struggle: 20th Century Practice and 21st Century Potential*. Boston: Porter Sargent, 2005.

Shridharani, Krishnalal. *War Without Violence: A Study of Gandhi's Method and Its Accomplishments*. New York: Harcourt, Brace, 1939.

Sibley, Mulford Q. *The Quiet Battle: Writings on the Theory and Practice of Non-Violent Resistance*. Boston: Beacon Press, 1963.

Stephan, Maria J., ed. *Civilian Jihad: Nonviolent Struggle, Democratization, and Governance in the Middle East*. Palgrave Macmillan Series on Civil Resistance. New York: Palgrave Macmillan, 2010.

Stephan, Maria J., and Jacob Mundy. "A Battlefield Transformed: From Guerilla Resistance to Mass Nonviolent Struggle in the Western Sahara." *Journal of Military and Strategic Studies* 8, no. 3 (2006): 1–32.

Summy, Ralph. "Nonviolence and the Case of the Extremely Ruthless Opponent." *Pacifica Review* 6, no. 1 (1994): 1–29.

Summy, Ralph, and Senthil Ram, eds. *Nonviolence: An Alternative for Defeating Global Terror(ism)*. New York: Nova Science, 2007.

Sutherland, Bill, and Matt Meyer. *Guns and Gandhi in Africa: Pan-African Insights on Nonviolence, Armed Struggle and Liberation in Africa*. Trenton, NJ: Africa World Press, 2000.

Tarrow, Sidney. *Power in Movement: Social Movements and Contentious Politics*, 2nd ed. Cambridge: Cambridge University Press, 1998.

Taylor Richard K. *Blockade: A Guide to Nonviolent Intervention*. Maryknoll, NY: Orbis Books, 1977.

Thalhammer, Kristina E., Paula L. O'Loughlin, Sam McFarland, Myron Peretz Glazer, Penina Migdal Glazer, Sharon Toffey Shepela, and Nathan Stoltzfus. *Courageous Resistance: The Power of Ordinary People*. New York: Palgrave Macmillan, 2007.

T'Hart, Marjolein, and Dennis Bos. *Humour and Social Protest*. Cambridge: Cambridge University Press, 2008.

Thoreau, Henry David. *Walden: On the Duty of Civil Disobedience*. New York: Rinehart, 1948. (Orig. pub. in 1854.)

Tilly, Charles. *Social Movements, 1768–2004*. Boulder: Paradigm, 2004.

Traynor, Ian. "From Belgrade to Baku, Activists Gather to Swap Notes on How to Topple Dictators." *The Guardian*, June 6, 2005.

Vinthagen, Stellan. "People Power and the New Global Ferment." *Open Democracy*, November 15, 2010. www.opendemocracy.net/stellan-vinthagen/people-power-and-new global-ferment. Accessed on November 16, 2010.

Weber, Thomas. "Nonviolence Is Who? Gene Sharp and Gandhi." *Peace and Change* 28, no. 2 (2003): 250–270.

Wehr, Paul, Heidi Burgess, and Guy Burgess, eds. *Justice Without Violence*. Boulder: Lynne Rienner, 1994.

Zunes, Stephen. "Egypt's Pro-Democracy Movement: The Struggle Continues." *Open Democracy*, February 8, 2011.

Zunes, Stephen. "Recognizing the Power of Nonviolent Action." *Foreign Policy in Focus*, March 2005.

Zunes, Stephen. "Unarmed Insurrections Against Authoritarian Government in the Third World: A New Kind of Revolution." *Third World Quarterly* 15, no. 3 (1994): 403–426.

Zunes, Stephen. "Weapons of Mass Democracy: Nonviolent Resistance Is the Most Powerful Tactic Against Oppressive Regimes." *Open Democracy*, September 16, 2009.

Zunes, Stephen, Lester Kurtz, and Sarah Beth Asher, eds. *Nonviolent Social Movements: A Geographical Perspective*. Oxford: Wiley-Blackwell, 1999.

The Contributors

Amr Abdalla is professor and vice rector at the UN-mandated University for Peace (UPEACE). Before arriving at UPEACE, he was senior fellow in the Peace Operations Policy Program, School of Public Policy, at George Mason University and professor of conflict analysis and resolution at the Graduate School of Islamic and Social Sciences. He practiced as a prosecuting attorney in Egypt from 1978 to 1987.

Yasmine Arafa has conducted research and evaluation of peacebuilding-related programs in Egypt, Morocco, Kenya, and Democratic Republic of Congo. She works as a consultant to the vice rector of the University for Peace.

Maciej Bartkowski is senior director for education and research at the International Center on Nonviolent Conflict (ICNC). He conducts research and writes on nonviolent movements and strategic nonviolent conflict and speaks regularly on civil resistance. He has taught in the United States, Central and Eastern Europe, and Central Asia, including at George Mason University where he currently holds the position of adjunct professor.

Howard Clark is an English nonviolent activist and independent peace researcher. He has worked at *Peace News* and since 2008, has been chair of War Resisters' International. He is a research fellow at the Centre for Peace and Reconciliation Studies, Coventry University, and a visiting faculty member at the UNESCO Centre for Philosophy of Peace, University Jaime I. He is author of *Civil Resistance in Kosovo* (2000); cocompiler (with April Carter and Michael Randle) of *People and Power Protest Since 1945: A*

Bibliography of Nonviolent Action (2006); and editor of *People Power: Unarmed Resistance and Global Solidarity* (2009).

Walter H. Conser Jr. is professor of both religious studies and history at the University of North Carolina Wilmington. He is author of a number of articles and books on religion and culture and coauthor (with Ronald M. McCarthy, David Toscano, and Gene Sharp) of *Resistance, Politics and the American Struggle for Independence, 1765–1775* (1986).

Tamás Csapody is assistant professor of moral philosophy at Semmelweis University and teaches peace studies at Eötvös Loránd University. He writes on nonviolence, alternative movements, conscientious objection, and civilian public service. He is coauthor (with László Vit) of *Hungary and the NATO Enlargement* (1999); and author of *Civil forgatókönyvek: Válogatott tanulmányok és publicisztikai írások (1983–2002)* (Civil Scenarios: Selected Essays and Writings on Publicism 1983–2002) (2002); and *Ne az én nvemben! Magyarorszag és az Iraqi háboru* (Not in My Name! Hungary and the Iraq War) (2004).

Fay Gadsden lectured in history at the University of Zambia for twenty-one years before leaving to start a publishing company and a bookselling business. She later became a part-time lecturer in the graduate studies program, Gender Studies Department, at the University of Zambia. She is author of book chapters and articles on the press in Kenya and education in Zambia and is on the editorial board of the newly established *Zambia Social Science Journal.*

Ishtiaq Hossain is associate professor, Department of Political Science, at the International Islamic University Malaysia (IIUM). He previously was senior lecturer in political science at the National University of Singapore and visiting professor at George Washington University and Waikato University. He is currently conducting research on politics and government in Muslim countries of South and Southeast Asia. He is coeditor with Mohsen Salih of *American Foreign Policy and the Muslim World* (2009).

Nikki Keddie is professor emerita of history at the University of California, Los Angeles (UCLA). She is author of *Women in the Middle East* (2007); *Modern Iran: Roots and Results of Revolution* (2006); and *Iran and the Muslim World: Resistance and Revolution* (1995) as well as books and articles about Iranian history and Sayyed Jamal ad-Din al-Afghani. She is editor of books about Middle Eastern women and religio-political trends in Iran and the Muslim world.

Mary Elizabeth King is professor of peace and conflict studies at the UN-affiliated University for Peace and distinguished scholar at the American University's Center for Peacebuilding and Development. She is Rothermere American Institute Fellow at Oxford University and a recipient of the Robert F. Kennedy Memorial Book Award for *Freedom Song: A Personal Story of the 1960s Civil Rights Movement* (1987). She is author of *The New York Times on Emerging Democracies in Eastern Europe* (2009); *A Quiet Revolution: The First Palestinian Intifada and Nonviolent Resistance* (2007); and *Mahatma Gandhi and Martin Luther King, Jr: The Power of Nonviolent Action* (2002).

Jason MacLeod is conducting research on the viability of nonviolent strategies and tactics to enlarge the prospects of the self-determination in West Papua. He teaches civil resistance at the School of Political Science and International Studies at the University of Queensland and in the master's course on nonviolent action at Sydney University. He taught community development at Monash University, the University of New England, and Christian Heritage College. He is author of several articles and book chapters on West Papua and nonviolent struggle.

Matt Meyer is an educator, activist, writer, and advocate of revolutionary nonviolent resistance. He is cofounding chair of the Peace and Justice Studies Association and serves as an editor and author associated with Africa World/Red Sea Press and PM Press. Meyer is a founding coconvener of the War Resisters International's Africa Working Group. He is coauthor together with Bill Sutherland of *Guns and Gandhi in Africa: Pan-African Insights on Nonviolence, Armed Struggle and Liberation* (2000); author of *Time is Tight: Transformative Education in Eritrea, South Africa, and the U.S.A.* (2007); coeditor with Elavie Ndura-Ouedraogo of *Seeds Bearing Fruit: Pan African Peace Action for the Twenty-First Century* (2010); and editor of *Let Freedom Ring: Documents from the Movements to Free U.S. Political Prisoners* (2009).

Jotham C. Momba is associate professor of political science and former head of the Department of Political and Administrative Studies at the University of Zambia. He also taught at Drew University and the University of Swaziland. He was president of the Organisation for Social Science and Research in Eastern and Southern Africa (OSSREA) from 2007 to 2011.

Yeshua Moser-Puangsuwan is Asia and Pacific research coordinator for the Landmine and Cluster Munition Monitor, a project of the International Campaign to Ban Landmines. He is a former course coordinator for Peace, Conflict Management and Human Rights at Mahidol University.

Gail M. Presbey is professor of philosophy at University of Detroit Mercy. Her areas of expertise are social and political philosophy as well as philosophy of nonviolence and cross-cultural philosophy. She also is involved in peace and justice studies and was executive director and president of Concerned Philosophers for Peace. She is editor of *Philosophical Perspectives on the "War on Terrorism"* (2007); coeditor with Karsten J. Struhl and Richard E. Olsen of *The Philosophical Quest: A Cross-Cultural Reader*; and coeditor with Daniel Smith, Pamela A. Abuya, and Oriare Nyarwath of *Thought and Practice in African Philosophy.*

Alfonso W. Quiroz is professor of history at Baruch College and Graduate Center, City University of New York. He writes on institutional, economic, and policy issues of modern and colonial Peru and Cuba, and is author of *Corrupt Circles: A History of Unbound Graft in Peru* (2008); coeditor with Mauricio A. Font of *The Cuban Republic and José Martí* (2006); and *Cuban Counterpoints: The Legacy of Fernando Ortiz* (2005). He is author of several articles on civil society and conflict in nineteenth-century Cuba. He was curator of the exhibits "A War in Perspective: Public Appeals, Memory, and the Spanish-American Conflict" at the New York Public Library (1998) and "Militant Metropolis: New York and the Spanish-American War" at the New York Historical Society (1998).

Malika Rahal is a researcher on the contemporary history of Algeria at the Institut d'histoire du temps présent (CNRS) in Paris. She is author of *Ali Boumendjel: Une affaire française, une histoire algérienne* (Ali Boumendjel: A French Affair, an Algerian history) (Paris, 2010, Algiers 2011).

Lee A. Smithey is associate professor of sociology at Swarthmore College where he coordinates the Program in Peace and Conflict Studies. He studies social conflict and social movements, especially ethnopolitical conflict and the use of nonviolent strategy and tactics. He is former chair of the Peace, War, and Social Conflict section of the American Sociological Association.

Thomas Weber is associate professor of politics and peace studies at La Trobe University. His conducts research on Mohandas Gandhi's life and thought and nonviolence theory and practice. He is author of *Gandhi's Peace Army* (1996); *On the Salt March* (1997); *Gandhi as Disciple and Mentor* (2004); *Gandhi, Gandhism and the Gandhians* (2006); and *Going Native: Gandhi's Relationship with Western Women* (2010). He is coeditor (with Yeshua Moser-Puangsuwan) of *Nonviolent Intervention Across Borders* (2000).

Index

419

About the Book

This unique book brings to light the little-known, but powerful roles that civil resistance has played in national liberation struggles throughout history.

Ranging from the American Revolution to Kosovo in the 1990s, from Egypt under colonial rule to present-day West Papua and Palestine, the authors of *Recovering Nonviolent History* consider several key questions: What kinds of civilian-based nonviolent strategy and tactics have been used in liberation struggles? What accounts for their successes and failures? Not least, how did nonviolent resistance influence national identities and socioeconomic and political institutions both prior to and after liberation, and why has this history so often been ignored? The story that emerges is a compelling one of the agency of thousands and even millions of ordinary people as they used nonviolent force in the course of struggles against foreign subjugation.

Maciej J. Bartkowski is senior director for research and education at the International Center on Nonviolent Conflict.